MySQL
Essential Skills

MySQL
Essential Skills

Dr. John Horn, Ph.D.
Michael Grey
Interstate Software, Inc.

McGraw-Hill/Osborne

New York   Chicago   San Francisco
Lisbon   London   Madrid   Mexico City
Milan   New Delhi   San Juan
Seoul   Singapore   Sydney   Toronto

The McGraw·Hill Companies

McGraw-Hill/Osborne
2100 Powell Street, 10th Floor
Emeryville, California 94608
U.S.A.

To arrange bulk purchase discounts for sales promotions, premiums, or fund-raisers, please contact **McGraw-Hill**/Osborne at the above address. For information on translations or book distributors outside the U.S.A., please see the International Contact Information page immediately following the index of this book.

MySQL: Essential Skills

1234567890 CUS CUS 01987654

ISBN 0-07-225513-7

Publisher   Brandon A. Nordin
Vice President & Associate Publisher   Scott Rogers
Editorial Director   Wendy Rinaldi
Acquisitions Editor   Nancy Maragioglio
Senior Project Editor   LeeAnn Pickrell
Acquisitions Coordinator   Athena Honore
Technical Editors   Brian Kaney, Jay Powers
Copy Editor   Marilyn Smith
Proofreader   Marian Selig
Indexer   Karin Arrigoni
Composition   John Patrus, Jean Butterfield
Illustrators   Kathleen Edwards, Melinda Lytle
Series Design   Jean Butterfield
Cover Design   Jeff Weeks

This book was composed with Corel VENTURA™ Publisher.

This book is dedicated to my wife, my partner, and my best friend, Jenny.
—John Horn

To my parents, Don and Georgia Miller;
my brothers and sisters-in-law, Dave and Donna and Bob and Carolyn;
and my nieces and nephews and their spouses: Ryan and Renee, Jason and Sarah,
Tiffany and Tommy, John and Melissa, Katie and Josh, and Peter and Crystal.
You couldn't ask for a better family.
—Michael Grey

About the Authors

John Horn is from Medicine Lodge, Kansas. He started programming on Apple computers during high school in 1983. Currently, he is the CEO of Interstate Software, the only MySQL training center in North America and the only "Gold Level" MySQL training, support, and consulting group in the world. Since 1994, he and his team have commercially supported everything from small web site databases to a MySQL database that is over half a terabyte (>500GB). They are the only MySQL training group that offers MySQL training on Linux, Solaris, and Windows. Interstate focuses on Open Source Solutions for the Enterprise and are also Novell and SuSE, Training and Business Partners. John is married to Jenny; they have one son, Kodi, and live in Kansas City, Missouri.

Michael Grey is a technical writer and instructor for Interstate Software. She has previously, among other things, written and executed software testing for RAID storage, been a webmaster, and attained the unusual combination of a bachelor's in computer science and a master's in English. Michael lives in the Kansas City, Kansas, area with a cat named Pixel, who, so far at least, has not walked through any walls.

About the Technical Editors

Brian Kaney, co-founder of Vermonster LLC, graduated from the University of Massachusetts with a bachelor's degree in engineering. While in college, he worked as a consultant for various companies in New England. He later co-founded Askfor.com, piloting a new middleware technology. In 2000 he co-founded Vermonster, a consulting company located in Boston, focusing on open software and open standards for the Enterprise.

Jay Powers is a graduate of the University of Vermont and has been working with open source technology for over seven years. He is experienced in designing and building web applications and web services. Before starting Vermonster, he worked as a technology director at Askfor.com, an Internet startup company. Prior to that, he worked as a director at AdSmart, a CMGI company. When Jay is not writing code, he enjoys riding around Boston on his fixed-gear Pinarello bicycle.

Contents

Acknowledgments

I've often heard the sentiment that no book is ever written alone, and this one is no exception. In addition to the invaluable expertise of my co-author, Dr. John Horn, there were many others who offered technical assistance, especially Jenny Horn, Kyle Sexton, Dennis Beckley, and last but never least, Brian McCullough.

In addition, there have been a myriad of friends who listened as I talked through explanations of things they didn't really understand and who put up with my deadline panics and general writer's anxiety, including but not limited to Chantel Austin, Vicki Hadley, Karen Burge, Jenny Crighton, and Rules.

I'd like to thank Nancy Maragioglio, Athena Honore, and LeeAnn Pickrell from McGraw-Hill/Osborne for shepherding me through the writing and editing process, especially Nancy for offering support, reassurance, and encouragement in just the right proportions. Also, kudos to our technical editors, Jay Powers and Brian Kaney, for keen eyes and truly constructive criticism, plus a special thanks to Brian for his kind contribution to the PHP material in Module 7.

When John suggested we write this book together, I had the vague notion that it would be fun. My bad. While "fun" is no longer a word I would connect to the experience, it has ultimately been enriching—though perhaps in the way that Dante was enriched by his sojourn through the Inferno. Seeing it on the shelf with our names on the cover will, I expect, be fun enough.

—*Michael Grey*

Introduction

Database Administration used to be the purview of computer professionals. The advent of Internet business and communication has opened the door to a variety of hobbyists and small business interests who want the informational power and convenience of computer data storage without having to commit to what amounts to career training in a particular database program in order to install and use it. MySQL has risen to the forefront as the multi-OS answer to the new database requirements of low cost and ease of operation, while at the same time remaining scalable enough for corporate use.

MySQL allows almost anyone to install and run a database, from the true beginner who wants a guestbook on their web site to the e-business needing storage for their shopping cart sales interface that will grow as their customer-base grows. It is simple and easy to use, yet allows for complex purposes. As your database needs grow, you will find MySQL has likely preceded you and the more you learn, the more versatile and powerful you will find this robust, approachable program. This book will provide you with the basic knowledge to install and set up, plan and design, and protect and administer your MySQL database. It gives you enough detail to progress without drowning you in minutia, and the hands-on projects create a quick learning curve that allows you to get your database up and running in a minimal amount of time.

Who Should Read This Book

This book is subtitled *Essential Skills,* and anyone whose requirements mandate a rapid entry into the MySQL world will be able to find the essential information required to get them moving forward in regards to that goal. More experienced users will be able to read between the lines in a way that the less experienced user will not, but on the whole, all effort has been expended to make the information detailed enough to provide context but, at the same time, not overwhelmingly encyclopedic. We will assume a basic familiarity with the operating system you choose to install MySQL on, and because of its nature, a slightly greater depth of knowledge is assumed for the Linux OS; however, a true database beginner can use this book as well as a more experienced database professional who is looking for a quick foothold into a new area of expertise.

What's in This Book

MySQL: Essential Skills is divided into eight modules, each covering a specific aspect of MySQL installation, operation, or administration.

Module 1: "Installing MySQL"

The first part establishes a common language by defining basic database terms as they are used in this text. We then move on to a discussion of open source software and how it relates to MySQL, and then to a discussion of the pertinent criteria in choosing a development and deployment operating system for your MySQL database.

You will then learn how to install MySQL on first the Windows then the Linux operating systems. The Windows installation section also covers installing MyODBC. Once MySQL is installed and running on your computer, you will learn how to use the MySQL command-line interface. The final section of this module outlines resources that may come in handy once your learning curve has taken you beyond the boundaries of essential skills.

Module 2: "Defining a Database"

This section covers database creation, table definition, and data insertion. The first section explains the essentials of MySQL data types, then segues into the preplanning needed to map out your database before creating it; thus, preventing some of the common mistakes that might require a later redefinition or re-creation of your tables.

The next section explains the syntax of database and table creation, as well as gives concrete examples of commands and what they accomplish. The final section of this module covers data insertion, and at the end of the included projects, you will have created a basic database that will allow you to experiment with subsequent data manipulation.

Module 3: "Manipulating the Database"

This module covers adding and changing the data and/or tables within the database constructed in the previous module. The first section covers commands that allow you to add new data in various forms to the database. The second section covers commands that allow you to change the structure of an existing table and/or add an index to an existing table.

The third section of this module explains the commands that allow you to modify the data already in a table, and the fourth and final section explains the commands necessary for either removing a table's data while leaving the table intact or removing a table, data and all, or deleting an entire database.

Module 4: "Basic Reporting"

This module covers the various uses of the basic commands used to select data from a table and display it in informative ways. You will learn how to choose the specific data you need to view then narrow that focus and display the required data in a meaningful manner.

Module 5: "Advanced Reporting"

The first section of this module covers a wide variety of functions used to control the flow of data, perform math on or with numerical data, manipulate and display character data, and display and manipulate representations of time from fractions of seconds to years.

The second and third sections show you how to order and group data from a table into meaningful displays to present reports and then how to connect data from two or more tables into an understandable and easily read format.

Module 6: "GUI Interfaces for Data-Handling and Administration"

Up until this point in the text, all interaction between the user and the database has taken place on the command-line interface. In this module, we will cover the MySQL Control Center and the new MySQL Administrator GUI interfaces.

The first section covers the functions currently available on the MySQL Administrator, which is still in Alpha testing and so subject to change. The second section covers the MySQLCC interface, which is in release and more stable. GUI interfaces allow you to interact with the database in a point-and-click environment, even if you are running on a Linux OS, instead of the GUI-driven Windows OS.

Module 7: "Interfacing with Programs"

This section gives an overview of PHP and touches on how it interfaces with MySQL in a web environment. You will learn how PHP can be used to allow a user to access a web page and either display or insert data to or from a MySQL database.

The second section deals with importing an existing Excel or Access database into MySQL, and also how to export or link MySQL data into Excel and/or Access in order to modify or view it in a more familiar environment.

Module 8: "Basic Administration and Backups"

This module covers the basic tools and actions needed for administrating a MySQL database in order to keep it secure and available for reliable use. The first section covers security in terms of access and command privileges and the creation and safekeeping of database backups.

The second section covers the correct procedures to follow in order to recover from a disaster using backups and a variety of commands to check, repair, and /or restore the database to a functional level again.

Appendixes

Appendix A contains the Mastery Check questions from the end of each chapter along with their respective answers. Appendix B contains the alphanumeric listing of the MySQL Reserved Words, which should enable you to avoid unfortunate or confusing naming conventions for database table and column names. Appendix C provides basic syntax and an overview of PHP for those users who have little or no experience with it.

Ask the Expert

Occasionally, more detailed information on a particular subject will be offered in an "Ask the Expert" section, which is couched in a question and answer format.

Progress Checks

Throughout each module, there will periodically be a list of questions, immediately followed by their answers at the bottom of the page, covering the material just discussed. If the questions are difficult to answer, or confusing, this is a sign you might want to review the previous material again before proceeding.

Mastery Checks

At the end of each module there are ten or more Mastery Check questions covering the most important points that should be gleaned from each module. The answers to the Mastery Check questions are in Appendix A in the back of the book.

Module 1

Installing MySQL

CRITICAL SKILLS

Although databases can be used for many complex things, they are basically places to store information in a standardized manner. The purpose of a database is to allow you to access data rapidly and to manipulate data so that you can present it in a meaningful and useful manner. A database can be as simple as a list of people who have visited a particular web site and signed the guestbook or as complicated as the financial records for a multinational corporation.

With the rise of e-commerce (buying and selling over the Internet), increasing numbers of people have found a need for a database that is cost-effective, fast, scalable, and easy to use. Judging from the manner in which MySQL is rising in popularity, for many people, it fills that need.

This module covers preparing to use MySQL and installing MySQL on your chosen operating system. First, we will clarify some basic definitions for common database terms and describe how MySQL works as open source software. Then you will find out why choosing a platform should be more than an exercise in brand loyalty. After that, you will go through the step-by-step projects for installing MySQL. Once you have MySQL installed, you will be introduced to its command-line interface. Finally, you will become familiar with the resources available after you have progressed beyond the boundaries of a beginner's guide.

CRITICAL SKILL
1.1 Know Basic Database Terms

Every area of study either evolves its own language or adopts familiar words to be used in a new context. Computer jargon is no exception, and the subject of databases has its usual share of seemingly ordinary words, which suddenly take on new meaning when you venture into this new realm.

Fortunately, the terms used to talk about databases are everyday words and easy to remember. The real confusion comes from the fact that, in a several cases, more than one word is used to refer to the same thing. However, there are occasionally subtle distinctions. For example, the terms *column* and *row* are usually used when referring to the dimensions of the database, and the terms *field* and *record* are usually used when referring to the contents of the database. But for all practical purposes, the words *column* and *field* mean the same thing, as do *row* and *record*, and the terms are used interchangeably. As long as you remember that the terms are basically interchangeable, you will get the gist of it.

Table 1-1 defines some common terms used with databases.

There is one more thing about MySQL terminology that leads to some degree of confusion. The MySQL AB (the official name of the company that maintains and distributes MySQL) developers decided to name everything to do with their program MySQL. The database server, the database client, and the default database that holds the login and other operational information are all forms of *MySQL*.

When you install and start MySQL, you are starting the MySQL Server (or Service). This means that the software that is the active part of the program, together with its settings and databases, is running and accessible.

Field	A single piece of information defined by type, length, and other attributes
Record	A single set of fields, which are ordered in a defined manner and related as a single set of information
Column	Used interchangeably with *field*, it also implies every instance of that field in every row of the database table
Row	Used interchangeably with *record*
Table	A finite set of defined, ordered columns (fields), which can contain any number of rows (records)
Relational database	A database in which data items and the relationships between them are gathered in a table or collection of tables, in which certain fields can be set as keys to aid data retrieval
Key	A field set as the specific piece of a record used for indexing the data for quicker retrieval
Index	Used interchangeably with *key*

Table 1-1 Common Terms Used with Databases

The next step usually involves communicating with the MySQL Service, and that is done via the MySQL Client. You open the MySQL Client by running a command on your computer's command line. You have probably guessed by now that the command to do that is also `mysql`. At this point, your normal command-line prompt is replaced by the MySQL Client prompt, which unsurprisingly, looks like this:

```
mysql>
```

When you run the command to show the default tables installed in MySQL, you see two tables listed: `test` and, once again, `mysql`.

In order to be clear in this book, when we refer to MySQL, we mean the entire program or the company that makes it. We will refer to the other three components as the MySQL Server, the MySQL Client, and the `mysql` database.

CRITICAL SKILL
1.2 Understand the Open Source and MySQL Relationship

Open source is one of today's hottest buzzwords, and for many, the choice to go with open source software takes on an almost crusading tone. However, the choices involving open source are not as black and white as some would have us think.

Open Source vs. Proprietary Software

Let's look at the two basic questions about open source:

- What does it mean by the word *free*?

- Why is it better or worse than the alternatives?

A common misconception is that open source software is always free of cost. Within a set of defined parameters (the Open Source Licensing Agreement), programs that are written as open source, or are innovations based on other open source code, can be packaged and sold. What open source does mean is that any open source program can be improved upon or used as the basis for another program, without needing to enter into complex contractual agreements to be allowed to even look at the source code. The source code is free in the sense of the intellectual property being open, or available, to all. The result is that a multitude of programmers can review, improve, and evolve popular programs.

A company may choose to release its product under a variety of open source licenses and most, including MySQL AB, do. This means that depending on the product, it can be literally free in the monetary sense, or it can be sold at varying levels of cost, as long as the original license for the software involved is transferred with the new product on which it is based.

Because so many programmers review the code, fix bugs and security issues, and add improvements of their own, open source programs tend to be more reliable and to have a faster development cycle (including quicker enhancements in response to user requests) than closed source, or proprietary, software. Using open source programs can also be more cost-effective. A company with proprietary software may charge hundreds or thousands of dollars per end user (licensing seat). In contrast, the Open Source License guarantees that open source software must be redistributable. Instead of buying a copy for each computer in your company that needs a particular program, you may be able to download it to each computer for free, or choose to buy one copy and have everyone throughout the workplace access it from a main server.

Why then would anyone buy copies of something they can get for free? There are some advantages to buying open source software rather than downloading it for free:

- The purchased package, unlike the freeware version, includes a warranty and, in most cases, support contracts.

- Other open source programs that dovetail well with the main program are often bundled into the packaged versions.

- You might want to support continuing improvements by the company that provides the software you use and depend on. Once you've found a program that is easily attainable, works well, and is cost-effective, it only makes sense to pay a reasonably affordable licensing fee to support the company that provides and improves on it.

Purchasing an open source package can lead to a faster, more convenient installation and a worry-free startup period.

MySQL As Open Source

MySQL AB subscribes to the open source view of software development and sales, and the company has what is referred to as a *dual-license* paradigm. If you are using MySQL on a small scale, you can download it for free. However, if you begin using the product on a more professional level, you are required to pay a reasonable licensing fee for its use. For some applications, the GNU General Public License (GPL) is adequate, but for others, a commercial license is more applicable. The MySQL web site (www.mysql.com) is the best place to investigate which licensing approach best applies to your situation.

MySQL AB's stated desire is that its database be affordable, available, and uncomplicated to use. The product should be always improving, while staying reliable, bug-free, and fast operating. Judging by the over 4 million active MySQL installations worldwide and over 35 thousand downloads per day, there are plenty of people willing to trust the results of the open source philosophy, given its obvious immediate rewards in terms of reliability and cost.

The relative youth of MySQL AB as a company (nine years' old) also supports the rapid development claims of open source in general and MySQL specifically. While protecting the intellectual property of source code seems instinctively advisable from a traditional, commerce-oriented point of view, MySQL's growth as a product that rapidly responds to its users' needs goes a long way toward positing that just because business has always been done in a way that seems right, that does not mean that it is the only or necessarily right way. Open source and companies willing to embrace that vision, like MySQL AB, appear to be here to stay, not only carving a place for themselves, but also perhaps shaping the way the future manufacturers of software do business.

There has been much made of the migration of various larger-sized companies to open source environments. Rather than indicating the death knell of proprietary software, it simply indicates that the point of viability for open source software in the business world has been reached and indeed passed. It has happened faster than most industry observers would have guessed, which arguably validates the claim of the open source community that rapid development is a hallmark of the open source software process.

CRITICAL SKILL
1.3 # Choose Your Development and Deployment Environments

You can install MySQL on both Windows and Linux platforms. Within the context of MySQL, there is little or no difference in the way it looks and feels to the user on either platform. However, the verbal battle continues between these two major operating systems (OSs). Lines are drawn in the sand, insults are hurled, and printed T-shirts are worn—all in the name of what each side fervently believes is the one true, best OS.

All the hoopla and proselytizing can make what should be a calm and logical decision seem difficult. Fortunately, there are some criteria to help you decide which OS to use for your MySQL database.

Applying Broad Criteria

To start the decision process, consider three broad criteria:

- The size of the project
- Whether equipment is already available or must be purchased
- The technological level of the participants

If, for instance, the project is a hobby or home-based business, and you already own an adequate PC complete with an operating system you are already familiar with, it might not make sense to change to another OS. You would only be adding time (learning all new software) and expense (new software at the very least and possibly a new, upgraded computer to run it on) to the project.

On the other hand, you might be a corporation that needs multiple computers for multiple users, with technologically aware employees. The upgrading to new equipment may already be viewed as a necessary cost of maintaining the competitive status of your company or its product. Then the next step of narrowing down the decision process is more important.

Narrowing the Decision

Here are seven basic areas that are often used to evaluate an OS:

- Ease of use
- Reliability
- Speed
- Functionality
- Integration with Microsoft technologies
- Availability of free/open source software
- Price

Let's take them one at a time.

Ease of Use

Ease of use can be argued from either side, but it has always been considered a given that Windows was easier to use because of its focus on user-friendliness. However, over time, the Linux side of the argument has progressed to the point that the difference, if any, is fairly negligible. What used to be a big issue is now pretty much an even draw.

Reliability

If reliability is defined as hours of continuous use without needing to reboot the system, then Linux is clearly the winner. However, for most users outside certain environments (like real-time displays of critical information or Internet servers), the occasional reboot is not a critical issue. And perhaps you normally shut down your computer on a fairly regular basis anyway. Once again, both sides come out fairly even, except for continuous use situations, where Linux has the advantage.

Speed

Speed is another variable that changes as rapidly as the latest advances in both hardware and software. Once again, certain areas of use (most notably Internet servers required to handle huge volumes of information transfers) may find the Linux side of the debate handles individual file transfers faster, especially in an Internet environment. However, for most uses, there is no practical difference in speed between the OSs.

It should be noted, however, that some programs operate faster on one OS than they do on the other. For example, MySQL, depending on the situation, can operate 30 to 50 percent faster on Linux than it does on Windows. If your database is being accessed by large numbers of users simultaneously, this could be very important. If only one or a few users access it at any given time, speed becomes less of a factor on which to base your decision.

Functionality

Functionality refers to the availability of programs to perform needed functions on a particular OS. This used to be a big bone of contention, with many more programs developed for the Windows OS than for Linux. These days, almost everything that can be done on one platform can be done with the other, although it is usually accomplished with different programs. There are more programs than ever that have been ported to work on both OSs. If the same program isn't available, usually other software can obtain the same end results.

So, if ease of use, reliability, speed, and functionality of the two OSs are more or less similar, we are still at a draw in the decision-making process, so let's continue.

Integration with Microsoft Technologies and Free/Open Source Software

Two areas where there will always be clear differences are integration with Microsoft technologies and availability of free or open source software. Windows will probably always come out ahead with regard to integration with Microsoft technologies. Linux will probably always come out ahead when you're considering the availability of free or open source software.

If you are already significantly invested in specific programs—through cost, industry standards, or experience in its use—it may make sense for you to stick with the OS that supports those programs. Occasionally, a specific program will function on both OSs. Then it is wise to look at how long it has been available for each OS. The one that has been available longer will be more robust and reliable, given that it has had more operational time for bug fixes and enhancements to occur.

Price

This leaves us with the final point of comparison: price. This is the one area where Linux is the undisputed winner. The development costs of software in an open source environment are often spread among many companies, and the licensing structure exists to promote that style of development (rather than enable a single company to recoup its much higher, individual development costs). Linux products are distributed free or at comparatively reduced fees, and they are often packaged in convenient bundles. If you decide to purchase the open source software, it is usually offered with support services at a much lower rate than proprietary software could ever afford to match.

Whether you are a private user or a company of whatever size, you can use the criteria described here to make an informed decision, without relying on the rhetoric of the entrenched proponents of both Windows and Linux. As in many areas, cost seems to be the overriding criteria, with the other six jockeying for place, depending on the type and complexity of your specific project. Whichever one you choose in the end, base that choice on reasons that make sense to you and apply to your specific situation.

Once you've decided on an OS, you're ready to install MySQL. Read the next "Critical Skill" section if you're using Windows, or skip to "Critical Skill 1-5" if you're installing MySQL on a Linux system.

CRITICAL SKILL
1.4 Install MySQL on Windows

To install MySQL on a Windows system, you need to have the following things available on your computer:

● Windows 95, 98, Millennium Edition (Me), NT, 2000, or XP

● A ZIP program to unpack the distribution file

● Enough space on the hard drive to unpack, install, and create your desired databases

If you are reading this section, you are presumably using one of the specified Windows OSs.

If you do not have a ZIP program currently installed on your computer, you can download one of a variety of programs available on the Internet, including many freeware or free trial versions. WinZip, a widely used version of this type of program, is user-friendly and reliable; a free trial version is available for download at http://www.winzip.com. Also, the registered version is comparatively inexpensive.

If you are going to install a database on your computer, you need to have enough room for it. It can be difficult for anyone to predict how large their databases may eventually grow. MySQL needs around 100 megabytes (MB) to install. Beginners are recommended to have at least 150MB to 200MB of free space before running the installation process. One of the pluses about MySQL is its ease of mobility. If your database outgrows its current location, you need only copy the current data to another, larger location (such as a newly installed hard drive), and then change the `datadir` setting. As long as you have around 200MB, you can start your database. If necessary, you can easily expand your database and change the settings for your database later.

Note that if you require tables larger than 4 gigabytes (GB), you will need to install MySQL on an NTFS or newer file system and use the commands `max_rows` and `avg_row_length` when creating the tables.

When you're using the Windows OS for your MySQL database, you'll also want to install MyODBC on your computer. Open Database Connectivity (ODBC) is a standardized Application Programming Interface (API) that allows you to connect to SQL databases. That means client programs can access many different kinds of databases or data sources. When connecting to MySQL from Windows, many programs require an ODBC connection, MyODBC is the ODBC designed by MySQL specifically to interface with all its supported platforms. Just to make things slightly more confusing, MySQL has a new term, Connector/ODBC, coined to cover its entire ODBC product line, but for simplicity, we use the term *MyODBC*.

Project
1-1

Project 1-1 Install MySQL on Windows and Start the MySQL Service

In this project, you will install MySQL on your Windows machine. Then you will start the MySQL service, so that you can start using MySQL.

NOTE

For the projects in this book, the MySQL installation default settings are more than adequate. The "Ask the Expert" section after the project covers questions about installing and running your database with the MySQL default settings.

Install MySQL on Windows and Start the MySQL Service

(continued)

Step by Step

1. Open a web browser and go to http://www.mysql.com/downloads/index.html.

2. Scroll down to MySQL database server & standard clients and click the link for the (highest numbered) **MySQL** *x.x* **-- Production release (recommended)**.

3. Scroll down to **Windows downloads** and click the **Pick a mirror** link at the end of the **Windows 95/98/NT/2000/XP/2003 (x86)** line.

4. Pick a mirror site close to you and click its link.

5. Select to save the file to My Downloads or another directory of your choice. After the download is complete, minimize your browser.

6. In Windows Explorer, go to My Downloads or the directory you chose and unzip the mysql-x.x.x-win.zip file. (You can either extract the files to a folder and save them in their unzipped format or install from within the ZIP program, which will save the files to a temporary folder during installation.)

```
WinZip - mysql-4.0.16-win.zip                                    _ □ ✕
File  Actions  Options  Help

  New      Open    Favorites    Add     Extract    View     Install    Wizard

 Name              Modified            Size   Ratio   Packed   Path
 Data.tag          10/20/2003 9:18 PM     115     6%      108
 Setup.exe         11/19/1997 3:09 PM  59,904    49%   30,729
 Setup.ini         10/20/2003 9:18 PM      67     0%       67
 _inst32i.ex_      11/19/1997 3:05 PM 300,178     0%  299,572
 _isdel.exe        11/19/1997 3:05 PM   8,192    54%    3,774
 _setup.dll        11/19/1997 3:08 PM  11,264    72%    3,108
 _sys1.cab         10/20/2003 9:18 PM 186,302    12%  163,557
 _user1.cab        10/20/2003 9:18 PM  45,173    75%   11,315
 data1.cab         10/20/2003 9:18 PM 23,316,...   0%  23,272...
 lang.dat          5/30/1997 11:31 AM   4,557    55%    2,065
 layout.bin        10/20/2003 9:18 PM     388    69%      120
 os.dat            5/6/1997 2:15 PM       417    62%      160
 setup.bmp         10/20/2003 9:15 PM  15,694    89%    1,793
 setup.ins         10/20/2003 9:15 PM  57,122    75%   13,998
 setup.lid         10/20/2003 9:18 PM      49     8%       45

 Selected 0 files, 0 bytes           Total 15 files, 23,443KB    ⚪ ⚪
```

7. Double-click Setup.exe. The MySQL Servers and Clients installer wizard opens. No input is required on the Welcome screen.

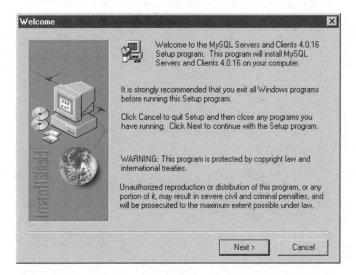

8. Click the Next button. The Information screen covers information about the configuration file (either my.cnf or my.ini) and the mandatory lines of information that are required for MySQL configuration. We'll discuss the configuration files briefly after your installation is complete.

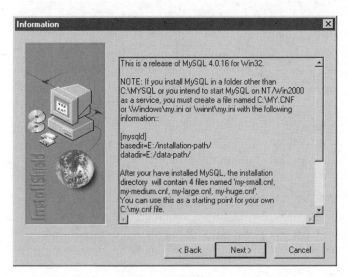

9. Click the Next button. The Choose Destination Location screen, shown next, appears.

(continued)

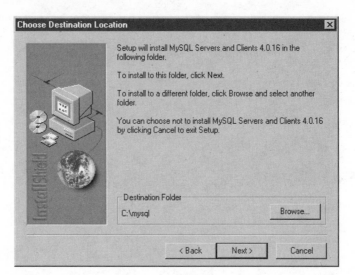

10. If possible, accept the default storage location and click Next. However, if you need to use a folder other than the default, click Browse and select it. After you choose the storage folder, the Setup Type screen appears.

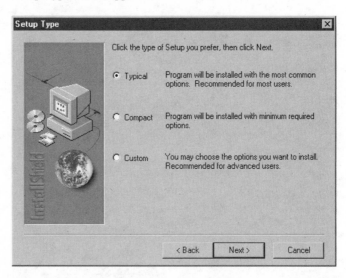

11. Make sure the radio button for Typical is chosen, and then click the Next button. Typical animated graphics will appear, indicating the progress of the installation. When it has completed, click the Finish button in the screen that appears.

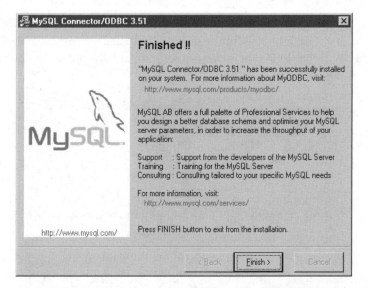

12. To start the MySQL service, open Windows Explorer to C:\mysql\bin and scroll down to winmysqladmin.exe.

NOTE

For later convenience, you may want to place a shortcut on your desktop by right-clicking the winmysqladmin.exe file, selecting Create Shortcut, and then dragging the resulting icon onto your desktop area.

(continued)

13. Double-click winmysqladmin.exe. The WinMySQLAdmin window flashes briefly on the screen and is replaced by the Quick Setup window. In this window, enter a user name and password. We recommend **root** as the user name and a password that is not a word found in the dictionary.

CAUTION

The user name and *unencrypted* password will appear in the my.ini file, which is located on the C:\ drive in either the \Windows or \WINNT folder, depending on your operating system. For security reasons, you may wish to make this password unique from your other passwords and also have a password on your screensaver to prevent unauthorized access.

14. Click the OK button. The MySQL traffic light appears in the tray on the right side of the Windows toolbar. The green (or bottom) light should be "on" (the most noticeable), indicating that the MySQL service is running. If the red (or top) light is on, right-click the traffic light and click either WinNT or Win9X, and then click Start the Service. The amber (or middle) light indicates that the service is in the process of shutting down or coming up, and it is usually only a momentary status indicator.

Project Summary

If you followed the steps in Project 1-1, you now have MySQL installed on your Windows computer. You also started the MySQL service, which should be running now.

In step 8 of the project, you saw that the Information screen of the installer wizard gives some basic, if slightly confusing, information about the two types of configuration files:

my.cnf and my.ini. The older name for the configuration files is my.cnf, and that filename is still supported. The newer name, and the name MySQL searches for first, is my.ini.

MySQL requires either the my.cnf or my.ini file in order to run. However, if you start MySQL for the first time without one of these files, the program will make the file for you, complete with default settings. MySQL recommends that novice users let its startup routine create the default configuration file for them. If you let the program create the my.ini file, you are operating with the MySQL recommended default settings.

Experienced users who may need different configuration settings can either use the program-generated configuration file (my.ini) or select one of the files provided in the \mysql\ directory: my-huge.ini, my-large.ini, my-medium.ini, or my-small.ini. See the "Ask the Expert" section after Project 1-2 for more information about changing configuration settings.

The WinMySQLAdmin Tool

Now that the MySQL service is installed and running, let's look at the type of information available from the WinMySQLAdmin tool. Right-click the traffic light in the toolbar tray and click Show Me. A window similar to Figure 1-1 will appear, with the traffic light in the upper-right corner.

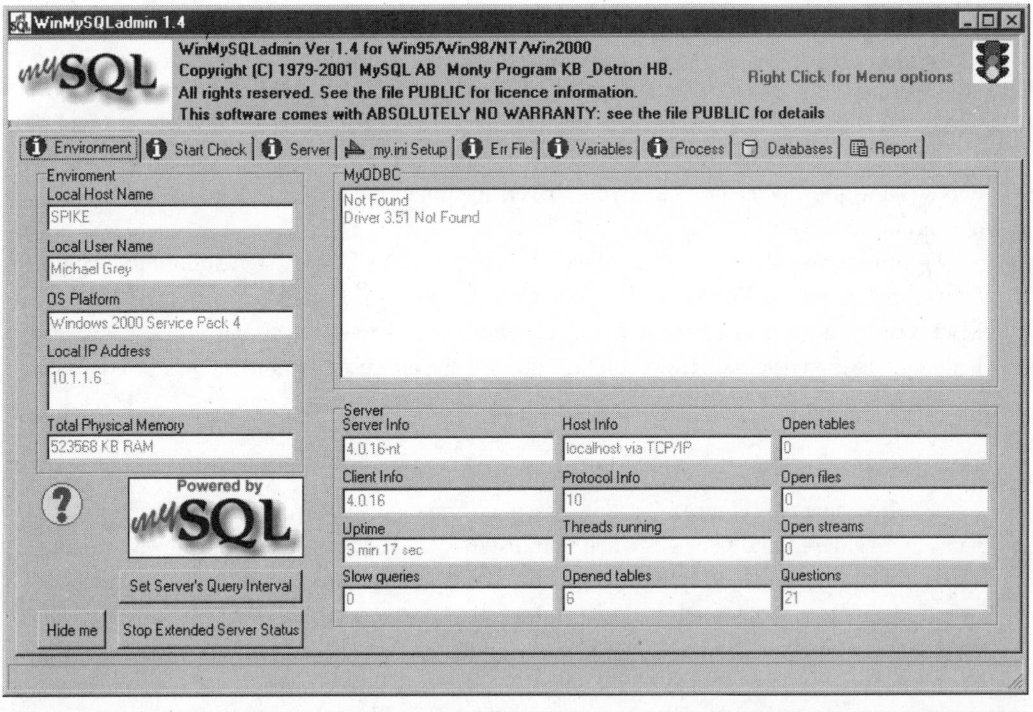

Figure 1-1 The default view of the WinMySQLAdmin tool before MyODBC has been installed

Right-clicking anywhere in this window gives you the following menu options:

- **Hide Me**   Use to minimize WinMySQLAdmin but leave it running to continue to collect data about the MySQL service. There is also a Hide me button in the lower-left corner of the WinMySQLAdmin window.

NOTE

Clicking the X button in the top-right corner of WinMySQLAdmin will close the WinMySQLAdmin window. It will not shut down the MySQL service.

- **Win9X or WinNT**   One or the other will be active, depending on your OS. Both lead to the next level of menu options.

- **Shutdown this Tool**   This closes WinMySQLAdmin but does not shut down the MySQL service.

- **Stop the Service**   This shuts down the MySQL service but does not close WinMySQLAdmin. It also activates the following two choices on the second level of menu options.

- **Start the Service**   This restarts the MySQL service.

- **Remove the Service**   This starts an uninstall wizard to remove MySQL from your computer.

If you choose Shutdown this Tool, Stop the Service, Start the Service, or Remove the Service, a window pops up, asking you for verification of the chosen procedure as a safety precaution.

Figure 1-1 also shows the rows of nine tabs at the top of WinMySQLAdmin: Environment, Start Check, Server, my.ini Setup, Err File, Variables, Process, Databases, and Report. The good news is that you do not need to know much about these tabs to start working with MySQL and building your first database. However, they do contain some useful information, so we will take a quick look at each of these tabs.

The Environment Tab

The Environment tab (Figure 1-1) shows basic information, such as the user and computer names you entered into your OS when you installed it. The Server section shows statistics like uptime (how long the MySQL service has been running since last started), the number of threads running, and the number of open tables. It also states what level of MySQL is currently installed and whether you have ODBC connections or an ODBC driver installed. The Not Found in the MyODBC window in Figure 1-1 means that there are no ODBC connections, and the Driver 3.51 Not Found means the ODBC Driver is not installed yet.

The Start Check and Server Tabs

The Start Check tab simply shows the system checks MySQL goes through when it starts the service. This information might be useful in debugging the database if it refuses to start.

The Server tab shows the number of processes that have been or are running and updates itself at regular intervals.

The my.ini Setup Tab

The my.ini Setup tab, shown in Figure 1-2, is interesting in several ways. It shows the my.ini file that MySQL created for you when it initially started up after installation, including some lines of code that are written in the correct format for use later, but commented out with a pound sign (#) until you decide that you need them.

The Pick-up and Edit my.ini values and Save Modifications buttons allow you to edit the my.ini file through this interface without using an outside text editor. Using these buttons is a safe way to edit the my.ini file, because you can't accidentally resave it to the wrong place.

If you want WinMySQLAdmin to automatically open and start MySQL any time you start or reboot your computer, you can click the Create ShortCut on Start Menu button.

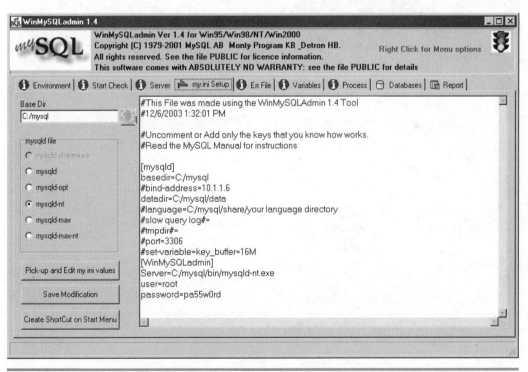

Figure 1-2 The my.ini tab has buttons to safely edit and resave the my.ini file.

The Err File, Variables, Process, and Report Tabs

The Err File, Variables, Process, and Report tabs show information that may be useful as you become more familiar with MySQL. You may want to take a glance at their current contents to familiarize yourself with the types of information they hold. It's not important that you understand it all, but do try to get an idea of where you can find particular information later if you have problems or want to view statistics.

The Databases Tab

The Databases tab shows all the individual databases set up within MySQL and their component table structure and keys. Initially, `mysql` and `test` are the default databases, and you should be able to see those.

Figure 1-3 shows the Databases tab with the `mysql` database selected (clicked in the Databases list in the upper left) and the `columns_priv` table selected (click in the Database

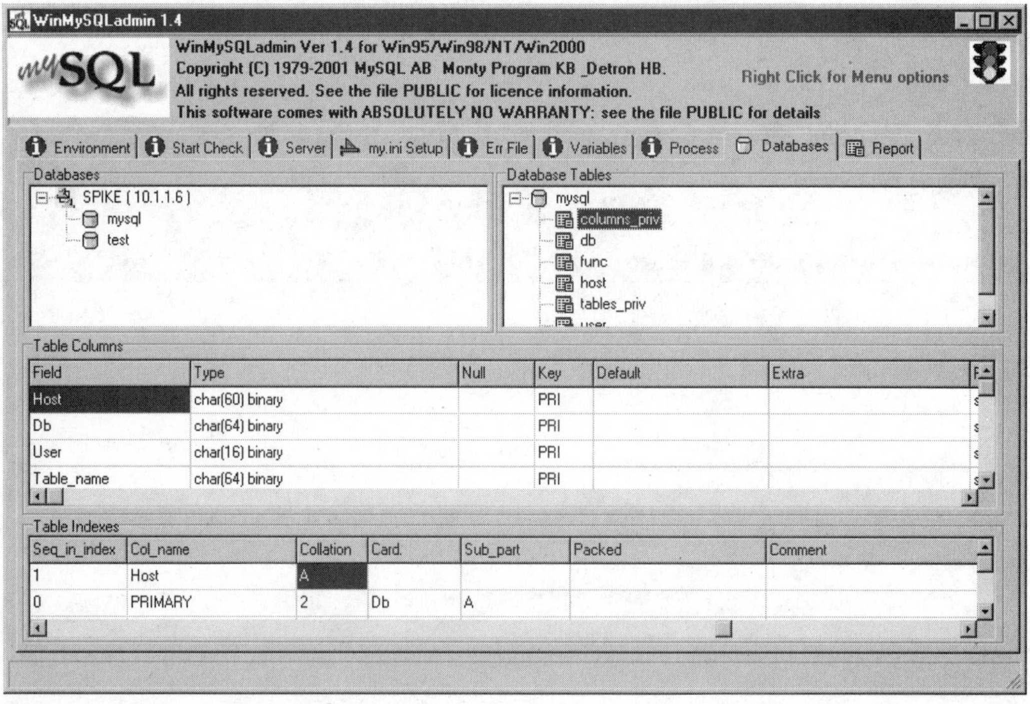

Figure 1-3 The Databases tab showing the columns_priv table information of the mysql database

Tables list in the upper right). The Table Columns list box shows how each field in the selected table (`columns_priv`) is defined. The Table Indexes list box shows what, if any, indexing key or keys have been set in the selected table.

If you select the `test` database, you will see that it does not have any tables defined yet.

The `mysql` database holds the user information for your MySQL service in general. For instance, information about the user name and password you entered during startup and the existence of the two default databases is stored here. Any subsequent users you allow access to the system and databases you build will be added to the information stored in `mysql`.

You should not alter the `mysql` database for experimental purposes. If you want to try commands before creating your first database, do your experimenting in the `test` database only. As the name suggests, that is its purpose.

As you saw on the Environment tab of WinMySQLAdmin, you do not have an ODBC driver installed yet. Let's take care of that now.

Project 1-2 Download and Install MyODBC on Windows

In this project, you will complete your setup on a Windows computer by downloading and installing MyODBC, which allows you to access databases from a Windows computer. We use MyODBC in Module 7.

Step by Step

1. Open a web browser and go to http://www.mysql.com/downloads/api-myodbc-3.51.html.

2. Scroll down to **Windows downloads** and click **Pick a mirror** at the right end of the **Driver Installer** line.

3. Choose a mirror location near you and click its link.

4. Select to save MyODBC-3.51.06.exe into My Downloads or another folder of your choice.

5. Close your browser and open Windows Explorer to My Downloads, or whatever folder you chose to use. Double-click MyODBC-3.51.06.exe.

6. The installer wizard will open, showing the MyODBC Welcome screen, which is shown next.

(continued)

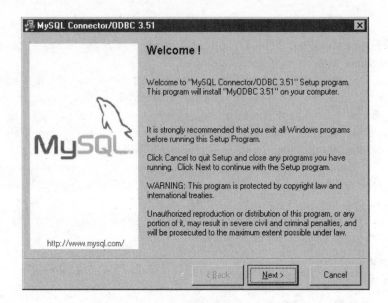

7. Click the Next button. The ReadMe screen opens.

8. Click the Next button. The Start Installation screen opens. It says to choose Next to continue or use the Back button to reenter installation information, but your memory hasn't fooled you—if you click the Back button, there is no place to enter any such information.

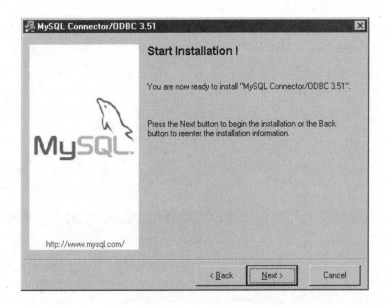

9. Click the Next button. The installation progress bars will show fleetingly, and then the Finished window appears.

10. Click the Finish button.

(continued)

11. To check the MyODBC installation, close WinMySQLAdmin (right-click, choose Win9X or WinNT, and then choose Shutdown this Tool).

12. Open WinMySQLAdmin, either by using the shortcut you placed earlier on your desktop or the one at Start | Programs | Startup | WinMySQLAdmin if you used the Create ShortCut on Start Menu button on the my.ini tab. If you haven't set up either of these options, locate winmysqladmin.exe in the C:\mysql folder and double-click it.

13. Once WinMySQLAdmin is open again, check the MyODBC window in the Environment tab. It will still say Not Found, as it did in Figure 1-1 because you have not set up any ODBC connections yet, but it will now list information about the ODBC driver and its .dll locations.

Project Summary

You now have both MySQL and MyODBC drivers installed on your Windows computer. MyODBC drivers allow a variety of programs to connect and interact with MySQL. You will learn more about MyODBC in Module 7, which covers GUIs and other Windows-related data-handling options.

Ask the Expert

Q: Why might I change the default settings in MySQL?

A: The two most common reasons for changing defaults are these:

- You see a performance decrease in the database's operation.
- You want to do something that requires a lot of resources.

If you notice a decrease in performance, it can often be solved by changed the amount of RAM specified in the my.cnf or my.ini file from the default setting of 8MB. This usually happens after the database has been in place for a while and is growing either in size or number of users. In that case, the change to the setting would be permanent. Some changes can be done temporarily, though. For instance, if you needed to insert a few million rows into your database, you could change the my.ini file settings to make doing this one thing easier. Then, when you are finished with the insertion, you could return the settings to the way they were for normal operation.

Q: When should I change the default settings in MySQL?

A: The important thing is to realize that at the beginner's level, you probably don't need to change them at all. They are certainly adequate to accomplish the projects in this book. However, later on, you may need to change them. Then you need to figure out the relative size of your MySQL database. Is it small, medium, large or huge? Even though this is a relative question, you should have a general idea of how big the database currently is or is going to be in the near future. For most noncorporate/commercial use, small or medium will probably be the answer to that question.

MySQL has included, in the download, four files that correspond to the potential size of your database. In other words, they give you four template files to start from: my-small.cnf, my-medium.cnf, my-large.cnf, and my-huge.cnf. Any of these files can replace the my.cnf file in Linux—the file is located in the /etc directory. In Windows, one of these files would replace the my.ini file. They all represent a starting point from which you can tailor the settings to meet your needs.

Q: What settings should I change?

A: We will assume that you are using the default table type in MySQL, which is MyISAM. (Module 2 covers table types.) The main setting you need to consider changing in the my.cnf or my.ini file is the key_buffer setting, which controls how much RAM is

(continued)

allocated for the storage of indexes. By default, it is set at 8MB. If you have a computer whose only function is to be your MySQL server, then the sum of the data size in the indexed columns may be greater than 8MB. If this happens, the MySQL application will need to swap to the hard drive to keep up because the buffer size is only 8MB. Swapping slows the performance of your database.

This buffer is the culmination of all of the indexed data (data size) from all of the tables in all of the databases running on the MySQL server. If the server has a total of 2GB of RAM, you may easily have over 1GB of unused RAM that is essentially sitting idle and can be used for this function. Remember that when you set these buffer settings, you are reallocating RAM, and this RAM will not be used for anything else. Once MySQL allocates a portion of RAM for itself, nothing else is allowed to use it, even if it is idle. If your computer is used for other things in unison with MySQL (including the operating system itself), then some RAM needs to be left for those operations.

Another setting you will probably change, once your real database is up and running, is one or more of the logging functions. Module 7 gives a more complete picture of the available settings with which you may alter your MySQL database should practical experience demonstrate the necessity. For now, simply remember that logging functions can be turned on and off in your my.cnf or my.ini file. By setting logs on and specifying their locations in the my.cnf or my.ini file, you save time by having logging taken care of automatically. It also means that you don't need to remember to turn on the logs. The one time you forget will likely be the one time you truly need the information gathered by the logging functions.

Q: **What other settings might I eventually change in the my.cnf or my.ini file?**

A: You can tell the MySQL server not to load variables and preallocate resources for table types you are not going to use, such as Berkeley (BDB) tables. You would do this by inserting the setting `skip-bdb`. If variables are loaded for a table type you are not using, part of your RAM still gets allocated for it, and once again, cannot be used by anything else (even other MySQL functions), which means you are reserving resources that will never get used.

You might also need to change which port the MySQL server uses. You can do this by inserting the setting `port=3306`, for instance, in the `[mysqld]` section of the file. You might want to do this for security reasons, or if you are running MySQL through an Internet host, you may be required to do it by your hosting company because of its setup. If you need to change the port number, you do it in the my.cnf or my.ini file. And if you do change the port number, you must remember to change which port the client is attempting to connect through in the client's settings. These topics will be covered in more detail in Module 8.

CRITICAL SKILL
1.5 Install MySQL on Linux

It's easy to install MySQL on a Linux OS. In order to download the files, you will need a Linux browser, an FTP program, or access to a Windows browser and FTP program.

Unlike with Windows installations, Linux users rarely need to install MyODBC (the ODBC designed by MySQL). MySQL's manual notes that ColdFusion is the only commonly used program that requires the MyODBC interface.

Before you install the database on your computer, make sure you have enough room for it. It can be difficult to predict how large a database may eventually grow. MySQL needs around 100 megabytes (MB) to install. Beginners are recommended to have at least 150MB to 200MB of free space before running the installation process. As long as you have around 200MB, you can start your database. If necessary, you can easily expand your database and change the settings for your database later.

Project 1-3 Download and Install MySQL on Linux

In this project, you will download MySQL, install it, and set a password. Depending on whether or not your Linux computer is set up to use a graphical interface (`startx`), you may use a Linux browser to download the necessary files, transfer the files using a file transfer program (FTP) to a MySQL mirror site (`ftp <close-ftp-site-from-list-on-MySQL-site>`), or use a browser on a Windows machine and an FTP to place them on your Linux machine.

NOTE

The screen captures for the Linux-related projects were taken by using a Windows-based program to view the Linux command line. Therefore, the window's appearance will differ slightly from that of a Linux-based one, but the command-line view is the same.

Step by Step

1. Open a browser and go to http://www.mysql.com/downloads/index.html.

2. Scroll down to **MySQL database server & standard clients** and click the link for the (highest numbered) **MySQL x.x -- Production release (recommended)**.

3. Scroll down to the box labeled **Linux RPM downloads**.

(continued)

4. Download the appropriate (for most users, Linux x86 RPM downloads) **Server** and **Client Program** RPMs to /usr/local/src.

5. From the /usr/local/src directory, you can install both the Server and Client packages at the same time with the following the RPM command:

```
rpm -i <server filename> <client filename>
```

```
Doc - SecureCRT                                                       _ □ ×
File  Edit  View  Options  Transfer  Script  Window  Help

[root@Doc src]# ls
httpd-2.0.47      MySQL-client-4.0.16-0.i386.rpm   php-4.3.3
httpd-2.0.47.tar  MySQL-server-4.0.16-0.i386.rpm   php-4.3.3.tar
[root@Doc src]# rpm -i MySQL-server-4.0.16-0.i386.rpm  MySQL-client-4.0.16-0.i386.rpm
warning: MySQL-server-4.0.16-0.i386.rpm: V3 DSA signature: NOKEY, key ID 5072e1f5
Preparing db table
Preparing host table
Preparing user table
Preparing func table
Preparing tables_priv table
Preparing columns_priv table
Installing all prepared tables
031212 11:24:48  /usr/sbin/mysqld: Shutdown Complete


PLEASE REMEMBER TO SET A PASSWORD FOR THE MySQL root USER !
This is done with:
/usr/bin/mysqladmin -u root password 'new-password'
/usr/bin/mysqladmin -u root -h Doc password 'new-password'
See the manual for more instructions.

Please report any problems with the /usr/bin/mysqlbug script!

The latest information about MySQL is available on the web at
http://www.mysql.com
Support MySQL by buying support/licenses at https://order.mysql.com

Starting mysqld daemon with databases from /var/lib/mysql
[root@Doc src]# █

Ready                              ssh1: 3DES  29, 17   29 Rows, 88 Cols  VT100        NUM
```

Alternatively, you can install them separately with the following two commands, which check to see if there are previous versions already installed, and if so, upgrades instead of running a full installation:

```
rpm -Uvh <server filename>
rpm -Uvh <client filename>
```

6. To verify that MySQL is installed and running, enter the following command:

```
mysqladmin -p ping
```

If MySQL is running, it will return the message "mysql is alive." If not, it will return an error message.

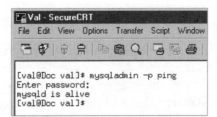

```
[val@Doc val]$ mysqladmin -p ping
Enter password:
mysqld is alive
[val@Doc val]$
```

7. As the screen showed when you ran the `rpm` command to install MySQL, there is no password on the database on initial startup. For security, it is important to set a password for the root MySQL user now by entering the following two commands, one at a time. The first command sets the root password as `pa55w0rd` (you should type your own chosen password in place of `pa55w0rd`). The second line sets the password of `root@localhost` (`hostname` determines the localhost name and places it in the `mysqladmin` command).

NOTE

Make sure to use the backtick to surround the word `hostname` rather than the single quotation mark. The backtick (`` ` ``) is usually located in the upper-left corner of the keyboard, with the tilde (~) as its shifted symbol.

```
/usr/bin/mysqladmin -u root PASSWORD pa55w0rd
/usr/bin/mysqladmin -u root -h `hostname` PASSWORD pa55w0rd
```

```
[root@Doc src]# /usr/bin/mysqladmin -u root password pa55w0rd
[root@Doc src]# /usr/bin/mysqladmin -u root -h `hostname` password pa55w0rd
[root@Doc src]#
[root@Doc src]#
[root@Doc src]#
```

8. Type **mysql -p** and press ENTER. The password prompt will come up.

9. Type your password and press ENTER. The prompt will change from the *localhost/directory* prompt to the `mysql` prompt.

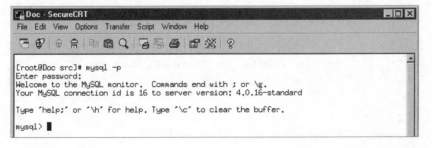

```
[root@Doc src]# mysql -p
Enter password:
Welcome to the MySQL monitor.  Commands end with ; or \g.
Your MySQL connection id is 16 to server version: 4.0.16-standard

Type 'help;' or '\h' for help. Type '\c' to clear the buffer.

mysql>
```

(continued)

Project Summary

You now have all the necessary software installed on Linux to proceed to the rest of the projects. Your computer has two default databases installed: `mysql` and `test`. MySQL has created a my.cnf file with default settings for you in the /etc directory. For information about why you might change from those defaults, see the "Ask the Expert" section that preceded "Critical Skill 1.5."

CRITICAL SKILL
1.6 Learn How to Use the Command Line

You may have heard arguments about working on the command line versus using a graphical user interface (GUI) client. These arguments tend to be all for using one or the other. The truth is that both have their strong and weak points.

The main argument you hear for GUIs is that they are faster and easier to use. That assertion is both true and false. GUIs do tend to have a shorter learning curve, since they follow the user-friendly principles we all have come to know and understand. So, in that sense, they are faster to use, especially at the beginning of your learning process. On the other hand, GUIs are programs that take a certain amount of time to start up and get ready to function. If you need to send only one command to MySQL, no matter how bad of a typist you are, it is often quicker and easier to do it from the command line than to open your GUI to execute it.

Our consideration here is which interface works as the better tool for learning how to use MySQL. It's nearly always true that if you need to type a command to get something done, you will have less difficulty remembering it later. This is usually not the case when you are using a point-and-click interface. The GUI seems simple and clear at the moment you are using it, but you'll often experience a complete memory blank when faced with the same task later. You can only make (and find later) so many notes with hurriedly scribbled syntax on them.

As you learn the basics of MySQL, this guide will focus solely on using the command line to communicate with MySQL through the MySQL Client. This is not because we're sadists, but because in the end, it will help you learn MySQL quicker and more effectively. Also, the same commands and responses are seen, whether you're operating in a Linux- or Windows-generated environment. It should make the overall concepts easier to grasp and remember, while reinforcing the underlying syntax and language patterns that make up MySQL administration, definition, and reporting tasks.

Once you can define a new database and its tables, edit their contents, and distill basic and more complex knowledge out of their contents using queries, then (in Module 6) you will return to the GUI. Then you will be armed with the foundation of knowledge that will allow you to use the GUI even more effectively. There will probably be moments when working on the projects ahead that you will be tempted to avoid the more time-consuming command-line typing, but repetition and practice are what turn bare-bones knowledge into instinctive skills, and none of the projects will require horrendous amounts of typing.

By the time you have reintroduced GUIs into your repertoire, you will not have to decide whether the GUI or the command-line method for using the MySQL Client will be faster or easier to accomplish a given task. At that point, it will be instinctive, because you will have developed the underlying experience—the muscles so to speak—that enable you to use the GUI to its fullest potential, instead of merely as an intellectual crutch. So, for all you GUI devotees, be patient; there is method in this command-line madness. For those of you used to a command-line approach, it's still the best way for you to acquire the basics you want, but for some things, the GUI will win out in the end, even with you.

Now let's take a look at running commands from the command line, so you'll be prepared for your command-line work in the following modules. Read either the section about using the command prompt in Windows or using it in Linux, depending on the OS on which you've installed MySQL.

Using the Command Prompt in Windows

To use the MySQL command line, you must first open a DOS window. An easy way to do this is by selecting Start | Run from the desktop, entering **cmd**, and clicking the OK button. You can also use the Command Prompt command from the Start | Programs menu. You may find it convenient to right-click the Command Prompt icon on the menu and make a shortcut, which you can then drag to your desktop for easy access.

When the Command Prompt window opens, type **cd \mysql\bin** and press ENTER. You are now in the directory with the MySQL executables. Type **mysql** and press ENTER to get to the command line mysql prompt.

```
Command Prompt (2) - mysql                               _ □ ×
Microsoft Windows 2000 [Version 5.00.2195]
(C) Copyright 1985-2000 Microsoft Corp.

C:\Documents and Settings\Michael Grey>cd \mysql\bin

C:\mysql\bin>mysql
Welcome to the MySQL monitor.  Commands end with ; or \g.
Your MySQL connection id is 56 to server version: 4.0.16-nt

Type 'help;' or '\h' for help. Type '\c' to clear the buffer.

mysql>
```

Now that you are at the MySQL command line prompt, let's look at a few commands that are essential. Type **help** and press ENTER. As shown in Figure 1-4, a list of all the MySQL commands appears, along with a backslash (\) shortcut for each. A backslash shortcut is an abbreviated way of typing a command using a backslash and a single letter. While it is not necessary to memorize them, learning the ones that correspond to the commands you use most often will save time by eliminating typing.

Notice that the help listing also includes a syntax reminder, which says that the command words must come first in the line and must end with a semicolon. In practice, only queries require the ending semicolon. You can enter other commands (help, for instance) without a semicolon, and they will still function properly. However, getting into the habit of using the semicolon, whether or not is required, will help you avoid problems.

```
mysql> help

For the complete MySQL Manual online visit:
   http://www.mysql.com/documentation

For info on technical support from MySQL developers visit:
   http://www.mysql.com/support

For info on MySQL books, utilities, consultants, etc. visit:
   http://www.mysql.com/portal

List of all MySQL commands:
   (Commands must appear first on line and end with ';')

help      (\h)     Display this help.
?         (\?)     Synonym for 'help'.
clear     (\c)     Clear command.
connect   (\r)     Reconnect to the server. Optional arguments are db and host.
ego       (\G)     Send command to mysql server, display result vertically.
exit      (\q)     Exit mysql. Same as quit.
go        (\g)     Send command to mysql server.
notee     (\t)     Don't write into outfile.
print     (\p)     Print current command.
prompt    (\R)     Change your mysql prompt.
quit      (\q)     Quit mysql.
rehash    (\#)     Rebuild completion hash.
source    (\.)     Execute a SQL script file. Takes a file name as an argument.
status    (\s)     Get status information from the server.
tee       (\T)     Set outfile [to_outfile]. Append everything into given outfile.
use       (\u)     Use another database. Takes database name as argument.

Connection id: 56  (Can be used with mysqladmin kill)

mysql>
```

Figure 1-4 The help listing of MYSQL commands and shortcuts in Windows

If you enter a command that requires a semicolon, such as show tables, without the semicolon and press the ENTER key, instead of executing the command, the MySQL Client displays an arrow-shaped prompt instead of the mysql prompt. The system will wait for the closing semicolon indefinitely.

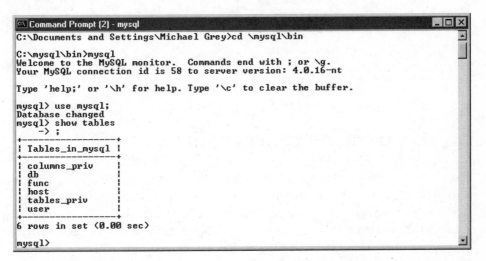

Once the concluding semicolon is entered, the command executes.

To return to the standard C:\ prompt, type either **EXIT** or **QUIT**. The MySQL Client will display bye, and then you'll exit the client.

```
Command Prompt (2)

mysql> use mysql;
Database changed
mysql> show tables
    -> ;
+-----------------+
| Tables_in_mysql |
+-----------------+
| columns_priv    |
| db              |
| func            |
| host            |
| tables_priv     |
| user            |
+-----------------+
6 rows in set (0.00 sec)

mysql> show tables;
+-----------------+
| Tables_in_mysql |
+-----------------+
| columns_priv    |
| db              |
| func            |
| host            |
| tables_priv     |
| user            |
+-----------------+
6 rows in set (0.00 sec)

mysql> quit
Bye

C:\mysql\bin>
```

Using the Command Prompt in Linux

At the end of Project 1-3, you entered a password and then ended up at the `mysql` prompt. To see some of the essential commands, type **help** and press ENTER. As shown in Figure 1-5, a list of all the MySQL commands appears, along with a backslash (\) shortcut for each.

The help screen also shows a syntax reminder, stating that the command words must come first in the line and must end with a semicolon. In practice, only queries require the ending semicolon. You can enter other commands (`help`, for instance) without a semicolon, and they will still function properly. However, it's a good idea to get into the habit of using the semicolon.

```
mysql> help

For the complete MySQL Manual online visit:
   http://www.mysql.com/documentation

For info on technical support from MySQL developers visit:
   http://www.mysql.com/support

For info on MySQL books, utilities, consultants, etc. visit:
   http://www.mysql.com/portal

List of all MySQL commands:
   (Commands must appear first on line and end with ';')

help      (\h)    Display this help.
?         (\?)    Synonym for `help'.
clear     (\c)    Clear command.
connect   (\r)    Reconnect to the server. Optional arguments are db and host.
edit      (\e)    Edit command with $EDITOR.
ego       (\G)    Send command to mysql server, display result vertically.
exit      (\q)    Exit mysql. Same as quit.
go        (\g)    Send command to mysql server.
nopager   (\n)    Disable pager, print to stdout.
notee     (\t)    Don't write into outfile.
pager     (\P)    Set PAGER [to_pager]. Print the query results via PAGER.
print     (\p)    Print current command.
prompt    (\R)    Change your mysql prompt.
quit      (\q)    Quit mysql.
rehash    (\#)    Rebuild completion hash.
source    (\.)    Execute a SQL script file. Takes a file name as an argument.
status    (\s)    Get status information from the server.
system    (\!)    Execute a system shell command.
tee       (\T)    Set outfile [to_outfile]. Append everything into given outfile.
use       (\u)    Use another database. Takes database name as argument.

Connection id: 16   (Can be used with mysqladmin kill)

mysql>
```

Figure 1-5 The help listing of MySQL commands and shortcuts in Linux

If you enter a command that requires a semicolon, such as show tables, without a semicolon, when you press ENTER, the command won't execute. Instead, you'll see an arrow-shaped prompt instead of the mysql prompt.

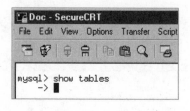

The system will wait for the closing semicolon indefinitely. Once the concluding semicolon is entered, the command executes.

```
Doc - SecureCRT
File  Edit  View  Options  Transfer

mysql> show tables
    -> ;
+-----------------+
| Tables_in_mysql |
+-----------------+
| columns_priv    |
| db              |
| func            |
| host            |
| tables_priv     |
| user            |
+-----------------+
6 rows in set (0.00 sec)

mysql> show tables;
+-----------------+
| Tables_in_mysql |
+-----------------+
| columns_priv    |
| db              |
| func            |
| host            |
| tables_priv     |
| user            |
+-----------------+
6 rows in set (0.00 sec)

mysql>




Ready
```

You can return to the standard prompt by typing either **EXIT** or `quit`. The MySQL Client will display bye and exit.

```
mysql> quit
Bye
[root@Doc src]# █
```

CRITICAL SKILL
1.7 Know Your Resources

The main sources for information regarding MySQL are available through the company web site at www.mysql.com. As you have seen, the company maintains a worldwide network of mirror sites for users not located near the company headquarters in Sweden. The site also offers company profiles, product listings, and information about various support and training services, as well as extensive documentation in a variety of forms. You can access most of this information via the tabs at the top of the MySQL home page.

When you click a tab, the subtopics of each tab topic appear in the stripe immediately below the chosen tab. While there is both useful and interesting information on all the tabs, clearly two of them—Downloads and Documentation—will be your most visited destinations. MySQL subtlety acknowledges this by choosing a darker color for those two tabs to make them easy to locate.

Downloads

The Downloads tab of the MySQL web site, as you have seen, contains a general overview page listing all the offered downloads and a page listing the worldwide mirror network. It works best to choose the download you are interested in, and then choose the closest mirror.

Aside from the MySQL database and the MaxDB (a supplementary database targeting large enterprise environments), several other items are offered:

- Graphical client interfaces

- APIs, both official (for C, Java and C++) and contributed (from Perl, Ruby, Python, .NET, and Ch)

- MySQL logos (with an explanation of when you can and can't post one on your web site without permission)

There are related downloads for Linux, FreeBSD, NetBSD, Solaris, SCO, Win32, NT, and OS/2, which you can explore, if your interests lead to any of those areas.

The final entries on the Downloads page are Contributed Software, Certified Hardware, and Certified Hosting. The Contributed Software downloads are applications and/or APIs developed by other companies to work in conjunction with MySQL. The Certified Hardware and Certified Hosting links feature companies that have entered into agreements with MySQL and have been certified to operate at certain predetermined levels or within predetermined agreements.

This page is arranged so that it can be searched by category or by keyword. The products listed on this page are described and have links to the sites where they can be obtained. Anyone can propose to add a link to these pages if they are registered with MySQL, but MySQL reviews the submissions before they are added to the site.

The More Information and Read Comments links lead to pages on the MySQL site. The Site or Publisher's Site links take you to where you can obtain the product and get information about cost or availability of trial versions.

Documentation

Now that you have MySQL installed, the Documentation tab on the MySQL web site, may prove useful. It contains links for the MySQL Reference Manual in several downloadable and online formats, mailing lists, articles, presentations, benchmarks, feature comparisons, and a searchable list of other MySQL-related sites.

The MySQL Reference Manual

The MySQL Reference Manual comes in two forms of PDF files (US Letter and A4). There is also a link to a softcover book, which can be purchased if you don't like the idea of printing out the 1,029-page PDF. For most beginning users, however, the style of writing and the depth of information provided in the manual can be intimidating. There are many assumptions about the reader's level of experience, which is why a beginner's guide such as this one is the easiest way to develop the experience required to make the advanced information accessible.

As the beginning MySQL user progresses in knowledge and experience to more advanced levels, the most useful part of the documentation may be the online searchable manual with user's comments, available at http://www.mysql.com/doc/en/index.html. The list of section topics on the left will expand to show the subtopics for easy navigating once you've gone through the initial pages. The search box in the upper-left corner allows for keyword searches and returns all instances within the manual. For a reminder, clarification, or brief explanation of an advanced command syntax or concept, this is undoubtedly the quickest way to find what you are looking for (providing you already have an understanding of the item in question and are simply looking for the details without explanation that manuals typically supply).

The last two indexes in the manual are the SQL Command, Type, and Function index and the Concept index. These indexes are worth putting in your browser bookmarks for the inevitable syntax reminder and concept clarification, as your experience with MySQL continues to progress.

The Mailing Lists

The mailing lists (http://lists.mysql.com/) are a way to obtain advice from other MySQL users. There are lists for general information, beginners, programmers, and application-specific questions. Lists can be a valued resource. Most members are genuinely helpful. Furthermore, the worldwide nature of the MySQL user base means that when you are trying to find an answer to a question, someone else is probably also online and may be able either to answer you or point you in the right direction.

MySQL recommends that all MySQL users join the Announcements list, which keeps you up-to-date on new releases and related products and services. It is not a high-volume list and is probably the best way to stay abreast of the improvements and innovations available with each new version.

Even if you have subscribed to a list before (and definitely if you haven't), read through the Frequently Asked Questions page at http://lists.mysql.com/faq.php in order to learn the eccentricities and etiquette of these lists. Realize that MySQL AB does not moderate these mailing lists and has no control over the quality of content or service.

Support & Consulting

Another resource from MySQL (and certainly the last resort for most noncommercial users) is available from the Support & Consulting tab of the MySQL web site. For the home user, it may be cost-prohibitive. For the commercial user, the situations and demands of your individual company's requirements will dictate which of the many levels of support available from MySQL you need and/or can afford.

Company

The Company tab of the MySQL web site lists MySQL partners who provide more in-depth support, consulting, and training in various locations around the world. You might be interested in this information if your MySQL usage becomes sophisticated enough to require professional-level training.

Module 1 Mastery Check

1. Which pairs of the following words mean the same thing: *row, field, key, record, index, column*?

2. What is the distinguishing feature of a relational database?

3. Is open source software always free of cost?

4. What are the seven criteria you should use to evaluate operating systems?

5. Of the seven criteria used to evaluate operating systems, which show the most difference?

6. In Windows, if you require tables larger than 4GB, on what type of file system will you need to install MySQL and what commands must be used when creating the tables?

7. In Linux, what is the command syntax for installing an .rpm file?

8. In Linux, what is the syntax on the two commands to set a password?

9. What does ODBC stand for and which OS is most likely to require it?

10. Why does this guide initially choose to use the command line to interface with MySQL instead of a GUI?

Module 2

Defining a Database

This module will explain the different types of data, their uses, and why it is important to define your data correctly. With an understanding of the different types of MySQL data types, you can plan your database and its tables, identifying the name, type, size, and special settings for each field. Next, you will learn the commands to create databases and tables in those databases. The projects in this module will lead you through creating a database with tables, and then loading data into your newly made database tables, which will give you the foundation for the projects in the later modules.

CRITICAL SKILL
2.1 Understand MySQL Data Types

You need to choose the correct data type when defining the fields of each record as you create the tables for your database. Some of the reasons that it is important to use the correct data type are straightforward. For instance, you can put numeric values in a text field, but you cannot use those values to do math. Therefore, any number you want to use for mathematical purposes (to total the number of items sold, for example) must be in a field that has been defined as some sort of numeric data type.

However, some of the reasons for choosing a particular data type for a field can be murkier. For example, you can make a text field that either is a fixed length or that automatically reflects the size of the data contained in it. The reasons why one would be better than the other are not immediately apparent, and indeed, usually depend on individual circumstances and requirements.

More than one company has called in expensive outside consulting support after several days of trying to troubleshoot a database problem, only to find that something as simple as the data type defining a field was all that was halting their database from proper functionality. So, taking the time to understand the various data types and selecting the most appropriate one can save you time, trouble, and sometimes money.

MySQL data types can be grouped into four sets: numbers, text, date and time, and defined group types. Table 2-1 lists the data types in each category.

Within each set of data types, the differences are not always clear from the word or partial word used in the code. For instance, on the surface, DATETIME and TIMESTAMP would seem to give you much the same information, and on a basic level, this is true. They both tell you time and date information; however, they do it in different formats and within different boundaries.

Before you start creating MySQL tables, you should understand the differences between data types and the reasons you might choose one data type over another. You don't need to memorize the details about each type. You can always check the tables provided here for information about code syntax and number boundaries.

Numbers	Text	Date and Time	Defined Group
Integers: INT, TINYINT, SMALLINT, MEDIUMINT, BIGINT	Normal strings: CHAR	Date and time: DATETIME	Enumerated lists: ENUM
Fixed decimals: NUMERIC, DECIMAL	Variable strings: VARCHAR	Date and time: TIMESTAMP	Sets of similar data: SET
Floating point: FLOAT, DOUBLE	Long text blocks: TINYTEXT, MEDIUMTEXT, TEXT, LARGETEXT	Date only: DATE	
	Binary Long Objects: BLOB, TINYBLOB, MEDIUMBLOB, LONGBLOB	Time only: TIME	
		Year only: YEAR	

Table 2-1 Data Types in MySQL

Number Data Types

The number data types cover a lot of ranges and byte sizes. Don't be intimidated by the wide variety of them. Make sure you understand the underlying concepts, and mark these pages for easy reference later.

Integers: TINYINT, SMALLINT, MEDIUMINT, INT, and BIGINT

An integer, in case it has been awhile since you were last forced to take a math class, refers to any of the natural numbers, the negatives of those numbers, or zero. There are five types of integer data in MySQL: TINYINT, SMALLINT, MEDIUMINT, INT, and BIGINT. Any of these types can be either *signed* or *unsigned*.

- A signed integer can hold both negative and positive numbers and zero.
- An unsigned integer can hold only positive numbers and zero.

The default value is signed. If you want the field to hold only positive numbers and zero, you must place UNSIGNED after the closing parenthesis:

```
<field_name> INT(width_value) UNSIGNED
```

The main difference between the integer data types is how much space each takes up. As a result of that specific size, the integer must hold numbers within a specific range. For instance, a TINYINT takes up only 1 byte of space. Because of this small space, it can hold only 256 sequential numbers: from 0 to 255, if unsigned, or from –128 to 127, if signed. In both these cases, the TINYINT holds 256 consecutive numbers, but the act of designating it as signed or unsigned radically changes which numbers it can hold.

If you define a field as TINYINT and the field's value exceeds the maximum size, the value will be edited to reflect the highest number possible. This means that any number larger than the upper range for that field will be automatically truncated. For instance, in a field defined as an unsigned TINYINT, any number 256 or larger will be entered in the field as 255. In the case of an automatically incremented field, such as one that contains customer numbers, it will flawlessly count from 1 to 255, and then repeat 255 for each entry thereafter. You might spend a lot of time and effort looking for the cause of the refusal to increment (since it's human nature to look for big causes before looking for little ones).

In the case of signed fields, the lower range works in the same way. No number smaller than the bottom of the range will be placed in the field.

Table 2-2 lists each integer type, along with the amount of bytes it takes up and the exact range of its signed and unsigned versions.

For a beginner, it can be difficult to guess just how big a particular range of numbers may need to grow. A good first rule of thumb is, when in doubt, make it bigger. However, if you were to consider only that, you would always choose the BIGINT data type, so there are other considerations.

Most people will probably never need an integer space that will hold a number that has more than 19 digits, which is the maximum in a BIGINT field. It is safe to assume (given that the people who wrote MySQL probably don't like typing any more than the rest of us) that the data type with the shortest designation, INT, is probably the one the MySQL developers expected to be used the most. In a number field that is not holding bar codes or accounting data of a corporation, the ability of a field to hold a number slightly over 4 billion is arguably adequate.

Integer Type	Bytes	Signed	Unsigned
TINYINT	1	–128 through 127	0 through 255
SMALLINT	2	–32,768 through 32,767	0 through 65,535
MEDIUMINT	3	–8,338,608 through 8,388,607	0 through 16,777,215
INT	4	–2,147,483,648 through 2,147,483,487	0 through 4,294,967,295
BIGINT	8	–9,223,372,036,854,775,808 through 9,223,372,036,854,775,807	0 through 18,446,744,073,709,551,615

Table 2-2 Integer Types in MySQL with Sizes and Ranges

But why shouldn't you just choose the largest integer range available so you don't ever need to worry about running out of room? The answers are storage and speed.

In an age where pocket calculators hold more memory and computing power than computers that filled entire rooms only 40 years ago did, it is easy to dismiss concerns about storage. Still, it is counterproductive and costly to use two or three times the space to store a field than necessary. Using an extra 2 bytes or 4 bytes doesn't seem like much when you are contemplating only a single record, but multiply that record times the hundreds, thousands, or more times it may appear in its table, and you begin to see a waste of space that you paid for yet are not using.

The other consideration is speed, and it involves something that most computer users don't think much about: read time. Consider for a moment listening to a music CD. If you want to listen to the next track, it takes only a moment for the head to move from track 2 to track 3, for instance; however, if you are at the beginning of a CD and decide you want to listen to a track at the end, it takes a few more moments for the head to move into place and the new music to begin. Movements similar to that happen in your computer hard drive all the time, although at a considerably faster speed than on your CD player. On a computer, the time saved when point A and point B are closer rather than farther happens in increments of time that are small enough to be an abstract concept to most of us.

If you have 1,000 records in a table on your database, and one of the fields is defined as INT, then each field takes up 4 bytes. If, instead, it is defined as SMALLINT (assuming that the field in question is not likely to exceed 65,535 places), each field takes up half that space. The database would be able to access any record from any other record faster at the 2-byte field size than at the 4-byte field size, simply because there is less ground to cover. An example of such a field is one destined to hold five-digit ZIP code numbers, where the largest number possible is theoretically 99999. Clearly, it will never go over the 65,535 upper limit, so any designation larger than SMALLINT is wasted space.

If you are the only person ever to access your database, then the speed consideration may involve amounts of time so small as to be unnoticeable. On the other hand, if your database exists online in a real-time environment, such as a company-wide intranet or on the Internet, many users may access the data simultaneously. In this case, the small increments of time saved by using the more appropriate field size could lead to less stress in the workplace or increased customer satisfaction. Users in any situation do not like to wait for a computer to give them the response they need.

As noted earlier, you should use TINYINT only when you are sure that the field you are defining will never need to hold a number bigger than 255 (unsigned) or 127 (signed). If you are concerned about storage and speed, choose your data types accordingly. However, most uses for beginners will easily fall into the INT data type, and there will be a clear reason for using one of the other data types. So, when in doubt, use INT.

NUMERIC and DECIMAL Data Types

The DECIMAL and NUMERIC types are interchangeable in MySQL. Both are defined as *fixed decimals*, which means the field is defined with a specific number of places to the right of the decimal point, as well as the total number of places in the whole field.

Despite the fact that these two types are intended to hold only numeric values, they are stored as characters; therefore, they should be used to store only numeric data and cannot be used for mathematical purposes. A company's annual report might be printed from accounting data stored in this data type. It creates a kind of safeguard in that the data, once saved in fields defined with this data type, cannot be accidentally manipulated mathematically.

The syntax for the fixed-decimal types is DECIMAL(w, d) or NUMERIC(w, d), where w equals the total number of digits in the entire number and d equals the number of places to the right of the decimal to display. You can use the type without specifying either of these, specify just one, or specify both. If you don't specify the number of digits in the number or decimal places, the defaults of ten digits without any decimal places will be used. Table 2-3 shows examples of code specifying the DECIMAL and NUMERIC types and what the displayed numbers might look like.

FLOAT and DOUBLE Data Types

The FLOAT and DOUBLE data types are alike, except DOUBLE is stored in twice the amount of bytes, so it has a larger range than FLOAT. These two data types differ from DECIMAL and NUMERIC in that their decimal point is floating rather than fixed.

FLOAT numbers are approximations, which means some numbers might not be able to be stored exactly in the internal format and must be approximated. For instance, the numeric value of pi is an example of a number that must always be an approximation.

FLOAT provides a means of representing noninteger numbers with fractional parts. For example, 9.876 would be represented in storage by the integer 9876 and a 1 to indicate the floating position of the decimal; 987.6 would be represented by storing the integer 9876 and

Syntax	Code	Display	Description
DECIMAL(w, d)	DECIMAL(5,2)	123.46	More decimal places than the field has room for makes the data round up. (5 digits, 2 decimal places)
NUMERIC(w, d)	NUMERIC(7,4)	123.4567	Exact fit. (7 digits, 4 decimal places)
DECIMAL(w)	DECIMAL(9)	123	No decimal specification defaults to 0 decimal places. (9 digits, 6 padded places to left of number)
DECIMAL	DECIMAL	123	Default is 10 digits, 0 decimal places. (10 digits, 7 padded places to left of number)

Table 2-3 Data Changed by Field Syntax When 123.4567 Is Inserted

a 3 to indicate its decimal position. This contrasts with fixed-point arithmetic, where decimals defined in each field do not move (there are a fixed number of decimal points in each field, whether or not the value inserted into the field needs a decimal point to be clearly expressed).

For monetary data or comparisons of strict equality between values, the FLOAT data type is not the best choice; for control of program loops, it is a bad choice.

The FLOAT (or DOUBLE) data type works well for holding scientific numbers, as you can see from the signed ranges listed in Table 2-4. If UNSIGNED is specified, then negative numbers are disallowed.

Text Data Types

Text can be any symbol that is used to communicate a concept. The alphabet comes to mind most readily, but symbols (such as punctuation marks) and numbers can be text, too. The caveat is, as we mentioned earlier, that numbers entered into a text field cannot be used to perform mathematical functions. A common example of text field that includes symbols and numbers as text is an address field. An address may contain a house number in numeric form, with a street name that also can contain a number and often punctuation, such as a period after an abbreviation or a space between words (as in 123 S. Broadway or 987 N. 21st).

Any number of text characters (alphabetical, numeric, or symbol characters) in a row is called a *string*. There are four types of strings that MySQL differentiates with separate data types: CHAR, VARCHAR, TEXT, and BLOB. The first three echo the three criteria of differentiation used for numeric data: fixed-length, variable-length, and long text strings. The fourth type, BLOB, is closely related to TEXT.

CHAR Data Type

The data type CHAR, which is short for *character* but usually pronounced like the word "car," is a fixed-length string. That means the text field has a designated length—it always takes up that amount of space in the database table record, whether or not the data placed in it is that length. For example, if a field is defined as being 20 characters long, and you place the name Molly (5 characters) in that field, the field is still 20 characters in length. Any remaining space (in this case, 15 characters) is padded to the right of the data until it is the correct fixed length.

Type	Signed Range
FLOAT	−3.402823466E+38 through −1.175494351E–38, 0, and 1.175494351E-38 to 3.402823466E+38
DOUBLE	−1.7976931348623157E+308 through −2.2250738585072014E–308, 0, and 2.2250738585072014E–308 through 1.7976931348623157E+308

Table 2-4 Ranges for Signed FLOAT and DOUBLE Data Types

This might lead you to believe this field, either printed or displayed onscreen, would look something like "Molly   " but MySQL has designed the CHAR data type so the trailing (or padded) spaces are automatically stripped off on output with the CHAR data type even though the TABLE stores the data type as "Molly   ".

The syntax for this data type is CHAR(*w*), where *w* specifies the field length and can be a number from 1 through 255. If you just specify CHAR, the field defaults to one character.

Any comparisons for sorting CHAR fields are not case-sensitive, by default. If you want case to be considered, you can add the BINARY option: CHAR(*w*) BINARY. But note that there is a trade-off when you make CHAR case-sensitive: the padded spaces are not stripped off automatically on output. However since you know the padding occurs to the right of the value, you can strip off any extra spaces when printing the data.

VARCHAR Data Type

The syntax for VARCHAR is similar to CHAR—VARCHAR(*w*)—and the value for *w* can also be any number from 1 through 255. However, unlike with the CHAR type, if the data a VARCHAR field contains is smaller than the specified field length, the field size shrinks to match. If a field is defined as VARCHAR(7) and you enter "James" in the field, the field in the database table record will be only five characters long. If you enter "Crighton," the field will still be only seven characters long, and the data in it will look like "Crighto," because it was truncated when it reached the defined upper limit. Like the CHAR data type, VARCHAR is not case-sensitive unless the BINARY option is specified: VARCHAR(*w*) BINARY.

NOTE

The VARCHAR data type actually stores its assigned value + 1. The extra byte is where the record width, represented in the syntax by *w*, is stored.

Both these data types have advantages and disadvantages. The VARCHAR type usually will take up less space than the CHAR type, because it varies its length to match the actual length of the data held in its fields. On the surface, this seems like a valid reason for choosing it above the other text types; however, this results in a slower access speed for that table. If all the fields are of a set length (as they are with CHAR), then the database can go directly to a given field in a table's record by use of a simple mathematical formula. With VARCHAR, the database must look for the field, because the space it takes up can vary from record to record. So, the fixed length of CHAR makes it faster to access, and the variable length of VARCHAR makes it take up less storage space.

Another consideration is that having one VARCHAR field in each of a table's records makes it necessary to treat all the records as if they were of varying length or, as it is sometimes referred to, *dynamic*. Also, in any varying-length table (a table with one or more varying-length fields in its records), any CHAR longer than three characters will be silently converted to VARCHAR.

A good rule of thumb is that you should put VARCHAR fields only in a table devoted to VARCHAR fields. Also, despite its variable nature, you should still try to define the VARCHAR field as close to a correct upper limit as possible. In other words, don't use a VARCHAR (255) when a VARCHAR (42) will do.

TEXT and BLOB Data Types

The data types TEXT and BLOB are related and most easily explained by contrasting them with one another. Text fields, similar to integer fields, come in different sizes. Table 2-5 shows the amount of bytes each type is stored in and how large a string can be placed in it.

The TEXT data types exist for strings that are longer than 255 characters, which is the upper limit for CHAR and VARCHAR. They are variable in length, so you can think of them as a VARCHAR field that is as long as the upper limit of LONGTEXT. The data types TINYTEXT and VARCHAR can be used interchangeably. If you insert data that is longer than the upper limit of the field, the data is truncated to fit. The TEXT types are not case-sensitive, which means the words *Chantel* and *chantel* are exactly the same from MySQL's viewpoint.

The BLOB data type (which has nothing to do with the 1950's horror classic) is essentially the same as the TEXT data types (see Table 2-5), except for one crucial point: The BLOB type is case-sensitive, which means that the words *Vicki* and *vicki* are not the same.

If you put the same set of data containing words that begin with both uppercase and lowercase letters into two tables, one of which has the field defined as a TEXT type and the other as a BLOB type, and then sorted the contents of each, the resulting output would be in different order. Depending on what you do with your database, that small difference may not matter. However, if your sorts come out differently than you expect, the field type of the string you are sorting on may be the culprit.

The VARCHAR BINARY data type can be used interchangeably with TINYBLOB, because the BINARY notation makes VARCHAR case-sensitive.

DATE and TIME Data Types

The DATE and TIME data types are all fairly similar, more like variations on a theme than different types. Both data types use a few basic notations and underlying rules that you need to understand to use them correctly.

Data Type	Size	Bytes
TINYTEXT and TINYBLOB	2^8-1	255
TEXT and BLOB	$2^{16}-1$	65,535
MEDIUMTEXT and MEDIUMBLOB	$2^{24}-1$	16,777,215
LONGTEXT and LONGBLOB	$2^{32}-1$	4,294,967,295

Table 2-5 TEXT and BLOB Data Type Sizes and Upper Limits (in Bytes)

The DATE and TIME data types use the following format:

YYYY-MM-DD HH:MM:SS

where:

- *YYYY* represents the year
- *MM* represents the month
- *DD* represents the day
- *HH* represents the hour
- *MM* represents the minute
- *SS* represents the second

The notation *M* serves as both minute and month, but generally, the range of numbers involved will make the difference between them clear. Also, the use of dash separators for the date and colon separators for the time clearly differentiates between them.

Although MySQL will try to interpret a date written in a different format (for instance, *YYYY-DD-MM HH:MM:SS*), it *always* expects to find the year in the leftmost position. This does not mean that you cannot have the year *displayed* on the right (*MM-DD-YYYY* or *DD-MM-YYYY*), but you must *store* it according to the MySQL expected format. (You will learn how to manipulate the display of date values in Modules 4 and 5.) Storing them in this format makes it easy to group together the same year's data.

If MySQL gets data for a date/time field that does not correlate with the required format, a zero value is inserted. (0000-00-00 00:00:00). You can also enter a zero value if you do not know the correct data to enter into a specific record; however, afterwards, it is impossible to tell whether the zero value was inserted because of unknown data during input or faulty data.

MySQL does minimal data checking on data input. It checks to see if the month value is between 0 and 12, and if the date value is between 0 and 31. Any further data checking is the responsibility of the user inputting the data. The zero values are allowed as placeholders for unknown data. For example, if you know the month and year of a person's birthday, but not the day, you can enter partial data with zeros for what is missing, and then complete the entry when the missing piece is available.

After the Y2K experience, most users understand why it's best to use a four-digit value for a year. However, MySQL will accept a two-digit value and deal with it using the following rules:

- Values in the range 0 through 69 will be interpreted and saved as 2000 through 2069.
- Values in the range 70 through 99 will be interpreted and saved as 1970 through 1999.

Because this rule of thumb will be correct only part of the time, you will save time and effort by adjusting two-digit years into a four-digit format before entering them into your database.

2

DATETIME, DATE, and TIMESTAMP Data Types

You should use the `DATETIME` type, rather than the `DATE` type, only when both the date and time parts are necessary. If all you need is the date, you can save 5 bytes of storage in each record by defining your field correctly. The `TIMESTAMP` type is slightly different. It gets the current time and places it in the `TIMESTAMP` field.

Table 2-6 shows the storage size, basic format, and start and end ranges supported by `DATETIME`, `DATE`, and `TIMESTAMP`. MySQL states that this range of dates is what is *supported*, which means you can enter dates outside the range, but MySQL does not guarantee they will function properly.

Prior to MySQL version 4.1, `TIMESTAMP` was stored as a pure number, without any separators or spaces. In version 4.1 and later, it is stored as a string, complete with separators. If you followed the appropriate project for your OS in Module 1, you have installed the latest version of MySQL, version 4.1.1 or above. If you are using an already installed, earlier version of MySQL, or have sought the advice of someone who is using a version prior to 4.1, the behavior of `TIMESTAMP` can be confusing.

TIMESTAMP and Automatic Updating   In the following cases, `TIMESTAMP` is updated to reflect the latest time a field or fields in a record has been changed in the following manner:

- An `INSERT` or `LOAD DATA INFILE` statement that does not specify a value for the `TIMESTAMP` column

- An `UPDATE` statement that does not specify a value for the `TIMESTAMP` column *and* one of the other columns has a change in value

- A `TIMESTAMP` value that is set to `NULL`

TIMESTAMP in MySQL Version 4.1 and Later   In version 4.1 and later, `TIMESTAMP` acts exactly like `DATETIME` . . . `TIMESTAMP` acts exactly like `DATETIME` with one exception. In versions later than 4.1, `TIMESTAMP` may be run in Maxdb mode, but there is no automatic update function.

In MySQL version 4.1 only, `TIMESTAMP` does not run in Maxdb mode at all, but if you are not running in Maxdb mode, it does still allow for an automatic update function.

Type	Bytes	Format	Start Date	End Date
`DATE`	3	`YYYY-MM-DD`	1000-01-01	9999-12-31
`DATETIME` and `TIMESTAMP` (version 4.1 and later)	8	`YYYY-MM-DD HH:MM:SS`	1000-01-01 00:00:00	9999-12-31 23:59:59
`TIMESTAMP` (prior to version 4.1)	4	`YYYYMMDDHHMMSS`	1970-01-01	Sometime in 2037

Table 2-6 Date and Time Sizes, Formats, and Ranges

If a statement updates fields with the same data that is already in them, TIMESTAMP will not automatically update, because MySQL ignores the update (for more efficient functioning).

TIMESTAMP Prior to MySQL Version 4.1   Prior to version 4.1, TIMESTAMP was stored as a number, so you could narrow the TIMESTAMP field by defining it with a specific width. The most popular widths, for reasons clearly seen in Table 2-7, are 6, 8, 12, and 14.

If you place a value of zero or a number greater than 14 in the parentheses designating width, MySQL sets the field width to 14. If you place an odd number in the parentheses designating width, it rounds up to the nearest even number.

So, if someone else's MySQL database will allow that person to do something with TIMESTAMP that yours does not, compare the versions—the difference probably lies there.

YEAR and TIME Data Types

The YEAR and TIME data types are simple. You use them when that data is all that you require for your database. Table 2-8 shows the basic size and range information for these two data types.

The YEAR data type can be given a length of either 2 or 4: YEAR (2) or YEAR (4). As mentioned earlier, the Y2K experience is the classic example of why YEAR (2) should not be used. That being said, if you choose to use it, the value range is similar to the range listed in Table 2-8, but not exactly. With YEAR (2), 0 through 69 represent the years 2000 through 2069, and 70 through 99 represent the years 1970 through 1999. Illegal YEAR values—years before 1901 and after 2155 or nonnumeric characters—are stored as zeros (0000).

NOTE

YEAR () allows input of either numeric or string values. However, if a two-digit YEAR () is defined as a number, its value range is 1–99 because when zero is specified, it will be interpreted as 0000 instead of 2000. If the YEAR () field is to be used mathematically, the four-digit version avoids this eccentricity.

Type and Size	Fomat
TIMESTAMP (14)	YYYYMMDDHHMMSS
TIMESTAMP (12)	YYYYMMDDHHMM
TIMESTAMP (10)	YYYYMMDDHH
TIMESTAMP (8)	YYYYMMDD
TIMESTAMP (6)	YYYYMM
TIMESTAMP (4)	YYYY
TIMESTAMP (2)	YY

Table 2-7   Effects of Narrowing the TIMESTAMP Field in MySQL Versions Prior to 4.1

Type	Bytes	Range	Format
YEAR	1	1901 through 2155	*YYYY*
TIME	3	−838:59:59 through 838:59:59	*HH:MM:SS* *HHMMSS* *MMSS SS* *HH:MM SS*

Table 2-8 Size, Range, and Formats for YEAR and TIME

The TIME data type has the basic format you might expect, but it also allows a variety of other formats, as shown in Table 2-8. What may be surprising is the large range, which is far outside the normal 24 hours in a day. This range allows for the storage of timing values, such as recording how long something has taken from beginning to end. Once again, if you try to enter a number that is outside this range, the value is stored as the closest upper or lower limit. For instance, 840:39:09 will be stored as 838:59:59, the upper limit. Invalid TIME values are stored as 00:00:00.

Defined Group Data Types: ENUM and SET

The ENUM and SET data types both involve a list or series of values defined when the field is defined. However, for ENUM and SET, it is better to think of the data type as the definition of a *column* of fields. This is because you specify all of the valid data items possible for every field in that table's column when you define the table. After that, only those defined values may be entered into any field in that column.

These two data types both store data as string values (a series of alphanumeric characters perceived as a whole), but they handle the storage differently. ENUM creates an index for the allowable values defined, and then stores the index number, rather than the data itself, in the record field. ENUM allows only one choice from the defined list, which makes it a much smaller value to store.

The SET data type also has defined allowable values, but it stores them as the values themselves. It will allow you to store multiple instances of those values within one field. Therefore, depending on the values and how many of them are stored in a given field, the length of the field may vary considerably. Table 2-9 shows the differences in storage.

So, why would you want to use either of these data types? A common use is for drop-down menus on web pages. The list of values you want in your drop-down menu would be the ENUM or SET you define. This approach offers a way to control what people can enter as a value for a particular column of fields in a database table. If you wanted the user to be able to input only

Type	Bytes	Storage Amounts	Defined Values Allowed
ENUM	1	Single value, using index number	0 through 65,535

Table 2-9 Storage Comparisons of ENUM and SET

one choice from the list of allowable values, you would use the ENUM data type. If you wanted the user to be able to input multiple choices from the list of defined values, you would use the SET data type.

Changes to the ENUM data type require an ALTER TABLE command. It is recommended that you use an ENUM to store only data that is unlikely to change very often. Putting a list of America's 50 states in an ENUM list would be an example of data that does not change very often and from which you might want a user to select only one choice.

ENUM sorts by its index number, so if you desire predictable sorting, you should define the initial list of values in alphabetic order. You can view the index number of an ENUM list by using the syntax `<column_name>+0`, as in the following statement:

```
SELECT <enum_column_name>+0 FROM <table_name>;
```

The output will give you a list of the index numbers for each record in the table, instead of the contents of the records themselves.

If you had a list of CD titles (64 or fewer) and wanted to instruct the user to choose up to five favorites, SET would be the ideal choice. Each user's record could list that user's input, from zero through five favorites, which would all be stored in a single field. The values in the SET field are comma-separated, making it possible to retrieve them from the database using a SELECT statement, and then parse the results to separate the data into its individual pieces. Modules 4 and 5 provide more information about handling and manipulating your data.

You now have a basic understanding of the MySQL data types. You've seen how they work, their uses, and their limitations, as well as why you might want to use them to store specific kinds of data. As stated previously, you do not need to memorize every detail of how they work. You just need to know how and why you might decide on one data type rather than another. When you need information about a specific data type, you can refer to this module.

Progress Check

1. What are the three basic number data types?

2. What are the four basic text data types?

3. What are the five date and time data types?

4. What are the two defined group data types?

---

1. The three basic number data types are INT (TINYINT, SMALLINT, MEDIUMINT, INT, and BIGINT), NUMERIC (or DECIMAL), and FLOAT/DOUBLE.
2. The four basic text data types are CHAR, VARCHAR, TEXT, and BLOB.
3. The five date and time data types are TIMESTAMP, DATETIME, DATE, YEAR, and TIME.
4. The two defined group data types are ENUM and SET.

CRITICAL SKILL
2.2 Plan Your Database

Before you actually create your MySQL database and tables, you need to plan how they will be set up. This planning involves choosing names for your database, tables, and the fields within the tables. You also need to decide which data type to assign to each field in your tables.

Of course, the plans you make for your database depend on the information it will contain. For the projects in this book, we will use a fictitious company and its data. Although the company may be whimsical, you will work through concrete examples that will make the learning process easier.

The fictional company is called DuckWear. As you might guess, this is an Internet-based company that sells a variety of costumes for pet ducks. Now it's time to put yourself in their shoes, or at least in the shoes of the DuckWear database administrator.

Naming Your Database

The first decision you need to make is what to call the DuckWear company's database. Database names need to be a compromise between the desire to convey information about the database's contents and the need to be concise. Naming a database too literally (like `db` or `data`, for instance) can lead to confusion later, when there are more databases running on the MySQL server or when someone else inherits the responsibility for maintaining the database.

MySQL has only a few rules for the name of a database:

- The name can have a maximum of 64 characters.

- The name cannot contain a forward slash (/), backslash (\), or a period (.).

We have decided it is logical to give the DuckWear company's database the name `duckwear`.

Naming Your Tables

Naming the individual tables (and the fields within them) in your database requires that you know what kinds of data you are going to store in them. As with the database name, the table name should tell you what it contains but also be concise.

Very specific names (like `duckwear_customer_information`, for instance) may be very informative, but they become increasingly annoying to type in on the command line. They take too long and give too many opportunities for typos. For most people, a name like `duck_cust` will be intuitive enough to be nearly as informative, yet much easier to type than the longer version. It is also common to store a brief description about the table in the comment section when creating tables by adding the syntax `comment="<comment string>"` to the `[table options]` part of the `CREATE TABLE` syntax. This can help you remember, or future administrators learn, the purpose of the table.

A MySQL table name can be a maximum limit of 64 characters and cannot use the forward slash (/), backslash (\), or period (.) characters. In addition, MySQL has a list of reserved words (see Appendix B) that are not recommended for use as names for tables or columns.

NOTE

The MySQL reserved words, for the most part, function as data types, commands, or predefined functions, and the improper use of them can cause syntax errors. There are ways around this. For instance, you can use a reserved word as a name by surrounding it with backticks or double quotation marks. However, the easiest approach is simply to avoid using reserved words for names. Appendix B provides a listing of the MySQL reserved words.

We have decided that all the table names in the duckwear database will start with duck_. The table of customer information will be named duck_cust.

Naming and Defining Fields

After working with the DuckWear CEO, you have come up with a list of information that should be included in the duck_cust table. It will include a customer number, customer name and address, the duck's name, and the duck's birth date. Now you need to decide on a name for each field and choose an appropriate data type and size for it.

Developing a system, or *convention*, that allows you to tell at a glance what table a specific field name belongs to can save you time and effort and work as a safeguard against inserting data into the wrong field by mistake. But be careful; if the system you develop is unnecessarily complicated, it may eventually become more of a hindrance than help, particularly if someone else becomes responsible for database maintenance. It needs to be logical but also clear enough that its patterns are easily recognized and emulated.

In the end, it all boils down to a matter of personal preference. Whichever convention you choose, the important thing is to stick to it. If you have a few names that defy convention, they will always be the ones you end up mistyping the most.

For the duck_cust table, all the words in field names will be separated by an underscore for easier readability, and the field names will start with the word cust.

NOTE

An alternative convention to enhance readability is to use uppercase letters to make the names clear, instead of using a separating underscore (for example, DuckCust for the table and CustDuckName for that field). However, if you are running your MySQL database on a Linux-based computer, remember that your OS is case-sensitive. This means that DuckCust and Duckcust are two different names.

You should write down your plans for each of your field names, type, size, and special settings. Having this information before you create a table will help you to avoid mistakes. You can alter a table's definitions after you have created it, but your work will be much easier if you don't need to make those kinds of changes later.

Table 2-10 shows the field listings for the duck_cust table and how they can best be defined.

Requiring Information with the NOT NULL Setting

You will notice many of the fields in Table 2-10 have the additional setting of NOT NULL. This means that data is required for these fields. Even if you do not know the correct data, some sort of default entry needs to be made. For example, you might enter "n/a" if you don't know the duck's name. That way, it is clear that the data was unknown and not accidentally left out.

Although the other fields for the customer address are set as NOT NULL, the one for the "plus 4" ZIP code is not. Since it is not absolutely necessary to have the plus 4 information in an address, it can be optional.

Similarly, a customer does not need to provide a preferred title like Mr. or Ms., even though DuckWear has politely decided to offer the choice in an attempt to use the correct title on a mailing label. And a customer may not have an apartment number, so this field can also be considered optional.

Information	Field Type	Field Size	Special Settings	Field Name
Customer number	MEDIUMINT	Default	NOT NULL AUTO_INCREMENT	cust_num
Customer title	TINYINT	Default		cust_title
Customer last name	CHAR	20	NOT NULL	cust_last
Customer first name	CHAR	15	NOT NULL	cust_first
Customer suffix	ENUM	Default		cust_suffix
Address	CHAR	30	NOT NULL	cust_add1
Apt. number	CHAR	10		cust_add2
City	CHAR	15	NOT NULL	cust_city
State	CHAR	2	NOT NULL	cust_state
ZIP code	CHAR	5	NOT NULL	cust_zip1
Plus 4	CHAR	4		cust_zip2
Duck's name	CHAR	25	NOT NULL	cust_duckname
Duck's birth date	DATE	Default		cust_duckbday

Table 2-10 Initial Fields for the DuckWear Customer Table (duck_cust)

Automatically Incrementing Fields

The field cust_num is defined as both NOT NULL and AUTO_INCREMENT, which means that every customer must have a number and that the number put in a newly created record will be automatically incremented by a value of one from the previous number inserted in that column. Since the MEDIUMINT data type has a maximum range of over 16 million, we can be fairly safe in assuming we will never run out of customer numbers, unless duck ownership increases drastically.

Defining Field Sizes

There are several fields that Table 2-10 lists as having the default field size. MEDIUMINT, TINYINT, ENUM, and DATE data types have specific sizes. However, the CHAR, or character, types need a specific length defined, and you must decide on the lengths of these fields before you create the table.

There is no definite rule of thumb for name, address, city, and similar field lengths. In some languages, longer names are more common than in others. Hyphenated last names may be common, for example, and these require more space to store. At best, the length you pick will be a guess that you hope will cover the majority of your customers. Try to think of the longest last name you know, and make your field slightly larger than that.

In other cases, you will know the field's length. For example, since the postal codes for states are all two letters, choosing to make the state field two characters is an easy decision.

Understanding Table Types

The default table type when you create a table is MyISAM. As a beginner, the MyISAM table is recommended, and that is what you are going to use with the projects in this book. MySQL can use several other table types (also called *engines*), and you should be familiar with the features that distinguish them. The available table types are shown in Table 2-11.

Table Type	Distinguishing Feature
ISAM	Original storage engine
MyISAM	Binary portable storage type; replaces ISAM
HEAP	Stored only in memory
BDB or BerkeleyDB	Transaction-safe tables with page locking
InnoDB	Transaction-safe tables with row locking
MERGE	Collection of MyISAM tables used as one table

Table 2-11 MySQL Table Types

Because most databases offer only one table type, the multiple table types offered by MySQL are often overlooked, particularly in the planning phase. The MyISAM table is a good place to start and has the advantage of being the default, but there are reasons why you might want to use one of the other table types, so we will look at each of them.

Regarding table types, MySQL has an eccentricity that you need to remember. If you specify a particular table type in MySQL, and it cannot comply with your request for some reason (for instance, if you turn off BDB and then forget and try to make a BDB table), MySQL will silently make the table MyISAM; that is, it will do it automatically and not tell you. So, if a table is not acting in the way you expect it to, it may be because of a silent conversion to MyISAM. However, in most of these situations, you will never become aware that such a conversion has happened, because the database will do what you want it to do.

MyISAM Tables

MyISAM is the default table type for MySQL. It was based on the old ISAM table type and has been extensively tested. It has table-level locking, which means during updating, no other user can access the same table. MyISAM also has many useful extensions that allow for checking and repairing tables, as well as accomplishing data recovery should your computer crash while writing to a file. The MyISAM table type allows for static, dynamic, and compressed table characteristics. It is the table version of the best of all possible worlds, because it fits most requirements while providing speed, ease of use, and reasonable security.

ISAM Tables

ISAM tables are popular in other databases and are an older table type. They will no longer be supported once MySQL reaches version 5.0, so even if you are using a pre-5.0 version of MySQL, now would not be a good time to start using ISAM tables.

HEAP Tables

HEAP tables use hashed indexes and are stored in memory. This makes them very fast, but because they are stored in memory, if your MySQL server crashes, you will lose all data stored in them. This makes them unsuitable for everyday storage. However, HEAP tables are useful for temporary tables, such as those that contain real-time statistics that are calculated anew each time the web page that displays them is loaded.

CAUTION

Because they reside in memory rather than having to be read from the hard disk, HEAP tables are very fast, but for most uses, the increased risk of data loss in the event of system crash does not justify the faster performance.

Transactional Tables: BDB and InnoDB

Transactional tables restrict the user access to varying amounts of information in a database when another user is accessing it, which is referred to as a *transaction*. Transactions give the user greater control when working with data by protecting the sections of the data being used for as long as the user's transaction is occurring.

There are advantages and disadvantages to using transactional tables, and you must weigh them in concert with your particular data-storage and data-access needs. The transactional table must keep track of what data is being used and when the user is finished with it in order to refuse other users simultaneous access to the same data. This requires that certain resources, like memory, be relegated to this process, which in turn affects things like the amount of memory available and the response time to a request. This is called *transaction overhead*. Table 2-12 summarizes the pros and cons of using transactional tables.

MySQL offers the two most commonly used transactional table types: BDB (or BerkeleyDB) and InnoDB.

BDB Tables   BDB, provided by SleepyCat (www.sleepycat.com), uses page-level locking. That means if one user is accessing a page from a table, no one else can access that table until that user is finished. This makes each transaction safer, but can lead to slower response time in some situations. In order to use BDB tables, you use a binary version of MySQL that has been compiled with BDB support or configure the MySQL source using the `withberkeleydb` option.

TIP

If you decide not to use BDB tables, start your MySQL server with the `skipbdb` option. This will free a lot of memory, since the BDB library and the memory MySQL would normally specify for its use will not be reserved on startup. Of course, this means that you will not be able to use BDB tables.

Currently, BDB is not used nearly as much as the alternative transactional table type, InnoDB.

Advantages	Disadvantages
Safer data because of automatic backups and recovery logs	Slower because of transaction overhead
Ability to ignore changes, if not run in auto-commit mode	Uses more disk space because of transaction overhead
Changes restored, if update fails	Uses more memory to do updates
Provides better concurrency	

Table 2-12 Pros and Cons of Using Transactional Tables (BDB and InnoDB)

InnoDB   InnoDB tables, made by Innobase Oy (www.innodb.com), are distributed under the GPL, as well as commercially. InnoDB features row-level locking (while a user is accessing a row, no one else can access that row), consistent nonlocking read in SELECT statements (to extract information from the database), and common table space for all tables (all TABLES are stored in the same area).

If you need commercial support or commercial licenses for your application and cost is a concern, you may not want to use InnoDB. Not using InnoDB will save you about 20 to 50 percent for licenses and support contracts. However, if data integrity is your primary concern, InnoDB provides MySQL with a transactional storage engine and crash-recovery capabilities.

InnoDB has been designed for maximum performance when processing large data volumes, so if your database includes large amounts of data and handles a lot of traffic, InnoDB may provide the speed and reliability you require. Also, any of the other disk-based, relational, database engines probably do not match its CPU efficiency. So, in a nutshell, most users that need a transactional database prefer the speed and features of InnoDB.

MERGE Tables

MERGE tables are two or more identical MyISAM tables joined by a UNION statement. You can only select, delete, and update from the collection of tables. If you drop the MERGE table, you are dropping only the MERGE specification. That means the MERGE table no longer exists, but the MyISAM tables it was constructed from and the data in them are still intact.

The most common reason to use MERGE tables is to get more speed. You can split a big, read-only table into several parts, and then put the different table parts on different disks. This results in faster access times, and therefore more efficient searches. Also, if you know exactly what you are looking for within the split parts, you can search in just one of the split tables for some queries, or if you need to search the entire table, use a MERGE command to access the parts as a whole.

Repairs on MERGE tables can be more efficient than on the same amount of data stored in any other table type, assuming that you have made it a MERGE table because of its size. It is faster to repair the individual files that are mapped to a MERGE file than to try to repair one huge file. MyISAM, and therefore MERGE, tables are represented as individual files on the hard drive. Using MERGE also allows you to work around your operating system's file-size limit.

However, there are some disadvantages to using MERGE tables:

- You can use only *identical* MyISAM tables for a MERGE table.

- The REPLACE command does not work.

- Key reads are slower, which negates the reason for having a key (or index) to read.

Because of the way they are constructed, MERGE tables sometimes require different syntax than other tables in order to manipulate them in the same fashion. This isn't a difficulty so much as it is just a fact about MERGE tables that you should remember. Obviously, MERGE tables will only be useful under special conditions; however, if your MyISAM tables develop growth-related restrictions, a MERGE table may be the most effective answer.

Now that you have learned about data types and how to plan a database, you next need to know about the actual commands for creating MySQL databases and tables. Then you can use the commands to set up our duckwear database.

Ask the Expert

Q: What are the main concerns I should consider in selecting a table type?

A: There are three main concerns you should consider when deciding on a table type: file size, data access, and data safety.

MyISAM, Merge, BDB are all subject to OS file size limits (although MERGE can to some extent work around that). HEAP and TEMPORARY (a table that is created for only as long as the current connection to the database is open) type tables are stored in memory and therefore subject to the amount of memory your computer has available. InnoDB tables are able to get around the file size limits completely, because they create a shared area that data is written across. For instance, if your InnoDB files are set at 2GB each and you have a 6GB table, InnoDB will spread that one table over all three files.

Data access is also a primary concern. The default table type for MySQL, MyISAM, has table-level locking, which means during an update operation, no other user can access any other record of the same table. BDB uses page-level locking, and during an update operation, no other user can access any other record residing in the same database page of that table, until the locking transaction issues a COMMIT statement. InnoDB, however, uses row-level locking. Row-level locking ensures that during an update operation, no other user can access that particular row, until the locking transaction issues a COMMIT statement. Therefore, InnoDB leaves more of the data available for other users to access, while still maintaining data security for the data in the row already being accessed. That being said, any of the table types will probably work fine for a web server, but in a local area network (LAN) application, the transactional table types (BDB and InnoDB) can cause unnecessary locking-contention issues, and a database is no fun when you are locked out of it.

Most users choose MyISAM if they need speed and InnoDB if they need data integrity. If your database requires both of these things in equal measure, you can use more than one table type, or any combination of these table types, in your database.

Remember to assess the needs of each table before building it. Even though MyISAM is faster and simpler than InnoDB, InnoDB is still fast when compared to any other database engine. With InnoDB you get transactions, speed, and integrity—three features not usually used in the same sentence. However, MyISAM is a good place to start for most of your applications, because its speed and simplicity will get your database up and running and it provides the most up-front options.

Progress Check

1. What are the table types MySQL allows you to use?

2. Which table type is the MySQL default?

3. Which table type is usually used to store large amounts of data?

4. What are the two transactional-based table types?

5. Which table should be used only to store temporary data?

CRITICAL SKILL
2.3 Create Your Database and Tables

So far, we've planned only one table, which contains customer information, for our DuckWear company's database. There are times when a certain set of data may be used repeatedly in various tables throughout a database. When it is clear that this may happen, you can make a separate table, so that the actual information needs to be stored only once. Other tables in the database store an *index* (or *key*) number to access the information.

For instance, if you wanted to store the full name of a state instead of its two-letter postal designation, you could create a table of the states with an automatically incrementing index number. Storing a digit from 1 to 50 takes up much less room than storing the entire name of any state. Later, when it is time to look at a printout of the customer data, the database could access the number in the State field and use it to reference the state name in the other table, so the name would be printed in the report instead of the number.

For the `duckwear` database, you will make a title table that allows customers to choose the title of address they prefer for their mailing label: Mr., Mrs., Ms., and so on, or none at all. (Given that it is increasingly difficult to correctly guess gender from looking at a name, it is wise to give your customers the choice.)

So, now you are making two tables in the `duckwear` database: `duck_cust` and `duck_title`. The data to be entered in them will be provided as you work your way through Project 2-1. However, first we need to look at the commands you will use to make the database and the tables.

---

1. The MySQL table types are ISAM, HEAP, BDB, InnoDB, MERGE, and MyISAM.
2. MyISAM is the default table type.
3. MERGE tables are used to store large amount of data.
4. BDB and InnoDB are transactional table types.
5. You should use the HEAP type only for temporary data.

Creating a Database

The full syntax for the command to create a database is very basic:

```
CREATE DATABASE [IF NOT EXISTS] <db_name>
```

Any portion of the syntax of a command within square brackets, [ ], is optional and, in this case, is merely a safeguard. Any portion of the syntax that is in all uppercase letters is a MySQL reserved word, and as stated earlier in this module, should not be used solely as a name, although you may use it as part of a name. For instance, INDEX is a reserved word, but you can name an index something like play_index, without needing any special notation.

If you try to create a database that already exists (and don't use the IF NOT EXISTS option), you will get a warning returned on the command line. If you use IF NOT EXISTS, there is no warning, but either way, the database is not created. So, the simplest syntax with which to create our DuckWear database is as follows:

```
CREATE DATABASE duckwear;
```

As mentioned in Module 1, MySQL will not process the command until the closing semicolon has been entered.

Creating a Table

The full syntax to create a table is a little more complex than the one to create a database:

```
CREATE [TEMPORARY] TABLE [IF NOT EXISTS] <table_name>
[(create_definition,...)] [table_options] [select_statement]
```

However, most of the syntax (as indicated by enclosing it in square brackets) is optional. The IF NOT EXISTS option works in the same manner as it does in a CREATE DATABASE statement.

The TEMPORARY option means that the table that is created will be visible only as long as the current connection to the database is open. When the connection is closed, even if by accident, the table will be deleted. An example of when you might use a temporary setting is to make a table where the data is a partial copy of data in another table. You can view the data in the table more clearly, and then delete the table after you have finished examining it.

There are a variety of options that go inside the create_definition parentheses, but we will only go over the ones that are used most frequently:

```
<column_name> <data type> [NOT NULL | NULL] [DEFAULT <default_value>]
[AUTO_INCREMENT]  PRIMARY KEY (<index_column_name>,...)
```

The column_name is used to define the columns of the table (or the fields of each record, if you prefer to think of them like that) and must have the column name and data type, which may be followed by several options:

● The NOT NULL/NULL choice, which determines whether or not the field requires data, as explained earlier in this module

- The ability to set a DEFAULT value (which the database uses in lieu of input data)

- AUTO-INCREMENT, which when set, automatically counts up when NULL is input into the column's field

- PRIMARY KEY, which indicates which column of fields will be used to form an index for faster access to the table's records

Any of these commands, if used, are contained inside the set of parentheses that enclose the *column_name* definitions and are separated by commas. If this seems confusing, don't panic; after the hands-on experience of Projects 2-1 and 2-2, it will all be clear.

The last two options in the CREATE TABLE command are *table_options* and *select_statement*. The most used table option is *type*, which specifies the table type (also referred to as *engine*) and determines by which rules the table operates. If you do not set a table type, your table is made with the MySQL default, MyISAM. For clarity, it is recommended that you specify the MyISAM table in a TYPE statement when you make a table. That way, there is no question as to your intentions, even though you have chosen to use the default type.

Correcting Mistakes in Commands

If you make a mistake in the syntax of the command itself or in the names within it, the command line will return an error statement. The error statement will try to give you some idea of what the difficulty is, but sometimes, especially for beginners, it does not seem all that helpful.

If you are sure of the overall syntax of the command, the most common errors should be checked first:

- A string that should be enclosed between single quotation marks but has only a single quotation mark on one side

- A double quotation mark where a single quotation mark should be

- A database, table, or field name that has been misspelled or, on Linux servers, a letter in uppercase rather than lowercase, or vice versa

- A dash where an underscore should be

- A CREATE statement that does not have one or both of the parentheses that surround the column descriptions

Especially on the longer commands, type in the command slowly and carefully, checking each line before pressing the ENTER key to go to the next line. If a typo slips past you, you cannot back up and correct it. If you do make a mistake, entering the ending semicolon without finishing the command will allow you to stop without creating a flawed table. To be absolutely sure that a flawed command is not accepted, you can type some gibberish before the semicolon to make sure that MySQL will return an error and not run the command.

Depending on you typing skills, it may save you a lot of frustration if you take advantage of already correct lines saved in the command-line history. Using the UP ARROW key will allow you to step back through the command history. Use this to back up to the beginning of the command and press ENTER. Repeat this for the next line until you get to the line with the error in it. At that point, you can use the ARROW and BACKSPACE keys to erase the error, and then type in the correct syntax. Continue to use the UP ARROW and ENTER keys until you run out of correctly entered lines of code, and then finish the command.

Formatting Table Data

When you're entering the data for a table, the form of the supplied data may not reflect the format rules of MySQL. You may need to do a certain amount of reformatting in order to enter data properly. Remember to format dates in the correct order ($YYYY:MM:DD$), replace any missing data with a zero (0), and list the record's fields in the order in which they were defined in the table.

The data you'll enter in Project 2-2 includes a name with an embedded apostrophe, which is the same as the single quotation that marks strings contained within the syntax. Work around this by putting two single quotation marks in the place where the apostrophe should go. For example, to insert the word *don't* as a string, type the string as `'don''t'`, using two single quotation marks between the letters *n* and *t*. This will prevent MySQL from confusing the apostrophe for a single quotation mark whose matching quotation mark is missing. You can also place a backslash (\) in front of a single quotation to *escape* it, or indicate that it is not one of a pair: `'don\'t'`.

Project 2-1   Create a Database and Tables with Data

In Project 2-1, you will gain experience with the CREATE DATABASE and CREATE TABLE commands. You will use the data types previously discussed and use the commands that allow you to inspect your databases, tables, table definitions, and table contents. You will need to press ENTER after typing each command (after entering the semicolon).

NOTE

The command lines in the project are shown with the reserved words in all uppercase in order to clarify the difference between the required and optional reserved words and the user-supplied names and values. As you will see in the illustrations that accompany the project steps, you may type the commands in with all lowercase letters, regardless of the operating system you are using. It is simply a matter of personal preference.

Step by Step

1. Open your MySQL client. In Windows, type **\mysql\bin\mysql**. In Linux, type **mysql -p**, and then enter **pa55w0rd**.

2. Type **CREATE DATABASE duckwear;**. The command line should say:

```
Query OK, 1 Row Affected
```

3. Type **SHOW DATABASES;**. The command line will return a list of databases.

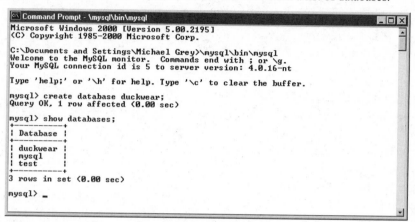

4. Specify which database to use and create your first table by typing the following commands:

```
USE duckwear;
CREATE TABLE duck_title(
title _num TINYINT NOT NULL AUTO_INCREMENT,
title _cust CHAR(4),
PRIMARY KEY(title_num)
) TYPE=MyISAM;
DESC duck_title;
```

The USE command will return Database Changed, the CREATE command will return Query OK, 0 rows affected, and the DESC command (short for describe) will return a description of the table duck_title.

(continued)

5. Create the duck_cust table by entering the following command:

```
CREATE TABLE duck_cust(
cust_num MEDIUMINT NOT NULL AUTO_INCREMENT,
cust_title TINYINT,
cust_last CHAR(20) NOT NULL,
cust_first CHAR(15) NOT NULL,
cust_suffix ENUM('Jr.', 'II', 'III','IV', 'V', 'M.D.','PhD'),
cust_add1 CHAR(30) NOT NULL,
cust_add2 CHAR(10),
cust_city CHAR(18) NOT NULL,
cust_state CHAR(2) NOT NULL,
cust_zip1 CHAR(5)NOT NULL,
cust_zip2 CHAR(4),
cust_duckname CHAR(25) NOT NULL,
cust_duckbday DATE,
PRIMARY KEY (cust_num)
)TYPE=MyISAM;
```

6. To verify the table creation, type **SHOW TABLES;**. The command line will return a list that now includes duck_cust and duck_title.

7. Type **DESC duck_cust;**. The command line will return a listing of all the properties of the columns in the duck_cust table.

NOTE

The display often wraps on the screen. In the example here, the display splits in the middle of the column that indicates whether a field's DEFAULT value is NULL. The last column of this display, Extra, has only one entry in it: the AUTO_INCREMENT setting for the cust_num column's fields. Take the time to study the display until the information and the explanatory headers above it make sense.

```
Select Command Prompt - \mysql\bin\mysql                                  _ □ ×
mysql> desc duck_cust;
+-----------------+--------------------+   +--------+-------+-----+
| Field           | Type               |   | Null   | Key   | De
fault | Extra      |                    |
+-----------------+--------------------+   +--------+-------+-----+
| cust_num        | mediumint(9)       |   |        | PRI   | NU
LL    | auto_increment |
| cust_title      | tinyint(4)         |   | YES    |       | NU
LL    |            |
| cust_last       | char(20)           |   |        |       |
|     |            |
| cust_first      | char(15)           |   |        |       |
|     |            |
| cust_suffix     | enum('Jr.','II','III','IV','U','M.D.','PhD') | YES |  | NU
LL    |            |
| cust_add1       | char(30)           |   |        |       |
|     |            |
| cust_add2       | char(10)           |   | YES    |       | NU
LL    |            |
| cust_city       | char(18)           |   |        |       |
|     |            |
| cust_state      | char(2)            |   |        |       |
|     |            |
| cust_zip1       | char(5)            |   |        |       |
|     |            |
| cust_zip2       | char(4)            |   | YES    |       | NU
LL    |            |
| cust_duckname   | char(25)           |   |        |       |
|     |            |
| cust_duckbday   | date               |   | YES    |       | NU
LL    |            |
+-----------------+--------------------+   +--------+-------+-----+
13 rows in set (0.00 sec)

mysql> _
```

Project Summary

In Project 2-1, you have used the correct syntax to create a database and the tables in it. You have practiced using the data types discussed at the beginning of this module. You have also learned a few basic commands to allow you to look at your database's tables, their layouts, and the contents of those tables.

CRITICAL SKILL

2.4 Insert Data into Tables

Placing data into a previously created table is accomplished with the INSERT command. The INSERT command performs this task one record or table row at a time. The inserted fields can be partially or completely specified. In the case of partially specified fields, MySQL inserts the default value into the unspecified field.

There are three basic variations on the INSERT syntax: INSERT . . . VALUES and INSERT . . . SET, which inserts specific values provided in the command code, and INSERT . . . SELECT, which inserts values provided in other tables:

```
INSERT INTO <table_name> [<column_name1[, <column_name2, . . .]
VALUES <column_value1>[, <column_value2>, . . .];
```

The INSERT . . . VALUES syntax requires a *table_name* value and it gives you the option of specifying a list of column names. The *column_name* values need to be listed in the order in which they appear in the actual table description. In addition, the list of *column_name*s and list of *column_value*s must match, respectively, or the data will be inserted into the wrong column. Because this version of the syntax inserts data in all the columns, you will find it is easier and less work to state only the *table_name*, letting MySQL attend to the *column_name* data. You can then focus on making sure the list of column_values is correctly ordered. If data is missing for a particular field, then use the NULL value, which will cause either the DEFAULT value to be inserted in that field or a marker value (such as 0 for a numeric field or "n/a" for a string field) to fill the place of the missing data:

```
INSERT INTO <table_name>
SET <column_name>=<column_value>[, <column_name>=<column_value>, . . .];
```

The INSERT . . . SET syntax allows you to put values in specified columns within a record, and the <column_name>=<column_value> format makes it easier to assure the correct match between column and data, especially if the record in question has a lot of fields. Any column not specified in the command will have the DEFAULT value inserted into it.

```
INSERT INTO <table_name> [<column_name1[, <column_name2, . . .]
SELECT <select_value> FROM <table_name>;
```

The INSERT . . . SELECT syntax allows you to use a SELECT command to read another table or tables and insert its data into the specified *table_name*. The *select_value* can be a wild card (*), an expression (i.e. *column_value*+3), or a *column_name* or list of *column_name*s. The column_names in each table description must be in respective order, and once again, any column not specified has the DEFAULT value placed into it.

As of MySQL version 4.1.0, all three of these INSERT syntaxes will allow the addition of the ON DUPLICATE KEY UPDATE clause at the end of the command but before the semicolon. This clause allows you to specify what will happen if the record you try to insert duplicates a key that has been designated as UNIQUE or PRIMARY by allowing you to update the specified field or fields of the unique record rather than insert a duplicate record. The following syntax shows this clause attached to the INSERT . . . VALUES syntax, but it can be used in the same position in all of the INSERT commands:

```
INSERT INTO <table_name> [<column_name1[, <column_name2, . . .]
VALUES <column_value1>[, <column_value2>, . . .]
 [ON DUPLICATE KEY UPDATE <column_name1>=<expression1>
 [, <column_name2>=<expression2>, . . .];
```

Project 2-2 Insert Data in Tables

Now that you have the beginning of your database, you can proceed to entering data. The text will supply you with the exact syntax for the first entry and a table listing the data for the rest of the entries.

Step by Step

1. You will begin, once again, with the simple duck_title table:

```
INSERT INTO duck_title
VALUES
(1, 'Mr.'),
(2, 'Ms.'),
(3, 'Mrs.'),
(4, 'Miss'),
(5, 'Sir'),
(6, 'Dame'),
(7, 'Dr.'),
(8, 'Lady'),
(9, 'None');
```

The command line shows the command and the return statement:

```
Query OK, 9 rows affected (0.02 sec)
Records: 9  Duplicates: 0  Warnings: 0
```

```
Command Prompt - \mysql\bin\mysql                                    _ □ X
mysql> insert into duck_title
    -> values
    -> (1, 'Mr.'),
    -> (2, 'Ms.'),
    -> (3, 'Mrs.'),
    -> (4, 'Miss'),
    -> (5, 'Sir'),
    -> (6, 'Dame'),
    -> (7, 'Dr.'),
    -> (8, 'Lady'),
    -> (9, 'None');
Query OK, 9 rows affected (0.02 sec)
Records: 9  Duplicates: 0  Warnings: 0

mysql> _
```

(continued)

2. To verify your data entry, use a SELECT command with the asterisk (*) wildcard symbol. Whenever an asterisk is used in a command, it can roughly be translated as "all that you find" or "everything," so the following command is the equivalent of saying, "Select everything in the table duck_title."

```
SELECT * FROM duck_title:
```

The resulting display allows you to examine the contents of the table and compare them with the command still visible above it. At this point, the table duck_title is completely loaded with the required data.

TIP

If you cannot remember the index number for any of the titles, you can use this SELECT command as a visual reminder.

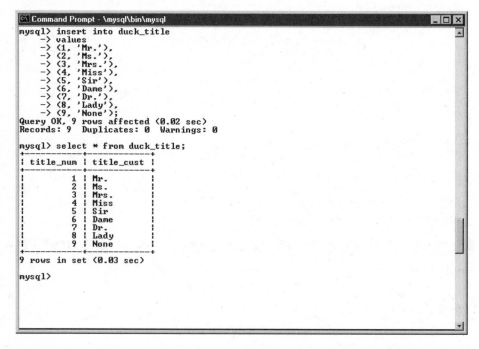

3. Insert the first of the customer records by typing in the following command:

```
INSERT INTO duck_cust
VALUES
(NULL, 8, 'Salisbury', 'Jenny', 0, '9 Wishing Well Court', 0,
 'Meadowlark Hill', 'KS', '67048', '1234', 'Spike', '1961:03:21');
```

The command line will return with Query OK, 1 row affected as long as you have carefully reproduced the command.

4. Verify the entry by using the SELECT statement on the duck_cust table:

```
SELECT * FROM duck_cust;
```

```
Command Prompt - \mysql\bin\mysql                                      _ □ X
mysql> insert into duck_cust
    -> values
    -> (null, 8, 'Salisbury', 'Jenny', 0, '9 Wishing Well Court', 0, 'Meadowlark Hi
ll', 'KS', '67048', '1234', 'Spike', '1961:03:21');
Query OK, 1 row affected (0.00 sec)

mysql> select * from duck_cust;
+---------+------------+-----------+------------+-------------+-----------+
---+------------+----------+-------------+-----------+----------+----------+
| cust_num | cust_title | cust_last | cust_first | cust_suffix | cust_add1 |
 | cust_add2 | cust_city     | cust_state | cust_zip1 | cust_zip2 | cust_duckna
me | cust_duckbday |
+---------+------------+-----------+------------+-------------+-----------+
---+------------+----------+-------------+-----------+----------+----------+
|         1 |          8 | Salisbury | Jenny      |             |           | 9 Wishing Well Cou
rt | 0         | Meadowlark Hill | KS       |     67048   | 1234      |    Spike
   | 1961-03-21 |
+---------+------------+-----------+------------+-------------+-----------+
---+------------+----------+-------------+-----------+----------+----------+
1 row in set (0.00 sec)

mysql> _
```

5. Insert the remaining customer data into the duck_cust table:

```
INSERT INTO duck_cust
VALUES
(NULL, 1, 'Irishlord', 'Red', 'III', '1022 N.E. Sea of Rye', 'A207',
 'Seacouver', 'WA', '98601', '3464', 'Netrek Rules', '1967:10:21');

INSERT INTO duck_cust
VALUES
(NULL, 4, 'Thegreat', 'Vicki', 0, '2004 Singleton Dr.', 0,
 'Freedom', 'KS', '67209', '4321', 'Frida Kahlo de Tomayo', '1948:03:21');

INSERT INTO duck_cust
VALUES
(NULL, 9, 'Montgomery', 'Chantel', 0, '1567 Terra Cotta Way', 0,
 'Chicago', 'IL', '89129', '4444', 'Bianca', '1971:07:29');

INSERT INTO duck_cust
VALUES
(NULL, 7, 'Robert', 'David', 'Sr.', '20113 Open Road Highway', '#6',
```

(continued)

```
'Blacktop', 'AZ', '00606', '1952', 'Harley', '1949:08:00');

INSERT INTO duck_cust
VALUES
(NULL, 5, 'Kazui', 'Wonko', 'PhD', '42 Cube Farm Lane', 'Gatehouse',
 'Vlimpt', 'CA', '45362', 0, 'Fitzwhistle', '1961:12:04');

INSERT INTO duck_cust
VALUES
(NULL, 6, 'Gashlycrumb', 'Karen', 0, '3113 Picket Fence Lane', 0,
 'Fedora', 'VT', '41927', '5698', 'Tess D''urberville', '1948:08:19');
```

6. Once you have all the data inserted, use the wildcard SELECT command to view the entire table.

```
SELECT * FROM duck_cust;
```

7. If the display is too confusing to read quickly and clearly, you can use a variation of the SELECT command to look at only one column at a time by replacing the asterisk with the column name. The following command will list only the contents of the cust_duckname column.

```
SELECT cust_duckname FROM duck_cust;
```

```
Command Prompt - \mysql\bin\mysql                              _ □ X
mysql> select cust_duckname from duck_cust;
+----------------------------+
| cust_duckname              |
+----------------------------+
| Spike                      |
| Netrek Rules               |
| Frida Kahlo de Tomayo      |
| Bianca                     |
| Harley                     |
| Fitzwhistle                |
| Tess D'urberville          |
+----------------------------+
7 rows in set (0.00 sec)

mysql>
```

Project Summary

In Project 2-2, after what was probably a certain amount of frustrating typos and omissions, you inserted data into both the `duck_title` and the `duck_cust` tables you created. You also used the most basic form of the `SELECT ... FROM` command to display some or all the records in a table. You now have the basic database required for the projects in the remaining modules.

In the preceding projects, you used several commands to choose and display information about your database tables. The `USE` command tells MySQL which database your subsequent commands refer to. The `SHOW` command tells MySQL to list either databases or tables. The `DESC` command requests a description of a specific table or a specific column within that table. The `SELECT ... FROM` command, as it was used in Project 2-2, requests the display of all of the records in a table. The basic syntax of these commands follows:

```
USE <database_name>;
SHOW <DATABASES | TABLES | GRANTS | PRIVILEGES>;
DESC <table_name> [<column_name>];
SELECT { * | <column_name> | <list of column_names>} FROM <table_name>;
```

The SELECT command can be used for more than displaying data on the command line and will be covered in more depth in Module 4. Now that you have completed Projects 2-1 and 2-2 and have your beginning database, you should take a moment to correlate the results with the steps you took. In the project, you saw how the display wrapped around because of the number of fields in each record, but the data is readable and corresponds with the headers above it.

Note that the initial entry of `NULL` in the values of the `INSERT INTO duck_cust` command in step 3 has caused the auto-incremented `cust_num` column to place a 1 in that row's field. Subsequent entries caused each record in succession to have a `cust_num` entry one digit higher than the one before it.

An 8 was entered in the `cust_title` column on the first record, and if you cross-reference that to the index 8 in the `duck_title` table, you get the word `Lady`, which matches the data in Table 2-13. This customer has only one address (no apartment number or other information), and so a 0 was entered into the `cust_add2` field. Similarly, there was no suffix to the customer's name, so it also had a 0 in its field.

Title	First Name	Last Name	Suffix	Address 1	Address 2	City	State	Zip Code	Plus 4	Duck's Name	Duck's Birthday
Lady	Jenny	Salisbury		9 Wishing Well Court		Meadowlark Hill	KS	67048	1234	Spike	03/21/1961
Mr.	Red	Irishlord	III	1022 N.E. Sea of Rye	A207	Seacouver	WA	98601	3464	Netrek Rules	10/21/1967
Miss	Vicki	Thegreat		2004 Singleton Dr.		Freedom	KS	67290	4321	Frida Kahlo de Tomayo	03/21/1948
	Chantel	Montgomery		1567 Terra Cotta Way		Chicago	IL	89129	4444	Bianca	07/29/1971
Dr.	David	Robert	Sr.	20113 Open Road Highway	#6	Blacktop	AZ	00606	1952	Harley	08/00/1949
Sir	Wonko	Kazui	PhD	42 Cube Farm Lane	Gatehouse	Vlimpt	CA	45362		Fitzwhistle	12/04/1961
Dame	Karen	Gashlycrumb		3113 Picket Fence Lane		Fedora	VT	41927	5698	Tess D'urberville	08/19/1948

Table 2-13 Raw Data for the duck_cust Table

The last customer entered into the database provided an opportunity to deal with a special character embedded in a string. Lady Gashlycrumb's duck is named `Tess D'urberville`, and the embedded apostrophe in that name required that you add an extra apostrophe in front of it in the command ('Tess D''urberville'). MySQL then knows to accept the apostrophe as a text character, which should be written to the field, rather than as a special character, which indicates the beginning or ending of a string. As explained previously in this module, you alternatively could have used a backslash ('Tess D\'urberville') and achieved the same result.

You can avoid having to put the zeros in the fields with no data if they have not been designated NOT NULL, but it requires that you type the column names, in the order you are putting the data in, to indicate where each insertion goes. If you are entering only a few fields, this can be useful. The following is an example of entering the same data as step 3, using the column names method to avoid entering zeros into fields where there is no data:

```
INSERT INTO duck_cust
(cust_title, cust_last, cust_first, cust_add1, cust_city,
cust_state, cust_zip1, cust_zip2, cust_duckname, cust_duckbday)
VALUES
(8, 'Salisbury', 'Jenny', '9 Wishing Well Court', 'Meadowlark Hill',
'KS', '67048', '1234', 'Spike', '1961:03:21');
```

If you compare this INSERT command with the one you used in step 3, you can see that only fields with actual data were inserted, but each field name had to be specified before the values to insert were listed. This results in more typing than you saved by not inserting zeros into the nonrequired fields.

As you can see in Figure 2-1, if you had entered this command immediately after the command in step 3, it would have duplicated the record with some interesting differences: The first record, which inserted zeros into the two fields with no information, saved nothing into the cust_suffix field and a string with the supplied 0 into cust_add2 field. The reason for the difference is that cust_suffix is an enumerated list and saves only those values that have been defined as acceptable. The string 0 is not one of those values. cust_add2 is a character string field, and so it can have the string 0 inserted into it.

In the second record, where no input was inserted into those two fields, however, the cust_suffix field and the cust_add2 field both contain the word NULL. Since the cust_suffix field was not designated NOT NULL, when the values for its enumerated list were defined, a NULL is the only thing besides the contents of that list that can be stored there. The end result, as far as output, is the same. However, the presence of the NULL indicator in a field means that the missing value may or may not have been intentionally left out. The presence of the string 0 or a blank field means that the data was intentionally left out of the INSERT command. More about the INSERT command will be covered in Module 3, as well as adding UPDATE and DELETE to your repertoire of commands.

```
Command Prompt - \mysql\bin\mysql                                    _ □ X

mysql> insert into duck_cust
    -> (cust_title, cust_last, cust_first, cust_add1, cust_city, cust_state, cust_z
ip1, cust_zip2, cust_duckname, cust_duckbday)
    -> values
    -> (8, 'Salisbury', 'Jenny', '9 Wishing Well Court', 'Meadowlark Hill', 'KS', '
67048', '1234', 'Spike', '1961:03:21');
Query OK, 1 row affected (0.00 sec)

mysql> select * from duck_cust;
+----------+----------+-----------+------------+-----------+-----------+----------
---+-----------+------------+-----------+------------+-----------+-----------
---+------------+
| cust_num | cust_title | cust_last | cust_first | cust_suffix | cust_add1
  | cust_add2 | cust_city      | cust_state | cust_zip1 | cust_zip2 | cust_duckna
me | cust_duckbday |
+----------+----------+-----------+------------+-----------+-----------+----------
---+-----------+------------+-----------+------------+-----------+-----------
---+------------+
|        1 |          |         8 | Salisbury | Jenny      |           | 9 Wishing Well Cou
rt | 0          | Meadowlark Hill | KS       |     67048 |      1234 |     Spike
   | 1961-03-21 |
|        4 |          |         8 | Salisbury | Jenny      |      NULL | 9 Wishing Well Cou
rt | NULL       | Meadowlark Hill | KS       |     67048 |      1234 |     Spike
   | 1961-03-21 |
+----------+----------+-----------+------------+-----------+-----------+----------
---+-----------+------------+-----------+------------+-----------+-----------
---+------------+
2 rows in set (0.00 sec)

mysql>
```

Figure 2-1 Allowing MySQL to fill some column data

Module 2 Mastery Check

1. Which TABLE type is the MySQL DEFAULT?

2. Which data types would you use to display the Date in one column and the Time in a separate column?

3. How does the VARCHAR data type differ from the CHAR data type?

4. What are the two main rules for naming a TABLE?

5. What is the syntax to create a database called `Angel` and a table in it called `Wesley` with a `TINYINT` column called `Fred`?

6. How do you display the databases in your MySQL Server?

7. How do you display the tables in a database called `Jet`?

8. How do you display the layout or specifications of a table called `Wraith` if you are already using the database in which it is housed?

9. How do you display the contents of a table called `horse` if you are already using the database in which it is housed?

10. If the `horse` table has the columns `bridle`, `saddle`, and `blanket`, how do you display the contents of `saddle` only?

Module 3

Manipulating the Database

This module will further your ability to interface with your newly made database. You will learn more ways to add new data to your database, as well as how to edit or add to existing data and create indexes to speed access to your data. This module will also show you how to remove either records from tables or entire tables from your database.

Add Data to Your Database

After you have a basic database, you will want to insert data into existing tables and add new tables. You can add data to your database in a variety of ways, in addition to using the INSERT command covered in the previous module.

Sometimes, an existing table can have all or nearly all the data you want to use in another table. In that case, it is easier and more efficient to create your new table by copying the old one and altering that copy. You can do this with one command, which defines the new table, and then fills it with the specified data. If you want to use data from just selected parts of another table, you can do that as well.

Occasionally, you may have data in a text file where the fields are separated by a common divider like a comma. You can use that file as a source to load all its data into a table with one command.

In this section, you will learn how to add data using both techniques: by copying a table and by using a text file as a source.

Copying a Table

In order to create a copy of a table so that you can alter it or experiment with it without endangering the original data, you can use the following command:

```
CREATE TABLE <new_table_name>
SELECT * FROM <old_table_name>;
```

NOTE

Remember that commands in MySQL are not ended until the semicolon. So the preceding code, despite being displayed on two lines, is only one command.

You can give your new table any name (new_table_name) you like, with just a few restrictions, as discussed in Module 2. As we suggested in that module, the name should clearly but succinctly reflect the table's intended use. For example, if it is an experimental copy of the original table, naming it with the original name followed by the word copy makes its function clear; a copy of duck_cust could be named duck_cust_copy.

As you learned in the previous module, the use of the asterisk (*), or wildcard symbol, means "everything." In this case, it is instructing MySQL to use not only the table definition data, but also all of the data the table contains. The only difference between the two tables, besides their names, is that if the old table had an index (or key), it does not transfer to the new table. If the new table needs the same or another index, you can create one for it, as explained in the "Creating an Index" section later in this module.

Copying Only Selected Columns from a Table

If you need a table that holds only part of the information in an existing table, you can specify the columns you want defined in the new table by using the following command:

```
CREATE TABLE <new_table_name>
SELECT <column_name1>, <column_name2> FROM <old_table_name>;
```

This example shows only two columns chosen, but you can list any number of columns, separated by commas.

The same basic result can be approached in a different way. You can choose to create the table first, and then use an INSERT command to populate the table with data, using this command:

```
CREATE TABLE <new_table_name> (
<column_name1> CHAR(15) NOT NULL,
<column_name2> CHAR(20) NOT NULL
)TYPE=MyISAM;
INSERT INTO <new_table_name>
SELECT <column_name1>, <column_name2> FROM <old_table_name>;
```

Copying to a Temporary Table

If you are creating a new table strictly to experiment with, and you won't need it after you've learned what you need to from it, you can create the copy as a temporary table by using the following syntax:

```
CREATE TEMPORARY TABLE <new_table_name>
SELECT * FROM <old_table_name>;
```

This copy of the old table will remain until the current session with the MySQL Client is ended. This is true whether the connection is severed on purpose or by accident, so keep that in mind if you are working with an unstable system.

Temporary tables are saved differently than permanent tables, and as a result, they do not show up in the output of the SHOW TABLES; command. If you leave your MySQL session connected and later find you have forgotten what you named the temporary table, use the arrow keys to search the command-line history for the command that created it.

Copying Only Selected Data from a Table

You can also use a more specific SELECT command to make a temporary or permanent table that holds only part of the data in the original table. Using the duck_cust table as an example, the following command will create a temporary table named temp_list, which displays only those customers who list the state KS in their customer record, and then print a display of their customer number and last name, from the temp_list table on the command line:

```
CREATE TEMPORARY TABLE tempKS_list
SELECT cust_num, cust_last FROM duck_cust
WHERE cust_state LIKE "KS";
SELECT * FROM tempKS_list;
```

Inserting Data from a Text File

Another option is to insert data into a table by using a file, such as a log file from your server, as a source. For this to work, the file must have the proper format—the data types and sizes, and the order of its arrangement, must match the table in order to load the entire file at one time. Also, it must be saved in a simple text file format, which usually means the file will have a .txt extension. Text files saved in more complex, word-processor formats, such as Word's .doc file format, have too many—and often invisible—formatting symbols that will corrupt data when it's loading. You can either design a table to hold the information that reflects the file's format, or edit the file so that its format fits an existing table in your database. This might seem like extra work, but the amount of time you will save by inserting multiple records this way usually outweighs the amount of time it takes to set up the file or a new table.

A comma-separated file is a text file in which each field of data in a record is separated from its neighboring fields with a comma (i.e. field1, field2, field3, and so on) The end of each record in the comma-separated field is indicated by an invisible Line Terminator, which you insert by pressing the ENTER key. Windows and Linux indicate the end of line differently, so you have to know your operating system and use the proper terminator in your commands. The Windows Line Terminator is "\r\n" and the Linux Line Terminator is "\n". The syntax for a command to use a comma-separated text file, saved in a Windows format, is as follows:

```
LOAD DATA INFILE '<full_path_to_text_file>'
INTO TABLE <table_name>
FIELDS TERMINATED BY ','
LINES TERMINATED BY '\r\n';
```

The path to the text file varies, depending on where you choose to save the file. The best place is somewhere you can easily remember, and of course, a shorter path is easier to type into the command line than a longer one.

In the FIELDS TERMINATED BY code, you can designate other separators:

- Colons, by using ' : '
- Semicolons, by using ' ; '
- Spaces, by using ' '

Another useful option when you insert data from a file is IGNORE <*numeric_value*> lines. Often, data stored in a file will have headers at the top. This option allows you to tell MySQL to skip over those lines and only load actual data. If the first line of your semi-colon-separated test file (duck.txt) is a series of column headers, and you do not want those headers placed in your table (quackers) as a record, you would use the IGNORE clause, as shown in the following example, using Linux Line Termination:

```
LOAD DATA INFILE '/documents/duck.txt'
INTO TABLE <quackers>
FIELDS TERMINATED BY ';'
LINES TERMINATED BY '\r\n'
IGNORE 1 LINES;
```

Project 3-1 Create Tables Using Existing Table Data

Now that you know the different ways of creating tables and adding data to new or existing tables, you will make practical use of these techniques. In this project, you will create a copy of an entire existing table, create a new table with columns from an existing table, create a temporary table from an existing table, insert data from an existing table into a newly created table, and finally, load data from a text file into an existing table.

Step by Step

1. Open a command-line window and log in to MySQL, using the **\mysql\bin\mysql -u root -p** command (Windows) or the **mysql** -p command (Linux), and then enter your password when prompted.

2. Type **USE duckwear**; and press the ENTER key.

3. Type in the following command to create a copy of the duck_cust table:

```
CREATE TABLE copy_duck_cust
SELECT * FROM duck_cust;
```

(continued)

4. Type in the following command to verify the creation of the copy of the duck_cust table, including its data:

```
SELECT * FROM copy_duck_cust;
```

Your table should be identical to the duck_cust table you created in Module 2.

```
mysql> select * from copy_duck_cust;
+-----------+-------------+-------------------+-------------+-------------+-------------+-------------+--
-----------+-------------+-------------------+-------------+-------------+-------------+-------------+--
                    +-------------+-------------------+
| cust_num  | cust_title  | cust_last         | cust_first  | cust_suffix | cust_add1
           | cust_add2   | cust_city         | cust_state  | cust_zip1   | cust_zip2   |
cust_duckname           | cust_duckbday     |
+-----------+-------------+-------------------+-------------+-------------+-------------+-------------+--
-----------+-------------+-------------------+-------------+-------------+-------------+-------------+--
                    +-------------+-------------------+
|         1 |           8 | Salisbury         | Jenny       |             | 9 Wishing Wel
1 Court    | 0         | Meadowlark Hill   | KS          | 67048       | 1234        |
Spike                   | 1961-03-21        |
|         2 |           1 | Irishlord         | Red         | III         | 1022 Sea of R
ye         | A207      | Seacouver         | WA          | 98601       | 3464        |
Netrek Rules            | 1967-10-21        |
|         3 |           4 | Thegreat          | Vicki       |             | 2004 Singleto
n Dr.      | 0         | Freedom           | KS          | 67290       | 4321        |
Frida Kahlo de Tomayo   | 1948-03-21        |
|         4 |           9 | Montgomery        | Chantel     |             | 1567 Terra Co
tta Way    | 0         | Chicago           | IL          | 89129       | 4444        |
Bianca                  | 1971-07-29        |
|         5 |           7 | Robert            | David       |             | 20113 Open Ro
ad Highway | #6        | Blacktop          | AZ          | 00606       | 1952        |
Harley                  | 1949-08-00        |
|         6 |           5 | Kazui             | Wonko       | PhD         | 42 Cube Farm
Lane       | Gatehouse | Ulimpt            | CA          | 46362       | 0           |
Fitzwhistle             | 1961-12-04        |
|         7 |           6 | Gashlycrumb       | Karen       |             | 3113 Picket F
ence Lane  | 0         | Fedora            | VT          | 41927       | 5698        |
Tess D'urberville       | 1948-08-19        |
+-----------+-------------+-------------------+-------------+-------------+-------------+-------------+--
-----------+-------------+-------------------+-------------+-------------+-------------+-------------+--
                    +-------------+-------------------+
7 rows in set (0.00 sec)

mysql>
```

5. Enter the commands to describe both the existing duck_cust table and the copy_duck_cust table and compare them:

```
DESC duck_cust;
```

```
ust' at line 1
mysql> desc duck_cust;
+-----------------+-------------------+     +------+-----+----
-------+-----------------+
| Field           | Type              |     | Null | Key | De
fault | Extra           |
-------+-----------------+
+-----------------+-------------------+     +------+-----+----
| cust_num        | mediumint(9)      |     |      | PRI | NU
LL      | auto_increment  |
| cust_title      | tinyint(4)        |     | YES  |     | NU
LL      |                 |
| cust_last       | char(20)          |     |      |     |
        |                 |
| cust_first      | char(15)          |     |      |     |
        |                 |
| cust_suffix     | enum('Jr.','II','III','IU','U','M.D.','PhD') | YES |   | NU
LL      |                 |
| cust_add1       | char(30)          |     |      |     |
        |                 |
| cust_add2       | char(10)          |     | YES  |     | NU
LL      |                 |
| cust_city       | char(18)          |     |      |     |
        |                 |
| cust_state      | char(2)           |     |      |     |
        |                 |
| cust_zip1       | char(5)           |     |      |     |
        |                 |
| cust_zip2       | char(4)           |     | YES  |     | NU
LL      |                 |
| cust_duckname   | char(25)          |     |      |     |
        |                 |
| cust_duckbday   | date              |     | YES  |     | NU
LL      |                 |
+-----------------+-------------------+     +------+-----+----
13 rows in set (0.13 sec)

mysql>
```

```
DESC copy_duck_cust;
```

```
mysql> desc copy_duck_cust;
+-----------------+-------------------+     +------+-----+----
-------+-------+
| Field           | Type              |     | Null | Key | De
fault | Extra |
+-----------------+-------------------+     +------+-----+----
-------+-------+
| cust_num        | mediumint(9)      |     |      |     | 0
       |       |
| cust_title      | tinyint(4)        |     | YES  |     | NU
LL      |       |
| cust_last       | char(20)          |     |      |     |
       |       |
| cust_first      | char(15)          |     |      |     |
       |       |
| cust_suffix     | enum('Jr.','II','III','IU','U','M.D.','PhD') | YES |   | NU
LL      |       |
| cust_add1       | char(30)          |     |      |     |
       |       |
| cust_add2       | char(10)          |     | YES  |     | NU
LL      |       |
| cust_city       | char(18)          |     |      |     |
       |       |
| cust_state      | char(2)           |     |      |     |
       |       |
| cust_zip1       | char(5)           |     |      |     |
       |       |
| cust_zip2       | char(4)           |     | YES  |     | NU
LL      |       |
| cust_duckname   | char(25)          |     |      |     |
       |       |
| cust_duckbday   | date              |     | YES  |     | NU
LL      |       |
+-----------------+-------------------+     +------+-----+----
13 rows in set (0.05 sec)

mysql> _
```

(continued)

NOTE

Remember that the only discrepancy between the two tables, other than their different names, is that the `duck_cust` table has the `cust_num` field set as PRIMARY and auto-incremented. This is because the index (or key) did not transfer to the copy of the table.

6. Create a table called `cust_names` using the table definitions and data from the `duck_cust` table. Type in the following command:

```
CREATE TABLE cust_names
SELECT cust_first, cust_last FROM duck_cust;
```

7. Display the new table's contents using the following command:

```
SELECT * FROM cust_names;
```

```
mysql> create table cust_names
    -> select cust_first, cust_last from duck_cust
    -> ;
Query OK, 7 rows affected (0.19 sec)
Records: 7  Duplicates: 0  Warnings: 0

mysql> select * from cust_name;
ERROR 1146: Table 'duckwear.cust_name' doesn't exist
mysql> select * from cust_names;
+------------+------------+
| cust_first | cust_last  |
+------------+------------+
| Jenny      | Salisbury  |
| Red        | Irishlord  |
| Vicki      | Thegreat   |
| Chantel    | Montgomery |
| David      | Robert     |
| Wonko      | Kazui      |
| Karen      | Gashlycrumb |
+------------+------------+
7 rows in set (0.00 sec)

mysql>
```

8. Create a similar table, but include the customer number field. You want to preserve the auto-incrementing key, so create the table, called `cust_num_names` first, and then insert data into it from the `duck_cust` table.

```
CREATE TABLE cust_num_names (
names_num MEDIUMINT(9) NOT NULL AUTO_INCREMENT,
names_first CHAR(15) NOT NULL,
names_last CHAR(20) NOT NULL,
PRIMARY KEY (names_num)
)TYPE=MyISAM;
INSERT INTO cust_num_names
SELECT cust_num, cust_first, cust_last FROM duck_cust;
```

9. View both the table contents and description by using the following commands:

```
SELECT * FROM cust_num_names;
DESC cust_num_names;
```

```
mysql> create table cust_num_names (
    -> names_num mediumint(9) not null auto_increment,
    -> names_first char(15) not null,
    -> names_last char(20) not null,
    -> primary key (names_num)
    -> )type=MyISAM;
Query OK, 0 rows affected (0.08 sec)

mysql> insert into cust_num_names
    -> select cust_num, cust_first, cust_last from duck_cust
    -> ;
Query OK, 7 rows affected (0.00 sec)
Records: 7  Duplicates: 0  Warnings: 0

mysql> select * from cust_num_names;
+-----------+-------------+-------------+
| names_num | names_first | names_last  |
+-----------+-------------+-------------+
|         1 | Jenny       | Salisbury   |
|         2 | Red         | Irishlord   |
|         3 | Vicki       | Thegreat    |
|         4 | Chantel     | Montgomery  |
|         5 | David       | Robert      |
|         6 | Wonko       | Kazui       |
|         7 | Karen       | Gashlycrumb |
+-----------+-------------+-------------+
7 rows in set (0.00 sec)

mysql> desc cust_num_names;
+-------------+-------------+------+-----+---------+----------------+
| Field       | Type        | Null | Key | Default | Extra          |
+-------------+-------------+------+-----+---------+----------------+
| names_num   | mediumint(9)|      | PRI | NULL    | auto_increment |
| names_first | char(15)    |      |     |         |                |
| names_last  | char(20)    |      |     |         |                |
+-------------+-------------+------+-----+---------+----------------+
3 rows in set (0.01 sec)

mysql>
```

Compare the cust_num column description in the output from the DESC copy_duck_cust; command in step 5 with the names_num column description here. You'll see that the auto-incrementing primary key did not duplicate in the copy process used to create the copy_duck_cust table. But since you specified it when making the names_num column, the key is set, so you do not need to re-create the index.

10. For marketing reasons, the sales department of DuckWear needs to know how many customers reside in a particular state. Use the following commands to make a temporary table to provide this data in an easily readable format:

```
CREATE TEMPORARY TABLE tempKS_list
SELECT cust_num, cust_last FROM duck_cust
WHERE cust_state LIKE "KS";
SELECT * FROM tempKS_list;
```

(continued)

The `tempKS_list` table has two customers and lists the required information: their customer numbers and last names.

```
Command Prompt - \mysql\bin\mysql -u root -p

mysql> create temporary table tempKS_list
    -> select cust_num, cust_last from duck_cust
    -> where cust_state like "KS";
Query OK, 2 rows affected (0.23 sec)
Records: 2  Duplicates: 0  Warnings: 0

mysql> select * from tempKS_list
    -> ;
+----------+-----------+
| cust_num | cust_last |
+----------+-----------+
|        1 | Salisbury |
|        3 | Thegreat  |
+----------+-----------+
2 rows in set (0.00 sec)
```

11. Type in the SHOW TABLES; command and press the ENTER key. The temporary table `tempKS_list` does not appear in the list of tables.

```
mysql> show tables;
+--------------------+
| Tables_in_duckwear |
+--------------------+
| copy_duck_cust     |
| cust_names         |
| cust_num_names     |
| duck_cust          |
| duck_title         |
+--------------------+
5 rows in set (0.08 sec)

mysql>
```

12. Type in the following command to demonstrate that the temporary table still exists:

    SELECT cust_num FROM tempKS_list;

```
mysql> select cust_num from tempKS_list;
+----------+
| cust_num |
+----------+
|        1 |
|        3 |
+----------+
2 rows in set (0.00 sec)

mysql>
```

13. Sever the current connection with MySQL by typing the **EXIT** command, and then reenter the MySQL Client using the same command you used in step 1.

14. Enter the SELECT command from step 12 again. As shown by the error message, the temporary table `tempKS_list` no longer exists in the `duckwear` database.

```
mysql> exit
Bye

C:\Documents and Settings\Michael Grey>\mysql\bin\mysql -u root -p
Enter password:
Welcome to the MySQL monitor.  Commands end with ; or \g.
Your MySQL connection id is 4 to server version: 4.0.16-nt-log

Type 'help;' or '\h' for help. Type '\c' to clear the buffer.

mysql> select cust_num from tempKS_list;
ERROR 1046: No Database Selected
mysql> use duckwear;
Database changed
mysql> select cust_num from tempKS_list;
ERROR 1146: Table 'duckwear.tempks_list' doesn't exist
mysql>
```

15. Create a text (.txt) file with the following information and format, using whatever word processor you are familiar with.

```
NULL ,Wolf ,Davidson
NULL ,Raccoon ,Danson
NULL ,Bob ,Filled
NULL ,Monte ,Billiards
NULL ,Jet ,Beauvais
NULL ,Kevin ,Seta
```

16. Save the file as **DataFile.txt** to a location on your hard drive that you can remember. In the example, the path will be \mysql\data\duckwear\DataFile.txt, but you could as easily save it to your normal file for documents.

(continued)

17. Enter the following commands to use the DataFile.txt file to insert data into the cust_num_ names table, replacing the /mysql/data/ portion of the path in the first command with the correct path to your DataFile.txt file. Also, if you are using a Linux system, replace the '\r\n' in the LINES TERMINATED BY syntax command with just '\n'.

```
LOAD DATA INFILE '/mysql/data/DataFile.txt'
INTO TABLE cust_num_names
FIELDS TERMINATED BY ','
LINES TERMINATED BY '\r\n';
```

18. Type in the SELECT statement to verify the insertion of names and the auto-incrementing of the customer number:

```
SELECT * FROM cust_num_names;
```

```
Command Prompt - /mysql/bin/mysql -u root -p
mysql> load data infile '/mysql/data/DataFile.txt'
    -> into table cust_num_names
    -> fields terminated by ','
    -> lines terminated by '\r\n';
Query OK, 6 rows affected (0.00 sec)
Records: 6  Deleted: 0  Skipped: 0  Warnings: 6

mysql> select * from cust_num_names;
+-----------+-------------+-------------+
| names_num | names_first | names_last  |
+-----------+-------------+-------------+
|         1 | Jenny       | Salisbury   |
|         2 | Red         | Irishlord   |
|         3 | Vicki       | Thegreat    |
|         4 | Chantel     | Montgomery  |
|         5 | David       | Robert      |
|         6 | Wonko       | Kazui       |
|         7 | Karen       | Gashlycrumb |
|         8 | Wolf        | Davidson    |
|         9 | Raccoon     | Danson      |
|        10 | Bob         | Filled      |
|        11 | Monte       | Billiards   |
|        12 | Jet         | Beauvais    |
|        13 | Kevin       | Seta        |
+-----------+-------------+-------------+
13 rows in set (0.00 sec)

mysql>
```

19. Open the DataFile.txt file in your word processor and save a copy of it as DataFile2.txt. Alter the DataFile2.txt file to reflect the changes shown in step 11 to emulate inconsistent file data.

20. Remove all the NULLs.

21. Replace the separating commas with colons and then add spaces in the following manner:

- Insert a space after the colon in the first and second lines
- Insert a space before the colon in the third and forth lines
- Insert a space (no colon or comma at all) in the fifth and sixth lines.

Save those changes.

22. Use the following command to load the DataFile2.txt file into the `cust_names` table.

```
LOAD DATA INFILE '/mysql/data/DataFile2.txt'
INTO TABLE cust_names
FIELDS TERMINATED BY ':'
LINES TERMINATED BY '\r\n';
```

NOTE

The preceding command shows the Windows format for the `LINES TERMINATED BY` indicator. If the file format is Linux in origin, the `LINES TERMINATED BY` indicator is `'\n'`.

Project Summary

In this project, you created `copy_duck_cust`, a copy of an entire existing table; `cust_names`, a new table with columns from an existing table; and `tempKS_list`, a temporary table from an existing table. All of these tables are still in your `duckwear` database, except for `tempKS_list`, which was erased when you severed the connection to the MySQL Client.

You also inserted data from an existing table, `duck_cust`, into a newly created table, `cust_num_names`, and finally, loaded data from text files, `DataFile.txt` and `DataFile2.txt`, into existing tables, `cust_num_names` and `cust_names`. However, there are few things you should remember about how the format of the field affects the format of the data in the database records. Figure 3-1 shows the data text file used in step 22 of the project. It contains the same data as the data text file used in step 15 but with differences in spacing and in choice of field terminator.

The common impulse, because you are taught to type normal sentences, is to put a space or sometimes even two after the punctuation mark. This can result in errors or inconsistencies in a supplied data file, especially if the data is created or supplied by individuals unfamiliar with database requirements. The first two entries in the text file in Figure 3-1 are formatted that way, with the space after the colon. The second two entries are formatted with the space before the separating colon. The last two entries have no separating punctuation at all, only a space. Figure 3-2 shows the result of the second `LOAD DATA INFILE` command. (The first seven entries were already in the table.)

As you can see, the first two entries from DataFile2.txt, with spaces after the separating colon, have been entered into the table with a space in front of the last names Davidson and Danson. The second set of entries from DataFile2.txt, with spaces before and not after the colon,

```
🖺 DataFile2.txt - Notepad
File  Edit  Format  Help
wolf: Davidson
Raccoon: Danson
Bob :Filled
Monte :Billiards
Jet Beauvais
Kevin Seta
```

Figure 3-1   DataFile2.txt showing different formats for field termination

(continued)

```
Command Prompt - /mysql/bin/mysql -u root -p
mysql> load data infile '/mysql/data/DataFile2.txt'
    -> into table cust_names
    -> fields terminated by ':'
    -> lines terminated by '\r\n';
Query OK, 6 rows affected (0.04 sec)
Records: 6  Deleted: 0  Skipped: 0  Warnings: 2

mysql> select * from cust_names;
+---------------+---------------+
! cust_first    ! cust_last     !
+---------------+---------------+
! Jenny         ! Salisbury     !
! Red           ! Irishlord     !
! Vicki         ! Thegreat      !
! Chantel       ! Montgomery    !
! David         ! Robert        !
! Wonko         ! Kazui         !
! Karen         ! Gashlycrumb   !
! Wolf          !  Davidson     !
! Raccoon       !  Danson       !
! Bob           ! Filled        !
! Monte         ! Billiards     !
! Jet Beauvais  !               !
! Kevin Seta    !               !
+---------------+---------------+
13 rows in set (0.00 sec)
```

have no extra spaces and resemble the format of the data loaded from the DataFile.txt file used in the project. The final two entries lacked the specified field-terminating colon, and as a result, both the first and last names were placed in the initial field, cust_first. Since nothing followed, the cust_last field was left blank on each entry.

In the next sections of this module, you will learn commands that will enable you to correct mistakes and omissions in both data fields and table definitions.

Figure 3-2 Results of loading DataFile2.txt into the cust_names table

Progress Check

1. What command would you use to view your newly created table's contents?

2. What does the following code create?

   ```
   CREATE TABLE newVampires
   SELECT * FROM vampires;
   ```

3. If you need to view a subset of a table's data and you need to apply a query or queries against it, what type of table should you create and what basic syntax will create it?

4. What does the following code accomplish?

   ```
   LOAD DATA INFILE '\documents\CityData.txt'
   INTO TABLE CoolCities
   FIELDS TEMINATED BY ' '
   LINES TERMINATED BY 'n';
   ```

---

1. To view a table's contents, use the command SELECT * FROM <table_ name>;.

2. It creates an identical copy of the table vampires, in both structure and data, where the only difference is that any key field specifications, or specifications dependent on the existence of the key field, have not been reproduced.

3. A temporary table should be created to apply queries against. The basic syntax is as follows:
```
CREATE TEMPORARY TABLE <temp_table _name>
SELECT <needed_field_name1>{, <needed_field_name2>, . . .]
[WHERE <where_value>'
```
4. It would insert all the data from the CitiesData.txt file, in which fields are terminated by spaces, into the CoolCities table.

CRITICAL SKILL
3.2

Change a Table's Structure and Add an Index

After you create a table, you may need to make changes to its columns or fields. You might also want to add an index, to speed up table searches.

Altering a Table

Sometimes, you will need to change a table's structure to correct a mistake. Other times, there may be a change in the requirements for a table or its contents. For example, your table might need another field (column) or changes to a field definition.

An example of when you might need to change a table's structure is after you make a new table by creating a copy of an existing table. As you learned in the previous section, if one of the fields copied into the new table was designated the auto-incrementing key, the key designation is lost. In addition, since you cannot have an auto-incrementing field without it also being defined as a key, the AUTO_INCREMENT function is lost. To fix the copied table, you will want to redefine a column as the key. You can make these kinds of changes by using the ALTER TABLE statement.

The ALTER TABLE syntax has four options:

- **ADD**   The ADD option allows you to add a field to a table's definition. It has two options of its own: FIRST and AFTER. The ADD FIRST option adds a field at the beginning of the table's record definition; the ADD AFTER option allows you to specify which field precedes the added field.

- **MODIFY**   The MODIFY option changes the format of a field. For instance, you could use this option to change a field from CHAR(5) to DECIMAL(5) or from CHAR(13) to CHAR(42).

- **CHANGE**   The CHANGE option renames fields and can be handy for clarifying contents or fixing a typo in the command used to create fields.

- **DROP**   The DROP option deletes a field, unless INDEX is specified, in which case the field named in the command remains, but it is no longer an index.

The basic variations of the syntax for ALTER TABLE and its options are as follows:

```
ALTER TABLE <table_name>
ADD <field_name> <field type> <one or more field options>,
ADD <field_name> <field type> AFTER <existing_field_name>,
ADD <field_name> <field type> FIRST,
ADD INDEX <field_name>,
MODIFY <field_name> <field type> <one or more field options>,
```

```
CHANGE <existing_field_name> <new_field_name> <field type>,
DROP <field_name>,
DROP INDEX <field_name>;
```

As you can see, you can specify more than one option in an ALTER TABLE statement. However, if you are making interrelated changes, make sure you list them in a logical order. For instance, if you are making a new field into the index key on a table, make sure you drop the old index first. The following command will alter a table called books, with the columns pub_date, title, surname, given_name, and publisher, by dropping the original index on the field pub_date and adding a new index on the surname field.

```
ALTER TABLE books
DROP INDEX pub_date,
ADD INDEX surname;
```

Care must be taken when dropping an index that the reserved word INDEX appears in the command. If the reserved word INDEX had been left out of the previous command, then the column pub_date, along with all of the data stored in it, would be dropped, instead of just the index, leaving the column and its data intact. Always double-check your syntax when using any form of a DROP clause.

The following command will alter the table authors by adding three new columns, changing the name of an existing column to match the last name_first initial naming convention, and modifying the definition of another column from a DATE format (*yyyy/mm/dd*) to a character string 10 spaces long.

```
ALTER TABLE authors
ADD Herbert_F CHAR(15),
ADD Pratchett_T CHAR(15),
ADD Gaiman_N CHAR(15),
CHANGE L_Hamilton Hamilton_L CHAR(15),
MODIFY pub_date CHAR(10);
```

Creating an Index

Indexes are created in order to make searching a table faster. It is akin to using an index to find information in a book, rather than looking at every page. The index allows you, figuratively speaking, to jump directly to the "page" that holds the information you seek.

For all table types except BDB, the index is held in memory. This fact alone speeds access, because the index can be searched without accessing the hard drive. Once the appropriate information has been located in the index, it gives the specific location on the hard drive where the requested data resides, allowing you to go directly there, instead of searching through the entire table.

You might decide to create an index for a table for many reasons. Here are some common indicators of when a table might need an index, which can act as cues.

- The table contains a large amount of data, requiring time to do an entire search.

- The data in the table is accessed frequently.

- The same field usually accesses the data in the table.

CAUTION

Indexing too much information can negate the advantages of the index. If the table and/or indexed field is large enough, the index itself can become too large. In that event, indexing only a portion of the field, such as the first few characters of a string, can allow you to shrink the size of the index back to the point where it regains the speed advantage.

To give a table an index, use the CREATE INDEX command. It can create an index on one or more fields, but you must remember that the order of the fields is reflected in the order of importance of the indexes. As long as you consider the order you will likely search in, it will be more efficient to have one index that covers fields a, b, and c than to have one a index, one b index, and one c index. If you make an a, b, c index but most of your searches are on the b and c fields, your index will not provide the faster results you were seeking by creating the index in the first place.

The simplest syntax for CREATE INDEX requires a name for the index and then a listing of the table and field or fields that compose the index.

```
CREATE INDEX <index_name> ON <table_name>(<field_name>, . . .);
```

An expanded syntax specifies a width for the field, which can save space without slowing the search process appreciably.

```
CREATE INDEX <index_name> ON <table_name>(<field_name>(width) . . .);
```

For instance, most names vary within the first ten characters. If your name field is defined as 25 characters, defining an index as (name(10)) would create a much smaller index than using all of the characters. This index would be only slightly slower to search, and it could even speed up insertions.

The CREATE INDEX command also has two options: FULLTEXT and UNIQUE.

```
CREATE FULLTEXT INDEX <index_name> ON <table_name>(<field_name>);
CREATE UNIQUE INDEX <index_name> ON <table_name>(<field_name>);
```

The FULLTEXT option is allowed only on CHAR, VARCHAR, and TEXT fields that are in MyISAM tables. As the name implies, FULLTEXT specifies an index that compares an entire string to another string. It is used only in conjunction with the MATCH function.

The UNIQUE option is more commonly used than FULLTEXT. It requires any addition to the index column's fields to be unique. If you try to insert or update a duplicate item into a UNIQUE column, an error message will be returned.

The CREATE INDEX command can add a forgotten index, let you set up an index that covers multiple fields, or allow you to redefine a deleted index with new criteria, which takes into account lessons learned by working with your database.

The table music has five columns: artist, title, label, release_date, and tracks_num. It was originally created with an index on the artist column, but you have found that you also need to search using the title column frequently. Because the titles vary in length and are occasionally quite long, the following command creates an index on the title column using the first nine characters, which makes the index smaller to store and should not extend the search time appreciably while possibly speeding insertions.

```
CREATE INDEX title_ndx ON music(title(9));
```

If you create a table, sales, and forget to incorporate an index into the definition of the order number, which must be UNIQUE to prevent any billing or shipping duplications, the following command will rectify the omission:

```
CREATE UNIQUE INDEX orderIndex ON sales(orderNum);
```

Ask the Expert

Q: Where are indexes used in commands?

A: Indexes are most often used in any command that has a WHERE clause. Indexes allow you to access data more quickly, but they also specify a certain item of data, or if the index is not defined as unique, certain sets of data. Any field of data that is a unique reference for its record is a candidate for indexing, especially if that field is the most likely way a user will identify or search for that record.

Q: Why would you make a multiple-field index?

A: A multiple-field index is useful when the most common field you search under is likely to have duplicate entries in your database, requiring other fields to be searched in order to narrow the results. The most classic example is a database where you search by

(continued)

name. If the record definition includes last and first names and middle initials, then a three-field index can come in handy.

In a large database of names, such as a telephone directory for a major city, a search for the last name Smith will usually find multiple records. Even if you narrow the search to Smith, George, it is probable that you will find many entries. If the search narrows to Smith, George, J, then the search is more likely to return only a few records that match all three fields. In such a case, an index a, b, c that consists of last, first, and middle initial fields would be ideal.

On the other hand, if you had a database with student, teacher, and school fields, and you searched for data by teacher or school as often as you did by student, then three separate indexes might make more sense. Certainly, a single multiple-field index would be counter-productive, because your search requirements seldom, if ever, require all three categories to narrow your search to the required data. Let your data and your accessing patterns dictate whether you need a single field index, several single-field indexes, or a multiple-field index. Remember, MySQL allows you to create new indexes easily after a table has been created, so it is possible to learn as you go, and create or drop indexes as experience dictates.

CRITICAL SKILL
3.3 Change Table Data

Now we are entering into what can be dangerous territory: changing data. If a small amount of data is changed accidentally, the results are usually easy to repair. You might even do it by hand if you are familiar enough with your data; however, if an unintentional mistake leads you to overwrite every record in a table or even your entire database, the process of returning it to its proper condition can be time-consuming.

To change table data, you can use the REPLACE INTO or UPDATE command. Here, you will learn when they should be used and what should be considered before using them.

Replacing Data

The REPLACE INTO command can be useful under specific circumstances, but if used without forethought, it can change much more than you intended it to change. When you use REPLACE INTO, the whole record is changed. If you do not specify data for all of the record's fields, then the default values for those unspecified fields are inserted into them. Therefore, it is recommended that you use this command only when you need to change an entire record.

The only way to recover from a REPLACE INTO that results in unintentional changes to your data is to have a backup copy of your database available. You will learn about making backups and restoring data from them in Module 8. Also, if the table you are replacing into does not have either a unique index or a primary key, then REPLACE INTO becomes the equivalent of an INSERT command, and it makes no sense to use it.

The REPLACE INTO command works in one of two ways:

- It inserts data into a specified record.

- If the data to be inserted violates key uniqueness, it deletes the existing record first and then inserts the replacement record.

The good news is that using REPLACE INTO to insert a record will keep you from inserting duplicate records into your table, providing they have a unique index or a primary key. The bad news can be that it accomplishes this by unilaterally deleting the existing record in favor of the new record, which it then inserts. If this is your intention, then using REPLACE INTO will save you time by taking two actions from one command. If it was not your intention, you could possibly delete a correct record and insert an incorrect one.

Also, if the table you are replacing into has multiple unique keys and the record you insert conflicts with multiple unique keys, multiple records will be deleted, and that one record will be inserted. In some cases, this may be a desirable result, and once again save you time and effort, but it also illustrates why you should be cautious when using the REPLACE INTO command.

None of this means that you should not use REPLACE INTO. It just means you should be careful and use it only if you are replacing an entire record in a table that has either a unique index (with single or multiple keys) or a primary key.

The syntax for the command is simple:

```
REPLACE INTO <table_name>
(<field_name1>, <field_name2>, <field_name3>, . . .)
VALUES
("value1", "value2", "value3", . . .);
```

NOTE

If REPLACE INTO inserts a record, it returns Query OK, 1 row affected. If it deletes a conflicting record, and then inserts its record, it returns Query OK, 2 rows affected. This makes it easy to determine if you are, intentionally or unintentionally, deleting rows while you are adding them.

For example, in a TABLE, fruits, you have columns number, fruit, color, and taste. The record with the unique number 42 contains incorrect information; it says that the color of the fruit, lime, is blue and that the taste is sweet. (42, lime, blue, sweet) The following command replaces the entire record with the correct information:

```
REPLACE INTO fruits
(number, fruit, color, taste)
VALUES
("42", "lime", "green", "sour");
```

Because this deletes the initial, incorrect record and then replaces it with the new, still unique record, the command will return `Query OK, 2 rows affected` to indicate the successful completion of the command.

Using the safe-updates Option

As you just learned, the REPLACE INTO command can dangerous, because it can alter an entire record or multiple records unintentionally. The UPDATE command, discussed next, can conceivably be much more destructive. Therefore, before you learn about UPDATE, you need to become familiar with the `safe-updates` option.

The `safe-updates` option, when added to your `my.ini` or `my.cnf` file, allows MySQL to refuse to run an UPDATE command that does not have a WHERE clause in it referencing a key column to specify which record needs to be changed. This can prevent table-wide updates that might ruin your data.

To add the `safe-updates` option, open your configuration file in either a word processor or your WinMySQLAdmin window's my.ini Setup tab, or whichever Linux word processor you use, and add the following lines of code at the bottom of the page:

```
[mysql]
safe-updates
```

Make sure you save the changes to your file, and then type **EXIT** to close your MySQL Client. Then open the MySQL Client in the normal fashion, and that will update your configuration file, making your databases protected by the `safe-updates` option.

With `safe-updates` in your configuration file, you will not be able to make a global change to a column—that is, put the same piece of data in every field in a column. If you need to make such a change, you can return to the command line and turn off the `safe-updates` option. If you are inside the MySQL Client, type **EXIT** to return to the command line. Once you are at the shell command line, type the following:

```
<path_to_mysql> --safe-updates=0;
```

The path to the `mysql` command for Linux and Windows users will be the same as the path used to normally start the MySQL Client.

Updating Data

The UPDATE command allows you to change a single, specific field or several specific fields, in a single record or many records at once. The basic syntax for changing a field or fields in a single record is as follows:

```
UPDATE <table_name>
SET <field_name>="data1"[, <field_name2>="data2", . . .]
[WHERE <key_field_name>="where_value"];
```

The WHERE clause clarifies which record in the column of the provided field name should be changed, and that field name is usually a key that allows you to narrow the range of which records you want to alter. Without the WHERE clause, data1 would be placed in the specified field of every record in the column of the specified table. MySQL version 4.1 and later will allow you to update multiple tables, which makes the WHERE portion of the code even more important, because you could conceivably update an entire database.

You can also use the UPDATE command to change many records at once, which can be a real timesaver. When you use UPDATE, MySQL does a comparison, and if the value set to update is the same as the value that is already in the field, then it skips the update, which also saves time. The syntax for updating many records at once is as follows:

```
UPDATE <table_name1>[, <table_name2>, . . .]
SET <field_name1>="data1"[, <field_name2>="data2", . . .]
[WHERE <key_field_name>="where_value"]
[ORDER BY . . .]
[LIMIT <row_count>];
```

As always, the syntax in the square brackets is optional, but in the case of the WHERE clause, it's only optional when safe-updates is not in effect. The ORDER BY and LIMIT options cannot be used when you are updating multiple tables.

The ORDER BY option allows you to set the order in which the rows will be updated. It is really of use only when used in conjunction with the LIMIT command.

The LIMIT option, which can be used without ORDER BY, sets a specific number of rows to be used in an UPDATE command. In MySQL versions before 4.0.13, the LIMIT option counted affected rows—that is, rows that satisfied the WHERE clause and had been changed—and stopped when that count equaled the row_count value. From MySQL version 4.0.13 on, the LIMIT option counts matched rows—that is, rows that match the WHERE clause criteria, whether or not they have been changed. This allows you to count rows that match the criteria but were not changed because they already had the updated value in the field or fields.

Customer number five in your duck_cust table has incomplete information in the cust_duckbday field. The year and month is there but not the date. (1949-08-00) Complete information can be placed in the field using the UPDATE command, as follows:

```
UPDATE duck_cust
SET cust_duckbday="1949:08:25"
WHERE cust_num=5;
```

If you also need to change the data in the suffix field to "V" for the same customer, accomplish both updates using the following command:

```
UPDATE duck_cust
SET cust_suffix="V", cust_duckbday="1949:08:25"
WHERE cust_num=5;
```

The `cust_zip2` field needs to be changed on customer numbers 9–14. The following command will update all of those records with the value "1958".

```
UPDATE duck_cust
SET cust_zip2="1958"
WHERE cust_num>=9;
```

Project 3-2 Make Changes to a Database

This project gives you hands-on experience with the commands and concepts discussed in the preceding section. You will make changes to your existing database structure and its data, using the ALTER TABLE, CREATE INDEX, UPDATE, and INSERT INTO commands, as well as set the SAFE-UPDATES option to see how it functions.

Step by Step

1. Open a command-line window and log in to your MySQL Client as in the previous projects. Specify using the `duckwear` database.

2. Use the following code to look at the contents of `cust_names` and `cust_num_names`:

```
SELECT * FROM cust_names;
SELECT * FROM cust_num_names;
```

Project
3-2

Make Changes to a Database

```
C:\ Command Prompt - /mysql/bin/mysql -u root -p

mysql> select * from cust_names;
+-------------+-------------+
| cust_first  | cust_last   |
+-------------+-------------+
| Jenny       | Salisbury   |
| Red         | Irishlord   |
| Vicki       | Thegreat    |
| Chantel     | Montgomery  |
| David       | Robert      |
| Wonko       | Kazui       |
| Karen       | Gashlycrumb |
| Wolf        | Davidson    |
| Raccoon     | Danson      |
| Bob         | Filled      |
| Monte       | Billiards   |
| Jet Beauvais |            |
| Kevin Seta  |             |
+-------------+-------------+
13 rows in set (0.00 sec)

mysql> select * from cust_num_names;
+-----------+-------------+-------------+
| names_num | names_first | names_last  |
+-----------+-------------+-------------+
|         1 | Jenny       | Salisbury   |
|         2 | Red         | Irishlord   |
|         3 | Vicki       | Thegreat    |
|         4 | Chantel     | Montgomery  |
|         5 | David       | Robert      |
|         6 | Wonko       | Kazui       |
|         7 | Karen       | Gashlycrumb |
|         8 | Wolf        | Davidson    |
|         9 | Raccoon     | Danson      |
|        10 | Bob         | Filled      |
|        11 | Monte       | Billiards   |
|        12 | Jet         | Beauvais    |
|        13 | Kevin       | Seta        |
+-----------+-------------+-------------+
13 rows in set (0.00 sec)

mysql>
```

(continued)

3. You can see that both tables have first name and last name columns, but `cust_names` does not have a customer number column. Use the following code to compare the description of the customer number columns in each table:

```
DESC cust_names;
DESC cust_num_names;
```

```
Command Prompt - \mysql\bin\mysql -u root -p                              _ □ ×
+-------------+---------------+--------------+
13 rows in set (0.07 sec)

mysql> desc cust_num_names;
+-------------+--------------+------+-----+---------+----------------+
| Field       | Type         | Null | Key | Default | Extra          |
+-------------+--------------+------+-----+---------+----------------+
| names_num   | mediumint(9) |      | PRI | NULL    | auto_increment |
| names_first | char(15)     |      |     |         |                |
| names_last  | char(20)     |      |     |         |                |
+-------------+--------------+------+-----+---------+----------------+
3 rows in set (0.07 sec)

mysql> desc cust_names;
+------------+----------+------+-----+---------+-------+
| Field      | Type     | Null | Key | Default | Extra |
+------------+----------+------+-----+---------+-------+
| cust_first | char(15) |      |     |         |       |
| cust_last  | char(20) |      |     |         |       |
+------------+----------+------+-----+---------+-------+
2 rows in set (0.00 sec)

mysql>
```

4. Use the following ALTER TABLE command to add the `names_num` column to the `cust_names` table definition and change the names of the other two columns:

```
ALTER TABLE cust_names
ADD names_num MEDIUMINT(9) PRIMARY KEY AUTO_INCREMENT FIRST,
CHANGE cust_first names_first CHAR(15),
CHANGE cust_last names_last CHAR(20);
```

5. Use the following commands to view how the table description and contents have changed:

```
DESC cust_names;
SELECT * FROM cust_names;
```

You see that a new column has been added and set as an auto-incrementing key, and the first and last name columns have had their names changed. When you compare the description of the `cust_names` table with the `cust_num_names` description, which you are trying to match, it is clear that none of the columns in `cust_names` have been set to NOT NULL.

```
mysql> desc cust_names;
+-------------+-------------+------+-----+---------+----------------+
| Field       | Type        | Null | Key | Default | Extra          |
+-------------+-------------+------+-----+---------+----------------+
| names_num   | mediumint(9)|      | PRI | NULL    | auto_increment |
| names_first | char(15)    | YES  |     | NULL    |                |
| names_last  | char(20)    | YES  |     | NULL    |                |
+-------------+-------------+------+-----+---------+----------------+
3 rows in set (0.00 sec)

mysql> select * from cust_names;
+-----------+-------------+------------+
| names_num | names_first | names_last |
+-----------+-------------+------------+
|         1 | Jenny       | Salisbury  |
|         2 | Red         | Irishlord  |
|         3 | Vicki       | Thegreat   |
|         4 | Chantel     | Montgomery |
|         5 | David       | Robert     |
|         6 | Wonko       | Kazui      |
|         7 | Karen       | Gashlycrumb|
|         8 | Wolf        | Davidson   |
|         9 | Raccoon     | Danson     |
|        10 | Bob         | Filled     |
|        11 | Monte       | Billiards  |
|        12 | Jet Beauvais|            |
|        13 | Kevin Seta  |            |
+-----------+-------------+------------+
13 rows in set (0.00 sec)

mysql> _
```

6. Use the ALTER TABLE command to set all three columns in cust_names to NOT NULL:

```
ALTER TABLE cust_names
MODIFY names_num MEDIUMINT(9) NOT NULL AUTO_INCREMENT,
MODIFY names_first CHAR(15) NOT NULL,
MODIFY names_last CHAR(20) NOT NULL;
DESC cust_names;
DESC cust_num_names;
```

Now the descriptions of cust_names and cust_num_names are identical.

```
mysql> desc cust_num_names;
+-------------+-------------+------+-----+---------+----------------+
| Field       | Type        | Null | Key | Default | Extra          |
+-------------+-------------+------+-----+---------+----------------+
| names_num   | mediumint(9)|      | PRI | NULL    | auto_increment |
| names_first | char(15)    |      |     |         |                |
| names_last  | char(20)    |      |     |         |                |
+-------------+-------------+------+-----+---------+----------------+
3 rows in set (0.10 sec)

mysql> desc cust_names;
+-------------+-------------+------+-----+---------+----------------+
| Field       | Type        | Null | Key | Default | Extra          |
+-------------+-------------+------+-----+---------+----------------+
| names_num   | mediumint(9)|      | PRI | NULL    | auto_increment |
| names_first | char(15)    |      |     |         |                |
| names_last  | char(20)    |      |     |         |                |
+-------------+-------------+------+-----+---------+----------------+
3 rows in set (0.00 sec)
```

(continued)

7. Use two SELECT commands to view and compare the data in both tables:

```
SELECT * FROM cust_num_names;
SELECT * FROM cust_names;
```

```
Command Prompt - /mysql/bin/mysql -u root -p

mysql> select * from cust_num_names;
+------------+-------------+-------------+
| names_num  | names_first | names_last  |
+------------+-------------+-------------+
|          1 | Jenny       | Salisbury   |
|          2 | Red         | Irishlord   |
|          3 | Vicki       | Thegreat    |
|          4 | Chantel     | Montgomery  |
|          5 | David       | Robert      |
|          6 | Wonko       | Kazui       |
|          7 | Karen       | Gashlycrumb |
|          8 | Wolf        | Davidson    |
|          9 | Raccoon     | Danson      |
|         10 | Bob         | Filled      |
|         11 | Monte       | Billiards   |
|         12 | Jet         | Beauvais    |
|         13 | Kevin       | Seta        |
+------------+-------------+-------------+
13 rows in set (0.01 sec)

mysql> select * from cust_names;
+------------+---------------+-------------+
| names_num  | names_first   | names_last  |
+------------+---------------+-------------+
|          1 | Jenny         | Salisbury   |
|          2 | Red           | Irishlord   |
|          3 | Vicki         | Thegreat    |
|          4 | Chantel       | Montgomery  |
|          5 | David         | Robert      |
|          6 | Wonko         | Kazui       |
|          7 | Karen         | Gashlycrumb |
|          8 | Wolf          |  Davidson   |
|          9 | Raccoon       |  Danson     |
|         10 | Bob           | Filled      |
|         11 | Monte         | Billiards   |
|         12 | Jet Beauvais  |             |
|         13 | Kevin Seta    |             |
+------------+---------------+-------------+
13 rows in set (0.00 sec)

mysql>
```

8. Before you use the UPDATE command to make the data in both tables match, open your configuration file (my.cfg or my.ini) and add the following code to the bottom of the file:

```
[mysql]
safe-updates
```

9. Exit the MySQL Client and open it again to update the configuration file. The safe-updates option is now running.

10. Choose your duckwear database with the USE command.

11. By examining the results of step 7, you can see that customers 8 and 9 have an extra space in front of their last names, and customers 12 and 13 need their first and last names placed into the correct fields. The following syntax uses both the UPDATE and REPLACE INTO commands to correct these discrepancies:

```
UPDATE cust_names
SET names_last="Davidson"
WHERE names_num=8;

UPDATE cust_names
SET names_last="Danson"
WHERE names_num=9;

UPDATE cust_names
SET names_first="Jet", names_last="Beauvais"
WHERE names_num=12;

REPLACE INTO cust_names
(names_num, names_first, names_last)
VALUES
("13", "Kevin", "Seta");
```

12. Use the **SELECT * FROM cust_names;** command to see the repaired table data.

```
Command Prompt - /mysql/bin/mysql -u root -p
mysql> update cust_names
    -> set names_last="Davidson"
    -> where names_num=8;
Query OK, 1 row affected (0.05 sec)
Rows matched: 1  Changed: 1  Warnings: 0

mysql> update cust_names
    -> set names_last="Danson"
    -> where names_num=9;
Query OK, 1 row affected (0.01 sec)
Rows matched: 1  Changed: 1  Warnings: 0

mysql> update cust_names
    -> set names_first="Jet", names_last="Beauvais"
    -> where names_num=12;
Query OK, 1 row affected (0.00 sec)
Rows matched: 1  Changed: 1  Warnings: 0

mysql> replace into cust_names
    -> (names_num, names_first, names_last)
    -> values
    -> ("13", "Kevin", "Seta");
Query OK, 2 rows affected (0.00 sec)

mysql> select * from cust_names;
+-----------+-------------+-------------+
| names_num | names_first | names_last  |
+-----------+-------------+-------------+
|         1 | Jenny       | Salisbury   |
|         2 | Red         | Irishlord   |
|         3 | Vicki       | Thegreat    |
|         4 | Chantel     | Montgomery  |
|         5 | David       | Robert      |
|         6 | Wonko       | Kazui       |
|         7 | Karen       | Gashlycrumb |
|         8 | Wolf        | Davidson    |
|         9 | Raccoon     | Danson      |
|        10 | Bob         | Filled      |
|        11 | Monte       | Billiards   |
|        12 | Jet         | Beauvais    |
|        13 | Kevin       | Seta        |
+-----------+-------------+-------------+
13 rows in set (0.00 sec)

mysql>
```

(continued)

13. In order to experiment with the LIMIT option of the UPDATE command, you need a table that has duplicate information. Since copy_duck_cust lost its key definition when it was made, you can use it. First, insert a duplicate row.

```
INSERT INTO copy_duck_cust
VALUES
(6, 5, 'Kazui', 'Wonko', 'PhD', '42 Cube Farm Lane', 'Gatehouse',
 'Vlimpt', 'CA', '46362', 0, 'Fitzwhistle', '1961:12:04');
```

14. Use the SELECT * FROM copy_duck_cust; command. You will see that there are now two identical records in the copy_duck_cust table.

```
Command Prompt - \mysql\bin\mysql -u root -p                           _ □ ×
: num_names              :
+-----------------------+
6 rows in set (0.08 sec)

mysql> select * from copy_duck_cust;
+----------+------------+-----------+-----------+-----------+------------+------------+--
+----------+------------+-----------+-----------+-----------+------------+------------+--
: cust_num : cust_title : cust_last : cust_first : cust_suffix : cust_add1 :
           : cust_add2  : cust_city : cust_state : cust_zip1 : cust_zip2 :
cust_duckname           : cust_duckbday :
+----------+------------+-----------+-----------+-----------+------------+------------+--
+----------+------------+-----------+-----------+-----------+------------+------------+--
:        1 :          8 : Salisbury : Jenny     :           : 9 Wishing Wel
1 Court    : 0          : Meadowlark Hill : KS    : 67048     : 1234
Spike      : 1961-03-21 :
:        2 :          1 : Irishlord : Red       : III       : 1022 Sea of R
ye         : A207       : Seacouver : WA        : 98601     : 3464
Netrek Rules : 1967-10-21 :
:        3 :          4 : Thegreat  : Uicki     :           : 2004 Singleto
n Dr.      : 0          : Freedom   : KS        : 67290     : 4321
Frida Kahlo de Tomayo : 1948-03-21 :
:        4 :          9 : Montgomery : Chantel  :           : 1567 Terra Co
tta Way    : 0          : Chicago   : IL        : 89129     : 4444
Bianca     : 1971-07-29 :
:        5 :          7 : Robert    : David     :           : 20113 Open Ro
ad Highway : #6         : Blacktop  : AZ        : 00606     : 1952
Harley     : 1949-08-00 :
:        6 :          5 : Kazui     : Wonko     : PhD       : 42 Cube Farm
Lane       : Gatehouse  : Ulimpt    : CA        : 46362     : 0
Fitzwhistle : 1961-12-04 :
:        7 :          6 : Gashlycrumb : Karen   :           : 3113 Picket F
ence Lane  : 0          : Fedora    : UT        : 41927     : 5698
Tess D'urberville : 1948-08-19 :
:        6 :          5 : Kazui     : Wonko     : PhD       : 42 Cube Farm
Lane       : Gatehouse  : Ulimpt    : CA        : 46362     : 0
Fitzwhistle : 1961-12-04 :
+----------+------------+-----------+-----------+-----------+------------+------------+--
+----------+------------+-----------+-----------+-----------+------------+------------+--
8 rows in set (0.00 sec)

mysql> _
```

15. You have been informed that Sir Wonko has two addresses and wants catalogs sent to both of them. His second address is 1630 Revello Drive, Shady Hill, CA 31626-2882. Use the following code to change only one of the two duplicate records and then verify the results:

```
UPDATE copy_duck_cust
SET cust_num=8, cust_add1="1630 Revello Drive", cust_add2=null,
 cust_city="Shady Hill", cust_zip1="31626", cust_zip2="2882"
WHERE cust_last="Kazui"
LIMIT 1;
SELECT * FROM copy_duck_cust
WHERE cust_last="Kazui";
```

Sir Wonko now has two addresses and a customer number for each, but the rest of his information is correctly duplicated in both records. Without the LIMIT clause, both records would have been changed, because both of them fit the WHERE criteria.

```
Command Prompt - \mysql\bin\mysql -u root -p                        _ □ ✕
mysql> update copy_duck_cust
    -> set cust_num=8, cust_add1="1630 Revello Drive", cust_add2=null, cust_city
="Shady Hill", cust_zip1="31626", cust_zip2="2882"
    -> where cust_last="Kazui"
    -> limit 1;
Query OK, 1 row affected (0.01 sec)
Rows matched: 1  Changed: 1  Warnings: 0

mysql> select * from copy_duck_cust
    -> where cust_last="kazui";
+----------+------------+------------+------------+------------+------------+
-----+------------+------------+------------+------------+------------+
--+------------+
| cust_num | cust_title | cust_last  | cust_first | cust_suffix | cust_add1
     | cust_add2  | cust_city  | cust_state | cust_zip1  | cust_zip2  | cust_ducknam
e | cust_duckbday |
+----------+------------+------------+------------+------------+------------+
-----+------------+------------+------------+------------+------------+
--+------------+
|        8 |            |          5 | Kazui      | Wonko      | PhD        | 1630 Revello Dr
ive | NULL       | Shady Hill | CA         |      31626 |       2882 | Fitzwhistle
  | 1961-12-04 |
|        6 |            |          5 | Kazui      | Wonko      | PhD        | 42 Cube Farm La
ne  | Gatehouse  | Ulimpt     | CA         |      46362 |          0 | Fitzwhistle
  | 1961-12-04 |
+----------+------------+------------+------------+------------+------------+
-----+------------+------------+------------+------------+------------+
--+------------+
2 rows in set (0.00 sec)

mysql> _
```

16. Now that all the records currently in copy_duck_cust are unique, create a unique index on the cust_num column using the following command:

```
CREATE UNIQUE INDEX copy_index ON copy_duck_cust(cust_num);
```

(continued)

17. Use the `DESC copy_duck_cust;` command to check that the `cust_num` column is now listed as the primary key.

```
Command Prompt - \mysql\bin\mysql -u root -p                                    _ □ ×
mysql> desc copy_duck_cust;
+-------------+----------------+---------------------------------------+-------+-----+---
------+--------+
| Field       | Type                                                   | Null | Key | De
fault | Extra |
+-------------+----------------+---------------------------------------+-------+-----+---
------+--------+
| cust_num    | mediumint(9)                                           |      | PRI | 0
       |       |
| cust_title  | tinyint(4)                                             | YES  |     | NU
LL     |       |
| cust_last   | char(20)                                               |      |     |
       |       |
| cust_first  | char(15)                                               |      |     |
       |       |
| cust_suffix | enum('Jr.','II','III','IV','V','M.D.','PhD')            | YES  |     | NU
LL     |       |
| cust_add1   | char(30)                                               |      |     |
       |       |
| cust_add2   | char(10)                                               | YES  |     | NU
LL     |       |
| cust_city   | char(18)                                               |      |     |
       |       |
| cust_state  | char(2)                                                |      |     |
       |       |
| cust_zip1   | char(5)                                                |      |     |
       |       |
| cust_zip2   | char(4)                                                | YES  |     | NU
LL     |       |
| cust_duckname | char(25)                                             |      |     |
       |       |
| cust_duckbday | date                                                 | YES  |     | NU
LL     |       |
+-------------+----------------+---------------------------------------+-------+-----+---
------+--------+
13 rows in set (0.00 sec)

mysql> _
```

18. Since the record for customer number 8 is now correct, insert it into `duck_cust`:

```
INSERT INTO duck_cust
SELECT * FROM copy_duck_cust
WHERE cust_num=8;
```

19. Alter the num_names table by dropping the `cust_num` field and verify the results:

```
ALTER TABLE num_names
DROP names_num;
SELECT * FROM num_names;
```

Now the num_names table has only two fields defined, instead of its previous three.

```
Command Prompt - \mysql\bin\mysql -u root -p
mysql> select * from num_names;
+-------------+-------------+
| names_first | names_last  |
+-------------+-------------+
| Jenny       | Salisbury   |
| Red         | Irishlord   |
| Vicki       | Thegreat    |
| Chantel     | Montgomery  |
| David       | Robert      |
| Wonko       | Kazui       |
| Karen       | Gashlycrumb |
| Wolf        | Davidson    |
| Racoon      | Danson      |
| Bob         | Filled      |
| Monte       | Billiards   |
| Jet         | Beauvais    |
| Kevin       | Seta        |
+-------------+-------------+
13 rows in set (0.01 sec)
```

Project Summary

In this project, you practiced using the ALTER TABLE, CREATE INDEX, REPLACE INTO, and UPDATE commands. You have learned that there are sometimes multiple ways of accomplishing the same data-altering results by using different commands.

With a certain amount of forethought, and occasionally a little cleaning up of the original source, you can use a file with consistent separators to load many records into a database with one command, thereby saving yourself a great deal of work.

You have placed the safe-updates option in your configuration file, in order to safeguard your database from being inadvertently overwritten. Earlier in this section, you learned the command-line instruction that turns off safe-updates temporarily, so that you can accomplish a global insert operation.

Using what you've learned in this section and practiced in this project, you can now add or drop indexes or column definitions; change field names; modify field types, sizes, or options; and update data within single or multiple records, all with existing tables.

Progress Check

1. What are the four main options to the ALTER TABLE command?

2. How do you add an index called Play_Index to a field called dramas in an existing table called Shakespeare?

3. What command syntax should you use when you need to put new values into an entire record in a table?

4. What do you place into your configuration file to guard against accidental global updates?

1. The four main ALTER TABLE options are ADD, MODIFY, CHANGE, and DROP.

2. You can add this index with the following command:

```
CREATE INDEX Play_Index ON Shakespeare(dramas);
```

3. To put new values into an entire record in a table, use the following syntax:

```
REPLACE INTO <table_name>
(<field_name1>[, <field_name2> , . . .])
VALUES
(<value1>[, <value2>, . . .)];
```

4. To guard against accidental global updates, add the following to the configuration file:

```
[mysql]
safe-updates
```

CRITICAL SKILL
3.4 # Remove a Table or Records

Similar to changing data, removing data can be serious business. For those of you using Linux, you are already familiar with the concept that deleted information is unrecoverable, but for Windows users, it must be emphasized that there is no equivalent to your OS's Recycle Bin. Unless you have a backup or some other form of a copy of your data, once that data is deleted, it is gone.

To remove data, you can use the DROP TABLE, DELETE, and TRUNCATE commands. The DROP TABLE command deletes entire tables, and we will look at that command first. The DELETE and TRUNCATE commands are somewhat similar, in that they both delete entire rows (or records) from a specified table; however, DELETE offers conditional syntax that allows you to specify which rows will be removed, and TRUNCATE always deletes all the rows in the table. Since DELETE is the more versatile command, we will cover it before TRUNCATE, and then contrast the simpler TRUNCATE command against it.

Dropping a Table

The DROP TABLE command allows you to completely remove one or more tables, including the data contained in them. The syntax is scarily simple, so be careful when using this command. It can be used to remove regular or temporary tables. In fact, there is a TEMPORARY option, beginning in MySQL version 4.1, which can safeguard against accidentally removing a permanent table because of a typo or momentary confusion over a correct name. The syntax is as follows:

```
DROP [TEMPORARY] TABLE [IF EXISTS] <table_name>[, <table_name2>,  . . ];
```

Adding the IF EXISTS option allows MySQL to return a warning instead of an error when the table specified in the command does not exist.

Deleting Table Contents

The DELETE command leaves the table definition intact, so you can work with that table after you have removed data from it.

The DELETE command has three optional clauses: WHERE, ORDER BY, and LIMIT clauses. It also has three optional keywords that do very specific things: LOW_PRIORITY, QUICK, and IGNORE. The basic syntax is as follows:

```
DELETE [LOW_PRIORITY] [QUICK] [IGNORE] FROM <table_name>
[WHERE <where_definition>
[ORDER BY . . .]
[LIMIT <row_count>;
```

As usual, all of the syntax within square brackets is optional, so at its most simple, the command could read:

```
DELETE FROM <table_name>;
```

However, if there is no WHERE clause, you will delete all of the records in the specified table.

The LOW_PRIORITY keyword is used when the speed of your database is more important than how long it takes the DELETE command to finish. It causes MySQL to delay the execution of the DELETE command until no other clients are reading from that table.

On MyISAM tables, the QUICK keyword may result in a faster DELETE command execution. It instructs the storage engine to delete all the effected records first and then complete the accompanying changes to the index later, instead of changing each index entry immediately after its correlating record deletion occurs. Depending on the tables involved, and the indexes defined on them, this may or may not result in an increase in speed.

Appearing first in MySQL version 4.1.1, the IGNORE keyword allows MySQL to ignore any errors that occur in the process of deleting data and cause them to be returned as warnings. The difference between the two is that errors will stop the command from executing, while warnings allow the command to continue. Therefore, IGNORE allows you to delete data, even when MySQL would otherwise not allow the DELETE command to execute.

If you know that errors will occur in the process of deleting data, but you are absolutely positive that you want to delete it regardless, then you can use the IGNORE keyword to override the automatic protection that MySQL provides and enforce your commands. The error messages will still appear couched as warnings, but the data will be deleted.

The WHERE, ORDER BY, and LIMIT clauses work the same way they do in the UPDATE command. In MySQL version 4.0, you can delete rows from multiple tables with a particular condition, but when deleting from multiple tables, the ORDER BY and LIMIT options do not apply.

NOTE

Before MySQL version 4.0, the DELETE command does not normally return the number of rows affected to the command line. If this information seems necessary or useful, and you are running a pre-4.0 version, adding the clause WHERE 1=1 to the syntax will cause MySQL to return the number of rows deleted.

Truncating Tables

Like the DELETE command, the TRUNCATE command removes data while leaving the table definition intact. The TRUNCATE command has a simple syntax with no options:

```
TRUNCATE TABLE <table_name>;
```

TRUNCATE functions by dropping the entire table and then re-creating it, which makes it much faster than the DELETE command, which works row by row. MySQL stores its data in a three-tiered system of files: .frm, .MYI, and .MYD. The .frm file holds the table definition; the .MYI holds the index information; and the .MYD holds the actual data. So, table duck_cust, which is found in the duckwear directory of the data directory in the mysql server, is contained in the duck_cust.frm, duck_cust.MYI, and duck_cust.MYD files. As long as the table definition file (*<table_name>*.frm) is valid, the table can be re-created, even if its data or index files have become corrupted.

CAUTION

If you have an active transaction or active table lock at the time the TRUNCATE command attempts to execute, you will get an error.

There are two behaviors of TRUNCATE that may or may not be negative:

- TRUNCATE does not return the number of rows affected. If you decide you need this information, then use the most basic form of the DELETE command, which gives the same overall result but does it row by row, allowing for a total count to be displayed in the RETURN statement once the command is finished. On the other hand, if you are absolutely sure that all of the data in a table needs to be deleted, it does not matter that the rows in the table are not counted and the count is not returned to the command line.

- If a column in a MyISAM or BDB table is set to AUTO_INCREMENT, once TRUNCATE re-creates the table, that table's handler may or may not resume the incrementing count where it left off. When you insert data into the table again, you will be able to tell which way the table responded to its re-creation. If it does not resume where it left off, it will restart the count from the beginning. If it does not reset, you can update the field using an ALTER TABLE command (ALTER TABLE *<table_name>* AUTO_INCREMENT=0) or drop and re-create the table.

If you just want to empty a table as quickly as possible, TRUNCATE is the command to use. If you want more control, use the DELETE command.

Project 3-3 Remove Data and Revisit Changing Data

This project gives you hands-on experience with the commands and concepts discussed in the preceding section. You will remove data from your existing database and revisit the changing of existing data, using the DROP TABLE, DELETE FROM, INSERT INTO, UPDATE, and TRUNCATE commands.

Step by Step

1. Drop the entire num_names table with its data from the duckwear database and use a SHOW command to verify the results:

```
DROP TABLE num_names;
SHOW TABLES;
```

```
mysql> drop table num_names;
Query OK, 0 rows affected (0.01 sec)

mysql> show tables;
+-------------------+
| Tables_in_duckwear |
+-------------------+
| copy_duck_cust    |
| cust_names        |
| cust_num_names    |
| duck_cust         |
| duck_title        |
+-------------------+
5 rows in set (0.00 sec)

mysql>
```

2. In the cust_num_names table, delete the data already contained in the duck_cust table: customer numbers 1 through 7. Then use a SELECT command to verify the results:

```
DELETE FROM cust_num_names
WHERE names_num<=7;
SELECT * FROM cust_num_names;
```

```
Command Prompt - /mysql/bin/mysql -u root -p                         _ □ ×

mysql> delete from cust_num_names
    -> where names_num<=7;
Query OK, 7 rows affected (0.07 sec)

mysql> select * from cust_num_names;
+-----------+-------------+------------+
| names_num | names_first | names_last |
+-----------+-------------+------------+
|         8 | Wolf        | Davidson   |
|         9 | Raccoon     | Danson     |
|        10 | Bob         | Filled     |
|        11 | Monte       | Billiards  |
|        12 | Jet         | Beauvais   |
|        13 | Kevin       | Seta       |
+-----------+-------------+------------+
6 rows in set (0.00 sec)

mysql>
```

3. Insert the remaining data of first and last names into the duck_cust table and check the results:

```
INSERT INTO duck_cust (cust_last, cust_first)
VALUES
("Davidson", "Wolf"),
```

(continued)

```
("Danson", "Raccoon"),
("Filled", "Bob"),
("Billiards", "Monte"),
("Beauvais", "Jet"),
("Seta", "Kevin");
SELECT * FROM duck_cust;
```

The auto-incrementing cust_num column has given each inserted record its unique customer number, and all fields in each record, other than cust_last and cust_first, have been filled with their default value, NULL.

```
Command Prompt - /mysql/bin/mysql --safe-updates=0 -u root -p                    _ □ ×
mysql> select * from duck_cust;
+----------+------------+--------------+--------------+-------------+-------------+------------+
+----------+------------+-------------------+------------+-------------+------------+------------+
| cust_num | cust_title | cust_last    | cust_first  | cust_suffix | cust_add1  |
|          | cust_add2  | cust_city    | cust_state  | cust_zip1   | cust_zip2  |
| cust_duckname         | cust_duckbday |
+----------+------------+--------------+--------------+-------------+-------------+------------+
+----------+------------+-------------------+------------+-------------+------------+------------+
|        1 |            | 8 | Salisbury | Jenny       |             | 9 Wishing Wel
l Court    | 0          | Meadowlark Hill | KS        | 67048       | 1234       |
Spike                  | 1961-03-21    |
|        2 | A207       | 1 | Irishlord | Red         | III         | 1022 Sea of R
ye         | A207       | Seacouver   | WA          | 98601       | 3464       |
Netrek Rules           | 1967-10-21    |
|        3 |            | 4 | Thegreat  | Vicki       |             | 2004 Singleto
n Dr.      | 0          | Freedom     | KS          | 67290       | 4321       |
Frida Kahlo de Tomayo  | 1948-03-21    |
|        4 |            | 9 | Montgomery | Chantel    |             | 1567 Terra Co
tta Way    | 0          | Chicago     | IL          | 89129       | 4444       |
Bianca                 | 1971-07-29    |
|        5 | #6         | 7 | Robert    | David       |             | 20113 Open Ro
ad Highway | #6         | Blacktop    | AZ          | 00606       | 1952       |
Harley                 | 1949-08-00    |
|        6 | Gatehouse  | 5 | Kazui     | Wonko       | PhD         | 42 Cube Farm
Lane       | Gatehouse  | Ulimpt      | CA          | 46362       | 0          |
Fitzwhistle            | 1961-12-04    |
|        7 |            | 6 | Gashlycrumb | Karen     |             | 3113 Picket F
ence Lane  | 0          | Fedora      | VT          | 41927       | 5698       |
Tess D'urberville      | 1948-08-19    |
|        8 | NULL       | 5 | Kazui     | Wonko       | PhD         | 1630 Revello
Drive      | NULL       | Shady Hill  | CA          | 31626       | 2882       |
Fitzwhistle            | 1961-12-04    |
|        9 |            | NULL | Davidson | Wolf       | NULL        |
           | NULL       |             |             |             | NULL       |
           | NULL       |             |
|       10 |            | NULL | Danson   | Raccoon    | NULL        |
           | NULL       |             |             |             | NULL       |
           | NULL       |             |
|       11 |            | NULL | Filled   | Bob        | NULL        |
           | NULL       |             |             |             | NULL       |
           | NULL       |             |
|       12 |            | NULL | Billiards | Monte     | NULL        |
           | NULL       |             |             |             | NULL       |
           | NULL       |             |
|       13 |            | NULL | Beauvais | Jet        | NULL        |
           | NULL       |             |             |             | NULL       |
           | NULL       |             |
|       14 |            | NULL | Seta     | Kevin      | NULL        |
           | NULL       |             |             |             | NULL       |
           | NULL       |             |
+----------+------------+--------------+--------------+-------------+-------------+------------+
+----------+------------+-------------------+------------+-------------+------------+------------+
14 rows in set (0.00 sec)

mysql> _
```

4. You now know that the last list of six customers live in the same apartment complex, so the addresses are all identical, except for their apartment numbers. By an amazing coincidence, they all named their ducks Quackers. The following syntax will allow you to update all six of their records at once:

```
UPDATE duck_cust
SET cust_title=9, cust_add1="1976 Stony Pointe Lane",
 cust_city="Elysium", cust_state="OK", cust_zip1="73102",
 cust_duckname="Quackers"
WHERE cust_num>=9;
```

5. The customers with numbers 9 through 14 live in apartments numbered 113, 243, 365, 142, 517, and 301, respectively. Using the following code as a guide, update each of their records with their correct apartment number:

```
UPDATE duck_cust
SET cust_add2="113"
WHERE
cust_num=9;
```

(continued)

6. Use a SELECT command to verify the results of the updated table:

```
SELECT * FROM duck_cust:
```

```
Command Prompt - /mysql/bin/mysql --safe-updates=0 -u root -p                    _ □ ✕
mysql> select * from duck_cust;
+-----------+-------------+-------------+-------------+-------------+-------------+--
-----------+-------------+-------------+-------------+
! cust_num ! cust_title ! cust_last   ! cust_first ! cust_suffix ! cust_add1
        ! cust_add2  ! cust_city   ! cust_state ! cust_zip1 ! cust_zip2 !
cust_duckname       ! cust_duckbday !
+-----------+-------------+-------------+-------------+-------------+-------------+--
-----------+-------------+-------------+-------------+
!        1 !           8 ! Salisbury  ! Jenny      !            ! 9 Wishing Wel
1 Court    ! 0          ! Meadowlark Hill ! KS      ! 67048     ! 1234     !
Spike                 ! 1961-03-21    !
!        2 !           1 ! Irishlord  ! Red        ! III        ! 1022 Sea of R
ye         ! A207       ! Seacouver  ! WA         ! 98601     ! 3464     !
Netrek Rules          ! 1967-10-21    !
!        3 !           4 ! Thegreat   ! Vicki      !            ! 2004 Singleto
n Dr.      ! 0          ! Freedom    ! KS         ! 67290     ! 4321     !
Frida Kahlo de Tomayo ! 1948-03-21    !
!        4 !           9 ! Montgomery ! Chantel    !            ! 1567 Terra Co
tta Way    ! 0          ! Chicago    ! IL         ! 89129     ! 4444     !
Bianca                ! 1971-07-29    !
!        5 !           7 ! Robert     ! David      !            ! 20113 Open Ro
ad Highway ! #6         ! Blacktop   ! AZ         ! 00606     ! 1952     !
Harley                ! 1949-08-00    !
!        6 !           5 ! Kazui      ! Wonko      ! PhD        ! 42 Cube Farm
Lane       ! Gatehouse  ! Ulimpt     ! CA         ! 46362     ! 0        !
Fitzwhistle           ! 1961-12-04    !
!        7 !           6 ! Gashlycrumb ! Karen     !            ! 3113 Picket F
ence Lane  ! 0          ! Fedora     ! UT         ! 41927     ! 5698     !
Tess D'urberville     ! 1948-08-19    !
!        8 !           5 ! Kazui      ! Wonko      ! PhD        ! 1630 Revello
Drive      ! NULL       ! Shady Hill ! CA         ! 31626     ! 2882     !
Fitzwhistle           ! 1961-12-04    !
!        9 !           9 ! Davidson   ! Wolf       ! NULL       ! 1976 Stony Po
inte Lane  ! 113        ! Elysium    ! OK         ! 73102     ! NULL     !
Quackers              ! NULL          !
!       10 !           9 ! Danson     ! Raccoon    ! NULL       ! 1976 Stony Po
inte Lane  ! 243        ! Elysium    ! OK         ! 73102     ! NULL     !
Quackers              ! NULL          !
!       11 !           9 ! Filled     ! Bob        ! NULL       ! 1976 Stony Po
inte Lane  ! 365        ! Elysium    ! OK         ! 73102     ! NULL     !
Quackers              ! NULL          !
!       12 !           9 ! Billiards  ! Monte      ! NULL       ! 1976 Stony Po
inte Lane  ! 142        ! Elysium    ! OK         ! 73102     ! NULL     !
Quackers              ! NULL          !
!       13 !           9 ! Beauvais   ! Jet        ! NULL       ! 1976 Stony Po
inte Lane  ! 517        ! Elysium    ! OK         ! 73102     ! NULL     !
Quackers              ! NULL          !
!       14 !           9 ! Seta       ! Kevin      ! NULL       ! 1976 Stony Po
inte Lane  ! 301        ! Elysium    ! OK         ! 73102     ! NULL     !
Quackers              ! NULL          !
+-----------+-------------+-------------+-------------+-------------+-------------+--
-----------+-------------+-------------+-------------+
14 rows in set (0.00 sec)

mysql>
```

7. Now that you have consolidated all your customer data into the duck_cust table, you no longer need the data in the cust_num_names table. Use the following command:

```
DELETE FROM cust_num_names;
```

You will get an error, because you ran a global command without the WHERE clause referencing a key field, and you have safe-updates in your configuration file.

```
mysql> delete from cust_num_names
    -> where 1=1;
ERROR 1175: You are using safe update mode and you tried to update a table witho
ut a WHERE that uses a KEY column
mysql>
```

8. You can allow this DELETE command to execute in one of two ways: either put a reference to a key field in a WHERE clause, as in WHERE cust_num>=1, or by temporarily turning off the safe-updates option (exit the MySQL Client, reenter it using the --safe-updates=0 command-line option, and then reenter the previous command). Choose whichever method you prefer.

9. Use the SHOW TABLES; command, and then the SELECT * FROM cust_num_names; command to check the results. You will see that the table still shows up in the database, but it is now an empty set.

```
Command Prompt - /mysql/bin/mysql --safe-updates=0 -u root -p           _ □ ×

mysql> show tables;
+--------------------+
| Tables_in_duckwear |
+--------------------+
| copy_duck_cust     |
| cust_names         |
| cust_num_names     |
| duck_cust          |
| duck_title         |
+--------------------+
5 rows in set (0.00 sec)

mysql> delete from cust_num_names
    -> where names_num>=1;
Query OK, 6 rows affected (0.11 sec)

mysql> show tables;
+--------------------+
| Tables_in_duckwear |
+--------------------+
| copy_duck_cust     |
| cust_names         |
| cust_num_names     |
| duck_cust          |
| duck_title         |
+--------------------+
5 rows in set (0.00 sec)

mysql> select * from cust_num_names;
Empty set (0.00 sec)

mysql>
```

10. You no longer need the data in the copy_duck_cust table either. Empty it using the TRUNCATE command, and then check the results:

```
TRUNCATE copy_duck_cust;
SELECT * FROM copy_duck_cust;
```

(continued)

TRUNCATE returns 0 rows affected, yet the table still exists as an empty set.

```
Command Prompt - \mysql\bin\mysql -u root -p
mysql> show tables;
+-------------------+
| Tables_in_duckwear |
+-------------------+
| copy_duck_cust    |
| cust_names        |
| cust_num_names    |
| duck_cust         |
| duck_title        |
+-------------------+
5 rows in set (0.00 sec)

mysql> truncate copy_duck_cust;
Query OK, 0 rows affected (0.10 sec)

mysql> select * from copy_duck_cust;
Empty set (0.00 sec)

mysql>
```

11. Use the DROP TABLE command to remove both of the empty tables from the database, and then check the results:

    ```
    DROP TABLE copy_duck_cust, cust_num_names;
    SHOW TABLES;
    ```

    Now, only the cust_names, duck_cust, and duck_title tables remain in the duckwear database.

```
Command Prompt - \mysql\bin\mysql -u root -p
mysql> show tables;
+-------------------+
| Tables_in_duckwear |
+-------------------+
| copy_duck_cust    |
| cust_names        |
| cust_num_names    |
| duck_cust         |
| duck_title        |
+-------------------+
5 rows in set (0.00 sec)

mysql> drop table copy_duck_cust, cust_num_names;
Query OK, 0 rows affected (0.00 sec)

mysql> show tables;
+-------------------+
| Tables_in_duckwear |
+-------------------+
| cust_names        |
| duck_cust         |
| duck_title        |
+-------------------+
3 rows in set (0.00 sec)

mysql>
```

Project Summary

In Project 3-3, you dropped entire tables, as well as deleted and truncated data from tables while leaving the tables intact. You revisited using the INSERT command to add data to single and multiple rows, and used the UPDATE command to update existing rows with new data. You finished by removing the extra tables created in earlier projects, leaving you with a clean database on which to base the projects in the next module, which covers basic reporting.

✓

Module 3 Mastery Check

1. How do you make a copy of the table wolfhounds, including its data?

2. If you have a table called sport and it has the fields football, basketball, soccer, and hockey, how do you make a table called ballgames without the hockey field?

3. What kind of table resides in memory and lasts only as long as the MySQL Client's current connection?

4. What does the following command accomplish?

```
LOAD DATA INFILE '\documents\games_stats.txt'
INTO TABLE stat_sheet
FIELDS TERMINATED BY ':'
LINES TERMINATED BY '\r\n';
```

5. What are the four options for the ALTER TABLE command and what do they do?

6. What command inserts only entire records into a table?

7. What does a table need to have in order to use the REPLACE INTO command and avoid inserting duplicate records?

8. What do you type on the command line to temporarily turn off the safe-updates option?

9. Which command allows you to insert data into specific fields within records?

10. What does the following command do?

```
UPDATE wine_list
SET color="red"
WHERE variety="Merlot";
```

11. Which command(s) removes a table and which command(s) removes only the data in the table?

12. How is TRUNCATE different from DELETE?

13. What does the following command do?

```
ALTER TABLE horse_gear
MODIFY num_code MEDIUMINT(9) PRIMARY KEY NOT NULL AUTO_INCREMENT,
MODIFY feed CHAR(15) NOT NULL,
CHANGE saddles_bridles tack CHAR(20) NOT NULL,
ADD blanket ENUM('Yes', 'No')
DROP color;
```

Module 4

Basic Reporting

This module deals with retrieving records from your database tables and presenting the data in them in a concise and informative display. You have already used the SELECT ... WHERE command to give you a basic view of your table's data. Here, you will learn how to refine your output by using more selective specifications. With a narrowed focus, you can present only the data you need in an easily accessible format.

Shape the Data from Your Tables to Fit Your Needs

While it can be true that the quality of an answer depends on the degree of detail in the question, there are things you, as the database administrator, can do to improve the effectiveness of the data you supply. When any request is made for specific data, you should give some thought to exactly what you are being asked to provide, and if the data you provide is going to lead to other, easily forecasted, requests.

For instance, if the sales department puts in a request for how many current customers live in a particular state or region, you may assume from past experience that the next request will involve a breakdown of those customers by city, and therefore decide to supply that information the first time around. You can also decide that ordering the output by the city name, which groups the customers in that city together, will make it easier for the sales department to draw conclusions from the data.

Always take a few moments to clarify what is being asked of you, and once you have that information, proceed to choose which fields from which tables will provide you with the appropriate collection of data.

As you've learned in previous modules, you can choose data from your database with the SELECT command. The SELECT command is used for two basic reasons. One is the reason you have been using it so far: testing. SELECT allows you to look at your tables quickly and easily in order to verify their content and the format of that content. The second reason is to shape the data from your tables into formats that are easier to read and use, defining the output to match the needs of your circumstances. This section will briefly review the SELECT command as you already know and use it, and then expand on its usefulness by adding some options to your repertoire that allow you to shape the data to fit your needs more closely.

Testing with the SELECT Command

Your use of SELECT so far has been to verify that the commands you used in your projects gave the desired results. You've used the wildcard form of SELECT (SELECT *) as a verifying test. Although this form is useful, it can present some problems. So, first we will look at when using SELECT * isn't appropriate. Then you will learn about another useful testing form of SELECT that uses the LIMIT option, which allows you to control how much data is returned.

Understanding the Problems with SELECT *

The basic SELECT command you have seen in previous modules has the following syntax:

```
SELECT [*] FROM <table_name>;
```

The asterisk (or wildcard) indicates choosing all of a table's columns.

The problem with using the wildcard is that you may be pulling up columns of information that you have no use for at the moment. In a small database, such as duckwear, this isn't much of a problem. However, if the duck_cust table held hundreds or even thousands of records, the importance of looking at only the fields you really need to examine becomes clear. Not only does using the wildcard complicate your output, but it also begins to affect your response time when your database has become large.

Another consideration relates to using SELECT * in code. When you write a piece of code using SELECT *, you are relying on the response to that code showing up in the order in which the table you are accessing is designed. If at some later point, you change the table in question—by adding, deleting, rearranging, or modifying a column's definition—then you will have unwittingly broken the code with the SELECT * in it. It is easy enough to do this with your own code, and even easier if someone else has taken over the administration of the database.

Because of these potential problems, you should use SELECT * only in testing. Even if you need all the fields in a table, when writing actual code that will be in use over time, you should call out the column names individually to avoid needless difficulties later in the life of your database.

Limiting Selections

The LIMIT option of the SELECT command allows you to specify a numeric quantity to control the amount of data you get from the command. You can also use it as a kind of scrolling stop.

The syntax for using the basic LIMIT option is as follows:

```
SELECT <column_name> FROM <table_name> LIMIT <numeric_value>;
```

Even if you use the SELECT * command, the output will produce only the number of lines of data specified in the LIMIT clause. For instance, you could issue the following command:

```
SELECT * FROM duck_cust LIMIT 9;
```

Figure 4-1 shows the results of using this command with the duck_cust table as it stands right now. As you can see, only the first 9 entries in the table appear, instead of the entire 14

```
Command Prompt - /mysql/bin/mysql -u root -p                    _ □ ×
mysql> select * from duck_cust limit 9;
+-----------+-------------+-------------+-------------+-------------+-------------+
+-----------+-------------+-------------+-------------+-------------+-------------+--
| cust_num | cust_title | cust_last | cust_first | cust_suffix | cust_add1 |
|          | cust_add2  | cust_city |            | cust_state | cust_zip1 | cust_zip2 |
| cust_duckname          | cust_duckbday |
+-----------+-------------+-------------+-------------+-------------+-------------+
+-----------+-------------+-------------+-------------+-------------+-------------+--
|       1 |           8 | Salisbury | Jenny     |           | 9 Wishing Wel
1 Court   | 0           | Meadowlark Hill | KS    |           | 67048     | 1234      |
Spike                    | 1961-03-21 |
|       2 |           1 | Irishlord | Red       | III       | 1022 Sea of R
ye       | A207        | Seacouver | WA        |           | 98601     | 3464      |
Netrek Rules             | 1967-10-21 |
|       3 |           4 | Thegreat  | Vicki     |           | 2004 Singleto
n Dr.    | 0           | Freedom   | KS        |           | 67290     | 4321      |
Frida Kahlo de Tomayo    | 1948-03-21 |
|       4 |           9 | Montgomery | Chantel  |           | 1567 Terra Co
tta Way  | 0           | Chicago   | IL        |           | 89129     | 4444      |
Bianca                   | 1971-07-29 |
|       5 |           7 | Robert    | David     |           | 20113 Open Ro
ad Highway | #6        | Blacktop  | AZ        |           | 00606     | 1952      |
Harley                   | 1949-08-00 |
|       6 |           5 | Kazui     | Wonko     | PhD       | 42 Cube Farm
Lane     | Gatehouse   | Ulimpt    | CA        |           | 46362     | 0         |
Fitzwhistle              | 1961-12-04 |
|       7 |           6 | Gashlycrumb | Karen   |           | 3113 Picket F
ence Lane | 0          | Fedora    | UT        |           | 41927     | 5698      |
Tess D'urberville        | 1948-08-19 |
|       8 |           5 | Kazui     | Wonko     | PhD       | 1630 Revello
Drive    | NULL        | Shady Hill | CA       |           | 31626     | 2882      |
Fitzwhistle              | 1961-12-04 |
|       9 |           9 | Davidson  | Wolf      | NULL      | 1976 Stony Po
inte Lane | 113        | Elysium   | OK        |           | 73102     | NULL      |
Quackers                 | NULL |
+-----------+-------------+-------------+-------------+-------------+-------------+
+-----------+-------------+-------------+-------------+-------------+-------------+--
9 rows in set (0.28 sec)
mysql>
```

Figure 4-1 Using the SELECT command with the LIMIT option

entries it contains. This demonstrates how the LIMIT option can be used to scroll through a table a few entries at a time.

You can also specify which record to begin with (the *offset*) and the total number of records you want to see (*count*), by using the following syntax:

```
SELECT * FROM <table_name> LIMIT <offset>, <count>;
```

For instance, you could use the following command:

```
SELECT * FROM duck_cust LIMIT 3, 4;
```

Figure 4-2 shows the results: the records starting with the record after 3 (customer number 4) and ending when the total number of records equals four (customer number 7).

```
Command Prompt - /mysql/bin/mysql -u root -p                           _ □ ✕

mysql> select * from duck_cust limit 3, 4;
+----------+------------+-----------+------------+------------+------------+--------
+------------+------------+------------+------------+------------+------------+--------
| cust_num | cust_title | cust_last | cust_first | cust_suffix | cust_add1
           | cust_add2  | cust_city | cust_state | cust_zip1  | cust_zip2  | cust_d
uckname    | cust_duckbday |
+----------+------------+-----------+------------+------------+------------+--------
+------------+------------+------------+------------+------------+------------+--------
|       4  |         9  | Montgomery | Chantel   |            |            | 1567 Terra Co
tta Way    | 0          | Chicago   | IL         | 89129      | 4444       | Bianca
           | 1971-07-29 |
|       5  |         7  | Robert    | David      |            |            | 20113 Open Ro
ad Highway | #6         | Blacktop  | AZ         | 00606      | 1952       | Harley
           | 1949-08-00 |
|       6  |         5  | Kazui     | Wonko      | PhD        |            | 42 Cube Farm
Lane       | Gatehouse  | Ulimpt    | CA         | 46362      | 0          | Fitzwh
istle      | 1961-12-04 |
|       7  |         6  | Gashlycrumb | Karen    |            |            | 3113 Picket F
ence Lane  | 0          | Fedora    | UT         | 41927      | 5698       | Tess D
'urberville | 1948-08-19 |
+----------+------------+-----------+------------+------------+------------+--------
+------------+------------+------------+------------+------------+------------+--------
4 rows in set (0.00 sec)

mysql> _
```

Figure 4-2 Using the LIMIT option with offset and count specifications

Using the LIMIT option of the SELECT command is handy for testing the results of commands, as well as scrolling through the table looking for results or content.

Shaping Data with the SELECT Command

After you have worked out what you need in a given piece of code and how you will go about displaying the data required, you will use forms of SELECT that shape the format of the data, rather than display it unfiltered. The DISTINCT option of the SELECT command is useful for removing duplicates from the results. The AS option lets you display columns with different names than they have in the table.

Removing Duplicates

The DISTINCT option allows you to cull out any duplicates in your reporting data. If you are looking for how many states you have customers in, for example, the list will be easier to compile if only one incidence of each state is reported.

The syntax for using the DISTINCT option is as follows:

```
SELECT [DISTINCT] <column_name> FROM <table_name>;
```

The DISTINCT option allows you to specify when you need to see only one incidence of a return value, which can make it much easier to draw conclusions from your output.

```
SELECT DISTINCT species FROM monsters;
```

For example, if the species column of the monsters table listed five vampires, three werewolves, two zombies, and one banshee, then this command would return the list vampire, werewolf, zombie, and banshee, editing out the repeating entries occurring in the species fields.

Renaming Columns for Display Purposes

The AS option allows you to give a column a new heading in the output of the SELECT command. It does not change the name of the column in the table, just defines an alias for the heading of that column's information in the output. This can be useful for clarity and security. Changing the display heading clearly labels the data in that column, and using an alias makes it harder for someone to access areas of the database where they do not have SHOW privileges in order to view table names and structures.

If, for instance, the name of a column is cust_duckname, you can change the header to DuckName for the output by using the following command:

```
SELECT cust_first, cust_last,
cust_duckname AS DuckName
FROM duck_cust;
```

If the new header contains spaces or special characters, then it must be enclosed within double quotation marks to indicate it is a string that should be handled as one unit of text. If you want to use Duck's Name as the header, which contains both a space and a special character (apostrophe), you would then use the following command:

```
SELECT cust_first, cust_last,
cust_duckname AS "Duck's Name"
FROM duck_cust;
```

Figure 4-3 shows the resulting output from the preceding command. The first two columns have their duck_cust field names as headers. However, the third column uses the name supplied with the AS option, rather than the duck_cust field name.

```
Command Prompt - /mysql/bin/mysql -u root -p                          _ □ X
Database changed
mysql> select cust_first, cust_last,
    -> cust_duckname as DuckName
    -> from duck_cust;
+------------+-------------+-----------------------------+
! cust_first ! cust_last   ! DuckName                    !
+------------+-------------+-----------------------------+
! Jenny      ! Salisbury   ! Spike                       !
! Red        ! Irishlord   ! Netrek Rules                !
! Vicki      ! Thegreat    ! Frida Kahlo de Tomayo       !
! Chantel    ! Montgomery  ! Bianca                      !
! David      ! Robert      ! Harley                      !
! Wonko      ! Kazui       ! Fitzwhistle                 !
! Karen      ! Gashlycrumb ! Tess D'urberville           !
! Wonko      ! Kazui       ! Fitzwhistle                 !
! Wolf       ! Davidson    ! Quackers                    !
! Raccoon    ! Danson      ! Quackers                    !
! Bob        ! Filled      ! Quackers                    !
! Monte      ! Billiards   ! Quackers                    !
! Jet        ! Beauvais    ! Quackers                    !
! Kevin      ! Seta        ! Quackers                    !
+------------+-------------+-----------------------------+
14 rows in set (0.44 sec)

mysql>
```

Figure 4-3 Using the AS option of the SELECT command

Progress Check

1. What are two reasons the SELECT * command should not be used except for testing purposes?

2. What does the LIMIT option of the SELECT command do?

3. What does the DISTINCT option of the SELECT command do?

4. What does the AS option of the SELECT command do?

---

1. One reason that the SELECT * command should not be used except for testing purposes is that you select more fields than your query actually requires, which clutters your output and may slow your response time. Another reason is that changing the order of the table columns can break the code, putting information in the wrong column headers.

2. The LIMIT option restricts the output of the SELECT command to a specific number of lines, or it can be used to scroll through a table by a specific number of lines at a time.

3. The DISTINCT option removes duplicated data from the output of the SELECT command.

4. The AS option creates an alias for the output headers of a column or columns from a table specified in a SELECT command.

4.2 Refine Your Data Selection

You can focus on particular areas of your database, viewing just the parts you need to see. You can also narrow your focus even smaller, to a specific record or field.

Focusing on Smaller Areas of Your Database

Several commands narrow the focus from your entire MySQL server to a specific database within it, and then to a specific table within that database. You've used these commands in the projects in preceding modules to work with the sample database and tables. These commands and their meanings are listed in Table 4-1.

Using WHERE to Narrow Your Focus

Once you have selected a particular column or columns of data to output, the WHERE clause of the SELECT command allows you to narrow your selection even more. You can choose to output only a specific record or field. For example, you can use it to specify a range or a single choice by focusing on a key (or index) value. This allows you to present the user with exactly the required data from your database.

NOTE

The WHERE clause can also be used in the same manner with the UPDATE and DELETE commands, to narrow their results.

Command	Meaning
SHOW DATABASES;	Shows all databases in the MySQL server
USE <database_name>;	Narrows the focus to the specified database
SHOW TABLES;	Shows all tables within the specified database
DESC <table_name>;	Lists the description of the specified table

Table 4-1 Commands That Focus on Areas of the Database

In the previous modules, you have learned about using some of the variations of the WHERE clause to narrow data to a precise item or range of items. Here, you will learn how to use the WHERE clause with conditions, which use operators or reserved words to return output based on comparisons.

The WHERE clause syntax is listed in the MySQL manual as [WHERE <*where_ definition*>], which is concise but not exactly detailed. Table 4-2 lists some, but not all, variations on the WHERE clause syntax with examples.

If each of the WHERE clauses listed in Table 4-2 were preceded by a SELECT * statement, the results would be a list of every record in the specified table that fits the criteria. Most of them, if read aloud, are self-explanatory, except for the last one, which selects records from a table where the data in the music_styles field begin with the letter *R*.

The next sections describe the operators and reserved words that you can use in WHERE clauses to refine your selections.

Syntax	Examples
WHERE <*column_name*><*operator*><*where_value*>;	WHERE car_color="green";
WHERE <*column_name*> IS <NULL/NOT NULL>;	WHERE graduation_date IS NULL;
WHERE <*column_name*><*operator*><*where_value*> AND <*column_name*><*operator*><*where_value*>;	WHERE release_date>=1964 AND vocal="John Lennon";
WHERE <*column_name*><*operator*><*where_value*> AND <*column_name*>BETWEEN <*numeric_where_value*> AND <*numeric_where_value*>;	WHERE car_maker="Chevrolet" AND car_year BETWEEN 1955 AND 1959;
WHERE <*column_name*><*operator*><*where_value*> OR <*column_name*><*operator*><*where_value*>;	WHERE series_code="BtVS" OR series_code="AtS";
WHERE <*column_name*> LIKE "<*comparison_value*>%";	WHERE music_styles LIKE "R%";

Table 4-2 Some Variations of the WHERE Syntax

Using Operators with WHERE

The WHERE clause allows you to use the six arithmetic and two logical operators listed in Table 4-3 as conditional comparisons. Any numeric field, such as the customer number, can be used in a WHERE clause with the numeric operators. You have already used <= and >= in the projects in Module 3.

Using the AND operator specifies that all the values involved in the comparison must be TRUE; using the OR operator specifies that at least one of the values in the comparison must be TRUE.

You can also use the reserved word BETWEEN in conjunction with the reserved word AND to establish a numeric range within which you want MySQL to select data.

Comparing Text with WHERE

The reserved word LIKE allows you to make comparisons with a portion of each field against a string value that you specify between double quotation marks. For instance, you could list all the fields in a column whose data begins with the same letter or letters.

The string comparisons in WHERE clauses are not case-sensitive by default. If you want to use case-sensitivity, you can add the BINARY option to the WHERE clause criteria:

```
WHERE BINARY <column_name><operator><where_value>;
```

This will allow MySQL to differentiate between strings where they vary because of case. For instance, you can use it to find only *don* and not *Don*, or in a LIKE wildcard search for "R%", so you will find *Rock* and *Reggae* but not *rock*.

Operator	Definition
=	Equal to
!=	Not equal to
<=	Less than or equal to
<	Less than
>=	Greater than or equal to
>	Greater than
AND	Both values true
OR	One or both values true

Table 4-3 Comparison Operators for the WHERE Clause

Progress Check

1. What are the six arithmetic and two logical comparison operators?

2. What reserved word allows you to compare strings for partially matching characters?

3. What code allows you to search a table called albums in the columns groups and release_dates for all records by Queen released between 1973 and 1976, giving you the data from the titles and sales fields.

4. How do you make a string comparison case-sensitive?

Project 4-1   Create Reports Using SELECT...WHERE to Refine Data

In Project 4-1, you will use the SELECT ... WHERE command with the LIMIT, DISTINCT, ORDER BY, and LIKE clauses to select and refine data from the duck_cust table as discussed in this module.

Step by Step

1. Open a command-line window and log in to MySQL, using the **\mysql\bin\mysql -u root -p** command (Windows) or the **mysql -p** command (Linux), and then enter your password when prompted.

2. Type **USE duckwear;** and press the ENTER key.

3. Use the following code as an example, select the customer number, first name, and last name, while scrolling through the entire duck_cust table four records at a time:

```
SELECT cust_num, cust_first, cust_last FROM duck_cust
LIMIT 0, 4;
```

(continued)

---

1. The six arithmetic operators used for comparison are equal to (=), not equal to (! =), less than or equal to (<=), less than (<), greater than or equal to (>=), and greater than (>). The two logical operators used for comparison are AND and OR.

2. The reserved word LIKE allows you to compare strings for partially matching characters.

3. The following code performs the search:

```
SELECT titles, sales FROM albums
WHERE groups="Queen" AND release_dates BETWEEN 1973 AND 1976;
```

4. You add the reserved word BINARY to the WHERE clause to perform case-sensitive comparisons.

The $<offset>$ variable of the LIMIT option is the only one that changes, and each subsequent command displays the next four records in the table until the last command, which displays the only two remaining records.

```
Command Prompt - /mysql/bin/mysql -u root -p                                    _ □ ✕

mysql> select cust_num, cust_first, cust_last from duck_cust
    -> limit 0,4;
+----------+------------+------------+
| cust_num | cust_first | cust_last  |
+----------+------------+------------+
|        1 | Jenny      | Salisbury  |
|        2 | Red        | Irishlord  |
|        3 | Vicki      | Thegreat   |
|        4 | Chantel    | Montgomery |
+----------+------------+------------+
4 rows in set (0.00 sec)

mysql> select cust_num, cust_first, cust_last from duck_cust
    -> limit 4,4;
+----------+------------+-------------+
| cust_num | cust_first | cust_last   |
+----------+------------+-------------+
|        5 | David      | Robert      |
|        6 | Wonko      | Kazui       |
|        7 | Karen      | Gashlycrumb |
|        8 | Wonko      | Kazui       |
+----------+------------+-------------+
4 rows in set (0.00 sec)

mysql> select cust_num, cust_first, cust_last from duck_cust
    -> limit 8,4;
+----------+------------+-----------+
| cust_num | cust_first | cust_last |
+----------+------------+-----------+
|        9 | Wolf       | Davidson  |
|       10 | Raccoon    | Danson    |
|       11 | Bob        | Filled    |
|       12 | Monte      | Billiards |
+----------+------------+-----------+
4 rows in set (0.01 sec)

mysql> select cust_num, cust_first, cust_last from duck_cust
    -> limit 12,4;
+----------+------------+-----------+
| cust_num | cust_first | cust_last |
+----------+------------+-----------+
|       13 | Jet        | Beauvais  |
|       14 | Kevin      | Seta      |
+----------+------------+-----------+
2 rows in set (0.00 sec)

mysql>
```

4. To test the function of the DISTINCT option, enter the following commands:

```
SELECT cust_duckname FROM duck_cust;
SELECT DISTINCT cust_duckname FROM duck_cust;
```

You'll see that the DISTINCT option filters out all repetition in the data fields.

```
Command Prompt - \mysql\bin\mysql -u root -p                    _ □ ✕

mysql> select cust_duckname from duck_cust;
+-------------------------+
| cust_duckname           |
+-------------------------+
| Spike                   |
| Netrek Rules            |
| Frida Kahlo de Tomayo   |
| Bianca                  |
| Harley                  |
| Fitzwhistle             |
| Tess D'urberville       |
| Fitzwhistle             |
| Quackers                |
| Quackers                |
| Quackers                |
| Quackers                |
| Quackers                |
| Quackers                |
+-------------------------+
14 rows in set (0.00 sec)

mysql> select distinct cust_duckname from duck_cust;
+-------------------------+
| cust_duckname           |
+-------------------------+
| Spike                   |
| Netrek Rules            |
| Frida Kahlo de Tomayo   |
| Bianca                  |
| Harley                  |
| Fitzwhistle             |
| Tess D'urberville       |
| Quackers                |
+-------------------------+
8 rows in set (0.00 sec)

mysql>
```

5. Display records where each customer's number, last name, state, and duck name are selected and use the AS option to change the header names, as follows:

Field	Header
cust_num	Cust. #
cust_last	Last Name
cust_state	State
cust_duckname	Duck's Name

```
SELECT cust_num AS "Cust.#", cust_last AS "Last Name",
  cust_state AS State, cust_duckname AS "Duck's Name" FROM duck_cust;
```

The output has the correct headers, but it still lists every customer in the database as if you had used the wildcard.

(continued)

```
Command Prompt - \mysql\bin\mysql -u root -p                          _ □ ×
mysql> select cust_num as "Cust.#", cust_last as "Last Name", cust_state as Stat
e, cust_duckname as "Duck's Name" from duck_cust;
+---------+-------------+-------+-------------------------+
! Cust.# ! Last Name   ! State ! Duck's Name             !
+---------+-------------+-------+-------------------------+
!       1 ! Salisbury   ! KS    ! Spike                   !
!       2 ! Irishlord   ! WA    ! Netrek Rules            !
!       3 ! Thegreat    ! KS    ! Frida Kahlo de Tomayo   !
!       4 ! Montgomery  ! IL    ! Bianca                  !
!       5 ! Robert      ! AZ    ! Harley                  !
!       6 ! Kazui       ! CA    ! Fitzwhistle             !
!       7 ! Gashlycrumb ! UT    ! Tess D'urberville       !
!       8 ! Kazui       ! CA    ! Fitzwhistle             !
!       9 ! Davidson    ! OK    ! Quackers                !
!      10 ! Danson      ! OK    ! Quackers                !
!      11 ! Filled      ! OK    ! Quackers                !
!      12 ! Billiards   ! OK    ! Quackers                !
!      13 ! Beauvais    ! OK    ! Quackers                !
!      14 ! Seta        ! OK    ! Quackers                !
+---------+-------------+-------+-------------------------+
14 rows in set (0.00 sec)

mysql>
```

6. Since you know that customer 8 is a repeat of the same duck at a different address (customer 6), you can remove it and get the desired output, using the following code:

```
SELECT cust_num AS "Cust.#",  cust_last AS "Last Name",
 cust_state AS State, cust_duckname AS "Duck's Name" FROM duck_cust
 WHERE cust_num!=8;
```

```
Command Prompt - \mysql\bin\mysql -u root -p                          _ □ ×
mysql> select cust_num as "Cust.#", cust_last as "Last Name", cust_state as Sta
te, cust_duckname as "Duck's Name" from duck_cust where cust_num!=8;
+---------+-------------+-------+-------------------------+
! Cust.# ! Last Name   ! State ! Duck's Name             !
+---------+-------------+-------+-------------------------+
!       1 ! Salisbury   ! KS    ! Spike                   !
!       2 ! Irishlord   ! WA    ! Netrek Rules            !
!       3 ! Thegreat    ! KS    ! Frida Kahlo de Tomayo   !
!       4 ! Montgomery  ! IL    ! Bianca                  !
!       5 ! Robert      ! AZ    ! Harley                  !
!       6 ! Kazui       ! CA    ! Fitzwhistle             !
!       7 ! Gashlycrumb ! UT    ! Tess D'urberville       !
!       9 ! Davidson    ! OK    ! Quackers                !
!      10 ! Danson      ! OK    ! Quackers                !
!      11 ! Filled      ! OK    ! Quackers                !
!      12 ! Billiards   ! OK    ! Quackers                !
!      13 ! Beauvais    ! OK    ! Quackers                !
!      14 ! Seta        ! OK    ! Quackers                !
+---------+-------------+-------+-------------------------+
13 rows in set (0.00 sec)

mysql>
```

7. Use a WHERE clause with numeric operators to list the names of customer numbers 10 and above. Also list customer numbers 3 and under plus those above, but not including, customer number 7. Additionally, use the AS option to change all four headers: cust_num to Number, cust_last to Last Name, cust_city to City, and cust_state to State.

```
SELECT cust_last, cust_first FROM duck_cust
WHERE cust_num>=10;
SELECT cust_num AS Number, cust_last AS "Last Name",
cust_city AS City, cust_state AS State FROM duck_cust
WHERE cust_num<=3 OR cust_num>7;
```

```
Command Prompt - /mysql/bin/mysql -u root -p                      _ □ ×

mysql> select cust_last, cust_first from duck_cust
    -> where cust_num>=10;
+-----------+------------+
| cust_last | cust_first |
+-----------+------------+
| Danson    | Raccoon    |
| Filled    | Bob        |
| Billiards | Monte      |
| Beauvais  | Jet        |
| Seta      | Kevin      |
+-----------+------------+
5 rows in set (0.09 sec)

mysql> select cust_num as Number, cust_last as "Last Name", cust_city as City,
    -> cust_state as State from duck_cust where cust_num<=3 or cust_num>7;
+--------+-----------+----------------+-------+
| Number | Last Name | City           | State |
+--------+-----------+----------------+-------+
|      1 | Salisbury | Meadowlark Hill | KS    |
|      2 | Irishlord | Seacouver      | WA    |
|      3 | Thegreat  | Freedom        | KS    |
|      8 | Kazui     | Shady Hill     | CA    |
|      9 | Davidson  | Elysium        | OK    |
|     10 | Danson    | Elysium        | OK    |
|     11 | Filled    | Elysium        | OK    |
|     12 | Billiards | Elysium        | OK    |
|     13 | Beauvais  | Elysium        | OK    |
|     14 | Seta      | Elysium        | OK    |
+--------+-----------+----------------+-------+
10 rows in set (0.00 sec)

mysql> _
```

8. Try changing the AND to an OR in the previous command. Then change the <= to >= and > to <:.

```
SELECT cust_num AS number, cust_last AS "last name",
cust_city AS city, cust_state AS state FROM duck_cust
WHERE cust_num<=3 AND cust_num>7;
```

```
SELECT cust_num AS number, cust_last AS "last name",
cust_city AS city, cust_state AS state from duck_cust
WHERE cust_num>=3 AND cust_num<7;
```

This first command completely changes the values of the output to an empty set. Changing the arithmetic operators gives you the previously missing data except for customer 7, plus customer number 3.

(continued)

```
Command Prompt - \mysql\bin\mysql -u root -p                                    _ □ ×
mysql> select cust_num as number, cust_last as "last name", cust_city as city, c
ust_state as state from duck_cust where cust_num<=3 and cust_num>7;
Empty set (0.00 sec)

mysql> select cust_num as number, cust_last as "last name", cust_city as city, c
ust_state as state from duck_cust where cust_num>=3 and cust_num<7;
+--------+------------+----------+-------+
| number | last name  | city     | state |
+--------+------------+----------+-------+
|      3 | Thegreat   | Freedom  | KS    |
|      4 | Montgomery | Chicago  | IL    |
|      5 | Robert     | Blacktop | AZ    |
|      6 | Kazui      | Ulimpt   | CA    |
+--------+------------+----------+-------+
4 rows in set (0.00 sec)

mysql>
```

9. Use the following code with equal to and not equal to operators to sort customers by region:

```
SELECT cust_num, cust_city, cust_state FROM duck_cust
WHERE cust_state="ok" OR cust_state="ks";

SELECT cust_num, cust_city, cust_state FROM duck_cust
WHERE cust_state="ca" OR cust_state="wa" OR cust_state="az";

SELECT cust_num, cust_city, cust_state FROM duck_cust
WHERE cust_state!="ca" AND cust_state!="wa" AND cust_state!="az" AND
cust_state!="ok" AND cust_state!="ks";
```

```
Command Prompt - \mysql\bin\mysql -u root -p                                    _ □ ×
mysql> select cust_num, cust_city, cust_state from duck_cust
    -> where cust_state="ok" or cust_state="ks";
+----------+---------------+------------+
| cust_num | cust_city     | cust_state |
+----------+---------------+------------+
|        1 | Meadowlark Hill | KS       |
|        3 | Freedom       | KS         |
|        9 | Elysium       | OK         |
|       10 | Elysium       | OK         |
|       11 | Elysium       | OK         |
|       12 | Elysium       | OK         |
|       13 | Elysium       | OK         |
|       14 | Elysium       | OK         |
+----------+---------------+------------+
8 rows in set (0.00 sec)

mysql> select cust_num, cust_city, cust_state from duck_cust
    -> where cust_state="ca" or cust_state="wa" or cust_state="az";
+----------+-----------+------------+
| cust_num | cust_city | cust_state |
+----------+-----------+------------+
|        2 | Seacouver | WA         |
|        5 | Blacktop  | AZ         |
|        6 | Ulimpt    | CA         |
|        8 | Shady Hill | CA        |
+----------+-----------+------------+
4 rows in set (0.00 sec)

mysql> select cust_num, cust_city, cust_state from duck_cust
    -> where cust_state!="ca" and cust_state!="wa" and cust_state!="az" and
    -> cust_state!="ok" and cust_state!="ks";
+----------+-----------+------------+
| cust_num | cust_city | cust_state |
+----------+-----------+------------+
|        4 | Chicago   | IL         |
|        7 | Fedora    | UT         |
+----------+-----------+------------+
2 rows in set (0.00 sec)

mysql>
```

NOTE

Despite being in all uppercase in the `duck_cust` table, the two-letter state designations do not need to be in uppercase for the string comparison to match, because the comparison was not designated with the `BINARY` option.

10. Check for missing duck birthday data with the following code:

```
SELECT * FROM duck_cust
WHERE cust_duckbday IS NULL;
```

You can see the customers who need to be sent letters asking for their duck's birth date.

```
Command Prompt - /mysql/bin/mysql -u root -p                        _ |□| x|
mysql> select * from duck_cust
    -> where cust_duckbday is null;
+-----------+------------+------------+-----------+------------+-----------+
-----------+------------+
| cust_num | cust_title | cust_last | cust_first | cust_suffix | cust_add1
           | cust_add2 | cust_city | cust_state | cust_zip1 | cust_zip2 | cust_duck
name | cust_duckbday |
+-----------+------------+------------+-----------+------------+-----------+
-----------+------------+
|        9 |          9 | Davidson  | Wolf      |        NULL |           | 1976 Stony Poin
te Lane | 113      | Elysium   | OK        |       73102 |      NULL | Quackers
        | NULL      |
|       10 |          9 | Danson    | Raccoon   |        NULL |           | 1976 Stony Poin
te Lane | 243      | Elysium   | OK        |       73102 |      NULL | Quackers
        | NULL      |
|       11 |          9 | Filled    | Bob       |        NULL |           | 1976 Stony Poin
te Lane | 365      | Elysium   | OK        |       73102 |      NULL | Quackers
        | NULL      |
|       12 |          9 | Billiards | Monte     |        NULL |           | 1976 Stony Poin
te Lane | 142      | Elysium   | OK        |       73102 |      NULL | Quackers
        | NULL      |
|       13 |          9 | Beauvais  | Jet       |        NULL |           | 1976 Stony Poin
te Lane | 517      | Elysium   | OK        |       73102 |      NULL | Quackers
        | NULL      |
|       14 |          9 | Seta      | Kevin     |        NULL |           | 1976 Stony Poin
te Lane | 301      | Elysium   | OK        |       73102 |      NULL | Quackers
        | NULL      |
+-----------+------------+------------+-----------+------------+-----------+
-----------+------------+
6 rows in set (0.08 sec)

mysql> _
```

11. List the customers in alphabetical order and change the headers in the display:

```
SELECT cust_last AS Last, cust_first AS First, cust_add1 AS Address,
  cust_add2 AS "Address 2", cust_state AS State, cust_zip1 AS Zip
  FROM duck_cust WHERE cust_num!=8 ORDER BY Last;
```

The `WHERE cust_num!=8` removes the repeat customer from the result set, and the `ORDER BY` makes the list appear in ascending alphabetical order.

(continued)

```
Command Prompt - /mysql/bin/mysql -u root -p                          _ □ ×

mysql> select cust_last as Last, cust_first as First, cust_add1 as Address,
    -> cust_add2 as "Address 2", cust_state as State, cust_zip1 as Zip
    -> from duck_cust where cust_num!=8 order by last;
+------------+---------+------------------------+-----------+-------+-------+
| Last       | First   | Address                | Address 2 | State | Zip   |
+------------+---------+------------------------+-----------+-------+-------+
| Beauvais   | Jet     | 1976 Stony Pointe Lane | 517       | OK    | 73102 |
| Billiards  | Monte   | 1976 Stony Pointe Lane | 142       | OK    | 73102 |
| Danson     | Raccoon | 1976 Stony Pointe Lane | 243       | OK    | 73102 |
| Davidson   | Wolf    | 1976 Stony Pointe Lane | 113       | OK    | 73102 |
| Filled     | Bob     | 1976 Stony Pointe Lane | 365       | OK    | 73102 |
| Gashlycrumb| Karen   | 3113 Picket Fence Lane | 0         | VT    | 41927 |
| Irishlord  | Red     | 1022 Sea of Rye        | A207      | WA    | 98601 |
| Kazui      | Wonko   | 42 Cube Farm Lane      | Gatehouse | CA    | 46362 |
| Montgomery | Chantel | 1567 Terra Cotta Way   | 0         | IL    | 89129 |
| Robert     | David   | 20113 Open Road Highway| #6        | AZ    | 00606 |
| Salisbury  | Jenny   | 9 Wishing Well Court   | 0         | KS    | 67048 |
| Seta       | Kevin   | 1976 Stony Pointe Lane | 301       | OK    | 73102 |
| Thegreat   | Vicki   | 2004 Singleton Dr.     | 0         | KS    | 67290 |
+------------+---------+------------------------+-----------+-------+-------+
13 rows in set (0.00 sec)

mysql> _
```

NOTE

The ORDER BY default is ascending, but you can force the issue by specifying ASC for ascending or DESC for descending after the field or fields specified as the ORDER BY value or values.

12. Remove the equal-to selection and order the output by ZIP code in descending order, using the following code:

```
SELECT cust_last AS last, cust_first AS first, cust_add1 AS address,
  cust_add2 AS "address 2", cust_state AS state, cust_zip1 AS zip
  FROM duck_cust ORDER BY Zip DESC;
```

```
Command Prompt - /mysql/bin/mysql -u root -p                          _ □ ×

mysql> select cust_last as last, cust_first as first, cust_add1 as address,
    -> cust_add2 as "address 2", cust_state as state, cust_zip1 as zip
    -> from duck_cust order by zip desc;
+------------+---------+------------------------+-----------+-------+-------+
| last       | first   | address                | address 2 | state | zip   |
+------------+---------+------------------------+-----------+-------+-------+
| Irishlord  | Red     | 1022 Sea of Rye        | A207      | WA    | 98601 |
| Montgomery | Chantel | 1567 Terra Cotta Way   | 0         | IL    | 89129 |
| Davidson   | Wolf    | 1976 Stony Pointe Lane | 113       | OK    | 73102 |
| Danson     | Raccoon | 1976 Stony Pointe Lane | 243       | OK    | 73102 |
| Filled     | Bob     | 1976 Stony Pointe Lane | 365       | OK    | 73102 |
| Billiards  | Monte   | 1976 Stony Pointe Lane | 142       | OK    | 73102 |
| Beauvais   | Jet     | 1976 Stony Pointe Lane | 517       | OK    | 73102 |
| Seta       | Kevin   | 1976 Stony Pointe Lane | 301       | OK    | 73102 |
| Thegreat   | Vicki   | 2004 Singleton Dr.     | 0         | KS    | 67290 |
| Salisbury  | Jenny   | 9 Wishing Well Court   | 0         | KS    | 67048 |
| Kazui      | Wonko   | 42 Cube Farm Lane      | Gatehouse | CA    | 46362 |
| Gashlycrumb| Karen   | 3113 Picket Fence Lane | 0         | VT    | 41927 |
| Kazui      | Wonko   | 1630 Revello Drive     | NULL      | CA    | 31626 |
| Robert     | David   | 20113 Open Road Highway| #6        | AZ    | 00606 |
+------------+---------+------------------------+-----------+-------+-------+
14 rows in set (0.00 sec)

mysql>
```

13. Make a list of customer names, cities, states, and ZIP codes with the output in ascending order by state and then city, using the following code:

```
SELECT cust_last AS last, cust_first AS first, cust_city AS city,
 cust_state AS state, cust_num AS number
 FROM duck_cust ORDER BY state, city ASC;
```

14. Repeat the command in step 13, but leave off the ASC.

```
mysql> select cust_last as last, cust_first as first, cust_city as city,
    -> cust_state as state, cust_num as number
    -> from duck_cust order by state, city;
+-------------+----------+----------------+-------+--------+
| last        | first    | city           | state | number |
+-------------+----------+----------------+-------+--------+
| Robert      | David    | Blacktop       | AZ    |      5 |
| Kazui       | Wonko    | Shady Hill     | CA    |      8 |
| Kazui       | Wonko    | Ulimpt         | CA    |      6 |
| Montgomery  | Chantel  | Chicago        | IL    |      4 |
| Thegreat    | Vicki    | Freedom        | KS    |      3 |
| Salisbury   | Jenny    | Meadowlark Hill| KS    |      1 |
| Davidson    | Wolf     | Elysium        | OK    |      9 |
| Danson      | Raccoon  | Elysium        | OK    |     10 |
| Filled      | Bob      | Elysium        | OK    |     11 |
| Billiards   | Monte    | Elysium        | OK    |     12 |
| Beauvais    | Jet      | Elysium        | OK    |     13 |
| Seta        | Kevin    | Elysium        | OK    |     14 |
| Gashlycrumb | Karen    | Fedora         | UT    |      7 |
| Irishlord   | Red      | Seacouver      | WA    |      2 |
+-------------+----------+----------------+-------+--------+
14 rows in set (0.01 sec)

mysql> _
```

You can see that the results are identical, because the ORDER BY default is ascending.

15. Use the following code to make a list of the last names beginning with the following partial characters:

```
SELECT cust_last AS LAST, cust_first AS FIRST,
cust_duckname AS DUCK,cust_num AS NMBR
FROM duck_cust WHERE cust_last LIKE "Dav%"
 OR cust_last LIKE "S%"
 OR cust_last LIKE "Be%";
```

The results are arranged in the order in which the records appear in the duck_cust table, which becomes clear when you look at the NMBR column.

16. Repeat the command in step 13, but add ORDER BY FIRST ASC to the end.

(continued)

This listing is arranged in ascending order by first name fields.

Project Summary

In this project, you used a variety of ways to manipulate and display the data in your tables, using the SELECT command in combination with the WHERE clause and a few simple options.

The LIMIT, DISTINCT, and AS options allow you to control how many records are displayed, whether specific fields are repeated in the display, and how the columns in the display table headers are labeled, respectively. The array of arithmetic operators and conditional reserved words (BETWEEN, LIKE, AND, and OR) enable you to use the WHERE clause to manipulate the display of table data to suit whatever need you require.

Now that you have had experience with these basic methods of reporting, Module 5 will cover increasingly complex ways to manipulate and present your data.

✓ Module 4 Mastery Check

1. What is the command to list all the data in the monsters table?

2. What is the command to list only the records with the values "vampire" and "werewolf" in the m_types field of the monsters table?

3. What does the following command do?

```
SELECT m_types FROM monsters LIMIT 13;
```

4. How do you view the records for the m_active field in the monsters table, starting with record 9 and listing the next 13 records?

5. How do you list each unique entry in the m_types field of the monsters table?

6. What is the code for listing the m_names, m_types, and m_active fields in the monsters table, using the headers Monster Names, Kind of Monster, and Day/Night/Both, respectively.

7. What are the two types of operators used for comparisons in the WHERE clause?

8. What are the four basic commands for viewing databases and tables?

9. What are two different ways that a WHERE clause could specify a numeric range of data between 42 and 113 in the field some_number?

10. How can you display entire records from the monsters table that contain "vampire" in the m_types field and a name beginning with the letter *D* in the m_names field?

11. How do you list m_numbers and m_names fields of every instance in the monsters table where you know the m_creators field should read "Joss" but due to a typo, the m_creators entry is not capitalized?

Module 5

Advanced Reporting

141

This module will expand on the report-generating skills learned in the previous module by explaining the most commonly used MySQL functions, including those for universal-, control flow–, aggregate-, mathematic-, string-, date-, and null-related manipulations of data. You will use the ORDER BY and GROUP BY clauses to focus your data output, and the JOIN commands to incorporate data from different tables into the same report.

CRITICAL SKILL

5.1 Use Functions in MySQL

In this skill, you will learn how to take advantage of many of the most-used functions in the MySQL arsenal. These functions allow you to quickly access and manipulate the data in your database tables. Using functions, you can define both simple and complex problems, and the MySQL functions will do the work for you.

Before you learn about the functions, you should be aware of how MySQL handles data in a mixed context. For instance, what if you were to give MySQL a nonsensical statement like this:

```
SELECT "3 bears"+"3 blind mice"+17;
```

MySQL would not give you an error for trying to add two strings to a number. Instead, it would ignore the string portion of the information, add the numeric portion of the information together, and return an answer of 23.

The MySQL database tries to interpret strings as numbers, if the context implies numbers, or as dates, if the context implies dates. It does this because MyISAM does not function with transactions, so it cannot roll back erroneous operations on a transactional level. Therefore, MySQL operates with a kind of doing-its-best philosophy. Occasionally, this may lead you to places you never intended to go when you place data in a mixed context; however, the side effect of this philosophy is that conversion functions are not necessary. MySQL will turn numbers into strings or strings into numbers automatically when the context requires it.

Using Universal Functions

Two functions within MySQL are so pervasive that they are universal: the IN function and the IF function. They are both applied to string and number values, used in the SELECT command, and involve kinds of comparisons.

IN Function

The IN function allows you to specify a comparison value for choosing table fields. It has the following syntax:

```
WHERE <comparison_field> IN(comparison_value1[, comparison_value2, … );
```

When the comparison matches, the fields specified in the SELECT command are chosen and returned to the command line. The comparison value does not need to be one of the fields specified in the SELECT portion of the command; it just needs to be in the WHERE ... IN portion.

For example, using the duck_cust table, to get a list with the customer number and first and last names for all the customers in a particular set of states, use the following code:

```
SELECT cust_num, cust_first, cust_last, cust_state
FROM duck_cust
WHERE cust_state IN("WA","CA","AZ");
```

The comparison works with number fields as well as strings. For example, the WHERE <comparison_field> IN value could be a list of customer numbers, like this:

```
SELECT cust_first, cust_last, cust_state
FROM duck_cust
WHERE cust_num IN(3,7,13,4,2);
```

As you can see, you can use the IN function only when you know the comparison values. It is practical when you don't need to list too many values. In theory, the list can be as long as you need it to be, but the longer the list, the less elegant the code and the more opportunity for mistakes in typing the comparison data into the command.

IF Function

The IF function allows you to set conditional evaluations with corresponding true and false values. Its syntax is as follows:

```
IF(<Boolean_test>, <value_if_true>, <value_if_false>)
```

The Boolean_test must evaluate to either a true (anything nonzero) or false (zero) value. The value_if_true and value_if_false can be a string, number, or date.

You can use the IF function more than once within a SELECT command by separating the functions with the standard comma separators.

The IF function is often used for creating columns for matrix-style reports or for counting instances of something (as opposed to adding up what those instances contain).

As an example, let's see how you could use the IF function to get information from a table with data about U.S. states. This table lists the population of each of the states last year and ten years ago, along with fields representing the capital city, number of congressional representatives, and region. Table 5-1 shows the table's fields and their defined types.

Field	Type
StateName	CHAR(15)
PopNow	INT
DecadePop	INT
NumReps	TINYINT
StateCap	CHAR(20)
Region	CHAR(15)

Table 5-1 Field Names and Types for the StatesPop Table

Suppose that you have received a request for a report that shows whether the population of each state is over or under 10 million, both now and a decade ago, listing the states by their regions. The following code will produce that report:

```
SELECT StateName AS State, Region,
IF(PopNow<10000000, "<10M",">10M") AS Current,
IF(DecadePop<1000000, "<10M",">10M") AS "Decade Ago",
FROM StatesPop
ORDER BY Region;
```

This gives you a report that has the following headers: State, Region, Current, and Decade Ago. The first two columns would hold the data from the StatesPop table, and the next two columns, depending on the range of their population, would hold either <10M or >10M.

As the code stands, if a state's population happens to be exactly 10 million, it will be placed in the greater-than 10 million category. This very well might be just fine for the type of data you are dealing with (population figures) and the generalized information required by the requested report. However, if you need a more detailed report, you can use more IF functions and more columns for the results. The following code gives you a report with more information.

```
SELECT StateName AS State, Region,
IF(PopNow<1000000, PopNow,"") AS "<1M Now",
IF(PopNow>1000000 AND PopNow<5000000, PopNow,"") AS "<5M Now",
IF(PopNow>5000000 AND PopNow<10000000, PopNow,"") AS "<10M Now ",
IF(PopNow>10000000 AND PopNow<15000000, PopNow,"") AS "<15M Now ",
IF(PopNow>15000000, PopNow,"") AS ">15M Now ",
IF(DecadePop<1000000, "<1M","") AS "<1M Then",
IF(DecadePop>1000000 AND DecadePop<5000000, "<5M","") AS "<1M Then",
IF(DecadePop>5000000 AND DecadePop<10000000, "<10M","") AS "<5M Then",
IF(DecadePop>10000000 AND DecadePop<15000000, "<15M","") AS "<15M Then",
IF(DecadePop>15000000, ">15M","") AS ">15M Then"
FROM StatesPop
ORDER BY Region;
```

This code returns a report that has 12 columns. For each state, it will display the state name and region, with population figures in Now and Then sections. All of the other columns in the Now and Then sections will remain blank, as indicated by the pair of double quotation marks with nothing between them.

IF functions can become as complicated as the permutations of your data and your grasp of conditional comparisons allow.

Using Control Flow Functions

Control flow functions allow you to set a value or condition, called a CASE, which is either compared against another value or evaluated as to its condition. You also specify a WHEN result for matching values or true conditions, and sometimes an alternate ELSE result for nonmatching values or false conditions. Control flow functions are normally used in situations where there is a specific set of results that apply to all, or nearly all, of the data. The IF function discussed in the previous section can also be considered a control flow function.

There are essentially two variations of the syntax for CASE...WHEN: one for comparing values and one for evaluating conditions.

The comparing values syntax looks like this:

```
CASE <value> WHEN <compare_value> THEN <result1>
[WHEN <compare_value2> THEN <result2> ...]
[ELSE <nonmatch_result>] END
```

The CASE *value* is specified in the code. The WHEN *compare_value* is drawn from the record of the table being read. The *result* is also specified in the code. As implied by the portion of the WHEN clause syntax in the square brackets, theoretically, you can have an unlimited number of WHEN clauses to compare the CASE value against. The square brackets around the ELSE clause indicate that it is also an optional part of the code. If it makes more sense in a particular situation for there to be no ELSE clause in the event of the CASE comparison not matching, you can omit the ELSE clause. The END is required in the syntax, and omitting it will cause a syntax error on the command line.

The conditional syntax is generally similar but the operational details of it differ:

```
CASE WHEN <condition> THEN <true_result1>
[WHEN <condition2> THEN <true_result2> ...]
[ELSE <false_result>] END
```

The CASE no longer has a specified value that the WHEN compares against. The WHEN has a condition, which is either true or false. If the condition is true, the *true_result* is used in the output. If the condition is false, and a *false_result* is supplied in the ELSE clause, it is used in the output.

In both variations of the CASE ... WHEN syntax, if no ELSE clause is specified and the comparison does not match or the condition is false, the NULL value will be returned.

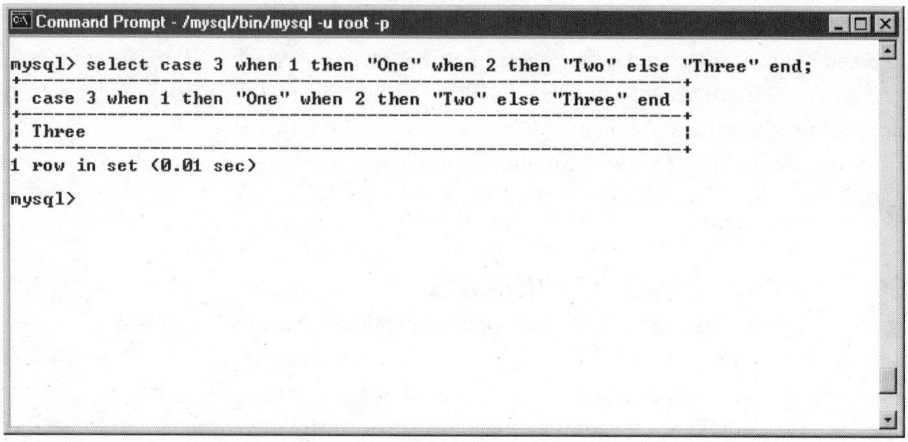

```
Command Prompt - /mysql/bin/mysql -u root -p                                    _ □ ×
mysql> select case 3 when 1 then "One" when 2 then "Two" else "Three" end;
+--------------------------------------------------------------------------+
| case 3 when 1 then "One" when 2 then "Two" else "Three" end |
+--------------------------------------------------------------------------+
| Three                                                                    |
+--------------------------------------------------------------------------+
1 row in set (0.01 sec)

mysql>
```

Figure 5-1 Using CASE...WHEN for comparing values

Here is an example of using the comparison value form of CASE...WHEN:

```
SELECT CASE 3 WHEN 1 THEN "One" WHEN 2 THEN "Two" ELSE "Three" END;
```

Figure 5-1 shows the resulting report. The value returned was the string Three, since the CASE value 3 did not match either of the comparison values (1 or 2) supplied in the WHEN clauses.

The following is an example of using CASE...WHEN for evaluating conditions:

```
SELECT CASE WHEN 9>7 THEN "TRUE" ELSE "FALSE" END AS "Results";
```

As shown in Figure 5-2, the value 9 is greater than the value 7, so the string TRUE was returned. The header for the report was Results, because it was specified using AS.

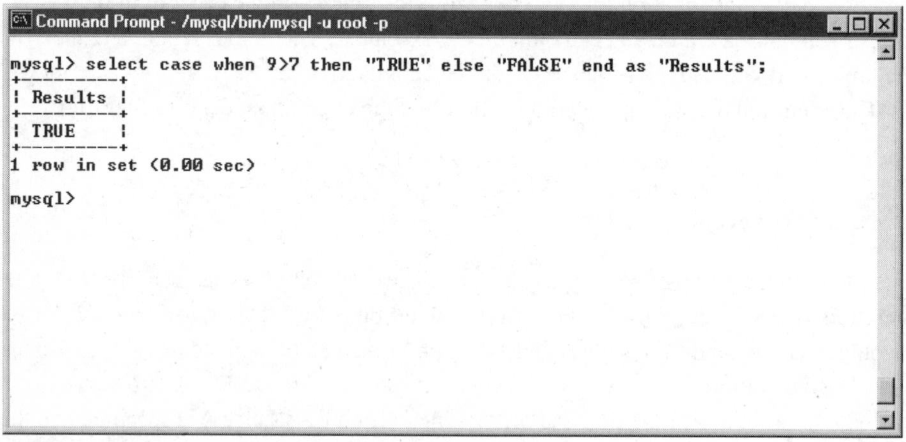

```
Command Prompt - /mysql/bin/mysql -u root -p                                    _ □ ×
mysql> select case when 9>7 then "TRUE" else "FALSE" end as "Results";
+---------+
| Results |
+---------+
| TRUE    |
+---------+
1 row in set (0.00 sec)

mysql>
```

Figure 5-2 Using CASE...WHEN for evaluating conditions

This example shows both variants of CASE...WHEN with no ELSE clause:

```
SELECT CASE "ferret" WHEN "cat" THEN "meow" WHEN "dog" THEN "woof" END;
SELECT CASE WHEN 4=5 THEN "large value of 4" END AS "results";
```

Figure 5-3 shows the results. Since the string "ferret" was not matched by the strings "cat" or "dog", and the condition 4=5 was evaluated as false, both lines of code returned NULL.

NOTE
The field type of the returned value is always the same as the field type of the result value following the first THEN in the command.

Using Aggregate Functions

This section describes *aggregate*, or collective, functions. These functions combine numbers by adding, averaging, or counting instances; give the high and low ranges of numbers; and provide a measurement of probability.

SUM, AVG, and COUNT

The SUM, AVG, and COUNT functions do what their names imply. Each action is performed on an expression, which can be as simple as a name indicating a column of fields or a more complex statement that has internal functions of its own.

```
Command Prompt - /mysql/bin/mysql -u root -p                              _ □ ×
mysql> select case "ferret" when "cat" then "meow" when "dog" then "woof" end;
+-----------------------------------------------------------------------+
| case "ferret" when "cat" then "meow" when "dog" then "woof" end |
+-----------------------------------------------------------------------+
| NULL                                                                  |
+-----------------------------------------------------------------------+
1 row in set (0.00 sec)

mysql> select case when 4=5 then "large value of 4" end as "results";
+---------+
| results |
+---------+
| NULL    |
+---------+
1 row in set (0.00 sec)

mysql>
mysql>
mysql>
mysql>
mysql>
mysql> _
```

Figure 5-3 Using CASE...WHEN without ELSE

The SUM function does simple addition of the content values in a column and returns a result. If there are no values in the specified column to add, it returns zero. However, if it references an empty set, where there are no rows in the specified table, SUM returns NULL. Here is an example:

```
SELECT SUM(num_sold) FROM Jan_sales;
```

The AVG function figures the averages of the specified expression, which means it adds all the value's contents together, and then divides that result by the number of instances added together in the first result. Here is an example:

```
SELECT student_name, AVG(quiz_scores) FROM class_scores;
```

The COUNT function adds the instances of the record field, as opposed to adding the value of the data in them. If the COUNT function is supplied with an expression (a field name, for instance), it will add one to its total for every non-NULL record field; however, if it is supplied with the asterisk wildcard (*), it starts at zero and adds one with each record it processes. This means that it does not matter whether the record field holds any data; it counts it regardless. Here is an example:

```
SELECT COUNT(renter_name) FROM apt_listings;
SELECT COUNT(*) FROM apt_listings;
```

The first of the two preceding commands would only add one to the COUNT if the rental listing showed a renter's name, so the count would end up showing the number of renters in the apartment complex. The second command would add one to the count for every record in the apt_listings table, so the count would end up showing how many apartments were in the complex, whether or not they were rented at the time.

MAX, MIN, and STD or STDDEV

The MIN and MAX functions evaluate the given fields and return the minimum or maximum value contained in them, respectively. They will evaluate both number and string types. Here is an example using a numeric field type:

```
SELECT MIN(rent_amount) from apt_listings;
SELECT MAX(rent_amount) from apt_listings;
```

This example would return the minimum rent amount and the maximum rent amount from the apt_listings table, giving you the costs of the cheapest and most expensive apartments.

Here is an example using a string field type:

```
SELECT MIN(StateName) FROM StatesPop;
SELECT MAX(StateName)FROM StatesPop;
```

This would return the first state name in an alphabetized list for MIN and the last state name in an alphabetized list for MAX.

NOTE

In the case of columns defined as ENUM and SET types, comparison is done using their string value, rather than their position relative to the set, as one might assume. MySQL has stated the intention to change a future version so that ENUM and SET are compared relative to their set position, but they do not function that way yet.

The STD and STDDEV functions are used for figuring standard deviation. They both function in the same way. The STDDEV function is provided only for compatibility with the Oracle database.

Calculating with Mathematical Functions

MySQL offers a wide variety of mathematical functions. Here, we will look at some of the more commonly used mathematical functions.

Trigonometry Functions

Simply put, *trigonometry* is the study of the properties of triangles. It is used in a variety of scientific disciplines like astronomy, geography, engineering. and physics. More specifically, the functions of trigonometry are used in calculus, linear algebra, and statistics.

DEGREES, RADIANS, and PI   The DEGREES and RADIANS functions deal with converting values. The DEGREES function returns the value of X converted into radians. The RADIANS function returns the value of X converted into degrees. Their syntax is as follows:

```
DEGREES(X)
RADIANS(X)
```

When you use the results of these two functions in a SELECT command—for instance, with a beginning value of 90 degrees—they will toggle their results between the two measurements. For example, RADIANS, given a value of 90 degrees, returns 1.5707963267949, and DEGREES, when given the value 1.5707963267949 radians, returns 90 degrees.

The function PI returns the value of pi. MySQL displays six decimal places as its default; however, internally, it uses the full double precision for computations. The function has parentheses, but no value is placed in them, as shown in the following syntax:

```
PI()
```

The SELECT PI(); command returns the value 3.141593.

SIN, COS, TAN, and COT   The SIN function is the trigonometric function sine. The COS function is the trigonometric function cosine. The TAN function is the trigonometric function tangent. The COT function is the trigonometric function cotangent. Their syntax is as follows:

```
SIN(X)
COS(X)
TAN(X)
COT(X)
```

In all of these functions, the value X is given in radians.

ASIN, ACOS, ATAN, and ATAN2   The ASIN function returns the arc sine of the value of X, meaning that the sine of the value it returns is the X supplied in the function. The ACOS function returns the arc cosine of the value of X, meaning that the cosine of the value it returns is the X supplied in the function. The ATAN function returns the arc tangent of the value of X, meaning that the tangent of the value it returns is the value X supplied in the function. Their syntax is as follows:

```
ASIN(X)
ACOS(X)
ATAN(X)
```

The ATAN function can also have two values input: X and Y. This returns the arc tangent of the two variables. As shown in the following syntax, MySQL allows you to use either the ATAN or ATAN2 notation when using this function, but the results are identical.

```
ATAN(X, Y)
ATAN2(X, Y)
```

NOTE

The ASIN function returns NULL if the supplied X value is not in the range of −1 to 1.

Logarithms and Powers

Logarithms started out as a way to multiply by adding before the advent of calculators. Powers are a convenient way of expressing large numbers by defining them as a smaller number raised to a stated power. For instance, 3^4 is equal to 3×3×3×3 or working it out the long way, 3×3=9, 9×3=27, 27×3=81. So, 3^4=81.

SQRT   The SQRT function returns the nonnegative square root of the supplied X value.

```
SQRT(X)
```

LOG, EXP, and POW   The LOG function returns the natural logarithm of the value X when it is supplied with only one value. When two values are supplied, it returns the logarithm of X for an arbitrary base supplied as the value B. That makes it the equivalent of LOG(X)/LOG(B).

```
LOG(X)
LOG(B, X)
```

NOTE

The two-value, arbitrary base version of LOG was added in MySQL version 4.0.3. In earlier versions, you must use LOG(X)/LOG(B) to reach the same result. The LOG2 function was also added in MySQL version 4.0.3. In earlier versions, you must use LOG(X)/LOG(2) to reach the same result.

The LOG10 function returns the logarithm of the supplied value X in base 10. The LOG2 function returns the logarithm of the supplied value X in base 2. LOG2 is useful for figuring out how much space, in bits, it takes to store a number.

```
LOG10(X)
LOG2(X)
```

The EXP function returns the value of e, which is defined as the base of natural logarithms, raised to the power of the supplied value X.

```
EXP(X)
```

The POW and POWER functions raise the value of X to the power of Y. This operation enables you to notate powers without the use of superscript notation. So, POW(2, 3) is equal to 2^3.

```
POW(X, Y)
POWER(X, Y)
```

MOD and %   The MOD function returns the modulo; that is, the remainder of the supplied value X divided by the supplied value M. You can also use the percent symbol (%) in place of MOD, which is the operator used for modulo in the C programming language.

```
MOD(X, M)
X % M
```

MySQL indicates that this function is safe to use with BIGINT values.

NOTE

In MySQL version 4.1 only, the syntax X MOD M is allowed, but it does not function in any version before or after.

ABS and SIGN   The ABS function returns the absolute value of the supplied value X.

```
ABS(X)
```

The SIGN function returns the sign of the supplied value X as –1, 0, or 1, depending on whether the value X is negative, zero, or positive, respectively. The SIGN function is used to test whether a given number X is positive, negative or zero. So, if the value of X were -42, the SIGN function would return a -1 value. If the value of X were 0, the SIGN function would return a 0 value. If the value of X were 9, the SIGN function would return a 1 value.

```
SIGN(X)
```

Rounding Functions

MySQL provides a lot of ways to deal with rounding numbers. The function ROUND is paradoxically the one that gives you the least control over how it goes about figuring your result.

ROUND, CEILING, FLOOR, and TRUNCATE   ROUND returns the supplied value X rounded to the nearest integer, and it has a two-variable form that allows you to specify, with the value D, the number of decimal places you want to round to. The syntax for the two versions of ROUND is as follows:

```
ROUND(X)
ROUND(X, D)
```

However, when the value in question is halfway between two integers (.5), the direction ROUND rounds is controlled by the C Library implementation, which varies depending on which operating system you are using. Some of operating systems always round up; some always round down; and some always round toward zero.

If you want more control over how your number is rounded, or you don't want to worry about how the particular operating system you're using deals with the 0.5 issue, you would be better off using TRUNCATE, CEILING, or FLOOR.

The CEILING function always rounds upwards. That means it returns the smallest integer value that is *not less* than the supplied value X.

```
CEILING(X)
CEIL(X)
```

NOTE

In MySQL version 4.0.6, the alias CEIL was added; however, the return value is converted to BIGINT.

The FLOOR function always rounds downward. That means that it returns the largest integer value *not greater* than the value of the supplied X.

FLOOR(X)

NOTE

The return value of the FLOOR function is converted to BIGINT.

The TRUNCATE function simply returns the supplied value X truncated to the number of decimal places equal to the supplied value D. If the supplied value for D is zero, there will be no decimal places returned.

TRUNCATE(X, D)

In the case of a negative number supplied for the D value, the whole part of the number is zeroed out. For instance, the command TRUNCATE(113, -2) returns the value 100; TRUNCATE(113, -1) returns the value 110.

Table 5-2 shows the rounding functions and results of using these functions with both positive and negative numbers. Remember that if you try the ROUND example with the .5 value on your system, you may get a different answer, depending on whether your computer's halfway default is to round up or down.

Positive	Result	Negative	Result
ROUND(7.5)	7	ROUND(-7.5)	-8
ROUND(7.53)	8	ROUND(-7.53)	-8
ROUND(7.49)	7	ROUND(-7.49)	-7
CEILING(7.5)	8	CEILING(-7.5)	-8
FLOOR(7.5)	7	FLOOR(-7.5)	-8
TRUNCATE(7.5, 0)	7	TRUNCATE(-7.5, 0)	-7

Table 5-2 Rounding Functions on Positive and Negative Numbers

Random Function

The RAND function has two versions: one with a specified value *N*, and one with no specified value. If no value *N* is specified, then RAND returns a value between zero and one. If a value *N* is specified, it is used as a seed value, which results in a repeatable sequence.

```
RAND()
RAND(N)
```

The RAND function is meant to be a quick and easy way to generate returns that are random enough for a given situation, and portable between identical versions of MySQL, rather than being a perfect random generator.

Random Numbers   If you use RAND with a specified *N* value, the result will be repeatable. For instance, the value returned for RAND(3) is, and will always be, 0.90576975597606. If no *N* value is specified, the return will be a more or less random number between zero and one.

If you run three RAND() commands, the return values may differ widely within the function's given range; however, the range between zero and one is a small enough sample, statistically speaking, for results to appear patterned. You can receive the same result twice in a row, for instance. The RAND function is not perfectly random, but it is serviceable for most requirements. Any time two commands in the RAND(*X*) syntax have the same *X* value, the result is always the same.

Random Strings   The RAND function can also be used to display a more or less random selection from a SELECT command by using it as the variable in an ORDER BY clause. The following example results in the random output of a single instance of the field cust_duckname from the duck_cust table:

```
SELECT cust_duckname FROM duck_cust ORDER BY RAND() LIMIT 1;
```

As long as your MySQL version is newer than 3.23, you can also use the RAND function with a wildcard SELECT statement, instead of needing to specify a column. The following example displays three adequately random, entire records from the duck_cust table's contents:

```
SELECT * FROM duck_cust ORDER BY RAND() LIMIT 3;
```

NOTE

If you use the RAND function in a WHERE clause, the RAND will be reevaluated every time the WHERE is executed.

Manipulating Strings with String Functions

String functions manipulate strings in some of the same ways mathematical functions manipulate numbers. They can add and subtract data from existing strings, make new strings, and edit the data already contained in strings. This section will cover the main string functions, and then cover those functions used to compare strings and manipulate the data in them.

Main String Functions

The main string functions are the ones most often used to handle strings and the information held in them. They add strings or portions of strings together, pick out parts of strings based on position or delimiters, search for strings in strings, change strings in other strings, and calculate the length of strings.

CONCAT   The CONCAT function is short for concatenate, which means to link together in a series or chain. Its syntax allows for one or more parameters that it will link together and return a result of a single string.

```
CONCAT(<string1>[, <string2>, … ])
```

If numeric data is supplied as an argument in CONCAT, it automatically converts the data into its equivalent string form. Also, if any of the supplied data is NULL, CONCAT returns the result NULL. Figure 5-4 shows some basic examples of the CONCAT function.

```
Command Prompt - /mysql/bin/mysql -u root -p                    _ □ ×
mysql> select concat("Duck", "Wear");
+------------------------+
| concat("Duck", "Wear") |
+------------------------+
| DuckWear               |
+------------------------+
1 row in set (0.00 sec)

mysql> select concat("Duck", "Wear", NULL);
+------------------------------+
| concat("Duck", "Wear", NULL) |
+------------------------------+
| NULL                         |
+------------------------------+
1 row in set (0.00 sec)

mysql> select concat("Duck", "Wear", 3000);
+------------------------------+
| concat("Duck", "Wear", 3000) |
+------------------------------+
| DuckWear3000                 |
+------------------------------+
1 row in set (0.00 sec)

mysql>
```

Figure 5-4 Basic examples of the CONCAT function

The CONCAT_WS function, which stands for CONCAT With Separator, allows you to use the first argument to indicate a separator for the rest of the arguments, and this separator will appear between the arguments in the resulting string.

```
CONCAT_WS(<separator>, <string1>[, <string2>, … ])
```

Unlike CONCAT, if a NULL appears in the strings supplied to the CONCAT_WS function, it is simply ignored. If, however, NULL is used as the indicated separator, a NULL value is returned. Figure 5-5 shows examples of using CONCAT_WS.

SUBSTRING and SUBSTRING_INDEX The SUBSTRING and SUBSTRING_INDEX functions both pick part of a string to return in a string result, but they operate based on different criteria. SUBSTRING makes its pick based on position within the string, and SUBSTRING_INDEX makes its pick based on delimiters and their occurrence within the string. The following syntax shows four variations of SUBSTRING and the single syntax for SUBSTRING_INDEX.

```
SUBSTRING(<string>, <position>)
SUBSTRING(<string> FROM <position>)
SUBSTRING(<string>, <position>, <length>)
SUBSTRING(<string> FROM <position> FOR <length>)
SUBSTRING_INDEX(<string>, <delimiter>, <count>)
```

The first two SUBSTRING syntax formats give the same result; the only difference is how they are written. These functions count in from the start of the string to the amount of the specified *position*, and beginning there, return the remainder of the string.

Figure 5-5 Examples of the CONCAT_WS function

The third and fourth SUBSTRING syntax formats are also variations that produce the same result. SUBSTRING functions with a *length* parameter count in to the place indicated by the *position* parameter, but they count from that place using the *length* parameter, and then return the string that lies between those two specified places. Figure 5-6 shows examples of the SUBSTRING function variations.

The SUBSTRING_INDEX function works in a similar manner, but it counts the specified *delimiter* instead of *position* within the *string*. If the *count* value is positive, SUBSTRING_INDEX returns the portion of the string that is to the left of, or before, the final *delimiter*. If the *count* value is negative, it returns everything to the right, or behind, the final *delimiter*. When the *count* is a positive number, the function counts the appearances of the *delimiter* starting from the left, or beginning, of the string. When the *count* is a negative number, SUBSTRING_INDEX counts the appearances of the *delimiter* starting from the right, or end, of the string. Figure 5-7 shows examples of using SUBSTRING_INDEX with both positive and negative *count* values.

INSTR, REPLACE, and LENGTH   The INSTR function, short for In String, returns the numeric position of the beginning of specified *substring* within the specified *string*.

```
INSTR(<string>, <substring>)
```

The REPLACE function takes three values: *string*, *from_string*, and *to_string*. It finds the portion of the *string* that matches the *from_string* value and replaces it with the *to_string* value, and then returns the new version of the *string*. If it does not find the specified *from_string* value, it returns the *string* value unaltered.

```
REPLACE(<string>, <from_string>, <to_string>);
```

Figure 5-6 Examples of the SUBSTRING function

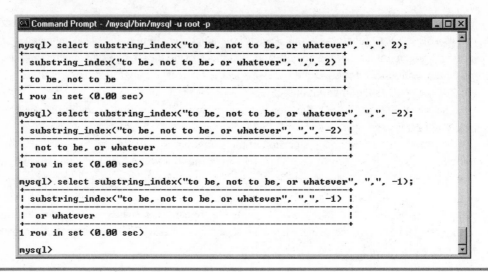

Figure 5-7 Examples of SUBSTRING_INDEX

The LENGTH function takes in a string and returns the numeric value of the length. If a character within the string takes multiple bytes to store, LENGTH counts those bytes separately.

```
LENGTH(<string>)
```

Figure 5-8 shows examples of INSTR, REPLACE, and LENGTH.

```
Command Prompt - /mysql/bin/mysql -u root -p
mysql> select instr("effulgent", "gent");
+-----------------------------+
| instr("effulgent", "gent") |
+-----------------------------+
|                          6 |
+-----------------------------+
1 row in set (0.00 sec)
mysql> select replace("effulgent", "gent", "gence");
+---------------------------------------+
| replace("effulgent", "gent", "gence") |
+---------------------------------------+
| effulgence                            |
+---------------------------------------+
1 row in set (0.00 sec)
mysql> select length("fulgent");
+-------------------+
| length("fulgent") |
+-------------------+
|                 7 |
+-------------------+
1 row in set (0.00 sec)
mysql> _
```

Figure 5-8 Examples of the INSTR, REPLACE, and LENGTH functions

Comparison String Functions

Comparison string functions allow you to compare two strings and get a return that tells you whether they are alike, not alike, or sometimes, partially alike.

LIKE   The LIKE function, in its most basic form, allows you to compare one specified string against another, resulting in the return of a one if true or zero if false. You can also use two wildcard values: percent (%) to match any number of characters, including zero characters, and underscore (_) to match one, and only one, character. If you are trying to search for one of those two wildcard symbols, you must use the escape symbol, the backslash (\), in front of the wildcard symbol you are comparing against. If you want to use a backslash in a comparison string, you can specify a different escape symbol with the ESCAPE clause.

```
<string> LIKE <pattern_string> [ESCAPE <'alternate_escape_character'>]
```

Figure 5-9 shows examples of the LIKE function, its wildcard symbols, and setting a different escape symbol.

STRCMP   The STRCMP function, short for String Comparison, takes two arguments, and returns a number depending on whether they partially match or don't match. If the two strings match, STRCMP returns a value of zero. If the first argument is a smaller value than the second argument, according to the current sort order, STRCMP returns a value of negative one. For any other comparison result, STRCMP returns a value of one.

```
STRCMP(<string1>, <string2>)
```

NOTE

Starting with MySQL version 4.0, STRCMP ceased to be case-sensitive unless one or both of the arguments are binary strings.

Figure 5-10 shows examples resulting in the three return values of STRCMP:

- In the first example, the strings "duck" and "Duck" return a value of 0, because STRCMP perceives them as matching since it is not case-sensitive.

- In the second example, the strings "duck" and "wolf" return a value of -1, because the first string "duck" comes before the second string "wolf" in an alphanumeric sort.

- In the third example, the strings "duck" and "bat" return a value of 1, because they do not match, nor is the first string smaller according to the sort order.

- In the fourth example, the two strings from the third example are in the reverse order, making "bat" the first string and "duck" the second string, and STRCMP returns a value of -1, because the first string comes before the second string in the sort order.

```
Command Prompt - /mysql/bin/mysql -u root -p                    _ □ ×

mysql> select "Monte!" like "Monte_";
+------------------------+
| "Monte!" like "Monte_" |
+------------------------+
|                      1 |
+------------------------+
1 row in set (0.00 sec)

mysql> select "Monte!" like "Monte\_";
+-------------------------+
| "Monte!" like "Monte\_" |
+-------------------------+
|                       0 |
+-------------------------+
1 row in set (0.00 sec)

mysql> select "Monte!Bass" like "Monte\_%";
+-----------------------------+
| "Monte!Bass" like "Monte\_%" |
+-----------------------------+
|                           0 |
+-----------------------------+
1 row in set (0.00 sec)

mysql> select "Monte_Bass" like "Monte\_%";
+-----------------------------+
| "Monte_Bass" like "Monte\_%" |
+-----------------------------+
|                           1 |
+-----------------------------+
1 row in set (0.00 sec)

mysql> select "Monte_Bass" like "Monte\_";
+----------------------------+
| "Monte_Bass" like "Monte\_" |
+----------------------------+
|                          0 |
+----------------------------+
1 row in set (0.00 sec)

mysql> select "Monte\Bass" like "M%!\Bas_" escape "!";
+--------------------------------------------+
| "Monte\Bass" like "M%!\Bas_" escape "!"    |
+--------------------------------------------+
|                                          1 |
+--------------------------------------------+
1 row in set (0.00 sec)

mysql> select "Michael\Base" like "M%!\Bas_" escape "!";
+---------------------------------------------+
| "Michael\Base" like "M%!\Bas_" escape "!"   |
+---------------------------------------------+
|                                           1 |
+---------------------------------------------+
1 row in set (0.00 sec)

mysql> _
```

Figure 5-9 Examples of the LIKE function

Manipulating String Functions

A variety of string functions allow you to manipulate the data in useful ways. The ones described here are some of the most useful string functions.

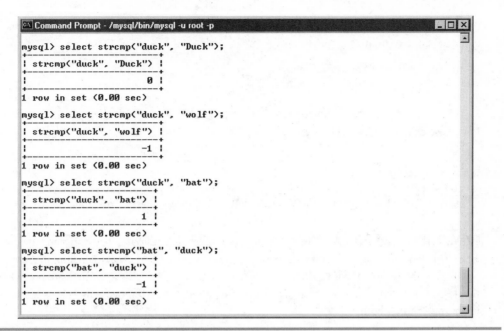

Figure 5-10 Examples of the STRCMP function

REVERSE and REPEAT

The REVERSE function takes in a *string* and returns it in reverse order.

REVERSE(<*string*>)

The REPEAT function takes in a *string* and a *count* and returns a string with the contents of the specified *string* repeated *count* times.

REPEAT(<*string*>, <*count*>)

For example, the command SELECT REVERSE("desserts"); returns the string value stressed. The command SELECT REPEAT("Love", 3); returns the string value LoveLoveLove.

LPAD, RPAD, UPPER, and LOWER

The LPAD and RPAD functions, short for Left Padding and Right Padding, respectively, take in a *string*, *length*, and *padding_string*, and return a string that contains the specified *string* enlarged using the *padding_string* until it equals the value of *length*. The LPAD function pads to the left of the string, and the RPAD function pads to the right of the string.

```
LPAD(<string>, <length>, <padding_string>)
RPAD(<string>, <length>, <padding_string>)
```

The UPPER and LOWER functions take in a string and convert it to all uppercase or all lowercase characters, respectively.

```
UPPER(<string>)
LOWER(<string>)
```

Figure 5-11 shows examples of the LPAD, RPAD, UPPER, and LOWER functions.

TRIM, LTRIM, and RTRIM   The TRIM function takes in a *remove_string* and a *string*, and trims the *remove_string* off the specified *string* at the beginning, end, or both, using the reserved word LEADING, TRAILING, or BOTH. If no specifiers are provided, the default is BOTH. If no *remove_string* is supplied, TRIM removes any spaces at the beginning, end, or both.

```
TRIM(<string>)
TRIM([[LEADING|TRAILING|BOTH] <remove_string> FROM] <string>)
```

```
Command Prompt - /mysql/bin/mysql -u root -p

mysql> select lpad("Arrow", 10, "->");
+-------------------------+
| lpad("Arrow", 10, "->") |
+-------------------------+
| ->->-Arrow              |
+-------------------------+
1 row in set (0.00 sec)
mysql> select rpad("Arrow", 13, "->");
+-------------------------+
| rpad("Arrow", 13, "->") |
+-------------------------+
| Arrow->->->->           |
+-------------------------+
1 row in set (0.00 sec)
mysql> select upper("caution");
+------------------+
| upper("caution") |
+------------------+
| CAUTION          |
+------------------+
1 row in set (0.00 sec)
mysql> select lower("DuckWear");
+------------------+
| lower("DuckWear") |
+------------------+
| duckwear          |
+------------------+
1 row in set (0.00 sec)
mysql>
```

Figure 5-11   Examples of the LPAD, RPAD, UPPER, and LOWER functions

If you are removing spaces from only one side of the string or the other, you can also use LTRIM or RTRIM, which take in a string and remove any spaces from the left or right side of the string, respectively.

```
LTRIM(<string>)
RTRIM(<string>)
```

Figure 5-12 shows examples of the TRIM, LTRIM, and RTRIM functions.

LEFT, MID, and RIGHT   The LEFT and RIGHT functions take in a *string* and *length*, and return the leftmost or rightmost *length* of the *string*, respectively. LEFT counts in to the value of *length* from the left, and RIGHT counts in to the value of *length* from the right.

```
LEFT(<string>, <length>)
RIGHT(<string>, <length>)
```

The MID function works exactly like the SUBSTRING(<string>, <position>, <length>) function, with the added bonus that it is shorter to type.

```
MID(<string>, <position>, <length>)
```

```
Command Prompt - /mysql/bin/mysql -u root -p                          _ □ ×
mysql> select trim("    Frankenduck    ");
+---------------------------+
| trim("    Frankenduck    ") |
+---------------------------+
| Frankenduck               |
+---------------------------+
1 row in set (0.00 sec)
mysql> select trim(leading "$" from "$$$$Money$$$");
+-------------------------------------+
| trim(leading "$" from "$$$$Money$$$") |
+-------------------------------------+
| Money$$$                            |
+-------------------------------------+
1 row in set (0.00 sec)
mysql> select ltrim("    $$$ Money $$$");
+-------------------------+
| ltrim("    $$$ Money $$$") |
+-------------------------+
| $$$ Money $$$           |
+-------------------------+
1 row in set (0.00 sec)
mysql> select rtrim("    $$$ Money $$$    ");
+-----------------------------+
| rtrim("    $$$ Money $$$    ") |
+-----------------------------+
|     $$$ Money $$$           |
+-----------------------------+
1 row in set (0.00 sec)
mysql> _
```

Figure 5-12 Examples of the TRIM, LTRIM, and RTRIM functions

Given the string "John Paul George Ringo", the LEFT, RIGHT, and MID functions work as follows:

- SELECT LEFT("John Paul George Ringo", 4) will return the string value "John", because it starts at the left of the string and selects the first four characters it finds.

- SELECT RIGHT("John Paul George Ringo", 5) will return the string value "Ringo", because it starts at the right of the string and selects the first five characters it finds.

- SELECT MID("John Paul George Ringo", 11, 6) will return the string value "George", because it counts in from the left of the string 11 places, starts counting anew from that eleventh place, and selects the next six characters it finds.

CHAR and ASCII   The CHAR function interprets the arguments as integers and returns the characters given by the ASCII code for those numbers. Null values are ignored.

```
CHAR(N, …)
```

The ASCII function takes in a string and returns the ASCII code value for the leftmost character in the string. If a numeric value is supplied instead of a string, MySQL will automatically convert it to its string equivalent. This function is case-sensitive.

```
ASCII(<string>)
```

As an example, the command SELECT CHAR(74, 101, 116) returns the string value "Jet". The command SELECT ASCII("James") returns the ASCII code value for the leftmost character of the string, in this case, 74. If either "Jet" or "James" had a lowercase *j*, the corresponding ASCII number would be 106.

Using Date Functions

The date functions allow you to manipulate time-related information. You can use them to specify date and time formats, and to get date and time information.

DATE_FORMAT

The DATE_FORMAT function takes in a *date* and a *format*, and then returns a string containing the *date* displayed in accordance with the specified *format*.

```
DATE_FORMAT(<date>, <format>)
```

You indicate the formatting by using a selection of symbols from a set of 22 specifiers, as shown in Table 5-3.

Specifier	Description
Day	
%a	Day of the week in 3-letter abbreviation (Sun, Mon, etc.)
%D	Day of the month abbreviated (1st, 2nd, etc.)
%d	Day of the month in 2-digit numeric indicator (00-31)
%e	Day of the month in numeric indicator (0-31)
%j	Day of the year in 3-digit display (001-366)
%W	Day of the week in full word (Sunday, Monday, etc.)
%w	Day of the week in numeric form (1=Sunday, 2=Monday, etc.)
Month	
%b	Month of the year in 3-letter abbreviation (Jan, Feb, etc.)
%c	Month of the year in numeric indicator (0-12)
%M	Month of the year in full word (January, February, etc.)
%m	Month of the year in 2-digit numeric indicator (00–12)
Year	
%X	Year in 4-digit numeric display, beginning with Sunday, for use with %V
%x	Year in 4-digit numeric display, beginning with Sunday, for use with %v
%Y	Year in 4-digit numeric display
%y	Year in 2-digit numeric display
Week	
%U	Week of the year (00–53), beginning with Sunday
%u	Week of the year (00–53), beginning with Monday
%V	Week of the year (01–53), beginning with Sunday, for use with %X
%v	Week of the year (01–53), beginning with Sunday, for use with %x
Hour	
%H	Hour in 2-digit, 24-hour time (00–23)
%h, %I	Hour 2-digit, in 12-hour time (01–12)
%k	Hour in 24-hour time (0–23)
%l	Hour in 12-hour time (1–12)

Table 5-3 DATE_FORMAT Specifiers

Minute	
%i	Minute in 2-digit display (00–59)
%p	Before noon or after noon (AM or PM)
Second	
%f	Microseconds in 6-digit display (000000–999999)
%S, %s	Seconds in 2-digit numeric indicator (00–59)
Time	
%r	Time in 12-hour display, formatted *HH:MM:SS*, with AM or PM
%T	Time in 24-hour display, formatted *HH:MM:SS*
Percent	
%%	Display of the percent symbol (%)

Table 5-3 DATE_FORMAT Specifiers *(continued)*

Figure 5-13 shows examples of the DATE_FORMAT functions using the specifiers %W, %M, %d, and %Y, which refer to the day of the week, the month name, the date, and the four-digit year, respectively.

NOW and INTERVAL

The NOW function does not take any arguments. It returns the current date and time in the following string format: *YYYY-MM-DD HH:MM:SS*. If you add a + 0, it returns the current date and time in the following numeric format: *YYYYMMDDHHMMSS*.

```
NOW()
NOW() + 0
```

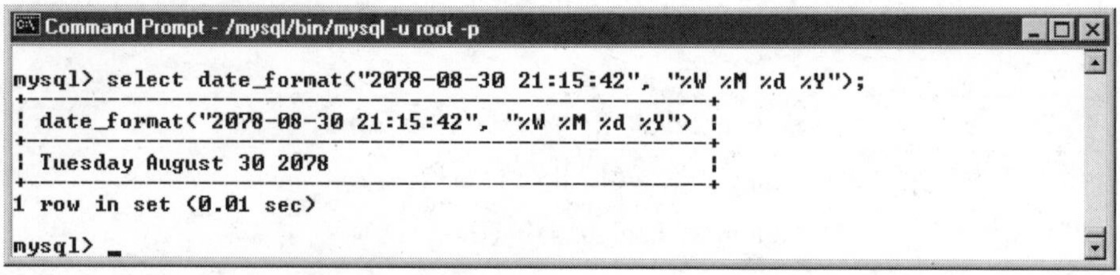

```
Command Prompt - /mysql/bin/mysql -u root -p                              _ □ ×
mysql> select date_format("2078-08-30 21:15:42", "%W %M %d %Y");
+--------------------------------------------------------+
| date_format("2078-08-30 21:15:42", "%W %M %d %Y")      |
+--------------------------------------------------------+
| Tuesday August 30 2078                                 |
+--------------------------------------------------------+
1 row in set (0.01 sec)

mysql>
```

Figure 5-13 Examples of the DATE_FORMAT function

You can add the INTERVAL clause to the NOW function by using the plus sign (+) and one of the following words with a *count* and date/time modifier: YEAR, MONTH, DAY, HOUR, MINUTE, or SECOND.

```
NOW() + INTERVAL <count> <date/time_modifier>
```

For example, NOW() + INTERVAL 8 DAY; returns the date and time eight days from the moment the command is run.

CAUTION

The INTERVAL modifiers are singular words, even if referring to multiple instances. Changing the INTERVAL modifiers to YEARS, MONTHS, DAYS, HOURS, MINUTES, or SECONDS will result in an error message.

DAYNAME, DAYOFWEEK, and DAYOFYEAR

The DAYNAME function takes in a string containing a *date* in the *YYYY-MM-DD* format, or a numeric *date* in the *YYYYMMDD* format, and returns the day of the week for the specified *date*. Any other format returns a NULL.

```
DAYNAME(<date>)
```

For example, the string version of the DAYNAME command SELECT DAYNAME ("2048-08-19") returns a value of Wednesday. The numeric version SELECT DAYNAME(20911204) returns a value of Tuesday.

The DAYOFWEEK function takes in a *date*, in either the string or numeric format, and returns a numeric value for the day of the week instead of a string value. It begins counting the day of the week with Sunday: 1=Sunday, 2=Monday, 3=Tuesday, 4=Wednesday, 5=Thursday, 6=Friday, and 7=Saturday.

```
DAYOFWEEK(<date>)
```

The DAYOFYEAR function takes in a *date*, in either the string or numeric format, and returns a numeric value for the day of the year. It begins counting on January 1, so 1=January 1 and so on until 365=December 31, unless it is a leap year, in which case, 366=December 31.

```
DAYOFYEAR(<date>)
```

For example, SELECT DAYOFWEEK("2048-08-19") returns the value 4, which corresponds with Wednesday. The command SELECT DAYOFYEAR(20911231) returns the value 365, because it is the last day of the year, given that 2091 is not a leap year.

Getting Information with Null-related Functions

Null-related functions are used to control the flow of data into your output. They allow you to make a return of a NULL value into a communicative output that has more meaning than a blank field.

IFNULL

The IFNULL function takes in two expressions, which can be string or numeric in format. If *expression1* is *not* NULL, the IFNULL function returns *expression1*. If *expression1* is NULL, the IFNULL function returns *expression2*. The return value does not alter the expression's type. For example, if you specify a string in the IFNULL function, a string is returned.

```
IFNULL(<expression1>, <expression2>)
```

NULLIF

The NULLIF function also takes in two expressions of either type. If *expression1* is equal to *expression2*, NULL is returned; otherwise, *expression1* is returned. In the NULLIF function, the *expression2* is never a return value.

```
NULLIF (<expression1>, <expression2>)
```

You can obtain the same result by using a CASE...WHEN statement like CASE WHEN *expression2=expression2* THEN NULL ELSE *expression1*, but plainly, the NULLIF function is the simpler, more efficient way of expressing the condition.

Figure 5-14 shows examples of the IFNULL and NULLIF functions. Since the syntax is almost identical, it's important to verify that you are using the one you actually need.

Progress Check

1. When do you use the control flow functions?

2. What actions do aggregate functions perform?

3. What main string function joins one or more strings together into a single string?

4. Which string functions compare?

5. Which two string functions change case?

6. What is the function used to control the way a date and/or time looks in the output?

7. The syntax of the command CASE WHEN *expression2=expression2* THEN NULL ELSE is the equivalent to what more concise function?

---

1. The control flow functions are used in situations where a specific set of results applies to all, or nearly all, of the data.

2. The aggregate functions combine numbers by adding, averaging, or counting instances; give the high and low ranges of numbers; and provide a measurement of probability.

3. The CONCAT function allows for one or more parameters that it will link together to return a result of a single string.

4. The LIKE and STRCMP functions do comparisons.

5. The UPPER and LOWER string functions change case to all uppercase or all lowercase, respectively.

6. The DATE_FORMAT function allows you to control the look of a date and/or time in your output.

7. It is equivalent to the NULLIF function.

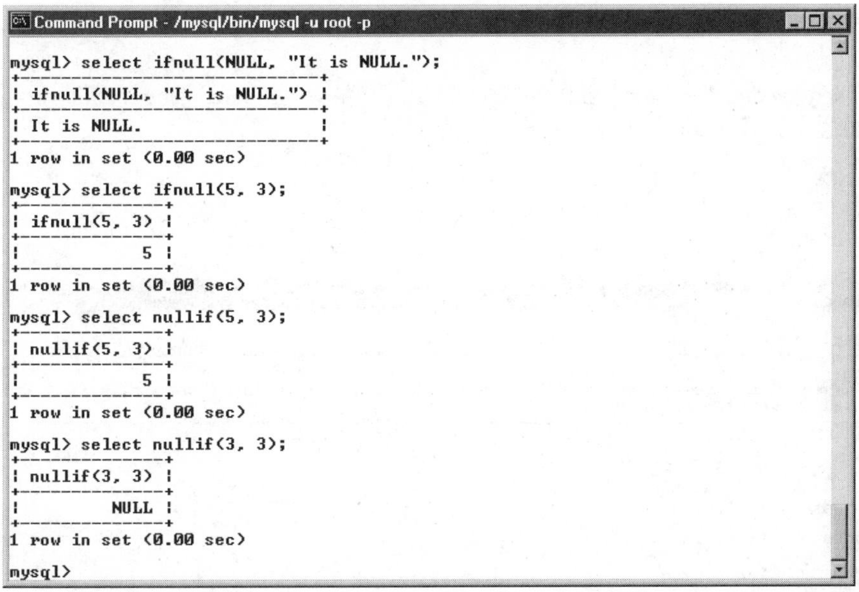

```
Command Prompt - /mysql/bin/mysql -u root -p                    _ □ ✕

mysql> select ifnull(NULL, "It is NULL.");
+-----------------------------+
| ifnull(NULL, "It is NULL.") |
+-----------------------------+
| It is NULL.                 |
+-----------------------------+
1 row in set (0.00 sec)

mysql> select ifnull(5, 3);
+--------------+
| ifnull(5, 3) |
+--------------+
|            5 |
+--------------+
1 row in set (0.00 sec)

mysql> select nullif(5, 3);
+--------------+
| nullif(5, 3) |
+--------------+
|            5 |
+--------------+
1 row in set (0.00 sec)

mysql> select nullif(3, 3);
+--------------+
| nullif(3, 3) |
+--------------+
|         NULL |
+--------------+
1 row in set (0.00 sec)

mysql>
```

Figure 5-14 Examples of the IFNULL and NULLIF functions

Project 5-1   Use MySQL Functions to Create Reports

This project gives you an overview of using MySQL functions and shows how some of them might be used in concert to produce more sophisticated output in your reports. To make use of some of the mathematical functions, you will begin by building a table that has more numeric content.

Step by Step

1. Create a table called `duck_sales`, using the following command

```
USE duckwear;

CREATE TABLE duck_sales(
design_num MEDIUMINT NOT NULL AUTO_INCREMENT,
design_name CHAR(20),
winter_sales INT,
spring_sales INT,
summer_sales INT,
fall_sales INT,
design_category CHAR(13),
```

(continued)

```
primary key(design_num)
)type=MyISAM;
```

2. Insert the data shown in Table 5-4 into the `duck_sales` table, using the following `INSERT` command as a template.

```
INSERT INTO duck_sales
VALUES
(NULL, 'Santa_Duck', 1067, 200, 150, 0, 'Holiday');
```

```
c:\mysql\bin\mysql.exe                                                    _ □ ×

mysql> select * from duck_sales;
+------------+------------------+-------------+-------------+-------------+-----
-----------+------------------+
| design_num | design_name      | winter_sales | spring_sales | summer_sales | fal
l_sales     | design_category  |
+------------+------------------+-------------+-------------+-------------+-----
-----------+------------------+
|          1 | Santa_Duck       |        1067 |         200 |         150 |
267 | Holiday          |
|          2 | Dr_Duck          |         970 |         770 |         561 |
486 | Profession       |
|          3 | Duckula          |          53 |          13 |          21 |
856 | Literary         |
|          4 | Fire_Duck        |         782 |         357 |         168 |
250 | Profession       |
|          5 | Bunny_Duck       |         589 |         795 |         367 |
284 | Holiday          |
|          6 | Duckspeare       |         953 |         582 |         336 |
489 | Literary         |
|          7 | Sherlock_Duck    |         752 |         657 |         259 |
478 | Literary         |
|          8 | Duck_O_Lantern   |          67 |          23 |          83 |
543 | Holiday          |
|          9 | Rodeo_Duck       |         673 |          48 |         625 |
52 | Profession       |
+------------+------------------+-------------+-------------+-------------+-----
-----------+------------------+
9 rows in set (0.00 sec)

mysql>
```

Name	Winter	Spring	Summer	Fall	Category
Santa_Duck	1067	200	150	267	Holiday
Dr_Duck	970	770	531	486	Profession
Duckula	53	13	21	856	Literary
Fire_Duck	782	357	168	250	Profession
Bunny_Duck	589	795	367	284	Holiday
Duckspeare	953	582	336	489	Literary
Sherlock_Duck	752	657	259	478	Literary
Duck_O_Lantern	67	23	83	543	Holiday
Rodeo_Duck	673	48	625	52	Profession

Table 5-4 Data for the `duck_sales` Table

3. Use the following code to make a report that lists only the categories Profession and Holiday.

```
SELECT design_name AS Name, design_category AS Category
FROM duck_sales
WHERE design_category IN("Profession", "Holiday");
```

```
c:\mysql\bin\mysql.exe                                                    _ □ X

mysql> select design_name as Name, design_category as Category
    -> from duck_sales
    -> where design_category in("Profession", "Holiday");
+----------------+------------+
| Name           | Category   |
+----------------+------------+
| Santa_Duck     | Holiday    |
| Dr_Duck        | Profession |
| Fire_Duck      | Profession |
| Bunny_Duck     | Holiday    |
| Duck_O_Lantern | Holiday    |
| Rodeo_Duck     | Profession |
+----------------+------------+
6 rows in set (0.00 sec)

mysql>
```

4. Use an `IF` function to evaluate which designs sell over 500 units during the winter sales quarter, using the following command to make a report that has name, category, and sales trend.

```
SELECT design_name AS Name, design_category AS Category,
IF(winter_sales>500, "Sells", "Slow") AS Trend
FROM duck_sales;
```

```
c:\mysql\bin\mysql.exe                                                    _ □ X

mysql> select design_name as Name, design_category as Category,
    -> if(winter_sales>500, "Sells", "Slow") as Trend
    -> from duck_sales;
+----------------+------------+-------+
| Name           | Category   | Trend |
+----------------+------------+-------+
| Santa_Duck     | Holiday    | Sells |
| Dr_Duck        | Profession | Sells |
| Duckula        | Literary   | Slow  |
| Fire_Duck      | Profession | Sells |
| Bunny_Duck     | Holiday    | Sells |
| Duckspeare     | Literary   | Sells |
| Sherlock_Duck  | Literary   | Sells |
| Duck_O_Lantern | Holiday    | Slow  |
| Rodeo_Duck     | Profession | Sells |
+----------------+------------+-------+
9 rows in set (0.00 sec)

mysql>
```

5. Use a `CASE...WHEN` function to indicate that the different categories have different sales trends, using the following command.

```
SELECT design_name AS Name,
CASE design_category
WHEN "Holiday" THEN "Seasonal"
```

(continued)

```
WHEN "Profession" THEN "Bi_annual"
WHEN "Literary" THEN "Random" END AS "Pattern"
FROM duck_sales;
```

```
c:\mysql\bin\mysql.exe                                                    _ □ ×

mysql> select design_name as Name,
    -> case design_category
    -> when "Holiday" then "Seasonal"
    -> when "Profession" then "Bi_annual"
    -> when "Literary" then "Random" end as "Pattern"
    -> from duck_sales;
+-------------------+------------+
| Name              | Pattern    |
+-------------------+------------+
| Santa_Duck        | Seasonal   |
| Dr_Duck           | Bi_annual  |
| Duckula           | Random     |
| Fire_Duck         | Bi_annual  |
| Bunny_Duck        | Seasonal   |
| Duckspeare        | Random     |
| Sherlock_Duck     | Random     |
| Duck_O_Lantern    | Seasonal   |
| Rodeo_Duck        | Bi_annual  |
+-------------------+------------+
9 rows in set (0.00 sec)

mysql>
```

6. Using the SUM function, make a report that shows the total sales numbers in each quarter.

```
SELECT SUM(winter_sales) AS "winter total",
SUM(spring_sales) AS "spring total",
SUM(summer_sales) AS "summer total",
SUM(fall_sales) AS "fall total"
FROM duck_sales;
```

```
c:\mysql\bin\mysql.exe                                                    _ □ ×

mysql> select sum(winter_sales) as "winter total",
    -> sum(spring_sales) as "spring total",
    -> sum(summer_sales) as "summer total",
    -> sum(fall_sales) as "fall total"
    -> from duck_sales;
+--------------+--------------+--------------+------------+
| winter total | spring total | summer total | fall total |
+--------------+--------------+--------------+------------+
|         5906 |         3445 |         2570 |       3705 |
+--------------+--------------+--------------+------------+
1 row in set (0.00 sec)
```

7. Use the same format, but find the average sales amount per sales quarter.

```
SELECT AVG(winter_sales) AS "winter avg ",
AVG (spring_sales) AS "spring avg ",
AVG (summer_sales) AS "summer avg ",
AVG (fall_sales) AS "fall avg "
FROM duck_sales;
```

```
c:\mysql\bin\mysql.exe                                          _□×
mysql> select avg(winter_sales) as "winter avg ",
    -> avg (spring_sales) as "spring avg ",
    -> avg (summer_sales) as "summer avg ",
    -> avg (fall_sales) as "fall avg "
    -> from duck_sales;
+-------------+-------------+-------------+-------------+
| winter avg  | spring avg  | summer avg  | fall avg    |
+-------------+-------------+-------------+-------------+
|    656.2222 |    382.7778 |    285.5556 |    411.6667 |
+-------------+-------------+-------------+-------------+
1 row in set (0.00 sec)

mysql> _
```

8. In order to alter the display of design_name without altering how it is stored in the table, use the REPLACE command to remove the underscores and insert spaces in their place.

```
SELECT REPLACE(design_name, "_", " ") FROM duck_sales;
```

Notice that the change was in the output, not in the record fields themselves.

```
c:\mysql\bin\mysql.exe                                          _□×
mysql> select replace(design_name, "_", " ") from duck_sales;
+---------------------------------+
| replace(design_name, "_", " ")  |
+---------------------------------+
| Santa Duck                      |
| Dr Duck                         |
| Duckula                         |
| Fire Duck                       |
| Bunny Duck                      |
| Duckspeare                      |
| Sherlock Duck                   |
| Duck O Lantern                  |
| Rodeo Duck                      |
+---------------------------------+
9 rows in set (0.00 sec)

mysql> select design_name from duck_sales;
+----------------+
| design_name    |
+----------------+
| Santa_Duck     |
| Dr_Duck        |
| Duckula        |
| Fire_Duck      |
| Bunny_Duck     |
| Duckspeare     |
| Sherlock_Duck  |
| Duck_O_Lantern |
| Rodeo_Duck     |
+----------------+
9 rows in set (0.00 sec)

mysql> _
```

9. Use the following command to produce a report called Sales Plan that replaces the underscores with spaces and concatenates the word *Sale* onto the names of the DuckWear outfits in the Literary and Holiday categories.

(continued)

```
SELECT CONCAT((REPLACE(design_name, "_", " ")), " ", "Sale") AS "Sales Plan"
  FROM duck_sales WHERE design_category!="Profession";
```

```
c:\mysql\bin\mysql.exe                                                    _ □ ×
mysql> select concat((replace(design_name, "_", " ")), " ", "Sale") as "Sales Pl
an" from duck_sales where design_category!="Profession";
+----------------------+
| Sales Plan           |
+----------------------+
| Santa Duck Sale      |
| Duckula Sale         |
| Bunny Duck Sale      |
| Duckspeare Sale      |
| Sherlock Duck Sale   |
| Duck O Lantern Sale  |
+----------------------+
6 rows in set (0.00 sec)

mysql> _
```

10. Enter the following command, which uses the basic mathematical operators to display a
yearly sales total for each of the DuckWear outfits in the duck_sales table.

```
SELECT REPLACE(design_name, "_", " ") AS Outfit,
winter_sales+spring_sales+summer_sales+fall_sales AS "Yearly Sales",
design_category AS Category
FROM duck_sales;
```

```
c:\mysql\bin\mysql.exe                                                    _ □ ×
mysql> select replace(design_name, "_", " ") as Outfit,
    -> winter_sales+spring_sales+summer_sales+fall_sales as "Yearly Sales",
    -> design_category as Category
    -> from duck_sales;
+---------------+--------------+------------+
| Outfit        | Yearly Sales | Category   |
+---------------+--------------+------------+
| Santa Duck    |         1684 | Holiday    |
| Dr Duck       |         2787 | Profession |
| Duckula       |          943 | Literary   |
| Fire Duck     |         1557 | Profession |
| Bunny Duck    |         2035 | Holiday    |
| Duckspeare    |         2360 | Literary   |
| Sherlock Duck |         2146 | Literary   |
| Duck O Lantern|          716 | Holiday    |
| Rodeo Duck    |         1398 | Profession |
+---------------+--------------+------------+
9 rows in set (0.00 sec)

mysql> select replace(design_name, "_", " ") as Outfit, winter_sales+spring_sale
s+summer_sales+fall_sales as "Yearly Sales", design_category as Category from du
ck_sales;
+---------------+--------------+------------+
| Outfit        | Yearly Sales | Category   |
+---------------+--------------+------------+
| Santa Duck    |         1684 | Holiday    |
| Dr Duck       |         2787 | Profession |
| Duckula       |          943 | Literary   |
| Fire Duck     |         1557 | Profession |
| Bunny Duck    |         2035 | Holiday    |
| Duckspeare    |         2360 | Literary   |
| Sherlock Duck |         2146 | Literary   |
| Duck O Lantern|          716 | Holiday    |
| Rodeo Duck    |         1398 | Profession |
+---------------+--------------+------------+
9 rows in set (0.00 sec)

mysql> _
```

NOTE

The second example in the illustration shows the same command entered without the line breaks. Notice that the result is the same. The line-break version of the code simply makes it easier to read, which makes it easier to comprehend and easier to debug if the command returns errors.

11. Enter the following DATE_FORMAT commands to experiment with the variety of results you can achieve.

```
SELECT DATE_FORMAT("2078-08-30 21:19:58", "%W %M %d %Y");
SELECT DATE_FORMAT("2078-08-30 21:19:58", "%a. %b %e, '%y");
SELECT DATE_FORMAT("2078-08-30 21:19:58", "%m-%e-%Y %l:%i%p");
SELECT DATE_FORMAT("2078-08-30 21:19:58", "%m-%e-%Y %h:%i%s%p %W");
SELECT DATE_FORMAT("2078-08-30 21:19:58", "%M %D,%Y %k:%i CST %W");
```

```
c:\mysql\bin\mysql.exe                                              _ | □ | X

mysql> select date_format("2078-08-30 21:19:58", "%W %M %d %Y");
+--------------------------------------------------+
| date_format("2078-08-30 21:19:58", "%W %M %d %Y") |
+--------------------------------------------------+
| Tuesday August 30 2078                            |
+--------------------------------------------------+
1 row in set (0.00 sec)
mysql> select date_format("2078-08-30 21:19:58", "%a. %b %e, '%y");
+-----------------------------------------------------+
| date_format("2078-08-30 21:19:58", "%a. %b %e, '%y") |
+-----------------------------------------------------+
| Tue. Aug 30, '78                                     |
+-----------------------------------------------------+
1 row in set (0.00 sec)
mysql> select date_format("2078-08-30 21:19:58", "%m-%e-%Y %l:%i%p");
+------------------------------------------------------+
| date_format("2078-08-30 21:19:58", "%m-%e-%Y %l:%i%p") |
+------------------------------------------------------+
| 08-30-2078 9:19PM                                    |
+------------------------------------------------------+
1 row in set (0.00 sec)
mysql> select date_format("2078-08-30 21:19:58", "%m-%e-%Y %h:%i%s%p %W");
+----------------------------------------------------------+
| date_format("2078-08-30 21:19:58", "%m-%e-%Y %h:%i%s%p %W") |
+----------------------------------------------------------+
| 08-30-2078 09:1958PM Tuesday                             |
+----------------------------------------------------------+
1 row in set (0.00 sec)
mysql> select date_format("2078-08-30 21:19:58", "%M %D,%Y %k:%i CST %W");
+----------------------------------------------------------+
| date_format("2078-08-30 21:19:58", "%M %D,%Y %k:%i CST %W") |
+----------------------------------------------------------+
| August 30th,2078 21:19 CST Tuesday                       |
+----------------------------------------------------------+
1 row in set (0.00 sec)
mysql>
```

(continued)

Project Summary

In this project, you applied some MySQL functions to a table of data. These examples gave you an idea of how the functions can be combined and layered to produce ever-increasingly complex and specific reports. Most of the time, the required syntax for the functions is straightforward, and when it is not, a small amount of experimentation allows you to refine it until the results match your requirements.

This project covered the use of the IN, IF, CASE...WHEN, SUM, AVG, REPLACE, CONCAT, and DATE_FORMAT functions. You used commands with more than one function nested inside them. You saw how you can make your output look the way you want it to, without changing the format in which your data is stored. The next skill will extend your knowledge in this area ever further.

CRITICAL SKILL
5.2 Order and Group Data

By default, MySQL returns data in the order in which it was placed into the table. Ordering and grouping data allows you to present reports in a form that conveys their information in a clear, easily readable manner.

Using the GROUP BY and ORDER BY Clauses

On the surface, the GROUP BY and ORDER BY clauses seem to be very similar, and in fact, they have much in common. Using one or the other arranges data in sequence by the specified column. Using both ORDER BY and GROUP BY together allows you to specify the sequence data is arranged in, and then group like data by referencing another specified column.

GROUP BY and ORDER BY have many similarities:

- They both cause data to be arranged in an order using a specified column as the arrangement basis.

- They both default to ascending order, but can be changed to descending order by using the DESC reserved word at the end of their syntax.

- They both can take the alias, or header name, established by an AS clause in the same command, instead of the actual field name.

- They both can take multiple columns as specifiers.

On the other hand, GROUP BY and ORDER BY have some differences:

- GROUP BY has an additional clause called HAVING, which you can use to filter the data even further.

- ORDER BY returns every instance of the specified field, but GROUP BY returns only one instance of each unique data item contained in the field.

Suppose that you have a table called monsters, which has a field m_type containing the following data: zombie, vampire, werewolf, mummy, and vampire. A SELECT command specifying the column m_type would return a different report depending on whether you used GROUP BY or ORDER BY to specify their output format.

```
SELECT m_type FROM monsters ORDER BY m_type;
```

This returns the entire set of five values, including the repetition of the data vampire.

```
SELECT m_type FROM monsters GROUP BY m_type;
```

This returns an edited set of four values, removing the repetition of the data vampire, grouping the repeated data into one instance.

If you are using both GROUP BY and ORDER BY in the same command, you must always place GROUP BY before ORDER BY, because that is required in the SELECT syntax.

Using Grouping Functions

Some functions are considered grouping functions, and their use can require a GROUP BY clause. All of the functions covered in the "Using Aggregate Functions" section earlier in this module fall in this category. If you use an aggregate or grouping function, and do not include a GROUP BY clause in the command, the result is the same as asking MySQL to group on all rows.

When you have a column in your output that is nongrouping and a column that is grouping, the GROUP BY clause is required. For instance, if you have a table called lazertag with the fields team, date, and score, and you want to make a report that shows the average score of each team listed in the table, you could use the following code:

```
SELECT team, AVG(score)
FROM lazertag
GROUP BY team;
```

The team column of the SELECT is nongrouping; it merely reports the data from the table without manipulating it. The score column is part of an AVG clause, which groups the data from all the rows of the column and averages them into one result. Since there is a mixture of grouping and nongrouping data specified in the output, a GROUP BY clause is necessary. Figure 5-15 shows the result of this command, plus the error that results if you try to run it without its GROUP BY clause.

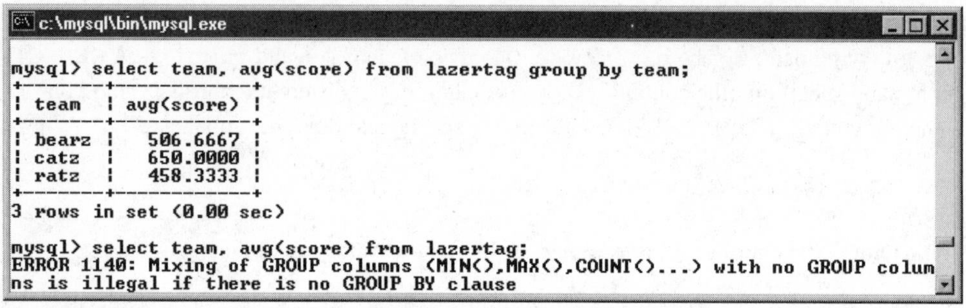

Figure 5-15 Using grouping and nongrouping columns

The error shown in Figure 5-15 gives a short list of the types of functions (MIN, MAX, COUNT) that require the GROUP BY clause. Here is a list of all of the functions that require the GROUP BY clause:

AVG	BIT_AND	BIT_OR
BIT_XOR	COUNT	GROUP_CONCAT
MIN	MAX	STD
STDDEV	SUM	VARIANCE

GROUP BY does not always operate intuitively, especially when it takes more than one field, so you may need to experiment until you become familiar with how it works. For example, consider these two commands:

```
SELECT team, score, date FROM lazertag GROUP BY team, date;
SELECT team, score, date FROM lazertag GROUP BY date, team;
```

Figure 5-16 shows how reversing the order of multiple GROUP BY fields in these commands changes the results. In the first example, the records are arranged by team, and then all the records from the same team are arranged by date. In the second example, all the records are arranged by date, and then all the records with the same date are arranged by team. The score field contents are just taken along for the ride.

```
c:\mysql\bin\mysql.exe                                                    _□X
mysql> select team, score, date from lazertag group by team, date;
+--------+-------+--------------+
| team   | score | date         |
+--------+-------+--------------+
| bearz  |   350 | 2040-01-01   |
| bearz  |   750 | 2040-01-02   |
| bearz  |   420 | 2040-01-03   |
| catz   |   450 | 2040-01-01   |
| catz   |   700 | 2040-01-02   |
| catz   |   800 | 2040-01-03   |
| ratz   |   500 | 2040-01-01   |
| ratz   |   600 | 2040-01-02   |
| ratz   |   275 | 2040-01-03   |
+--------+-------+--------------+
9 rows in set (0.00 sec)

mysql> select team, score, date from lazertag group by date, team;
+--------+-------+--------------+
| team   | score | date         |
+--------+-------+--------------+
| bearz  |   350 | 2040-01-01   |
| catz   |   450 | 2040-01-01   |
| ratz   |   500 | 2040-01-01   |
| bearz  |   750 | 2040-01-02   |
| catz   |   700 | 2040-01-02   |
| ratz   |   600 | 2040-01-02   |
| bearz  |   420 | 2040-01-03   |
| catz   |   800 | 2040-01-03   |
| ratz   |   275 | 2040-01-03   |
+--------+-------+--------------+
9 rows in set (0.00 sec)

mysql>
```

Figure 5-16 Reversing the order of GROUP BY fields changes the results.

Screening Results with HAVING

GROUP BY also allows you to further filter the data by adding a HAVING clause; however, you should not use the HAVING clause when a WHERE clause will suffice. You should use the HAVING clause as the criteria only to determine which record or records *sent from* the GROUP BY clause should be used in the output. The WHERE clause should be used as the criteria to determine which record or records should be *sent to* the GROUP BY clause.

The following shows two variations of the HAVING clause:

```
SELECT team, AVG(score) FROM lazertag GROUP BY team;
SELECT team, AVG(score) FROM lazertag GROUP BY team HAVING AVG(score)>=600;
SELECT team, AVG(score) FROM lazertag GROUP BY team HAVING team="bearz";
```

As shown in Figure 5-17, the resulting report lists the average score for each team playing lazertag, and then two variations of the HAVING clause further distill that information to display which team's average score was under 600, and then the average score of the bearz team.

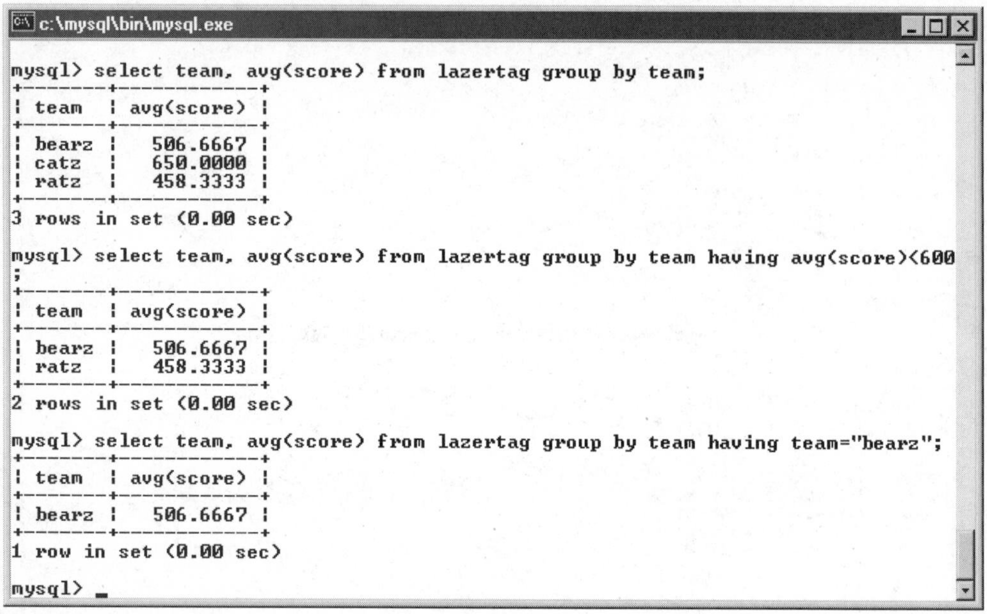

```
C:\ c:\mysql\bin\mysql.exe                                        _ □ ✕

mysql> select team, avg(score) from lazertag group by team;
+-------+-------------+
| team  | avg(score)  |
+-------+-------------+
| bearz |    506.6667 |
| catz  |    650.0000 |
| ratz  |    458.3333 |
+-------+-------------+
3 rows in set (0.00 sec)

mysql> select team, avg(score) from lazertag group by team having avg(score)<600
;
+-------+-------------+
| team  | avg(score)  |
+-------+-------------+
| bearz |    506.6667 |
| ratz  |    458.3333 |
+-------+-------------+
2 rows in set (0.00 sec)

mysql> select team, avg(score) from lazertag group by team having team="bearz";
+-------+-------------+
| team  | avg(score)  |
+-------+-------------+
| bearz |    506.6667 |
+-------+-------------+
1 row in set (0.00 sec)

mysql> _
```

Figure 5-17 Examples of the GROUP BY HAVING clause

Progress Check

1. Which must come first in the SELECT syntax: GROUP BY or ORDER BY?

2. Which of the grouping clauses has the HAVING clause?

3. What is the main difference in the output of the GROUP BY and ORDER BY clauses?

4. What keeps the grouping functions from grouping on all rows?

5. When does using one of the grouping functions require also using the GROUP BY clause?

---

1. GROUP BY must always come before ORDER BY in the SELECT command syntax.

2. The HAVING clause is part of the GROUP BY clause.

3. The ORDER BY clause returns all the fields in a specified column; the GROUP BY clause returns only the unique instances in the specified column, editing out repeated data.

4. The grouping functions need to have a GROUP BY clause to avoid grouping on all rows.

5. If there is a nongrouping field specified in addition to the grouping field, the GROUP BY clause is required.

Project 5-2 Use ORDER BY and GROUP BY

The ORDER BY and GROUP BY clauses of the SELECT command are used to manipulate your data output into more clearly understandable formats specifically focused for the intended audience. This project will give you practical experience with these clauses, as well as with using the HAVING clause in conjunction with GROUP BY to further distill your data's presentation.

Step by Step

1. Use ORDER BY to list all the designs in duck_sales arranged by their category.

```
SELECT design_name, design_category FROM duck_sales
ORDER BY design_category;
```

```
c:\mysql\bin\mysql.exe
mysql> select design_name, design_category from duck_sales
    -> order by design_category;
+----------------+-----------------+
| design_name    | design_category |
+----------------+-----------------+
| Santa_Duck     | Holiday         |
| Bunny_Duck     | Holiday         |
| Duck_O_Lantern | Holiday         |
| Duckula        | Literary        |
| Duckspeare     | Literary        |
| Sherlock_Duck  | Literary        |
| Dr_Duck        | Profession      |
| Fire_Duck      | Profession      |
| Rodeo_Duck     | Profession      |
+----------------+-----------------+
9 rows in set (0.00 sec)

mysql>
```

2. Use two ORDER BY fields to display the design names within each category in a sorted order.

```
SELECT design_name, design_category FROM duck_sales
ORDER BY design_category, design_name;
```

```
c:\mysql\bin\mysql.exe
mysql> select design_name, design_category from duck_sales
    -> order by design_category, design_name;
+----------------+-----------------+
| design_name    | design_category |
+----------------+-----------------+
| Bunny_Duck     | Holiday         |
| Duck_O_Lantern | Holiday         |
| Santa_Duck     | Holiday         |
| Duckspeare     | Literary        |
| Duckula        | Literary        |
| Sherlock_Duck  | Literary        |
| Dr_Duck        | Profession      |
| Fire_Duck      | Profession      |
| Rodeo_Duck     | Profession      |
+----------------+-----------------+
9 rows in set (0.00 sec)

mysql>
```

(continued)

Project
5-2

Use ORDER BY and GROUP BY

3. Use the following GROUP BY clause to list only the unique states in the cust_state column of the duck_cust table.

```
SELECT cust_state FROM duck_cust
GROUP BY cust_state;
```

4. Use the following GROUP BY clause to list only the unique cities and states in the cust_city and cust_state columns of the duck_cust table.

```
SELECT cust_city, cust_state FROM duck_cust
GROUP BY cust_state;
```

This command results in a list of states identical to the results of the command in step 3; however, in the case of CA, there is more than one city in the table, so it does not give a complete listing of the cities. Grouping by state, MySQL displays only the city from the first CA state record it finds.

5. Change the GROUP BY field to cust_city, to list all the unique cities and their states, including both cities from CA.

```
SELECT cust_city, cust_state FROM duck_cust
GROUP BY cust_city;
```

```
c:\mysql\bin\mysql.exe

mysql> select cust_state from duck_cust
    -> group by cust_state;
+------------+
| cust_state |
+------------+
| AZ         |
| CA         |
| IL         |
| KS         |
| OK         |
| UT         |
| WA         |
+------------+
7 rows in set (0.00 sec)

mysql> select cust_city, cust_state from duck_cust
    -> group by cust_state;
+----------------+------------+
| cust_city      | cust_state |
+----------------+------------+
| Blacktop       | AZ         |
| Shady Hill     | CA         |
| Chicago        | IL         |
| Meadowlark Hill| KS         |
| Elysium        | OK         |
| Fedora         | UT         |
| Seacouver      | WA         |
+----------------+------------+
7 rows in set (0.00 sec)

mysql> select cust_city, cust_state from duck_cust
    -> group by cust_city;
+----------------+------------+
| cust_city      | cust_state |
+----------------+------------+
| Blacktop       | AZ         |
| Chicago        | IL         |
| Elysium        | OK         |
| Fedora         | UT         |
| Freedom        | KS         |
| Meadowlark Hill| KS         |
| Seacouver      | WA         |
| Shady Hill     | CA         |
| Ulimpt         | CA         |
+----------------+------------+
9 rows in set (0.00 sec)

mysql>
```

6. Using the following SELECT command with WHERE, GROUP BY and HAVING clauses, list the design_name or names in the Literary design_category that have winter_sales over 700, in order of most sales to least sales.

```
SELECT design_name, design_category, winter_sales
FROM duck_sales
WHERE design_category="Literary"
GROUP BY winter_sales DESC HAVING winter_sales>700;
```

```
c:\mysql\bin\mysql.exe                                              _ □ ×
mysql> select design_name, design_category, winter_sales
    -> from duck_sales
    -> where design_category="Literary"
    -> group by winter_sales desc having winter_sales>700;
+---------------+-----------------+---------------+
| design_name   | design_category | winter_sales  |
+---------------+-----------------+---------------+
| Duckspeare    | Literary        |           953 |
| Sherlock_Duck | Literary        |           752 |
+---------------+-----------------+---------------+
2 rows in set (0.00 sec)

mysql>
```

Project Summary

In this project, you used GROUP BY and ORDER BY clauses to control the output of your SELECT commands. You specified both single and multiple fields, and also used the HAVING clause to further refine the output of your GROUP BY clause.

Although the syntax for each of these clauses is simple, the ways in which they can be utilized can result in increasingly complex manipulations. Using them, you can produce specific reports of a table's contents and see how its fields relate to each other.

Project
5-2

CRITICAL SKILL
5.3 Join Data in Multiple Tables

Sometimes, the data you need for a report exists in more than one table. When you select data from more than one table, it is called *joining*. One way to show you are selecting fields from specific tables is to specify both the table and field name in the command, separated by a period: *table_name.field_name*. Alternatively, you can use one of several JOIN functions. This section covers Cartesian products, simple or INNER JOINS, and the LEFT JOIN, and RIGHT JOIN functions.

When you are joining data from more than one table and selecting a field from a table, you must list that table in the FROM clause of the SELECT command. If any of the fields within the tables you are selecting happen to have the identical field name (such as cust_num), you must specify the table name, and then the desired field name, separated by a period, as shown in the previous paragraph.

Understanding Cartesian Product vs. Simple Join Operations

A *Cartesian join* is when every field in one table is joined with every field in another table. For instance, if a table called here held the values One and Two, and a table called there held the values a, b, and c, a Cartesian join of those two tables would result in the report shown in Figure 5-18. The information repeats itself until all the permutations of the join are covered. Because there is so much repetition of data, this type of join is rarely useful.

The following example shows a simple joining of two tables without using a formal JOIN function:

```
SELECT here.stuff, there.stuff
FROM here, there
WHERE here.Ndex=there.Ndex;
```

The results, shown in the first example in Figure 5-19, use the primary key fields called Ndex in each table to match up the data in the fields called stuff. The third entry in the there table, the value c, does not appear in the results, because there is not a corresponding third value and resulting matching index number in the here table.

The second example in Figure 5-19 shows the result of the same code after a third field, Three, is added to the here table. The command is the same, but now the tables have the same number of matching records, so the results differ. This type of join risks a result with incomplete data, unless you know without question that the tables involved are of equal size.

Figure 5-20 shows how the same result can be achieved using the INNER JOIN function with its ON clause replacing the WHERE clause in the previous example. Using a formal JOIN function this way has the advantage of better communicating your intentions to subsequent maintainers of the code.

```
SELECT here.stuff, there.stuff
FROM here INNER JOIN there
ON here.Ndex=there.Ndex;
```

```
c:\mysql\bin\mysql.exe

mysql> select * from here, there;
+------+-------+------+-------+
| Ndex | stuff | Ndex | stuff |
+------+-------+------+-------+
|    1 | One   |    1 | a     |
|    2 | Two   |    1 | a     |
|    1 | One   |    2 | b     |
|    2 | Two   |    2 | b     |
|    1 | One   |    3 | c     |
|    2 | Two   |    3 | c     |
+------+-------+------+-------+
6 rows in set (0.00 sec)

mysql>
```

Figure 5-18 A Cartesian join

```
c:\mysql\bin\mysql.exe                                          _ □ ×
mysql> select here.stuff, there.stuff
    -> from here, there
    -> where here.Ndex=there.Ndex;
+-------+-------+
| stuff | stuff |
+-------+-------+
| One   | a     |
| Two   | b     |
+-------+-------+
2 rows in set (0.00 sec)

mysql> select here.stuff, there.stuff
    -> from here, there
    -> where here.Ndex=there.Ndex;
+-------+-------+
| stuff | stuff |
+-------+-------+
| One   | a     |
| Two   | b     |
| Three | c     |
+-------+-------+
3 rows in set (0.00 sec)

mysql>
```

Figure 5-19 Results from simple joins

These examples join tables that have identical column names, and so they require the
table_name.field_name syntax to make their meaning clear to MySQL. As shown in
Figure 5-21, if the `stuff` column in the `there` table is renamed `junk`, those fields no longer
need to have the table specified in the SELECT command. However, since both tables still have a
key field named `Ndex`, the table must be specified when they are used in the ON clause. You can
choose to use the table specification syntax only when necessary for the sake of brevity in the
code, or you can always use it to make the intentions of the code clearer and more consistent.

Deciding Whether to Use LEFT JOIN or RIGHT JOIN

Continuing with the examples from the previous section, Figure 5-22 shows what happens
when a fourth value, d, has been added to the `junk` table, causing `junk` and `stuff` to once
again contain a different number of rows. In the first example in Figure 5-22, the results of the
LEFT JOIN is identical to the results of the previous INNER JOIN. The value d is left off of
the results, because it has no corresponding index value in the other table.

```
c:\mysql\bin\mysql.exe                                          _ □ ×
mysql> select here.stuff, there.stuff
    -> from here inner join there
    -> on here.Ndex=there.Ndex;
+-------+-------+
| stuff | stuff |
+-------+-------+
| One   | a     |
| Two   | b     |
| Three | c     |
+-------+-------+
3 rows in set (0.00 sec)

mysql> _
```

Figure 5-20 Using an INNER JOIN function

```
c:\mysql\bin\mysql.exe                                      _ □ ×

mysql> select stuff, junk
    -> from here inner join there
    -> on here.Ndex=there.Ndex;
+-------+------+
| stuff | junk |
+-------+------+
| One   | a    |
| Two   | b    |
| Three | c    |
+-------+------+
3 rows in set (0.00 sec)

mysql> _
```

Figure 5-21 Specifying the table name only when necessary

In order to make it show in the results, you must use either a LEFT JOIN or RIGHT JOIN, depending on how the fields and tables are arranged in the commands. In the second example in Figure 5-22, the JOIN has been changed from an LEFT JOIN to a RIGHT JOIN. Since the here table is listed first in the SELECT line, the there table is on its right, and since the

```
c:\mysql\bin\mysql.exe                                      _ □ ×

mysql> select stuff, junk
    -> from here left join there
    -> on here.Ndex=there.Ndex;
+-------+------+
| stuff | junk |
+-------+------+
| One   | a    |
| Two   | b    |
| Three | c    |
+-------+------+
3 rows in set (0.00 sec)

mysql> select stuff, junk
    -> from here right join there
    -> on here.Ndex=there.Ndex;
+-------+------+
| stuff | junk |
+-------+------+
| One   | a    |
| Two   | b    |
| Three | c    |
| NULL  | d    |
+-------+------+
4 rows in set (0.00 sec)

mysql> select junk, stuff
    -> from there left join here
    -> on here.Ndex=there.Ndex;
+------+-------+
| junk | stuff |
+------+-------+
| a    | One   |
| b    | Two   |
| c    | Three |
| d    | NULL  |
+------+-------+
4 rows in set (0.00 sec)

mysql>
```

Figure 5-22 Using RIGHT and LEFT JOIN on noncorresponding tables

there table has more rows, a RIGHT JOIN instructs MySQL to place a NULL value in the table across from any value in the right table that has no corresponding value in the left table.

The LEFT JOIN works in precisely the opposite way, as demonstrated in the third example in Figure 5-22. In this example, the here and there tables have swapped sides, necessitating a LEFT JOIN to have the value d to appear in the result.

Deciding whether to use LEFT JOIN or RIGHT JOIN to mold your information into its desired form depends on how the information is stored in its tables and how the desired format of the results differs from the original format. Often, you will need to experiment to get the results you want. The best way to understand how the JOIN commands work is to try them in simple ways, which will provide the insight you need to know how to use them in more complex combinations.

Project 5-3 Combine Table Data with JOIN

In this project, you will work through a few examples of JOIN functions using the DuckWear tables.

Step by Step

1. Use the following command to create a report that shows the correct customer title from the duck_title table, and the customer's last name and state from the duck_cust table. Sort the data by the state field.

```
SELECT duck_title.title_cust, duck_cust.cust_last,
duck_cust.cust_state
FROM duck_title, duck_cust
WHERE duck_title.title_num=duck_cust.cust_title
ORDER BY duck_cust.cust_state;
```

This command is syntactically correct but cumbersome and overly specific.

```
c:\mysql\bin\mysql.exe                                          _ □ ×

mysql> select duck_title.title_cust, duck_cust.cust_last, duck_cust.cust_state
    -> from duck_title, duck_cust
    -> where duck_title.title_num=duck_cust.cust_title
    -> order by duck_cust.cust_state;
+------------+------------+------------+
| title_cust | cust_last  | cust_state |
+------------+------------+------------+
| Dr.        | Robert     | AZ         |
| Sir        | Kazui      | CA         |
| Sir        | Kazui      | CA         |
| None       | Montgomery | IL         |
| Lady       | Salisbury  | KS         |
| Miss       | Thegreat   | KS         |
| None       | Davidson   | OK         |
| None       | Danson     | OK         |
| None       | Filled     | OK         |
| None       | Billiards  | OK         |
| None       | Beauvais   | OK         |
| None       | Seta       | OK         |
| Dame       | Gashlycrumb| UT         |
| Mr.        | Irishlord  | WA         |
+------------+------------+------------+
14 rows in set (0.00 sec)

mysql>
```

(continued)

NOTE

Unless a command uses fields from tables that have the same name, the
`table_name.field_name` syntax is not necessary and can lead to errors
due to typos.

2. Create the same report using the `JOIN` function in the following command.

```
SELECT title_cust, cust_last, cust_state
FROM duck_title RIGHT JOIN duck_cust
ON title_num=cust_title
ORDER BY cust_state;
```

This produces a report that is identical to the one you created in step 1.

```
c:\mysql\bin\mysql.exe                                            _□×

mysql> select title_cust, cust_last, cust_state
    -> from duck_title right join duck_cust
    -> on title_num=cust_title
    -> order by cust_state;
+------------+-----------+------------+
| title_cust | cust_last | cust_state |
+------------+-----------+------------+
| Dr.        | Robert    | AZ         |
| Sir        | Kazui     | CA         |
| Sir        | Kazui     | CA         |
| None       | Montgomery| IL         |
| Lady       | Salisbury | KS         |
| Miss       | Thegreat  | KS         |
| None       | Davidson  | OK         |
| None       | Danson    | OK         |
| None       | Filled    | OK         |
| None       | Billiards | OK         |
| None       | Beauvais  | OK         |
| None       | Seta      | OK         |
| Dame       | Gashlycrumb| UT        |
| Mr.        | Irishlord | WA         |
+------------+-----------+------------+
14 rows in set (0.00 sec)

mysql> _
```

3. As a sales promotion, DuckWear is going to give away one each of the nine outfits in the
`duck_sales` table to the corresponding oldest account numbers. Using the following
command, create a report that lists the customer number, last name, duck's name, and the
outfit that will be their prize.

```
SELECT cust_num, cust_last, cust_duckname, design_name
FROM duck_cust RIGHT JOIN duck_sales
ON cust_num=design_num;
```

```
c:\mysql\bin\mysql.exe                                                    _ □ X

mysql> select cust_num, cust_last, cust_duckname, design_name
    -> from duck_cust right join duck_sales
    -> on cust_num=design_num;
+----------+------------+---------------------------+----------------+
| cust_num | cust_last  | cust_duckname             | design_name    |
+----------+------------+---------------------------+----------------+
|        1 | Salisbury  | Spike                     | Santa_Duck     |
|        2 | Irishlord  | Netrek Rules              | Dr_Duck        |
|        3 | Thegreat   | Frida Kahlo de Tomayo     | Duckula        |
|        4 | Montgomery | Bianca                    | Fire_Duck      |
|        5 | Robert     | Harley                    | Bunny_Duck     |
|        6 | Kazui      | Fitzwhistle               | Duckspeare     |
|        7 | Gashlycrumb| Tess D'urberville         | Sherlock_Duck  |
|        8 | Kazui      | Fitzwhistle               | Duck_O_Lantern |
|        9 | Davidson   | Quackers                  | Rodeo_Duck     |
+----------+------------+---------------------------+----------------+
9 rows in set (0.00 sec)

mysql>
```

4. Create a report listing the outfit won, then the address to send it to using the duck_sales and duck_cust tables.

```
SELECT design_name, cust_add1, cust_add2, cust_city, cust_state,
  cust_zip1, cust_zip2
FROM duck_sales LEFT JOIN duck_cust
ON cust_num=design_num;
```

```
c:\mysql\bin\mysql.exe                                                    _ □ X

mysql> select design_name, cust_add1, cust_add2, cust_city, cust_state, cust_zip
1, cust_zip2
    -> from duck_sales left join duck_cust
    -> on cust_num=design_num;
+--------------+----------------------+----------+--------------+------+
| design_name  | cust_add1            | cust_add2| cust_city    | cust_|
| state | cust_zip1 | cust_zip2 |
+--------------+----------------------+----------+--------------+------+
| Santa_Duck   | 9 Wishing Well Court | 0        | Meadowlark Hill | KS
|    67048  | 1234      |
| Dr_Duck      | 1022 Sea of Rye      | A207     | Seacouver    | WA
|    98601  | 3464      |
| Duckula      | 2004 Singleton Dr.   | 0        | Freedom      | KS
|    67290  | 4321      |
| Fire_Duck    | 1567 Terra Cotta Way | 0        | Chicago      | IL
|    89129  | 4444      |
| Bunny_Duck   | 20113 Open Road Highway | #6    | Blacktop     | AZ
|    00606  | 1952      |
| Duckspeare   | 42 Cube Farm Lane    | Gatehouse| Ulimpt       | CA
|    46362  | 0         |
| Sherlock_Duck| 3113 Picket Fence Lane | 0      | Fedora       | UT
|    41927  | 5698      |
| Duck_O_Lantern | 1630 Revello Drive | NULL    | Shady Hill   | CA
|    31626  | 2882      |
| Rodeo_Duck   | 1976 Stony Pointe Lane | 113    | Elysium      | OK
|    73102  | NULL      |
+--------------+----------------------+----------+--------------+------+
9 rows in set (0.00 sec)

mysql>
```

(continued)

Project Summary

The choice between using a LEFT JOIN or a RIGHT JOIN usually revolves around the comparison made in the ON clause and whether the tables involved have a different number of rows. If the table with the least rows is on the left of the FROM clause, a LEFT JOIN will result in a report that has only that many rows. If a RIGHT JOIN is used in those circumstances, the resulting report will have some of the SELECT fields padded with NULL, as there will be no corresponding entries in the shorter table. If the tables have the same amount of rows and the comparison fields are all full, you can use an INNER JOIN, although most of the time, a LEFT or RIGHT JOIN will return the same result.

✓ Module 5 Mastery Check

1. What does the following command return?

```
SELECT ep_title AS Album, Band,
IF(Release>1964 and Release<=1969, "60's"," ") AS Beatles Era,
IF(Release>1979 and Release<1990, "New Wave"," ") AS "Hair Band Era",
FROM RecordCollection
ORDER BY Band;
```

2. What is the purpose of the CASE...WHEN function?

3. What are the four ways to control how a column of fields rounds off numeric content?

4. What does the code LPAD sale_price, 5, "$" return, when sale_price contains a string value of 9.95?

5. From a table called cust_orders that has the columns cust_num, design_num, design_name, quantity, and price, make a report that shows the total quantity of outfits bought by cust_num 13.

6. What would the following code return?

```
concat_ws(" … ", "There can be", "Only ONE")
```

7. When is it required that you use the *table_name.field_name* syntax in your JOIN clause?

8. Can you use only the ORDER BY clause in the SELECT syntax?

9. Which function returns the current date and time on the computer on which you are working?

10. What does the following command do?

```
SELECT Range, AVG(height) FROM Mountains GROUP BY Range
HAVING Range="Rockies";
```

le 6

Data Handling

nistration

or

ter

Graphical user interfaces (GUIs) are often the quickest and most efficient way to interface with MySQL. Now that you have had some experience with using MySQL from the command line and have a basic understanding of how SQL commands go together to communicate with your database, you're ready to try the GUI approach.

In this module, you will learn how to use two GUIs provided by MySQL AB: MySQL Administrator and MySQL Control Center (MySQLCC). MySQLCC has plenty of hours of practical use behind it, and the newest offering from MySQL AB, MySQL Administrator, is a welcome addition with many useful and convenient features.

NOTE

There are a variety of other GUIs for MySQL available, both for sale and for free. As you gain experience working with your database, you may find one of them better fits your needs.

CRITICAL SKILL
6.1 Use MySQL Administrator

MySQL Administrator is a visual console that allows you easy access to a variety of administrative tasks, as well as performance and data structure information. It provides a point-and-click environment for speedy and simple command access, as well as a real-time visual interpretation of your database's performance.

NOTE

This section refers to MySQL Administrator version 1.0.3 Alpha. Because of the rapid development in the open-source environment, you may download a later version.

The Alpha designation means that this is a new product from MySQL AB that has only been tested on a limited number of machines. The likelihood of undiscovered bugs in the code means that you should back up all important data before using MySQL Administrator in a production environment. If you find a bug in the program, you can participate in the open source development cycle by reporting it to MySQL AB as described on their Report a Bug page at http://bugs.mysql.com/.

As shown in Figure 6-1, MySQL Administrator has three components in its basic layout: a menu bar, a sidebar list, and a main window display. As you would expect, the menu bar hosts the program's drop-down menus. The sidebar lists the available information displays, and the main window to its right shows the information for the item selected in the sidebar.

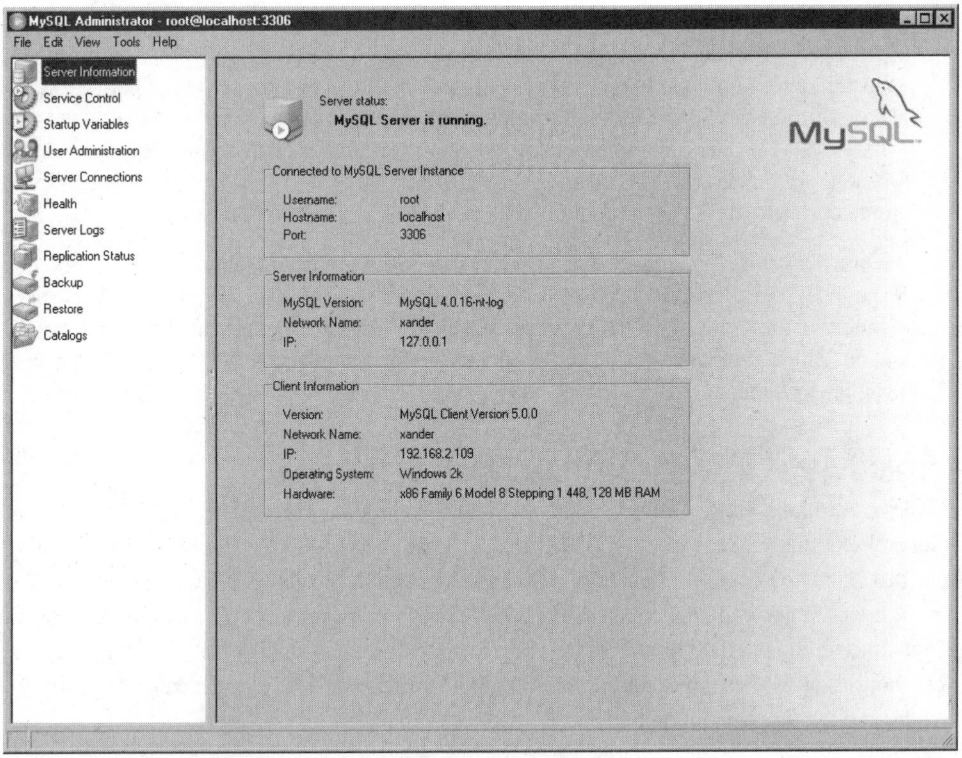

Figure 6-1 The MySQL Administrator opening window

Choosing MySQL Administrator Menu Options

Five drop-down menus are available from the MySQL Administrator menu bar:

- **File**   This menu has five options, which may or may not be available, depending on the information shown in the main window. The first three options allow you to open a new connection to a database, manage your database connections, and save the current database connection. Choosing the Manage Connection or Save Connection option opens the Connections page of the Options dialog box, which is discussed in the next section. The final two options are Export Page, which is only available when applicable and Close, which shuts down the MySQL Administrator tool.

- **Edit**   This menu has an item to open the Options dialog box, which is discussed in the next section. It also offers the standard Cut, Copy, and Paste functions.

- **View**   This menu provides options for opening the same information displays listed in the sidebar, which are discussed in the "Viewing Information in MySQL Administrator" section.

- **Tools** This menu has two options: one to access the MySQL command-line and another to access the standard command-line window for the OS on which MySQL Administrator is installed (as you have been using in previous modules to gain access to you MySQL database). The MySQL Command Line Client option opens a command-line window where the `mysql` command has already been input. The current connection operating in MySQL Administrator, for instance `root`, is entered as user, allowing you to simply type in the corresponding password and gain access to the MySQL Client.

- **Help** This menu has four options. You can open a searchable Help document in a separate window, report a MySQL Administrator bug should you find one, and launch a new browser window to go to the MySQL AB web site. In addition, of course, you'll find the About option, which gives you version and proprietary information about the MySQL Administrator program you are using.

Setting MySQL Administrator Options

MySQL Administrator's Options dialog box offers options in three categories: Administrator, General Options, and Connections. This dialog box appears with the Connections category options when you choose either File | Manage Connection or File | Save Connection, as shown in Figure 6-2. You can also open the Options dialog box by selecting Edit | Options. You can adjust the settings in the Options dialog box to control some aspects of MySQL Administrator. The buttons at the bottom of the dialog box allow you to apply or discard changes you've made, and to close the dialog box.

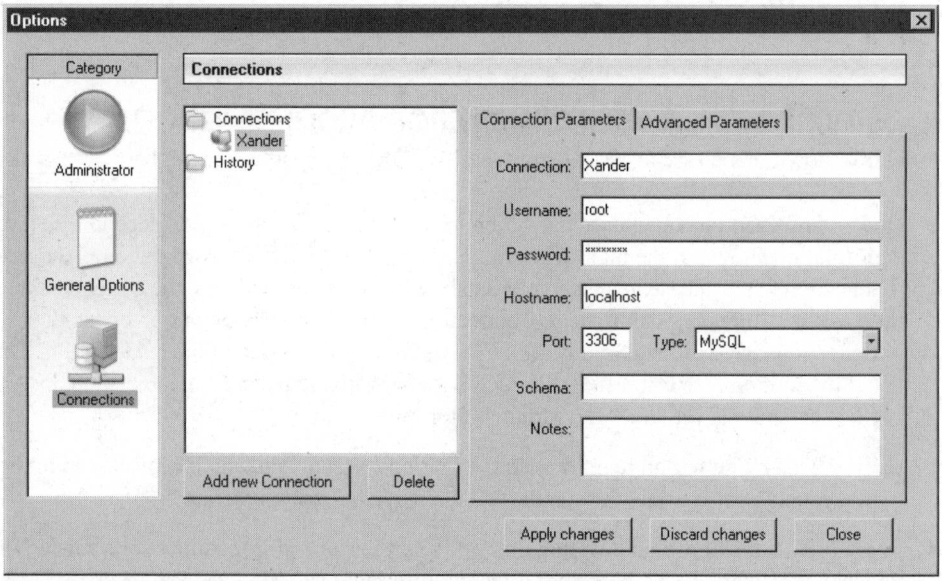

Figure 6-2 The Connections category of the Options dialog box

Administrator Options

The Administrator Options category of the Options dialog box allows you to make two choices: whether or not to show the global privileges and the table/row privileges within the displays in the MySQL Administrator program. Any changes you make can be either applied or discarded, so you can experiment without making actual changes to your database.

General Options

The General Options category of the Options dialog box has four option areas:

- **Applications Startup**   This section allows you to choose whether to show the tip of the day and whether to store window positions.

- **Language**   This section theoretically allows you to choose the language MySQL Administrator runs in; at this time, it lists only English.

- **Connection Passwords Storage**   This section has a check box to indicate if you want the connection passwords stored and a drop-down list that allows you to choose either plain text or obscured formatting for those stored passwords.

- **Font**   This section allows you to choose another font and font size in place of the default MS Sans Serif 8 used by MySQL Administrator, and also to choose a different character set from the ones installed on the server.

Connection Options

The Connections category of the Options dialog box (see Figure 6-2) shows all the stored connections and allows you to access and edit them, as well as view their histories. You can also add and save new connections from this dialog box.

NOTE

Connections are automatically added to the History file, but you must intentionally save them by clicking Apply Changes in order for them to remain in the Connections file.

You can edit the connection in both the Connections and History file by using the fields in the Options dialog box: Connection (the name of the connection), Username, Password, Hostname, Port, Type (connection protocol), Schema, and Notes. In the Notes field, you can add notes to clarify the intended use of a specific connection. On a database with more than one administrator, adding notes can take the guesswork out of the reasoning or purpose behind a connection or connections. This can also be helpful for clarifying your intentions for future administrators.

NOTE

MySQL Administrator ignores the Schema field because other MySQL GUI programs use that field.

The Advanced Parameters tab in the Connections category of the Options dialog box allows you to choose a compression protocol, return the number of found rows instead of affected rows, ignore spaces after function names (which effectively makes them reserved words), enable LOAD DATA LOCAL handling (which allows a user to access files on the local machine that the server has read access to, raising obvious security issues), and set the number of seconds a connection can be inactive before it is disabled.

Some of the early versions of MySQL Administrator do not have the Advanced Parameters tab enabled. To access these settings in those versions, go to File | New Instance Connection…, and then click the Details button in the Connect to MySQL Server Instance dialog box, as shown in Figure 6-3.

The following three paragraphs give you a frame of reference for the Toolbar links. Take a moment to familiarize yourself with their location and dropdown menu contents.

The Toolbar Edit dropdown, as mentioned previously, has a link to the Options window. It also has links to the standard Cut, Copy and Paste functions. The View dropdown has text links to all of the Icons listed in the Sidebar Index and those displays of information will be discussed in the Basic Areas of Information section immediately following this one.

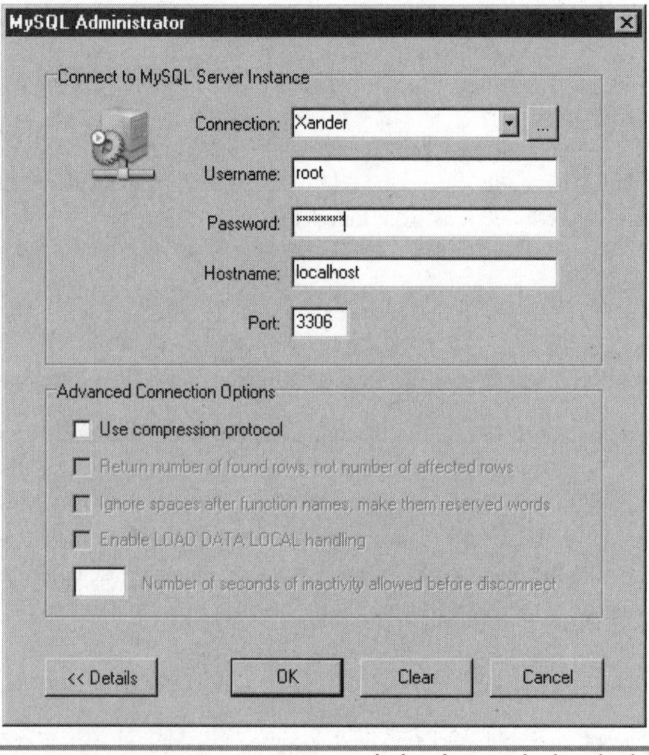

Figure 6-3 The Connect to MySQL Server Instance dialog box with details displayed

The Tools dropdown has two links: MySQL Command Line Client and a standard Command Line Window for the OS that MySQL Administrator is installed on. The MySQL Command Line Client link opens a command line window where the `mysql` command has already been input. The current connection operating in MySQL Administrator, for instance `root`, is entered as user, allowing you to simply type in the corresponding password and gain access to the MySQL Client. The other link opens a normal Command Line Window such as you have been using to gain access to your MySQL database previously in these lessons.

The final dropdown link on the Toolbar is Help. Help has four links allowing you to pull up a searchable Help document in a separate window, report a My SQL Administrator Bug should you find one, launch a new browser window to go to the MySQL AB web site, and of course, the About link, which gives you version and proprietary information about the MySQL Administrator program you are using.

Viewing Information in MySQL Administrator

To view information in MySQL Administrator, select the area of interest in the sidebar, and the information will appear in the main window on the right. Most of the areas of information have more than one tab in the main window. The following sections describe each area of information.

Server Information

The Server Information display (see Figure 6-1), provides four areas of information:

- **Server Status**   Whether the MySQL server is running or disconnected.

- **Connected to MySQL Server Instance**   The username, host name, and connecting port by which the active instance of connection to the server had been made.

- **Server Information**   The version of MySQL running on the server, along with its network name and IP address.

- **Client Information**   The client version, network name, and IP address, as well as the OS it is running on and the hardware's CPU information.

Service Control Information

The Service Control information display has two tabs: Stop/Start Service and Configure Service. For security reasons, Service Control functions work only if you are connected to MySQL via the localhost. That is, you must be physically using the computer on which your MySQL Server and MySQL Administrator are installed; you cannot be logged in from another computer on a network or from a remote location. This means that only someone logged in to the server that the database is hosted on can change these functions, or start or stop the service.

Start/Stop Service Tab   The Start/Stop Service tab, shown in Figure 6-4, has an icon and text indicating whether the service is running or stopped. It also has a single button, which either starts or stop the service, depending on the current condition. An animated progress bar indicates that the starting or stopping process is occurring, and it disappears when the desired state has been reached. The bottom part of this tab contains a Log Messages window, where all the messages sent during startup or shutdown are displayed.

Configure Service Tab   The Configuration Service tab, shown in Figure 6-5, is divided into three areas:

- **Service Settings**   This area has a check box that, if checked, allows MySQL to start up automatically whenever the server it is running on starts. It also allows you to edit the name that the computer uses to refer to the program and add a description of that service if desired.

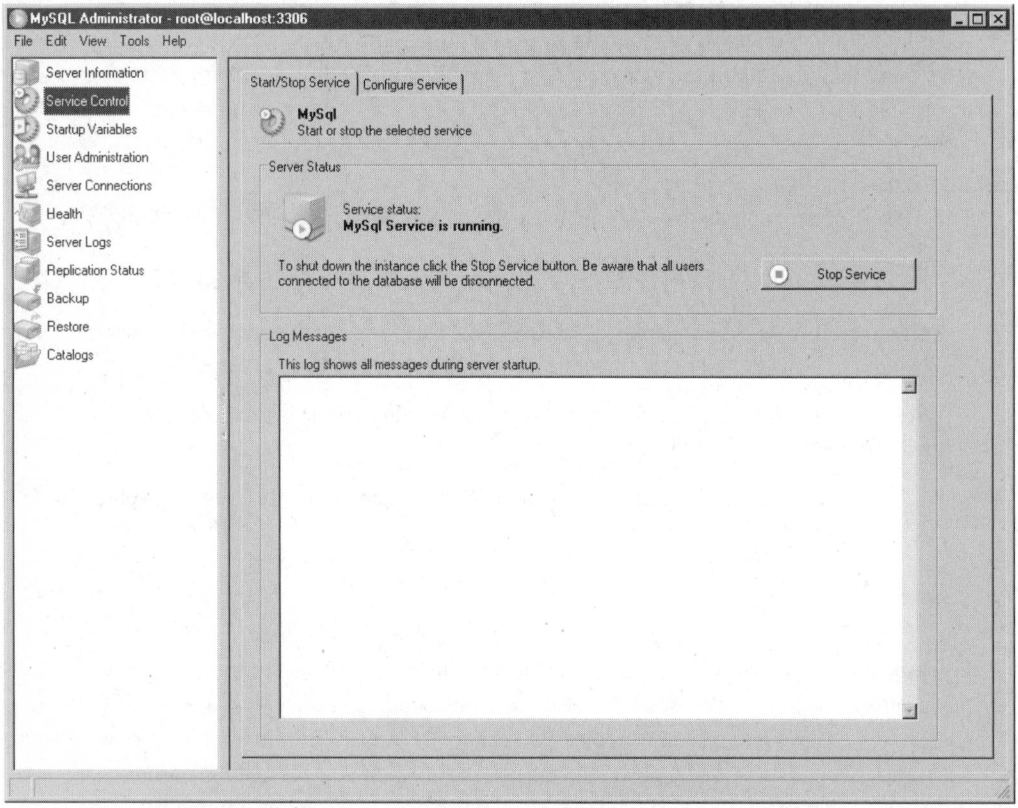

Figure 6-4 The Service Control display with the Start/Stop Service tab selected

- **Configuration Files**   This area allows you to see and edit the path to the MySQL configuration file, and edit the name of the configuration file section used for the current instance of the server. Unless you are running multiple servers, it is doubtful you will need to change the Section Name setting here.

- **Server Features**   This area consists of four check boxes and an editable display of the path to the binary executable file that starts the service. The four options the check boxes allow you to choose are support for InnoDB, support for BDB, allowing named pipes, and enabling debug information. The use of named pipes on anything other than a server making connections on a localhost is not recommended.

CAUTION

Using Debug Information causes the server to slow down and should only be used when debugging is really needed. If you enable Named Pipes, the Debug Information option is not available.

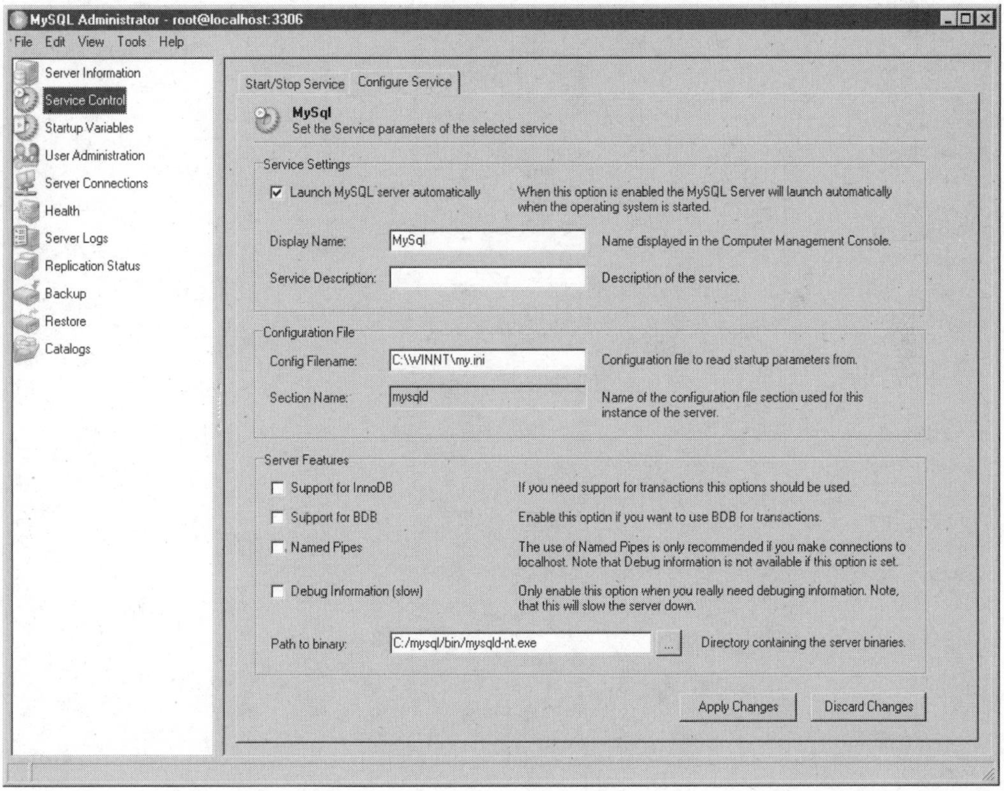

Figure 6-5 The Service Control display with the Configure Service tab selected

When you select the Apply Changes button to save changes you've made on the Configure Service tab, the changes do not take effect until the next time the server is shut down and restarted.

Startup Variables Information

The Startup Variables information display, shown in Figure 6-6, allows you to view and alter a number of the variables that MySQL reads at startup from the configuration file (my.ini or my.cnf). The variables are presented on nine tabs. You can make changes to the configuration file here, instead of opening the file in a word processing program and changing it by hand, which can cut down on typos. For security reasons, the Startup Variables functions can be accessed only if you are connected via the localhost. This way, only someone logged in to the server on which the database is hosted can change the startup variables.

As with the Configure Service tab in the Server Control information display, any changes you make here do not take effect until the server is stopped and started again (because the configuration file is read only when the server is started).

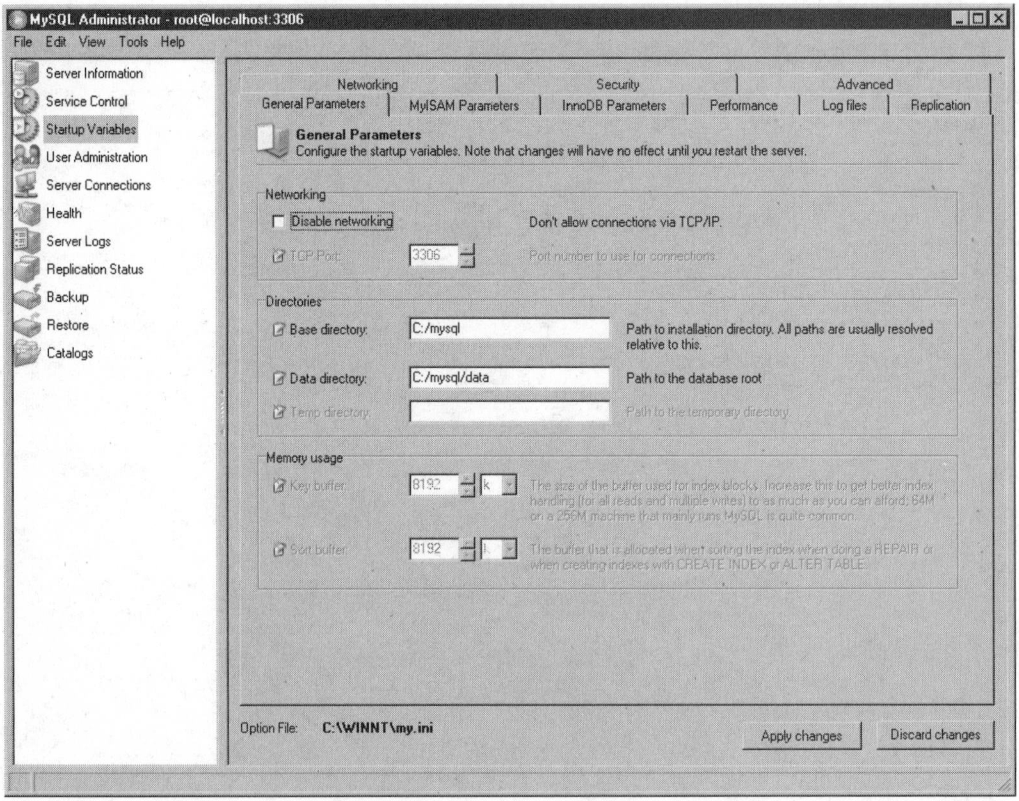

Figure 6-6 The Startup Variables display with the General Parameters tab selected

General Parameters Tab   The General Parameters tab (see Figure 6-6) has three areas:

- **Networking**   This section allows you to disable networking, which means that the server will no longer accept TCP/IP connections. It also allows you to set the TCP port to a different number than the default.

- **Directories**   This area allows you to specify or edit the path for three directories: Base, Data, and Temp. The Base directory is where the installation directory for MySQL is located. The Data directory is where the data for MySQL is located. The Temp directory is where MySQL stores temporary data. This option can be used to store data on a drive separate from the executable program to increase storage space or spread the hardware failure risk factor.

- **Memory Usage**   This area is used to set the key buffer and sort buffer sizes. Both of these values affect how indexes are handled. Altering them in keeping with your computer's parameters can enhance index handling, as well as enhance the REPAIR command and index creation when using the CREATE INDEX or ALTER TABLE command.

NOTE

For advice on when to change buffer sizes, see the "Ask the Expert" section in this module.

MyISAM Parameters Tab   The MyISAM Parameters tab has three areas:

- **General**   This area has two options. One allows concurrent inserts in MyISAM tables. The other allows external locking, which would enable you to test (but not repair) MyISAM tables on a running MySQL Server, by using the myisamchk script (discussed in Module 8).

- **Fulltext Search**   This area allows you to change four parameters related to fulltext searches: minimum word size, maximum word size, query expansion, and the path for a Stopword file that is created rather than using the built-in one.

- **Advanced Settings**   This area has four options. The Block Size setting refers to MyISAM index pages. The Extra Sort File Size setting refers to the point where MySQL decides to use the slower but safer key cache index create method. The Max Sort File Size setting refers to the maximum size that a temporary file made while creating an index can reach before MySQL decides not to use the faster sort index method to create an index. The Number of Repairs setting refers to the number of threads that MySQL can use when repairing a MyISAM table.

Ask the Expert

Q: When should I change the size of my key and index buffers?

A: One of the reasons MySQL is so popular is that its default settings are adequate for most users and applications. The power and speed of MySQL make up for systems with scarce resources; however, if you encounter performance issues, you might consider changing the `key_buffer_size` setting.

By default, 8MB of RAM is allocated for key and index buffers. MyISAM tables use this setting; InnoDB uses the `innodb_buffer_pool_size` for its indexes. You should note that if you set both sizes, the system will allocate both, whether you use it to create indexes or not. So, by default `key_buffer_size` and `innodb_buffer_pool_size` are set to 8MB. The two settings take 16MB of RAM from the system and reserve that space for their own use, even if it is never used. This may not be a problem for newer computers, as most have enough memory that 8 to 16MB will probably not be missed. The larger the setting, the larger the indexes you can keep in memory, and this makes searching the tables to which those indexes refer faster.

However, as your application grows, so does your need for large buffers. MySQL recommends 25 percent of physical RAM as a rule of thumb for key buffer allocation. If you have 1GB of RAM, it is not unheard of to allocate 256MB for the key buffer setting. Setting your buffer size too large has consequences though. Performance may decrease because the computer is expending too many resources on performing memory management.

This is where the MySQL Administrator health monitors come in. Use these monitors to check resource usage during your database's most stressful periods. If your resources are not regularly approaching 80 percent, then leave the default settings unaltered. Simply monitor your system on a regular basis (weekly, monthly, or even quarterly, depending on how quickly the size and demands on your database changes). Don't be afraid to experiment with adding more memory to your buffers and then monitoring how significantly, if at all, your system is impacted.

NOTE

Setting the value of Number of Repairs to 1 disables parallel thread repair, which may result in a slower repair process.

InnoDB Parameters Tab   The InnoDB Parameters tab has a variety of areas dealing with the options available when using InnoDB tables. The check box at the top of the tab allows you to deactivate InnoDB tables. As mentioned in Module 2, if you have decided that you are not going to use InnoDB tables, deactivating them saves space, frees allocated memory, and speeds up the startup process.

Performance Tab   The Performance tab allows you to alter four options dealing with query cache:

● **Query Cache Limit**   This option sets an upper limit to the size of result that is cached. Any result larger than the limit is not cached.

● **Minimal Size of Result**   This option sets the smallest unit into which results are cached.

● **Cache Size**   This option refers to the amount of allocated memory set aside to hold results from old queries.

● **Cache Type**   This option has a dropdown menu that allows you to choose from several query cache types or no result caching at all.

Log Files Tab   The Log Files tab has four areas:

● **Activate Logging**   This section allows you to enter a log name for any or all of the six types of logs listed: Binary, Query, Error, Slow Queries, Update, and ISAM. If the logging functions are turned on and there are no names entered, MySQL will use default names for each of these log types.

● **Binlog Options**   This section allows you to name the file where the last binary log files are stored and to set the maximum binary log size, which signals MySQL to rotate to a new log file when this size is reached. Rotating a log means that the current full log is saved under a different name, and the current log file is then emptied and ready to fill again.

● **Slow Query Log Options**   This section allows you to set the number of seconds MySQL uses to determine whether a query has taken too long and is deemed to be slow. An entry is written into the Slow Query log every time a query takes longer to execute than the number of seconds set.

● **Advanced Log Options**   This section allows you to specify if you want MySQL to log queries that are executed without using indexes, to log noncritical warnings, or to log only in short format, which filters out extra information sent to the Update and Slow Query logs. It also allows you to set the number of days after which MySQL will rotate expired logs.

Replication Tab   *Replication* is an automated process where a main server, called the *master*, replicates specified data onto another server or servers, called *slaves*. You can set up replication in order to maintain more than one copy of the data on a running server, to protect against catastrophic hardware or software failure. The Replication tab offers a wide variety of settings for both the master and slave computers that control the replication process.

Networking Tab   The Networking tab allows you to set and/or edit variables that deal with accessing MySQL over a network. The five areas it covers are General, Memory, Timeout Settings, Advanced, and Naming. Fine-tuning these settings on a busy network can remarkably enhance the performance of your MySQL database. If you are logged in to your database as root, then you are by default the system administrator of the MySQL server; however, if your database exists in a corporate network environment, then it is advisable to consult with the network's system administrator before altering any of these settings. For the vast majority of users, the MySQL default settings will be the best choice unless slow performance issues arise.

Security Tab   The Security tab allows you to turn on or off seven security-related functions:

- **Safe User Create**   This option prohibits a user who does not have write access to the `mysql.user` table from creating new users.

- **Disable Grant Tables**   This option allows MySQL to start without accessing the grant tables, which results in all users being given full access to all tables (see Module 8).

TIP

If you forget the root password to a MySQL database, restarting it without the grant tables (`--skip-grant-tables`) allows you to establish a new root password. See Module 8 for details.

- **Make all tables read-only**   This option allows visual access to the tables without endangering data integrity. The only exceptions are replication threads and users with `SUPER` privileges.

- **Deactivate SHOW DATABASE Commands**   This option prevents users from accessing any database they do not already know the name of.

- **Use Old Passwords**   This option switches the password encryption to the old, pre-version 4.0 methods, which is sometimes necessary when importing data from an older version of MySQL.

- **Secure Authentication**   This option prevents access to any user whose password is encrypted in the preversion 4.1 methods.

- **Enable LOAD DATA LOCAL INFILE**   This option allows you to turn on or off the permission to load data from a file in this manner.

Advanced Tab   The Advanced tab has five areas:

- **Localization**   These options allow you to set the language, the default character set, the default collation, and a path to a character set directory.

- **Thread Specific Settings**   These options allow you to fine-tune threads to improve database performance.

- **Insert Delayed Settings**   These options allow you to fine-tune insert operations to improve database performance.

- **General**   These options cover a range of advanced settings. You can print a symbolic stack trace on a failure to flush tables, or set a specified interval for MySQL to flush all tables. You can set up a signal to aid in debugging. You can set a lower priority for INSERT, DELETE, and UPDATE commands than for SELECT commands. You can specify a memory lock, which rules out swapping. You can use the old LOAD DATA command in the binary log, which means the data already in the file is not saved. You can disable the stack trace. You can also set a default week format, set an open files limit, and set a maximum error count to limit the amount of errors and/or warnings that can be saved for a particular statement.

- **Various**   As you might guess from the name, these are a mixture of settings that do not fit under any of the other tab headings but still are useful startup variables to access through the GUI.

User Administration

The User Administration display allows you to add new users, delete existing users, and view and change the privileges of users. When you click the User Administration icon in the sidebar, an additional sidebar panel appears beneath the main one, as shown in Figure 6-7. Labeled User Accounts, this sidebar displays all users. When you double-click a user name, any subcategories for that user (for instance, host names the user may connect from) are displayed. If subcategories appear for a user, it means that he or she has restricted privileges that are related directly to the specified hosts. Above the list of users is a text box with a magnifying glass icon. To search for a specific user, type the beginning letters or full name of a user in the text box.

As shown in Figure 6-7, the User Administration display has three tabs: User Information, Schema Privileges, and Resources. If you've set the MySQL Administrator options to show global privileges and table/column privileges (in the Administrator Options category of the Options dialog box, accessed by choosing Edit | Options), the display will also include two additional tabs: Global Privileges and Table/Column Privileges.

User Information Tab   When none of the users in the User Accounts sidebar are highlighted, all of the input fields in the User Information tab (see Figure 6-7) are grayed out and unavailable. Choosing a user or clicking the New User button at the bottom of the window activates all the fields. The display is divided into two areas: User Information and Additional Information. The User Information area allows you to add or change the user name and password.

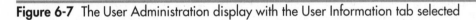

Figure 6-7 The User Administration display with the User Information tab selected

CAUTION

Although MySQL allows you to add users without supplying a password, it is not recommended to do so for security reasons.

The Additional Information fields are Full Name, Description, Email, Contact Information, and Icon. None of this information is required, but the more users your database has, the more useful the additional information becomes, especially when future administrators take over maintenance duties.

NOTE

If you click the Load Icon From Disk button next to the Icon field, you can assign your own icon for the user. The file you choose must be 48 by 48 pixels and in the PNG (Portable Network Graphics) format.

When editing an existing user account or adding a new user, the Apply Changes and Discard Changes buttons at the bottom of the window allow you to save or abandon any changes you have made. If you made changes to a user account, and then click another user without applying or discarding the changes, a MySQL Administrator pop-up window will prompt you to save or abandon the changes.

Global Privileges Tab   As noted earlier, the Global Privileges tab is available in the User Administration display only if you have selected the Show Global Privileges check box in the Administrator Options tab of the MySQL Administrator Options dialog box. The Global Privileges tab will show the selected users privileges in an Assigned Privileges list and the other privileges in an Available Privileges list. You can alter the user's privileges by moving them between these lists by means of arrow buttons. You can move single or multiple privileges by highlighting them and then clicking the single arrow button that points in the direction of the appropriate list, or move all of the privileges by clicking the desired double-arrow button.

Schema Privileges Tab   The Schema Privileges tab is always visible in the User Administration display. It is similar to the Global Privileges tab described in the previous section, except for an additional list labeled Schema, which shows all of the individual databases in your MySQL database. Once you select a specific database, the privileges in the Available Privileges list can be transferred into or out of the Assigned Privileges list, using the arrow buttons.

Table/Column Privileges Tab   Like the Global Privileges tab, the Table/Column Privileges tab is only available when the Show Table/Column Privileges check box is selected in the Administrator Options tab of the Options dialog box. It looks and functions like the Schema Privileges tab, except its leftmost list box is labeled Schemata and contains the individual databases, which you can double-click to see the tables within the databases and the columns within the tables. The available privileges differ on each of these levels, and you can set assigned privileges at any of these levels.

Resources Tab   The Resources tab allows you to manage MySQL's resources by limiting the number of user resources in three specific areas: questions, updates, and connections. By entering a number into the max_questions, max_updates, or max_connections fields, you limit the amount of drain each user can put on the system within one hour.

Server Connections Information

The Server Connections display allows you to view your connections, or threads, to the server or, if you have the privileges, to see all the connections to the server. It has two tabs: Threads and User Connections, which show the same information but in different formats. Figure 6-8 shows the Threads tab.

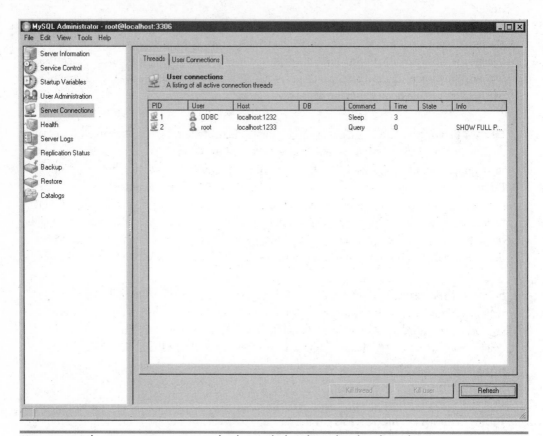

Figure 6-8 The Server Connections display with the Threads tab selected

Threads Tab   The Threads tab shows all the threads attached to the server. This means multiple threads from the same user may be visible, depending on his or her interaction with the database. At the bottom of the Threads tab display there are three buttons: Kill Thread, Kill User, and Refresh. The Refresh button is always available, and it updates the display of the threads at the moment it is clicked. The Kill Thread button remains grayed out and inoperative until a thread is highlighted in the display by clicking it. You can stop the highlighted thread by clicking the Kill Thread button or by right-clicking the highlighted thread and choosing Kill Thread from the pop-up menu. You are allowed to select multiple threads. The Kill User button is inactive on this tab's display.

NOTE

You need SUPER privileges to view and kill other users' threads, and you cannot kill your own threads.

User Connections Tab   The User Connections tab also displays the threads connected to the server; however, instead of only displaying each thread separately, it shows both the number of threads that the selected user has at any given time and a list of each separate thread of that user. Like the Threads tab, the User Connections tab can be updated by clicking the Refresh button. When a user is highlighted in the upper window, the Kill User button becomes active and using it will stop all the threads of that user with a single click. When a single thread or multiple threads are highlighted in the list of user threads, the Kill Thread button becomes active and using it will stop any threads that are selected.

Health Information

The Health display, shown in Figure 6-9, provides graphical and statistical views of MySQL's performance and status. The Health information is divided among four tabs: Connection Health, Memory Health, Status Variables, and System Variables.

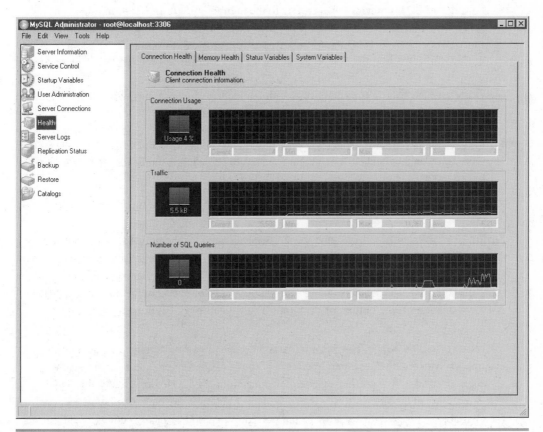

Figure 6-9 The Health display with the Connection Health tab selected

Connection Health Tab   The Connections Health tab shows information about MySQL connections in two different ways. There is a vertical bar graphic, which displays percentages, and an X,Y axis chart, which scrolls from right to left with time. The tab has three sections:

- **Connection Usage**   This refers to the maximum number of simultaneous client connections allowed.

NOTE

If the Connections Usage gets close to 100% on a regular basis, you should consider raising the maximum number of connections allowed. You can do this from the Startup Variables display's Networking tab, in the Max Connections field.

- **Traffic**   This refers to the amount of usage at a given moment.

- **Number of SQL Queries**   This refers to the number of SQL queries running at any given moment.

   Current, Minimum, Maximum, and Average statistics are listed under each display.

Memory Health Tab   The Memory Health tab includes two sections, which use the same graphical and statistical format as the Connection Health tab:

- **Query Cache Hitrate**   This shows the ratio between the number of SELECT queries that were and were not cached. The higher the hit rate percentage, the better the performance of the server.

- **Key Efficiency**   This shows information about the key buffer.

Status Variables Tab   The Status Variables tab shows a wide range of statistics concerning the status of the MySQL Server. The sidebar lists a variety of variables grouped in five sections: General, Performance, Networking, Commands Executed, and Miscellaneous. Each section has subsections you can select to see the corresponding information in the main display. There is a Refresh button at the bottom of the window to gather up-to-the-moment information.

System Variables Tab   The System Variables tab shows a wide range of statistics and information concerning the system operation of the MySQL Server. The sidebar lists the variables grouped in five sections: General, Connections, SQL, Memory, and Table Types. Select a section in the sidebar to see the related information in the main display. If the icon for a variable is a page with a yellow pencil poised over it, the variable is editable, and double-clicking it opens a pop-up window that allows you to change the value. Set and Abort buttons allow you to save or abandon any changes to the variable made in the pop-up window. This tab also has a Refresh button to gather the most current information.

Server Logs

The Server Logs display contains information about three logs, as shown in Figure 6-10. The display format for each log includes a left pane showing events and a right pane showing page content. You can use the Pages bar at the top of the display as a rough navigation method for longer logs, by clicking at the beginning, middle, or end of the log. The Search and Save Log Page buttons at the bottom of the window open pop-up windows allowing you to search the log file and save the currently displayed page, respectively. The Refresh button allows you to gather an up-to-the-moment image of the log file.

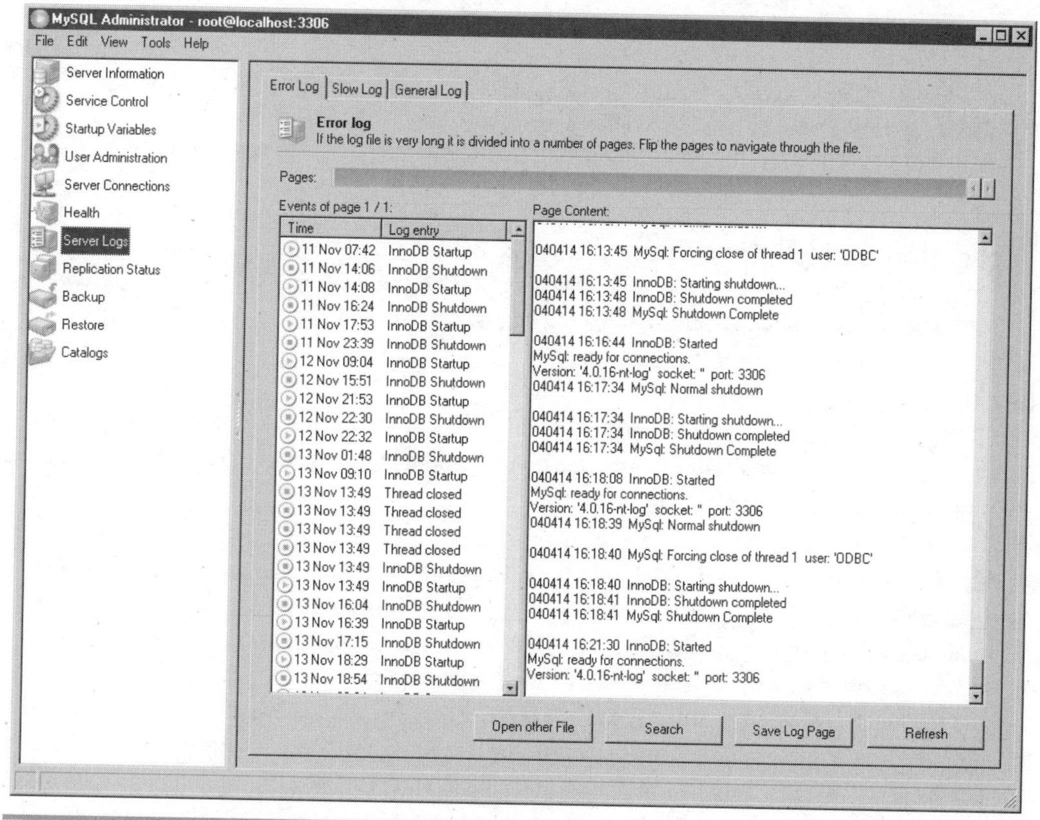

Figure 6-10 The Server Logs display with the Error Log tab selected

There is a tab for each log:

- **Error Log**   This tab displays the MySQL Server's Error log, which contains start and stop information, as well as the critical errors that occur while running.

- **Slow Log**   This tab displays the log containing all the commands that took longer than a specified amount of time to execute. For this log to exist, you must enable it, using the Startup Variables display's Log Files tab, which contains the Slow Queries Log field in the Activate Logging area.

- **General Log**   This tab displays the Query log file containing general query information. Like the Slow log, this file must first be enabled for this tab to be functional. You can enable the Query log file using the Startup Variables display's Log Files tab, which contains the Query Logfile Name field in the Activate Logging area.

NOTE

If one of the Server Logs tabs is disabled, the log file may not be enabled on the MySQL Server, or the log file may exist on a different computer than the one on which MySQL Administrator is running. The Alpha version of MySQL Administrator allows you to read only the log files stored on the computer on which it is installed.

Replication Status Information

If you have a replication process set up for your MySQL Server, the Replication Status display will give you an overview of the replication status.

Backup

The Backup display, shown in Figure 6-11, allows you to create and execute backup projects. It is a graphic interface for the `mysqldump` command that we will cover in Module 8, with the added advantage of saving the projects.

Backup Project Tab   When you select the Backup Projects tab, another sidebar panel appears below the main sidebar on the left. This sidebar lists the saved backup projects. The main display area has two panes: on the left, the pane labeled Schemata lists the individual databases, and the pane on the right shows the contents of the backup. You can move data into the Backup Content list by using the arrow buttons between the two panes.

The New Project button at the bottom of the window clears the display so a new project can be specified. The Save Project button is enabled when the New Project button is selected or when data is altered in an existing project. The Execute Backup Now button is enabled any time a project is selected in the sidebar list.

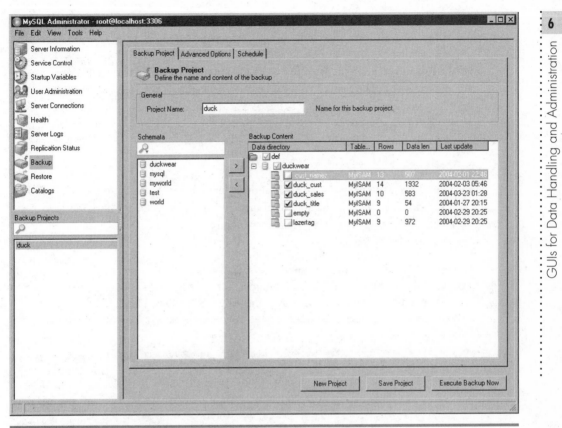

Figure 6-11 The Backup display with the Backup Project tab selected

Advanced Options Tab   The Advanced Options tab allows you to specify how your backup should be executed. It is arranged into two areas: Backup Execution and Output File Options. The Backup Execution area offers four choices:

- **Lock All Tables**   This option is crucial to getting a consistent picture of your MyISAM tables.

- **Single Transaction**   This option is crucial to getting a consistent picture of your InnoDB tables.

- **Normal Backup**   This option causes each table to be backed up independently, which can lead to inconsistent backups and should be avoided.

- **Backup Selected Schemata**   This option completely overrides your Backup Content specifications and backs up all of the tables of the selected schemata. This should be used on schemas where tables are often added.

The Output File Options area has options that allow you to select the format of the output file and to choose to include or exclude certain commands and information.

Schedule Tab The Schedule tab will eventually allow you to perform an automatic, scheduled backup at a specific interval of time, but this feature is not yet available in the current Alpha version. If the feature uses the `crontab` command to achieve its end result, this will be a Linux-specific feature, but by the time the tool reaches the Production version, the Schedule tab may be available on Windows systems as well.

Restore

The Restore display, shown in Figure 6-12, allows you to restore backups you've made. Click the Open Backup File button at the bottom of the window and select a .sql backup file to restore. Click the Start Restore to begin the restoration process.

The Restore display has two tabs:

●   **General** This tab contains options for how the backup will be restored. When you select a backup file, MySQL Administrator automatically fills in the File to Restore field. In the Alpha version of MySQL Administrator, the Target Schema and Backup File Type are also selected automatically, because there is only one option available for each field.

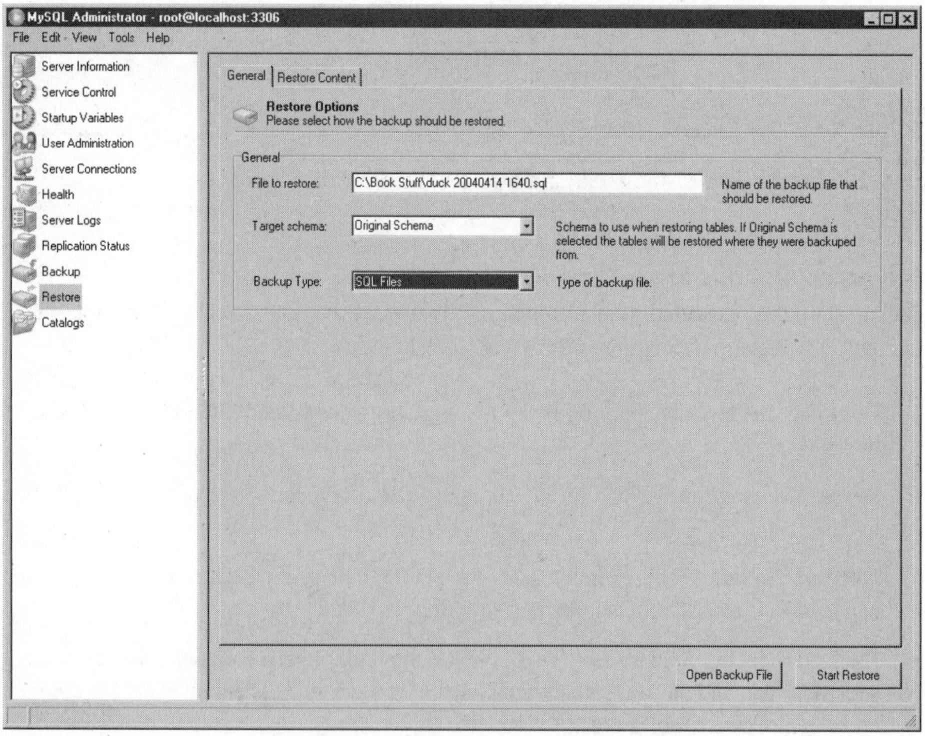

Figure 6-12 The Restore window with General tab displayed

- **Restore Content**   This tab displays the contents of the backup file that has been selected for restoration.

Catalogs Information

The Catalogs display allows you to select a database (schema) and view its tables (schemata), as well as the details of the table's construction, as shown in Figure 6-13. It has three tabs: Schema Tables, Indices, and Users. All three tabs have a Refresh button at the bottom of the window.

Schema Tables Tab   The Schema Tables tab allows you to view a database's tables and columns. When a database is selected in the Schemata sidebar that appears beneath the main one on the left, the list of tables for that database is displayed in the upper pane of the main display. When you select a table from that list, the details about that table are displayed in the lower pane's four tabs:

- **Columns**   This tab shows the description of the selected table.

- **Indices**   This tab shows any index fields the table may have.

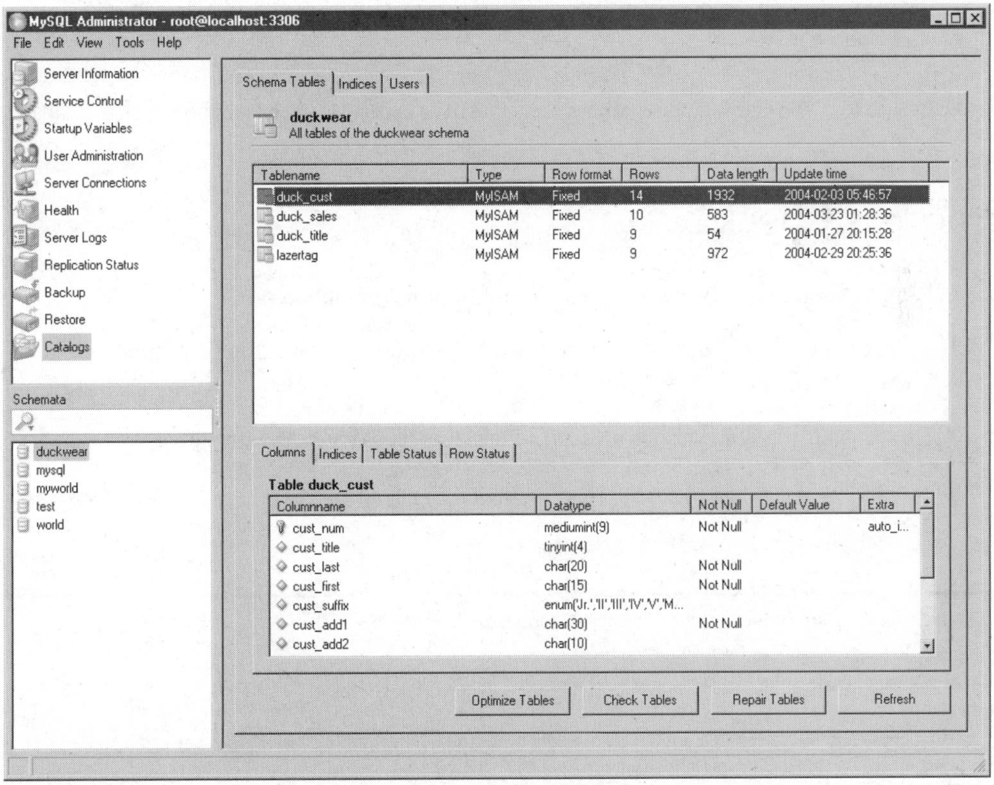

Figure 6-13 The Catalogs display with the Schema Tables tab selected

- **Table Status** This tab shows the table type, the row format, the next available auto-increment number, any CREATE options specified, and comments (if any exist for the table).

- **Row Status** This tab shows both data and time information. The Data section shows Number of Rows, Average Row Length, Data Length, Max Data Length, Index Length, and Data Free fields. The Time section shows the Create, Update, and Check Times fields.

The buttons at the bottom of the window allow you to perform certain tasks related to the tables: optimizing, checking, and repairing tables.

Indices Tab The Indices tab is similar but more comprehensive than the Indices tab in the Schema Tables tab. Where the Indices tab in the Schema Tables tab lists the index field or fields for a specific table, the Indices tab of the Catalog display lists all of the index fields for the entire selected database. Double-click a table name to see the column name of the index.

NOTE

The Alpha version lists all the indices for all the databases on the server, regardless of which database is selected.

Users Tab The Users tab lists all the users that have access privileges to the selected database.

Progress Check

1. Why shouldn't you always leave the Debug Information option on?

2. If the Connections Usage percentage gets close to 100%, what is the first thing you should you do?

3. How do you view the various areas of information in MySQL Administrator?

4. When should you use MySQL Administrator?

---

1. Leaving the Debug Information on can affect the performance of the server.

2. You should increase the Max Connections number.

3. In the sidebar to the left, you select the area your interested in and that information will appear in the main window on the right.

4. You should use it if you prefer a GUI interface over the command line for administration tasks like setting buffer sizes, monitoring system health, and maintaining user accounts and privileges.

Project 6-1 Download and Install MySQL Administrator on Windows

In this project, you will download MySQL Administrator and install it on your Windows machine. The functions that allow you to monitor your system's health will be useful in choosing whether to change your database settings and to check things like peak usage. The user administration function gives you a quick overview of your database's users and their privilege settings, which makes administration more convenient and less time-consuming. You can also use MySQL Administrator to start and stop the MySQL server. Many MySQL Administrator functions will become clear only as your grasp of and experience with MySQL grows over time. Some options are so specialized you may never need them, but should the need arise, MySQL Administrator gives you quick and easy access to them without having to look up the command-line syntax.

Step by Step

1. Open a web browser and go to the MySQL AB web site for downloading MySQL Administrator: http://www.mysql.com/downloads/administrator.html.

2. Click the **Pick a mirror** link under the **Windows downloads** section.

NOTE

The MySQL Administrator program is in the Alpha stage, and as such, there is only one version available, but if there are multiple versions to choose from, select the one marked (Recommended) or failing that, the newest version.

3. Pick a mirror site close to your location and click the accompanying HTTP or FTP link to download the .zip file and save it to your hard disk. Once the file download is complete, you may close your browser if desired.

4. Go to the directory where you saved the .zip file and open it using your ZIP program. When your ZIP program opens, you can either install the downloaded program from inside the ZIP program, using temporary directories, or extract it to a file, and then install from there.

(continued)

5. Double-click the Setup.exe file. After the initial "preparing to install" message, you will see the Welcome screen of the MySQL Administrator InstallShield Wizard.

6. Click the Next button to proceed with the installation. The License Agreement window appears. Click the radio button to agree to the terms of the license.

7. Click the Next button. The next window, titled Readme Information, supplies a URL (http://bugs.mysql.com) for reporting any bugs found. Make a note of this address (or mark this page in this book).

8. Click the Next button. The Destination Window appears next. It allows you to install MySQL Administrator in another directory, if necessary.

9. If you want to use another directory, click the Change button and browse for a more appropriate location. Otherwise, leave the default destination folder. Click the Next button to proceed to the Setup Type window.

(continued)

10. Unless you have overriding factors that prompt you to require a Custom installation, click the Typical radio button, and then click the Next button to proceed to the Ready to Install the Program window.

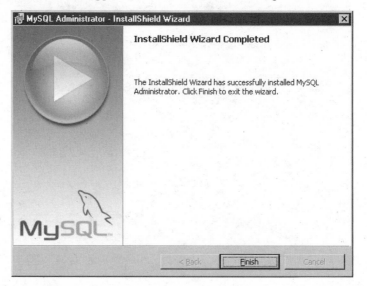

11. If the information displayed is not correct, use the Back button to correct it. When the information displayed is correct, click the Install button, The InstallShield Wizard Completed window will appear when the installation is complete.

12. Click the Finish button to close the installation wizard.

Project Summary

In this project, you installed the MySQL Administrator program on your system. Clicking the MySQL Administrator shortcut icon placed on your system's desktop will open the program and allow you to explore the various windows discussed in the preceding sections of this module. Even though there may be some unpredictable behavior or incomplete features, because the program is still in its Alpha version, the MySQL Administrator program will allow you to view information and statistics about your MySQL Server, as well as access and edit many useful settings.

CAUTION

MySQL Administrator is in Alpha release. In accordance with open source principles of development, MySQL AB has released the code to users in order to further its development process. Back up your database regularly in case of a mishap and report bugs to MySQL AB to speed improvements to this program.

Project 6-2 Download and Install MySQL Administrator on Linux

In this project, you will download MySQL Administrator and then install it on a machine running the Linux OS. The functions that allow you to monitor your system's health will be useful in choosing whether to change your database settings and to check things like peak usage. The user administration function gives you a quick overview of your database's users and their privilege settings, which makes administration more convenient and less time-consuming. You can also use MySQL Administrator to start and stop the MySQL server. Many MySQL Administrator functions will become clear only as your grasp of and experience with MySQL grows over time. Some options are so specialized you may never need them, but should the need arise, MySQL Administrator gives you quick and easy access to them without having to look up the command-line syntax.

Step by Step

1. Open a browser and go to http://www.mysql.com/downloads/administrator.html. Scroll down to **Linux downloads** and click the **Pick a mirror** link.

2. Choose the closest mirror site and click the HTTP or FTP link. Download the taz.gz file to /usr/local/src. Once the file download is complete, you may close your browser if desired.

NOTE

The MySQL Administrator program is in the Alpha stage, and as such, there is only one version available, but if there are multiple versions to choose from, select the one marked (Recommended) or failing that, the newest version.

(continued)

3. Open a command-line window and change directory to /usr/local/src. The file you downloaded should be named something like mysq-administrator-1.*x.xx*-linux.tar.gz. tar.

4. Change directory to /usr/opt (where the FAQ.txt on MySQL Administrator suggests installing the program) and untar and install the file, using the following command (replace the instances of the letter *x* in the version identifier with the corresponding numbers in the file you downloaded).

```
tar -xzvf /usr/local/src/mysql-administrator-1.x.xx-linux.tar.gz.tar
```

5. Start the program by running the following command.

```
/opt/mysql-administrator/bin/mysql-administrator
```

6. Fill in the Username, Password, and Hostname fields in the MySQL Administrator window that pops up, and then click the Connect button to open the GUI and connect it to your server.

Project Summary

Even though there may be some unpredictable behavior or incomplete features because the program is still in its Alpha version, MySQL Administrator will allow you to view information and statistics about your MySQL Server, as well as access and edit many useful settings; however, MySQL does not recommend using it in a production environment at this time.

CRITICAL SKILL
6.2 Use MySQL Control Center

The MySQL Control Center (MySQLCC) is a GUI that allows you easy access to the databases, tables, and data on your MySQL Server. It provides a point-and-click environment for speedy and simple command access, as well as a visual overview of your database design and contents. It supplies you with a syntax-highlighting text editor for constructing queries and allows you to do some database and table management. MySQLCC also allows you to view and change some server variables.

NOTE

This section refers to MySQL Control Center version 0.9.4-beta.

Everything that can be accomplished in MySQLCC can be accomplished using the command line. MySQLCC is simply a tool for those users more familiar with or more comfortable with a GUI interface. There are some specific situations in which MySQLCC will be easier or simpler to use than the command line. For instance, reading large amounts of data in each record is easier using a GUI interface than using the command line; when long lines continue to the next line, correlating a field with its header can be difficult. As you experiment with MySQLCC, you will develop your own preferences for using the GUI and using the command line.

MySQLCC can appear with a main Control Center window and a separate Console Manager window, as shown in Figure 6-14 (with the Console Manager window minimized). Whether there are separate MySQLCC windows depends on the MDI setting in the program's Options menu, as described shortly.

Choosing MySQLCC Menu Options

The menu bar at the top of the Control Center window has five drop-down menus:

- **Console**   This menu has only one option: Exit. Choosing Exit causes MySQLCC to close; it's equivalent to clicking the Close button (with the X) in the upper-right corner of the window.

- **Options**   This menu has four choices: MDI, Themes, Fonts, and General. These are discussed in the next section.

- **HotKeys**   This menu contains only the option to open the HotKey Editor, which lets you edit the existing hotkeys (shortcut keys) or add new ones.

- **Window**   This menu has an option for toggling the display of the Console Manager. It also has options that allow you to close only the window that is currently highlighted or

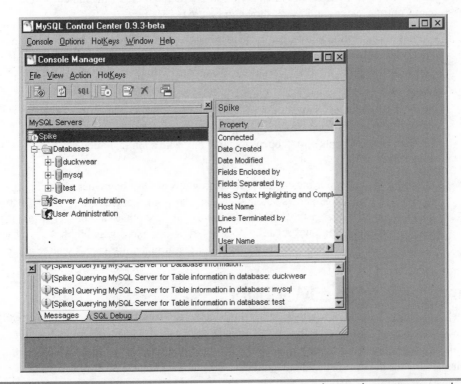

Figure 6-14 The main Control Center window with a minimized Console Manager window

6

GUIs for Data Handling and Administration

close all the windows that are currently open in MySQLCC. There are also two options for arranging the windows when you have more than one of them open and wish to navigate between them: Cascade and Tile.

● **Help**   This menu, ironically enough, offers very little in the way of help. It does show information on the version number of MySQLCC you are running and a list of names and e-mail addresses of those who contributed to the design of the program.

Selecting MySQLCC Options

You can select the following options from the Options menu to control some aspects of MySQLCC:

● **MDI**   This option runs MySQLCC in MDI (Multiple Document Interface) mode. When you choose MDI, you'll see a message noting that MySQLCC needs to be restarted before it reflects the change you just made. When MySQLCC is in MDI mode, a Console Manager window will appear within a Control Center window. When not in MDI mode, there is no main Control Center window; only a Console Manager window appears. This is normally referred to as SDI (Single Document Interface) mode, but MySQLCC does not use that acronym. The SDI Console Manager window has some of the menu choices from the main Control Center window, as shown in Figure 6-15.

● **Themes**   This option allows you to choose between six different themes that change the appearance of the MySQLCC windows. The changes take place immediately (you don't need to restart the program), so it is easy to experiment to decide which theme you prefer.

● **Fonts**   This option allows you to choose the font, style, size, and effects for the application and printer fonts. The application fonts are the ones used for text in all of the MySQLCC windows. The printer fonts are those used for documents sent to the printer from MySQLCC. The Query Editor Fonts option opens a dialog box with a tab that allows you to view and change a few variables regarding the Query Editor.

● **General**   This option brings up the same dialog box as choosing Query Editor Fonts, but displaying a tab that allows you to view and alter some general information, including paths to sound files, language, size of the History file, and other variables. The dialog box has tabs containing variables regarding queries, plug-ins, and syntax highlighting. These tabs have Apply or Cancel buttons for saving or discarding any changes you've made.

Using the Console Manager

Whether or not you run MySQLCC in MDI mode, the Console Manager functions in nearly the same manner. If the program is in MDI mode, the Console Manager's menu bar holds the File, View, Action, and HotKeys menu, as shown in Figure 6-16. If it is not in MDI mode, the menu bar adds the two menus that would have been in the main Control Center window's menu bar: Options and Help.

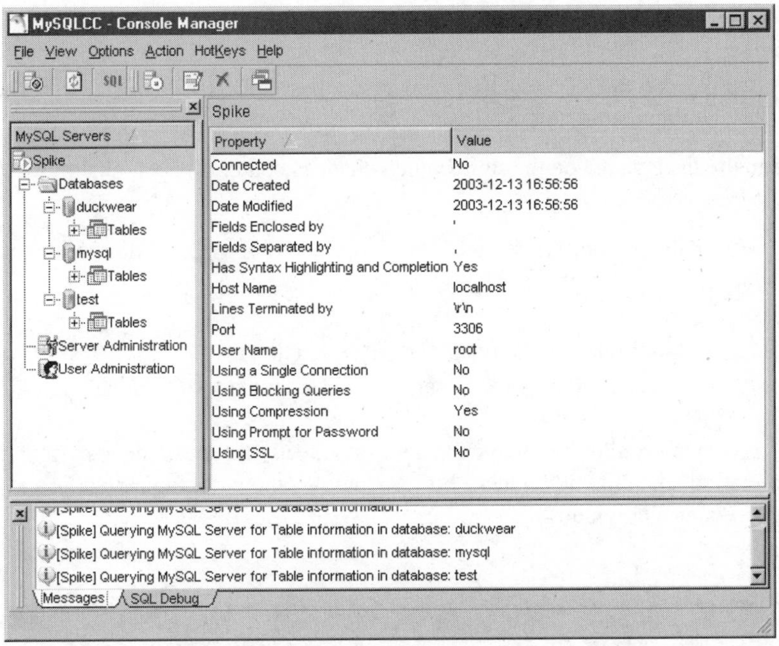

Figure 6-15 MySQLCC when the MDI option is not selected

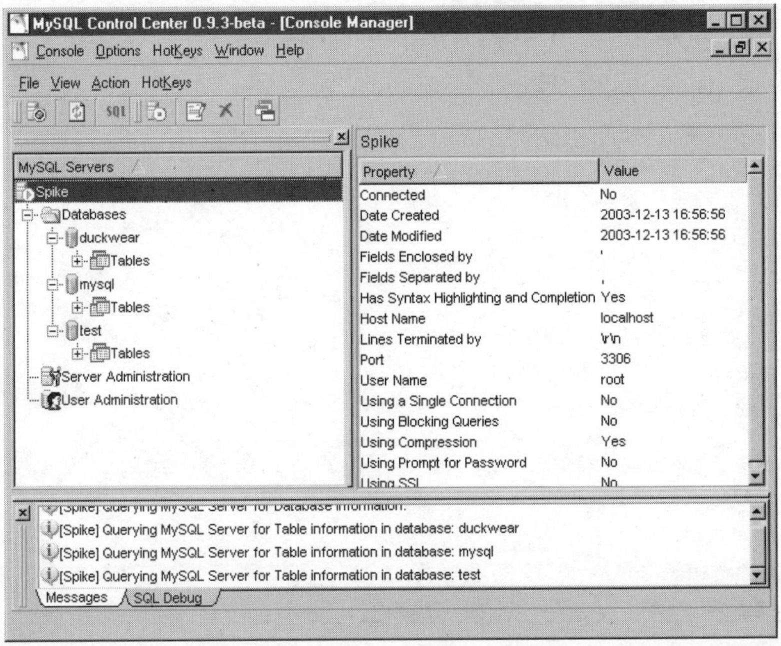

Figure 6-16 The Console Manager window in MDI mode with main Control Center window

The Console Manager window consists of three areas of information:

- The tree pane on the left, which shows the databases on your MySQL Server (or servers), plus User Administration and Server Administration categories

- The main display area on the right, which changes contents depending on what is selected in the tree pane

- The pane at the bottom, which holds messages and SQL debug information, each on its own tab

Using the Console Manager Menus and Toolbar

The Console Manager window's menu bar has four menus (in MDI mode):

- **File** This menu allows you to open a new connection, refresh the current display of information, open the SQL Query Editor window (shown in Figure 6-17), and close the Console Manager window.

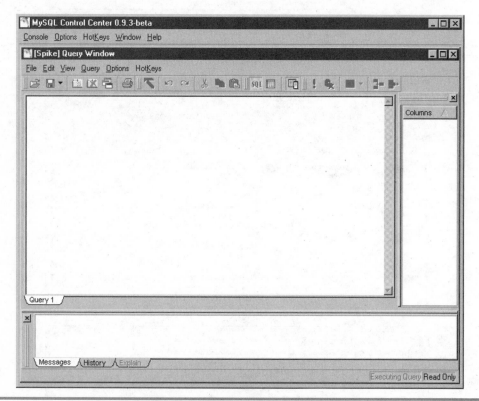

Figure 6-17 The SQL Query Editor window

- **View**   This menu allows you to turn on and off the tree and message displays in the Console Manager window. Their display can also be turned off using the Close button in the upper-right corner of each display, but the View drop-down is the only place when they can be turned back on.

- **Action**   This menu changes depending on what is selected in the tree pane. It provides the same options as the Console Manager window's toolbar buttons, described in the next sections.

NOTE

If you can't find a particular function in the Action menu, it may because you do not have the corresponding area selected in the tree pane.

- **HotKeys**   This menu has an option for the HotKeys Editor, which works in the same way as it does when accessed from the main Control Center window.

The Console Manager toolbar buttons change depending on what is selected in the tree pane, as described in the next section. However, in all these displays, the first three buttons are always the same.

These buttons, from left to right, allow you to add new connection definitions and variables, refresh the current display, and open the SQL Query Editor (see Figure 6-17).

Viewing Information and Performing Actions

You can select seven levels of information in the MySQLCC tree pane:

- Server
- Databases
- Specific database
- Tables
- Specific table
- Server administration
- User administration

Server-level Information   When the server level of information is selected in the tree, the display of information in the right window is server-related, as shown in Figure 6-18.

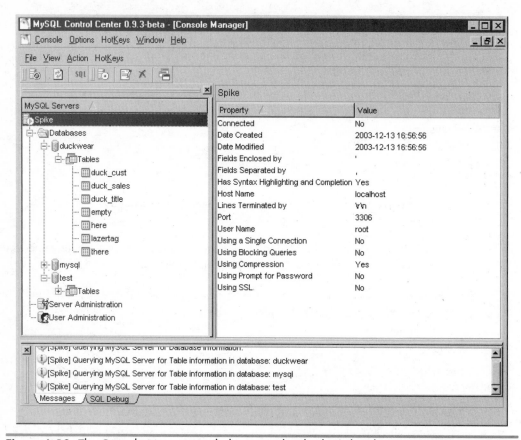

Figure 6-18 The Console Manager with the server level selected in the tree pane

Along with the first three standard toolbar buttons (described in the previous section), the toolbar in this view contains four buttons related to the server information.

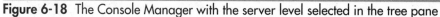

The server-level toolbar buttons perform the following tasks:

- **Disconnect or Connect**   Clicking the button performs either action, depending on the current status between the GUI and the server.

- **Edit**   Opens a window allowing variables to be accessed.

- **Delete**   Deletes the currently saved server connection information.

- **New Window from Here**   Opens a new instance of the Control Manager window.

Database-level Information   When the databases level of information is selected in the tree pane, the display of information in the right window is about the database in general, as shown in Figure 6-19.

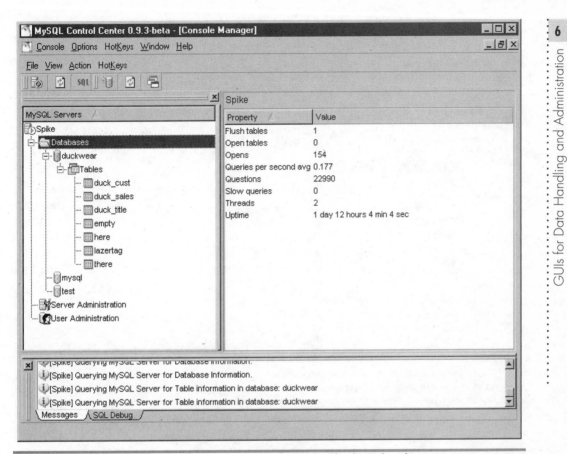

Figure 6-19 The Console Manager with the databases level selected in the tree pane

The Console Manager toolbar buttons in the database-level view, from left to right, create a new database, refresh the existing display, and open a new instance of the Control Manager window.

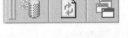

Specific Database Information   When you've selected a specific database in the tree pane, the display of information in the right window is the same as the information shown at the databases level (see Figure

6-19). The toolbar buttons, from left to right, disconnect or connect to the specific database, drop the specific database, and open a new instance of the Control Manager window.

Tables-level Information   When the tables level of information is selected in the tree pane, the display of information in the right window shows all the tables for the database, as shown in Figure 6-20.

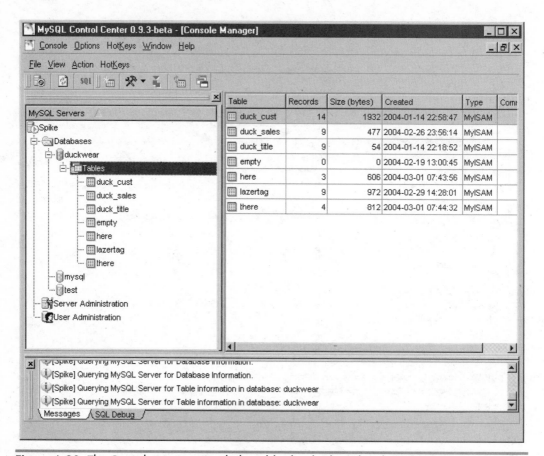

Figure 6-20 The Console Manager with the tables level selected in the tree pane

The toolbar buttons in this view, from left to right, open a window that allows you to define a new table for the database, display the Tools menu, allow you to import tables, refresh the tables, and open a new instance of the Control Manager window.

The Tools menu that opens when you click the Tools button on the toolbar offers Analyze, Check, Optimize, Repair Tables, and SHOW CREATE options. The SHOW CREATE option brings up a list of current tables to run the SHOW CREATE command on. By choosing a table and one of the Tools options, MySQLCC automatically composes the necessary SQL commands and sends them to the database, relieving you of having to remember the correct syntax. You can click the History tab at the bottom of the window to see a listing of SQL commands sent to the database. The SHOW CREATE command ultimately brings up a Query window showing the command used to create the specified table.

Specific Table Information   When you've selected a specific table in the tree pane, the display on the right shows all the column definitions for the table, as shown in Figure 6-21. The toolbar in this view contains nine buttons related to the server information.

These toolbar buttons represent the bulk of MySQLCC's table definition and data editing capabilities. They work as follows:

- **Open Table**   Opens a menu with two options: Return All Rows and Return Limit. Return All Rows brings up a Query window with the data contents of the selected table, as shown in Figure 6-22. This window allows you to insert and delete rows, change column definitions, and edit data on an individual field basis, as well as perform various other table- and data-related functions. The Return Limit option brings up a dialog box asking for a limit number, and then displays only that many records.

Field	Type	Null	Key	Default
cust_num	mediumint(9)		PRI	
cust_title	tinyint(4)	YES		
cust_last	char(20)			
cust_first	char(15)			
cust_suffix	enum('Jr.','II','III','IV','\	YES		
cust_add1	char(30)			
cust_add2	char(10)	YES		
cust_city	char(18)			
cust_state	char(2)			
cust_zip1	char(5)			
cust_zip2	char(4)	YES		
cust_duckname	char(25)			
cust_duckbday	date	YES		

Figure 6-21   The Console Manager with a specific table selected in the tree pane

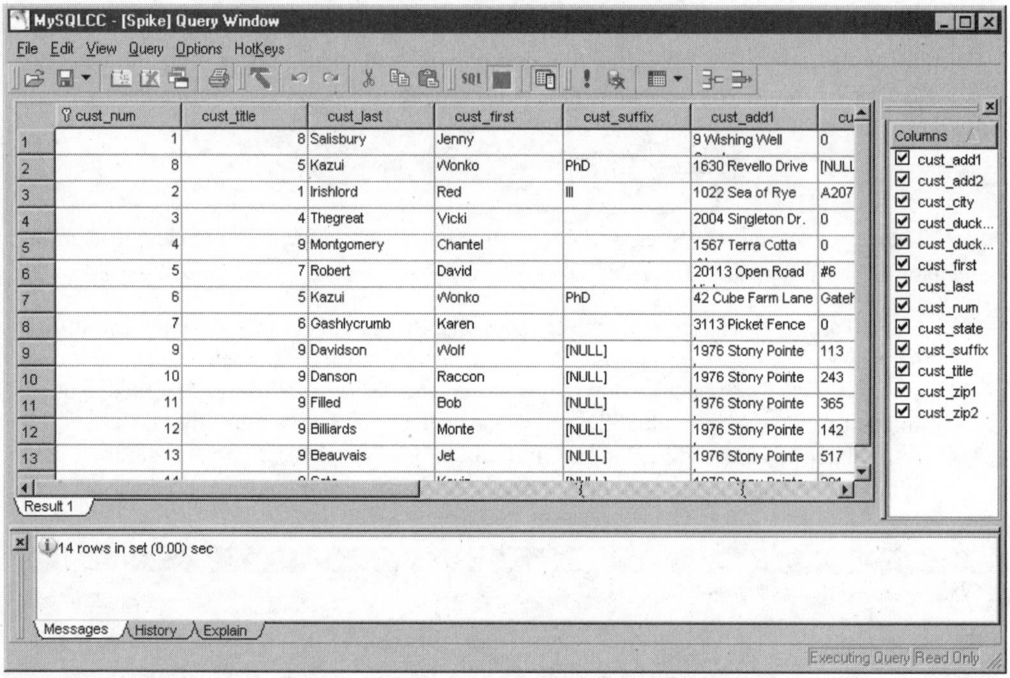

Figure 6-22 The Query window displaying all rows in a table

- **Edit Table** Brings up an editing window that allows you to edit a table by row or column, including changing the table definition, as shown in Figure 6-23.

- **Properties** Brings up a display of general properties for the specified table, but only for viewing. You cannot make any changes in the Properties window.

- **Export** Allows you to export table information.

- **Tools** Opens the Tools menu, described in the previous section.

- **Empty Table** Removes all the data from a table, permanently, while leaving the table definition intact.

- **Drop Table** Removes the table and its data from the database permanently.

- **Rename Table** Allows you to change the name of the selected table.

- **Refresh Fields** Gets up-to-date information from the database for the table display.

Server Administration Information When you've selected Server Administration in the tree pane, the display to the right is essentially the same as the information displayed in the databases and specific database levels (see Figure 6-19).

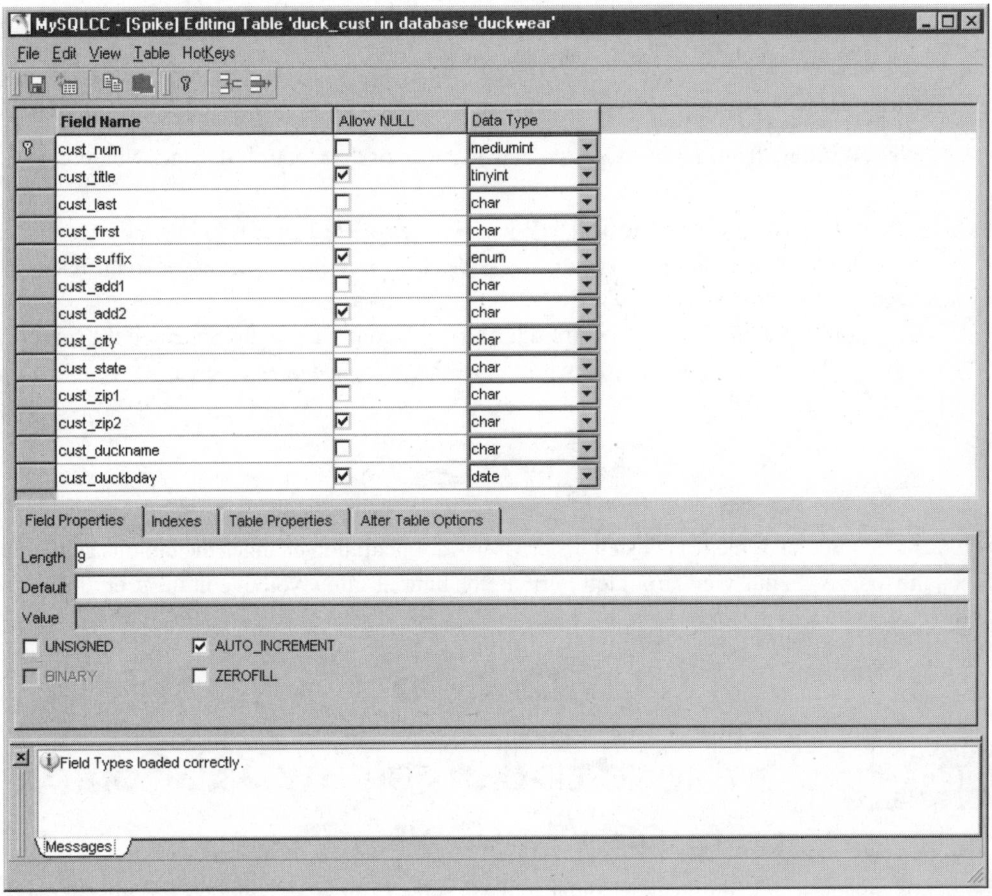

Figure 6-23 The window for editing a table

The toolbar in this view contains seven buttons related to administering the server.

The Server Administration toolbar buttons perform the following tasks:

- **Show Process List**   Brings up the Administration window with the Process List tab displayed.

- **Show Status**   Brings up the Administration window with the Status tab displayed.

- **Show Variables**   Brings up the Administration window with the Variables tab displayed.

- **Flush**   Opens a menu with nine options that you can choose to flush the database.

- **Ping**   Checks to see if the `mysqld` process is alive and returns a message to the Message window at the bottom of the Administration window.

- **Shutdown**   Closes the MySQL Client after verification.

- **New Window from Here**   Opens a new instance of the Control Manager window.

User Administration Information   When you've selected User Administration in the tree pane, the display to the right is essentially the same as the information displayed in the databases and specific database levels (see Figure 6-19).

The toolbar buttons in this view, from left to right, connect and disconnect to the server supplying a list of the users, add a new user, refresh tables, and open a new instance of the Control Manager window.

Selecting one of the users listed under User Administration changes the buttons available on the toolbar. In this view, from left to right, the buttons allow you to edit the user, delete the user, and add a user.

Project 6-3 Download and Install MySQL Control Center on Windows

In this project, you will download and install MySQLCC on your Windows machine. Now that you have had hands-on experience using the command line with MySQL, you may opt to use the GUI interface at times, depending on your personal preference. Logging in on the command line to execute a single command will probably still be faster; however, viewing and interpreting data in a multicolumn table will be easier in MySQLCC because of the wrap-around format for long lines of data when using the command line.

Step by Step

1. Open a web browser and go to the download page of the MySQL AB web site for MySQLCC: http://www.mysql.com/downloads/mysqlcc.html.

2. Click the **Pick a mirror** link under the **Windows downloads** section.

3. Pick a mirror site close to your location and click the accompanying HTTP or FTP link to download the .zip file and save to your hard disk. Once the file download is complete, you may close your browser if desired.

4. Go to the directory where you saved the .zip file and open it using your ZIP program. When your ZIP program opens, you can either install the program from inside the ZIP program, using temporary directories, or extract it to a file, and then install from there.

5. Double-click the Setup.exe file.

6. The Welcome to the MySQL Control Center Installation Wizard window appears. It has standard reminders about closing other programs before beginning the installation process.

(continued)

7. Click Next to proceed. The Licensing Agreement window appears with MySQL's GNU agreement. Click the radio button to accept the license agreement.

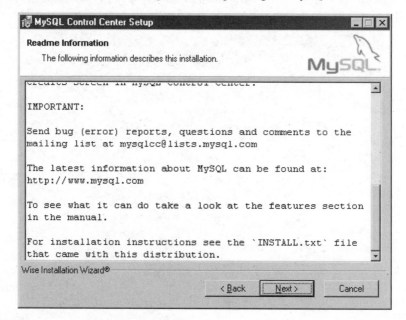

8. Click the Next button. The Readme Information window appears. It has some basic installation information, including where to report bugs in MySQLCC.

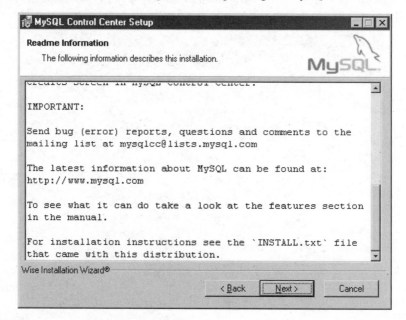

9. Click the Next button to proceed. The Destination Folder window that appears next allows you to change the installation location, if you have compelling need to do so. If you need to change the installation directory, click the Browse button and select a new path.

10. After you specified either the default location or a new one, click the Next button to proceed. The Select Features window appears. This window allows you to decline to install some of the language features for MySQLCC.

(continued)

11. All of the Language features combined do not take up a great deal of space on the disk, so unless disk space is incredibly dear, click the Next button and leave all the features marked for installation. The Ready to Install the Application window appears, giving you a chance to click the Back button and change your earlier selections, if necessary.

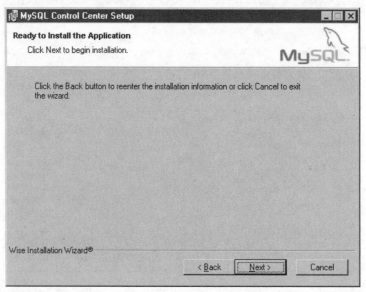

12. When your selections are correct, click the Next button to proceed with the installation. A progress bar will indicate the installation progress, and then you'll see a window reporting that MySQLCC has been successfully installed.

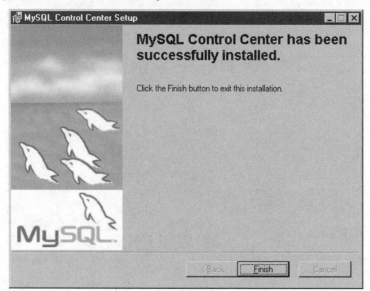

13. Click the Finish button to finalize the installation process.

14. MySQLCC has installed a shortcut icon on your desktop. Double-click it to open MySQLCC.

Project Summary

In this project, you installed MySQLCC. Now, you can use it to interface with your database in a point-and-click, visually-oriented environment. In some circumstances, this will be preferable to working on the command line.

Project 6-4 Download and Install MySQL Control Center on Linux

In this project, you will download and install MySQLCC on a computer that runs the Linux OS. Now that you have had hands-on experience using the command line with MySQL, you may opt to use the GUI interface at times, depending on your personal preference. Logging in on the command line to execute a single command will probably still be faster; however, viewing and interpreting data in a multicolumn table will be easier in MySQLCC because of the wrap-around format for long lines of data on the command line.

Step by Step

1. Open a browser and go to http://www.mysql.com/downloads/mysqlcc.html. Scroll down to **Linux downloads** and click the **Pick a mirror** link.

2. Choose the closest mirror site and click the HTTP or FTP link. Download the taz.gz file to /usr/local/src. Once the file download is complete, you may close your browser if desired.

3. Open a command-line window and change to the /usr/local/src directory. The file you downloaded should be named something like mysqlcc-0.*x.x*-linux-glibc2*x*.tar.gz.tar.

4. Untar and install the file, using the following command. (Replace the instances of the letter *x* in the version designation with the corresponding numbers in the file you downloaded).

```
tar -xzvf mysqlcc-0.x.x-linux-glibc2x.tar.gz.tar
```

5. Start the program by running the following command.

```
/usr/local/src/mysqlcc-0.9.4-linux-glibc22/mysqlcc
```

6. Fill in the Username, Password, and Hostname fields in the pop-up window labeled MySQL Administrator, and then click the Connect button to open the GUI and connect it to your server.

Project Summary

In this project, you installed MySQLCC. Now, you can interface with you database in a point-and-click, visually oriented environment. In some circumstances, this will be preferable to working on the command line.

✓

Module 6 Mastery Check

1. What is an Alpha version release?

2. How do MySQLCC and MySQL Administrator differ?

3. How can you change or set Hot Keys with MySQLCC?

4. What happens when you select different levels on the tree pane of MySQLCC?

5. What is the MySQL recommendation for buffer size?

6. Which of these two GUIs allows you to start and stop the MySQL server by pressing a button?

7. What four areas of system health can you monitor with MySQL Administrator?

8. Where do you go in MySQL Administrator to set up a variety of system logs?

9. How do you change the main display window in MySQLCC?

10. What causes buttons to appear and disappear from the toolbar in MySQLCC?

Module 7

Interfacing with Programs

CRITICAL SKILLS

7.1   Use PHP and MySQL

7.2   Separate Database Functions from Application Code

7.3   Import MySQL Data into Excel and Access

This module deals with three programs that commonly interface with MySQL: PHP, Microsoft Excel, and Microsoft Access. PHP and MySQL are often jointly used in dynamic web sites, where information is displayed or accepted in a real-time environment. Information stored in Excel and Access is often migrated to MySQL, as users' data storage and manipulation needs become more sophisticated and demanding. However, you may need to bring some data into Excel or Access. For example, some users prefer to use Access as a front end to view or manipulate their MySQL-stored data, because they are already familiar with its GUI.

If you are interested in using any of these programs with MySQL data, this module will explain how to do that. We will assume that you already have some familiarity with the program.

CRITICAL SKILL
7.1 Use PHP and MySQL

PHP is a scripting language whose most common use is creating dynamic web pages. It is common to see PHP and MySQL working together in web sites and web-based applications. PHP is fairly easy to learn and quick to use, making it one of the fastest growing web languages, and it is now making inroads into larger enterprise applications. This means that the same technology that makes a hobbyist's web site can also be used to power large, business-critical web software.

This skill will focus on how you can use PHP to interface with a MySQL database. At the time of this book, version 5 of PHP is just about ready for production. Therefore, we will also cover the new, improved, MySQL-specific functions found in this new PHP release.

Introducing PHP

PHP stands for Pre-Hypertext Processor. *Hypertext*, a concept Tim Berners-Lee is credited with creating, is the linking of text documents following protocols and standards. One example of hypertext is the Hypertext Markup Language (HTML). PHP, in conjunction with a web server like Apache or Microsoft Internet Information Services (IIS), allows developers to dynamically alter or produce the markup language (HTML) just prior to sending it to the client (the web browser), where it is rendered as a web page. This allows for the real-time insertion of information as simple as the current date and time or as complex as current database contents.

Uses for PHP

PHP has many uses, most involving some type of markup language and the Internet. For example, PHP can be used in HTML applications where a standard web browser is the intended destination. It can also be used with the Wireless Markup Language (WML) where a wireless device (such as a mobile handset) is the intended destination.

One of the newer developments in web technology is web services, including Simple Object Access Protocol (SOAP) and Remote Procedure Calls using the XML standard (XML-RPC). Web services use the same protocols used for HTML, but some other application is the intended destination, instead of a person's web browser. Typically, you use this for data exchanges between applications or systems. PHP can also be used to create command-line scripts and more traditional client/server programs, using a project called PHP-GTK (for GIMP Tool Kit).

PHP Coding

PHP is a loosely typed language. That means its variables (string, integer, Boolean, and so on) are determined by their context, unless specifically defined. This is important when updating or inserting information into the database, as you will see later in this section. PHP's syntax is similar to Perl's syntax: variables begin with a dollar sign ($) and code segments end with a semicolon (;).

PHP processing instructions are enclosed in <?php ?> tags, similar to the XML recommendation for processing instructions (<?xml ?>). (There are other tags and variations for enclosing PHP code, but it is recommended that you use the standard full PHP tags for clarity and consistency in your code.) Comments within PHP code are preceded by double forward slash marks (//).

For more information about PHP basics and syntax, see Appendix C of this book. If you would like to learn about PHP in more detail, visit http://www.php.net or read a PHP-specific book such as *PHP 4: A Beginner's Guide* by William McCarty (McGraw-Hill/Osborne). Also, you can see what PHP code looks like and how others are using the language by examining coding examples provided by a reputable source. One great resource for high-quality code is PEAR (http://pear.php.net).

Project 7-1 Create a Web Interface to Accept and Display Information

As a basic introduction to PHP, this project will show you how to make a simple web interface to accept information from a user over the Internet and then display it on the web page dynamically. Once this has been accomplished, we will talk more in-depth about using PHP to interface with MySQL and expand on this project in both the following text and project.

Step by Step

1. In a text editor, open a new file and type in the following code:

```
<html>
<body>
<?php
echo "<h1>Hello ".$_REQUEST['name']."</h1>";
?>
<h2>A Simple Example</h2>
<form action="simple.php" method="post">
<label>Name <input name="name"/></label>
</form>
</body>
</html>
```

(continued)

2. Save the file as **simple.php**. Depending on your text editor, it may try to place another file extension (`.txt` for instance) after `.php`. If this occurs, rename the file to remove the unwanted extension.

3. Load the file onto your Internet server, using your normal means, and view the `simple.php` page with your web browser.

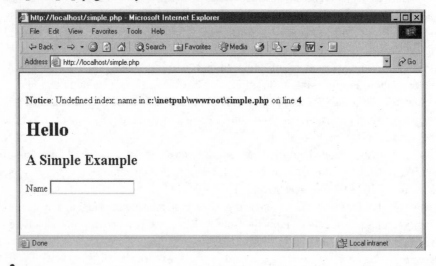

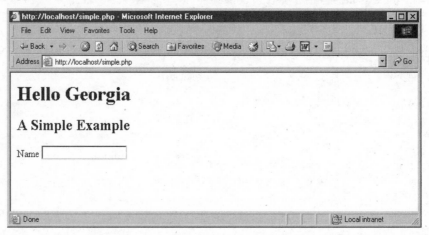

When you initially load this page, you will see a warning at its top, because the `name` variable has not been set.

4. Type **Georgia** into the Name text box and press the ENTER key. The warning should disappear, and "Hello Georgia" should appear at the top of the page.

Project Summary

In Project 7-1, you wrote a PHP script and used it to display a dynamic web page on the Internet. You also submitted data over the Internet and placed it on the web page. This is a simple form of a PHP-generated, dynamic web page. In the following sections, you will use this experience as a stepping-stone to creating a web interface to access your MySQL database and display its contents on a web page.

Connecting to a Database

Assuming you are in an environment where PHP is already configured to support MySQL, the first step is to establish a communication link to the MySQL Server. You can use two functions for this:

- `mysql_connect()` creates a new link to the server. This method automatically closes the connection when the PHP script is finished running.

- `mysql_pconnect()` creates a persistent connection, which means that the function will look for a previous link and use it instead of creating a new one. This method does not automatically close the connection when the script ends; the connection remains open until you send a command to close it.

Both functions return a resource handler if the connection is a success, and a Boolean false otherwise. The resource handler should be stored as a variable for subsequent actions.

`mysql_connect()` has the following syntax (the optional arguments are enclosed in brackets `[ ]`).

```
link = mysql_connect(server, [username], [password],
    [new], [flags])
```

The *server* parameter is the name of the server where the MySQL database server is located. *username* and *password* are the user name and password to use when connecting, respectively. *new* is a Boolean parameter that forces a new link; that is, if your script calls `mysql_connect` multiple times, using a `True` value for *new* creates a new link each time. The *flags* parameter is one or more of the following constants: `MYSQL_CLIENT_COMPRESS`, `MYSQL_CLIENT_IGNORE_SPACE`, and `MYSQL_CLIENT_INTERACTIVE`.

`mysql_pconnect()` takes the same arguments as `mysql_connect()`, except `mysql_pconnect()` does not have the *new* parameter.

CAUTION

If you use the `pconnect` method, you will be responsible for housekeeping regarding connection links. This means your program needs to keep track of the connections and close them when they are no longer needed; otherwise, you could use up all of the available connections or open numerous, redundant links, thereby wasting resources.

Here is an example of connecting to a server running on Windows, using the user and password you set up in Module 1 of this book. Notice that this example uses the compression flag (MYSQL_CLIENT_ COMPRESS) for more efficient communication.

```php
<?php

    $link = mysql_connect('localhost', 'root',
        'pa55w0rd', false, MYSQL_CLIENT_COMPRESS);

    if ($link === false)
        {
        echo 'Connection failure!';
        }
    else
        {
        echo 'Connection success!';
        }

?>
```

NOTE

The indentations and blank lines in the PHP code examples are used in accordance with style standards and are meant to make the code easier to read. However, they are not necessary to make the code function properly.

Checking Your Connection

Now that you are connected to a MySQL Server, you can verify that the server is running by using the ping function, mysql_ping(), which has the following syntax:

```
boolean = mysql_ping(link)
```

The link parameter is an integer that represents the query resource link (or connection) identifier.

Make sure the MySQL Server is running, and then execute the following script.

```php
<?php
    $link = mysql_connect('localhost', 'root', '', false,
                    MYSQL_CLIENT_COMPRESS);
    $alive = mysql_ping();

    if($alive) {
        echo "It's Alive!\n";
    } else {
        echo "MySQL is not alive\n";
    }
?>
```

You should see the "It's Alive!" text.

If you stop the MySQL Server and try this script, you'll see warnings like these (the warning lines have been truncated, but you get the idea):

```
PHP Warning:  mysql_connect(): Can't connect to local MySQL ...
PHP Warning:  mysql_ping(): Can't connect to local MySQL ...
PHP Warning:  mysql_ping(): A link to the server could ...
MySQL is not alive
```

In PHP, if a MySQL function fails, it produces a warning. This information is very useful to a programmer, but not so useful to the end user. In fact, it actually may be dangerous, because it gives away information about the database. Having warnings such as these show up on a dynamic web page, in place of the data that would have displayed if there were no problems, places in public view information that might be used to compromise your database security. For this reason, you might want to suppress PHP warnings.

All PHP warnings can be suppressed using a configuration setting that specifies error levels; some can be suppressed on a perfunction basis by appending an at symbol (@) to the beginning of the function name, as shown in this example:

```php
<?php
    $link = @mysql_connect('localhost', 'root', '', false,
        MYSQL_CLIENT_COMPRESS);
    $alive = @mysql_ping();

    if($alive)
        {
        echo "It's Alive!\n";
        }
    else
        {
        echo "MySQL is not alive\n";
        }
?>
```

When you run this code, you do not see the internal warnings; only the echo statements appear. Later in this module, you will learn about methods for dealing with PHP errors.

Listing Available Databases and Tables

Once you're connected to your MySQL Server, you can use a PHP command that is the equivalent of SHOW DATABASES in MySQL. The mysql_list_dbs() command allows you to retrieve the database names on your server. It has the following syntax:

```
result = mysql_list_dbs([link])
```

The `link` parameter is an integer that represents the query resource link (or connection) identifier. This is optional. If it's not supplied, PHP will attempt to use the most recently created resource link.

This function returns a resource pointer to a result. You will learn how to use a resource pointer when we cover the `mysql_fetch_row()` function later in this module. The following code is an example using the `mysql_list_dbs()` command to list databases.

```php
<?php
    $link = mysql_connect('localhost', 'root', '', false,
        MYSQL_CLIENT_COMPRESS);
    $result = mysql_list_dbs($link);

    while ($row = mysql_fetch_array($result))
        {
        echo $row[0] . "\n";
        }
?>
```

The "`\n`" newline character works if the script is typed on the command line. If you save this script into a file and run it through a browser, replace the "`\n`" with a "`<br>`" to output a newline character. When you run this script, it will produce the following results:

```
duckwear
mysql
test
```

You can also find your list of tables using a PHP command that is the equivalent to the MySQL SHOW TABLES command: `mysql_list_tables()`. This function, like the `mysql_list_dbs()` function, returns a resource pointer.

```
result = mysql_list_tables(database, [link])
```

The `database` parameter is a string type that specifies the name of the database whose tables you want to list. The `link` parameter is the optional query resource link (or connection) identifier. If you don't supply a link, PHP will attempt to use the most recently created resource link.

The following example lists the tables of the `mysql` database.

```php
<?php

    $link = mysql_connect('localhost', 'root', '', false,
        MYSQL_CLIENT_COMPRESS);
    $result = mysql_list_tables('mysql', $link);

    while($array = mysql_fetch_row($result))
```

```
    {
    echo $array[0]."\n";
    }
?>
```

The results of the previous script will be as follows:

```
columns_priv
db
func
host
tables_priv
user
```

Selecting a Database

Now that you know which databases are available, you can set your default database. The equivalent of the MySQL USE DATABASE command in PHP is the mysql_select_db() function, which has the following syntax:

```
mysql_select_db(database, [link])
```

The database parameter is a string type that specifies the name of the database to use. The link parameter is the optional query resource link identifier. Again, if you don't supply this parameter, PHP will attempt to use the most recently created resource link.

You can still use the full name to a database field with the dot nomenclature (for example, mysql.user) to access tables. However, if you use mysql_select_db() to set the default database, you can then refer to each table by its name only.

The following script sets the default database to duckwear.

```
<?php
    $link = mysql_connect('localhost', 'root', '', false,
        MYSQL_CLIENT_COMPRESS);
    mysql_select_db('duckwear', $link);
?>
```

Issuing Queries

Now that you can list the table names and fields, you can issue any SQL query. The basic PHP command for issuing queries is mysql_query(). This command sends the SQL statement to the server, waits for a full result set, and returns to the script. It has the following syntax:

```
result = mysql_query(sql, [link])
```

The sql parameter is a string type that is the SQL statement to send to the server. The link is the optional resource link. If is not supplied, PHP will attempt to use the most recently created resource link.

Note that since you are using the client library to send the statement to the server on a perfunction-call basis, you do not need to include the trailing semicolon in the SQL statement. This is the incorrect syntax:

```
$sql = 'SELECT * FROM test;'; // incorrect
```

And this is the correct syntax:

```
$sql = 'SELECT * FROM test';   // correct
```

The mysql_query() function will wait and store the entire results in memory before returning to the script. If you expect large results from your query, consider using the PHP function mysql_unbuffered_query(). This function has the same syntax as mysql_query(), but will stream the results back to the script as they come from the database.

The following are examples of issuing queries:

```
<?php
    $result = mysql_query('SELECT * FROM table_name');
    $result = mysql_unbuffered_query('SELECT * FROM bigtable_name');
?>
```

The return of both functions is a link to a resource identifier, providing access to the results by using one of the methods described in the next section.

Dealing with Result Resources

You can use a host of methods to deal with the results of a query. If the query is not selecting data (that is, a command like DELETE, INSERT, UPDATE, and so on), you typically just verify that the command was successful.

```
<?php
    $result = mysql_query('DELETE FROM testing');
    if ($result)
        {
        echo "Successfully deleted";
        }
    else
        {
        echo "Deletion failed!";
        }
?>
```

L 7-20

For selection queries where you expect some results back, you typically use one of the mysql_fetch functions, which are described in Table 7-1.

Fetch Function	Description
mysql_fetch_row	Fetch a single row as an anonymous array, following the column order.
mysql_fetch_array	Fetch the entire result set (multiple rows if applicable), accessed as an anonymous array following the column order.
mysql_fetch_assoc	Fetch the result set as a hash array, following a *key = value* format, where the field name is the *key*.
mysql_fetch_object	Fetch the result set as a PHP object, where the variable is the field name, as in $result_row->fieldname = value.

Table 7-1 Variations of the PHP mysql_fetch Function

Fetching a Row   Use mysql_fetch_row() when you expect a single row of results. It has the following syntax:

```
array = mysql_fetch_row(result)
```

The result parameter is the resource link, which indicates where the result set can be found.

The following is an example of using mysql_fetch_row().

```php
<?php
    $link = mysql_connect('localhost', 'root', '', false,
        MYSQL_CLIENT_COMPRESS);
    mysql_select_db('mysql');
    $sql = 'SELECT count(*) FROM user';
    $result = mysql_query($sql, $link);
    $array = mysql_fetch_row($result);
    echo "There are ".$array[0]."\n";
?>
```

This script will return the number of database users, similar to this:

```
There are 4
```

Fetching Multiple Rows   The other three mysql_fetch functions are useful when you expect a number of rows back. It is common to use these functions within a looping control structure, like a while loop.

NOTE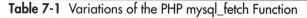

It is possible to manually keep track of, and move, the result set pointer thereby looping around the results, but the mysql_fetch_array(), mysql_fetch_assoc(), and mysql_fetch_object() functions are a bit easier to use and subject to fewer human errors.

The `mysql_fetch_array()` function returns a row of results as an array, and then moves the pointer to the next row. If there is no row to return, the function returns false. It has the following syntax:

```
array = mysql_fetch_array(result, [result type])
```

The *result* parameter is the result resource. The *result* type is an integer that determines what kind of array to return. The valid *result* types (constants) include the following:

- `MYSQL_ASSOC` returns an associative array, where the keys are the field names.
- `MYSQL_NUM` returns an anonymous array, where the key is an integer starting with 0 and incrementing to the total number of fields requested.
- `MYSQL_BOTH`, the default, returns a hybrid.

An alternative to calling `mysql_fetch_array()` with the `MYSQL_ASSOC` flag is the more specific `mysql_fetch_assoc()` function. It behaves like `mysql_fetch_row()` and has the following syntax:

```
array = mysql_fetch_assoc(result)
```

The *result* parameter is the resource link, which indicates where the result set can be found.

To capture the results as PHP objects instead of an array, you can use the `mysql_ fetch_ object()` function. It returns the current row as an object, and then advances the data pointer to the next row. If there are no rows to return, this function will return false. It has the following syntax:

```
object = mysql_fetch_object(result)
```

The *result* parameter is the resource link, which indicates where the result set can be found.

The following is an example of using the various `mysql_fetch` functions. (The "`\t`" outputs a tab character.)

```php
<?php
    $link = mysql_connect('localhost', 'root', '', false,
        MYSQL_CLIENT_COMPRESS);
    mysql_select_db('duckwear');

    $sql = 'SELECT cust_last, cust_first, cust_city, cust_state
        FROM duck_cust';

    $result = mysql_query($sql, $link);
    echo "Fetching a row using mysql_fetch_row:<br>";
```

```php
$row = mysql_fetch_row($result);
echo "\t".$row[0];
echo "\t".$row[1];
echo "\t".$row[2];
echo "\t".$row[3];
echo "<br>";

// The next line clears out data from $row for the next example.
unset($row);

echo "\n\nFetching all the rows using mysql_fetch_array:<br>";
$result = mysql_query($sql, $link);
while ($row = mysql_fetch_array($result))
    {
    echo "\t".$row[0];
    echo "\t".$row[1];
    echo "\t".$row[2];
    echo "\t".$row[3];
    echo "<br>";
    }

// The next line clears out data from $row for the next example.
unset($row);

echo "<br>Fetching all the rows using mysql_fetch_assoc:<br>";
$result = mysql_query($sql, $link);
while ($row = mysql_fetch_assoc($result))
    {
    echo "\t".$row['cust_last'];
    echo "\t".$row['cust_first'];
    echo "\t".$row['cust_city'];
    echo "\t".$row['cust_state'];
    echo "<br>";
    }

echo "<br>Fetching all the rows using mysql_fetch_object: <br>";
$result = mysql_query($sql, $link);
while ($row = mysql_fetch_object($result))
    {
    echo "\t".$row->cust_last;
    echo "\t".$row->cust_first;
    echo "\t".$row->cust_city;
    echo "\t".$row->cust_state;
    echo "<br>";
    }
?>
```

```
http://localhost/test7.php - Microsoft Internet Explorer                    _ 8 X
File   Edit   View   Favorites   Tools   Help
Back  ·  →  ·  ⊗  ⊘  ⌂  ⊘ Search  ⊛ Favorites  ⊛ Media  ⊛  ⊗·  ⊣  ⊚  ·  ⊟
Address ⊡ http://localhost/test7.php                                    ▼   ⊘ Go

Fetching a row using mysql_fetch_row:
Salisbury Jenny Meadowlark Hill KS

Fetching all the rows using mysql_fetch_array:
Salisbury Jenny Meadowlark Hill KS
Irishlord Red Seacouver WA
Thegreat Vicki Freedom KS
Montgomery Chantel Chicago IL
Robert David Blacktop AZ
Kazui Wonko Vlimpt CA
Gashlycrumb Karen Fedora VT
Kazui Wonko Shady Hill CA
Davidson Wolf Elysium OK
Danson Raccoon Elysium OK
Filled Bob Elysium OK
Billiards Monte Elysium OK
Beauvais Jet Elysium OK
Seta Kevin Elysium OK

Fetching all the rows using mysql_fetch_assoc:
Salisbury Jenny Meadowlark Hill KS
Irishlord Red Seacouver WA
Thegreat Vicki Freedom KS
Montgomery Chantel Chicago IL
Robert David Blacktop AZ
Kazui Wonko Vlimpt CA
Gashlycrumb Karen Fedora VT
Kazui Wonko Shady Hill CA
Davidson Wolf Elysium OK
Danson Raccoon Elysium OK
Filled Bob Elysium OK
Billiards Monte Elysium OK
Beauvais Jet Elysium OK

⊡ Done                                                    ⊞ Local intranet
```

Figure 7-1 Fetching results from queries

NOTE

To include comments that are longer than one line, you can start the comment with /* on the first line and end it with */ several lines later, instead of placing // at the beginning of each line.

Figure 7-1 shows the results of the example. Notice that the first function returns only the first row, whereas the other three functions return all the rows in the table, due to the `while` loop.

Project 7-2   Create a Web Interface for a Database

Since you have used PHP successfully in Project 7.1 to create a dynamic web page, now you can take it one step further and use it to access and display information by creating a simple web interface for your `duckwear` database. This project will show you how to combine PHP and HTML to display your data in a web-accessible manner.

Step by Step

1. In a text editor, open a new file and type in the following script:

```
<html>
<body>
<H3>This is the current DuckWear customer list.</H3>
<?php
    $link = mysql_connect('localhost', 'root', '', false,
        MYSQL_CLIENT_COMPRESS);
    mysql_select_db('duckwear');

    $sql = 'SELECT cust_last, cust_first, cust_city, cust_state
        FROM duck_cust';

    echo "Last Name| First Name| City| State|:<br><br>";
    $result = mysql_query($sql, $link);
    while ($row = mysql_fetch_array($result))
        {
        echo "\t".$row[0]."\t|";
        echo "\t".$row[1]."\t|";
        echo "\t".$row[2]."\t|";
        echo "\t".$row[3]."\t|";
        echo "<br>";
        }
?>
</table>
</body>
</html>
```

2. Save the file as **duckwear.php**, remembering to verify that no unwanted file extension has been added to its name when you save it.

3. Load the file onto your Internet server, using your normal means, and view the duckwear.php page with your web browser.

This is the current DuckWear customer list.

Last Name| First Name| City| State|:

Salisbury | Jenny | Meadowlark Hill | KS |
Irishlord | Red | Seacouver | WA |
Thegreat | Vicki | Freedom | KS |
Montgomery | Chantel | Chicago | IL |
Robert | David | Blacktop | AZ |
Kazui | Wonko | Vlimpt | CA |
Gashlycrumb | Karen | Fedora | VT |
Kazui | Wonko | Shady Hill | CA |
Davidson | Wolf | Elysium | OK |
Danson | Raccoon | Elysium | OK |
Filled | Bob | Elysium | OK |
Billiards | Monte | Elysium | OK |
Beauvais | Jet | Elysium | OK |
Seta | Kevin | Elysium | OK |

(continued)

Project Summary

In Project 7-2, you made an Internet interface between your MySQL database and the Internet. Your page has requested data from the database over the Internet and displayed the up-to-the-moment copy of it on the web page.

Handling Errors

In the previous examples, you checked the result resource and caused the PHP script to exit and issue your own error statement in the event it was false. You can use the actual server error code and message that the MySQL server returns, and log the actual server error code and message to aid in debugging problems. This is accomplished by using the mysql_error() and mysql_errno() functions. Both functions return information for the last attempted MySQL function call.

The mysql_error() function returns the error string directly from the MySQL Server. If there isn't an error, this function returns an empty string. The mysql_errno() function returns the MySQL error code number, instead of the error message string. If an error has not occurred, it will return a numeric value of zero (0). These functions have the following syntax:

```
mysql_error(link)
mysql_errno(link)
```

The *link* parameter is the query resource link identifier.

The following script demonstrates using both of these error-handling commands.

```php
<?php
//Open and check your connection
    $link = mysql_connect('localhost', 'root', '', false,
        MYSQL_CLIENT_COMPRESS);
    if (mysql_errno())
        {
        echo "MySQL Connection Error ".mysql_errno().":
            ".mysql_error()."\n";
        die();
        }
//Select a database and check the selection
    mysql_select_db('duckwear');
    if (mysql_errno())
        {
        echo "MySQL Databse Selection Error ".mysql_errno().":
            ".mysql_error()."\n";
        die();
        }
//Define query string
    $sql = 'SELECT cust_last, cust_first, cust_city, cust_states
```

```
        FROM duck_cust';    $result = mysql_query($sql, $link);
//Check for query error and display error message then die
   if (mysql_errno())
      {
      echo "MySQL Query Error ".mysql_errno().":
      ".mysql_error()."\n";
      die();
      }
//Display data by row while there are rows in table
   while ($row = mysql_fetch_assoc($result))
      {
      echo "\t".$row['cust_last'];
      echo "\t".$row['cust_first'];
      echo "\t".$row['cust_city'];
      echo "\t".$row['cust_state'];
      echo "\n";
      }
?>
```

Since the `cust_states` field does not exist in the `duckwear` table, you can expect to return an error. Running this script would output the following message:

```
MySQL Query Error 1054: Unknown column 'cust_states' in 'field list'
```

Progress Check

1. What are the opening and closing tags for a PHP script?

2. What functions can you use to create a link or connection to your MySQL database, and what is the difference between them?

3. What function verifies whether or not the MySQL database is connected?

4. What are the two functions for error handling?

---

1. The opening and closing tags for a PHP script are `<?php` and `?>`.

2. The `mysql_connect()` or `mysql_pconnect ()` function is used to create a link, or connection, to MySQL. The former creates a new link with each call, and the latter creates a persistent link that remains open until closed.

3. The `mysql_ping ()` function verifies whether the MySQL database is connected.

4. The two functions for error handling are `mysql_error ()` and `mysql_errno ()`.

Good Design Concepts

This section will touch upon some good design concepts, like using escape strings, type casting and general security concerns. In the early days of PHP, it was common to see scripts written where the namespace was shared using a server setting called `register_globals`, which used to have a default value of on. This meant that a form variable would be accessed in the PHP script via its name. So, if you had the code `<input name="field1"/>` in the HTML, you would access it in PHP as `<?php echo $field1 ?>`. This was quickly recognized as a security issue, because the variables are essentially posted to the Internet. It is it highly recommended that you keep the `register_globals` setting off and instead, to use *and parse* the super-globals. PHP has access to HTTP `post` and `get` variable from a web page via these variables called `super globals`. They include `$_POST`, `$_GET` and `$_REQUEST` (a combination of the previous two).

Separating Logic and HTML Coding

Another good design concept involves the separation of the logic and HTML coding. The script in Project 7-1 mixed the business/database logic with the HTML code. That is generally a bad idea, because it makes maintaining larger projects a nightmare. Therefore, it is recommended that all the database and business logic be separate from the HTML and presentation logic. You can accomplish this simply by writing your code in two separate files: a logic file and a template file.

Here is an example of a logic file named simple2.php:

```php
<?php
    /* All our business logic would reside here
    including database calls and queries.*/
    $var1 = 'More Information';

    // Now you call in the presentation template(s)
    include "simple2.tpl.php";
?>
```

The following is an example of a template file named simple2.tpl.php:

```html
<html>
    <body>
        <h1>This is mostly an HTML file</h1>
        <p>We suggest using HTML only for content; to make
        the page look nice, or for layout, use CSS and the
        CSS box model.</p>
        <h1><?php echo $var1; ?></h1>
        <p>It is okay to sprinkle PHP in the template as in
        the preceding line, but just for presentation purposes.
        </p>
    </body>
</html>
```

The simple2.php file calls the simple2.tpl.php file, making it possible to use one template file for a site's look and layout while calling it from multiple pages. This reduces repetitive code, saving space and making it easier to alter the look and layout by changing one template file that automatically changes all the pages that call it.

TIP

You may want to review some of the more robust templating projects available for PHP, including Smarty (http://smarty.php.net), PHPTAL (http://phptal.sf.net), and PHP Savant (http://www.phpsavant.com).

In the interests of simplicity and to encourage a quick learning curve, the projects in this module do not use this advise, but for ease of maintenance in a real-world, production environment, you should try to design your code with this separation in mind.

Maintaining Web Security

Using the raw information for the client is generally a bad idea. Cleaning the variable and using the type-casting functions are recommended. This allows your web interface to run while obfuscating critical information (names, passwords, and so on) to make it harder for someone to illegally access your sever. You can do this with `sprintf`-like functions, regular expressions, or by using some of the following built-in MySQL functions:

`intval($var)`	Get the integer value of `$var`
`floatval($var)`	Get the float value of `$var`
`strval(var)`	Get the string value of `$var`
`settype($var, type)`	Set the `$var` to one of the following types: Boolean, integer, float, string, array, object, or null

Here is an example of using a type-casting function to ensure you get a string type for this value, no matter what the content may be. This way, even if numbers are supplied as input, they will be saved in a string format because of the forced type-casting indicated by the use of `strval($_REQUEST['name'])`.

```php
<?php
    $name = strval($_REQUEST['name']);
?>
<html>
<body>
<?php echo "<h1>Hello ".$name."</h1>"; ?>
<h2>A Simple Example</h2>
<form action="simple.php" method="post">
```

```
<label>Name <input name="name"/></label>
</form>
</body>
</html>
```

Using type casting makes sure the data type is correct, but you also should make sure the data is not harmful by checking it for special characters that will make the INSERT fail or for embedded SQL commands (MySQL injections) that could unintentionally initiate destructive actions over the web interface. (See the "Ask the Expert" section for more on MySQL injections.)

Suppose you are inserting a name into a database using a web form like the following. The insert.html file, the file that calls the PHP file, would look like this:

```
<html>
   <body>
      <form action="insert.php" method="post">
         <fieldset>
            <legend>Enter Your Name</legend>
            <label>First Name
               <input type="text" name="cust_first"/></label><br/>
            <label>Last Name
               <input type="text" name="cust_last"/></label><br/>
         </fieldset>
      </form>
   </body>
</html>
```

The insert.php file, the file that the HTML calls, would look like this:

```
<?php
// Connection code
   $link = mysql_connect('localhost', 'root', '', false,
      MYSQL_CLIENT_COMPRESS);
   if (mysql_errno())
      {
      echo "MySQL Connection Error ".mysql_errno().":
         ".mysql_error()."\n";
      die();
      }

   $cust_first = strval($_REQUEST['cust_first']);
   $cust_last = strval($_REQUEST['cust_last']);
   $sql = "INSERT INTO duck_cust (cust_first, cust_last)
             VALUES ('$cust_first', '$cust_last')";

   $result = mysql_query($sql, $link);
```

```
?>

<html>
    <body>
        <h1>Successfully Inserted Data!</h1>
    </body>
</html>
```

If the user enters a value with a single apostrophe ('), the insertion would fail. A good way to prevent this is to use the `mysql_quote()` function, which has the following syntax:

```
string = mysql_escape_string (variable)
```

The `variable` parameter is a string that defines the variable to escape.

The following example allows users to input special characters by using the `mysql_escape_string()` function.

```php
<?php
    // Connection code
    $link = mysql_connect('localhost', 'root', '', false,
                MYSQL_CLIENT_COMPRESS);
    if (mysql_errno())
    {
      echo "MySQL Connection Error ".mysql_errno().":
                ".mysql_error()."\n";
      die();
    }

    $cust_first = strval($_REQUEST['cust_first']);
    $cust_last = strval($_REQUEST['cust_last']);

    $sql = "INSERT INTO duck_cust (cust_first, cust_last)
                VALUES (mysql_escape_string($cust_first),
                        mysql_escape_string($cust_last));
    $result = mysql_query($sql, $link);
?>
<html>
    <body>
        <h1>Successfully Inserted Data!</h1>
    </body>
</html>
```

Now if a user types in an apostrophe for a name, like D'urberville, the escape function will convert it to D\'urberville, preventing an insertion error.

Ask the Expert

Q: **What are SQL injections, and how can I prevent them?**

A: *SQL injections* are when a user inputs an SQL query instead of the expected information. If unprotected against this sort of attack, the database will accept the input string and unintentionally send a command to the database. This can result in faulty data or even the deletion of a table or an entire database.

If you have a web-based deletion function, where your PHP code would delete a customer based on a provided customer number, it would probably look something like the following example:

```php
<?php
// Connection code goes here
    $cust_num = strval($_REQUEST['cust_num']);
    $sql = "DELETE FROM duck_cust
            WHERE cust_num=".$cust_num;
    $result = mysql_query($sql);
?>
```

You are verifying the data by making sure that the $cust_num is a string, but someone can still post a value that contains a harmful SQL query, like this:

```
    "bogus")'; DROP DATABASE duckwear;
```

If this string were inserted, it would be read and run like any other command and result in dropping your entire database. This kind of security issue is called SQL-injection.

To prevent this, you should use the mysql_escape_string() function discussed in this module, as shown in the following example:

```php
<?php
// Connection code goes here...

    $cust_num = strval($_REQUEST['cust_num']);
    $sql = "DELETE FROM duck_cust
            WHERE cust_num=".mysql_escape_string($cust_num);
    $result = mysql_query($sql);
?>
```

This prevents the string from being interpreted as a command that would drop the entire duckwear database, and it provides another layer of security for your database/web interface.

Using the MySQL Improved Interface (PHP 5 only)

One of the major advances in the latest version of PHP (PHP 5) is a new object model, which provides a much fuller feature set for object-oriented developers. This version offers MySQL-related functions that can be run in object mode, as well as the ability to bind parameters.

Procedural Mode and Object Mode

The new model includes `mysqli` functions, such as `mysqli_connect()`, which can be run in either procedural or object mode. Procedural mode is similar in syntax to the original `mysql` functions discussed earlier in this module.

Here is an example of the connection syntax using object mode:

```php
<?php
    $mysqli = new mysqli("localhost", "root", "", "duckwear");
// check connection
    if (mysqli_connect_errno())
        {
        echo "Connect failed:". mysqli_connect_error()."\n";
        die();
        }
    $mysqli->close();
?>
```

Here is an example of the connection syntax using procedural mode:

```php
<?php
    $link = mysqli_connect("localhost", "root", "", "duckwear");
// check connection
    if (!$link)
        {
        echo "Connect failed:". mysqli_connect_error()."\n";
        die();
        }
    mysqli_close($link);
?>
```

Notice that the procedural style requires the link to be passed around, while the object-oriented style creates a database object.

Binding Parameters

One of the major features missing from the original `mysql` library was the ability to bind parameters. You often find yourself looping around data, while issuing an INSERT command each iteration. Without binding, you would need to issue a full INSERT command each iteration, which is processor- and bandwidth-intensive. The binding method handles these difficulties.

Binding data adds information to a stack or an array. You can use the `mysqli_stmt_bind_param()` to accomplish this. The command is then issued using wildcards to describe where the data should go. Then the command is executed once with the statement and data array. The database server interprets the SQL statement and quickly substitutes the information from the array.

When binding parameters, you need to indicate the type of parameter. The following are some of the available binding parameters:

i	The value is expected as an integer.
d	The value is expected as a double.
s	The value is expected as a string.
b	The value is expected as a BLOB.

The following is an example of using binding parameters.

```php
<?php
    $mysqli = new mysqli("localhost", "root", "pa55w0rd", "duckwear");

    if (mysqli_connect_errno())
        {
        echo "Connect failed:". mysqli_connect_error()."\n";
        die();
        }

    $sql = 'INSERT into duck_cust (cust_first, cust_last)
        VALUES (?, ?)';
    $sth =& $mysqli->prepare($sql);
    if ($mysqli->errno())
    {
        echo "Prepare failed: ". $mysqli->errno() .":".
                $mysqli->error()."\n";
        die();
    }
// In this example, you are using two strings, hence
// the first parameter is "ss".
    $sth->mysqli_stmt_bind_param('ss', 'Kodi', 'Evil');
    $sth->mysqli_stmt_bind_param('ss', 'Austin', 'Miller');
    $sth->mysqli_stmt_bind_param('ss', 'Isabella', 'Smith');
    $sth->execute();
    if ($mysqli->errno())
        {
        echo "Execute failed: ". $mysqli->errno() .":".
            $mysqli->error()."\n";
        die();
        }
?>
```

At the time of the writing of this book, PHP 5 was not yet in production, so the command names and behavior could differ. However, it is available for downloading and experimentation, and production release is imminent. For more information, visit the `mysqli` section of the online PHP documentation.

Progress Check

1. What are four functions to force type casting of variables?

2. What function prevents SQL injections?

3. What is the new function for creating a link or connection with MySQL in PHP 5?

4. What are four type indicators for binding parameters with the new `mysqli_stmt_bind_param()` function and what types do they represent?

CRITICAL SKILL
7.2 # Separate Database Functions from Application Code

In web-based projects, it is not unusual to work in mixed environments, where the database, web server, or operating system may vary. Sometimes, you find yourself migrating to different technologies after an application has been developed. Separation between application code and database-specific functions makes these issues more manageable. This separation is sometimes referred to as *abstraction*. ODBC is an example of database abstraction on a system level. It is definitely acceptable to set up MyODBC and connect using PHP's ODBC functions to your MySQL database. However, using MyODBC instead of the native MySQL client libraries can result in severe performance degradation—as much as 30 percent. Fortunately, there is another option for database abstraction.

Implementing application-level database abstraction takes advantage of native client libraries and provides a unified interface to the database functions. This skill will look at the PEAR::DB abstraction module, which supports ODBC databases using the ODBC API.

---

1. Four functions that force type casting of variables are `intval()`, `floatval()`, `strval()`, and `settype()`.

2. The `mysql_escape_string` prevents SQL injections.

3. The new function for creating a link or connection with MySQL in PHP 5 is `mysqli_connect()`.

4. The four binding parameter types mentioned are `i` for integer, `d` for double, `s` for string, and `b` for BLOB.

Installing PEAR::DB

First, you need to install the base PEAR libraries. PEAR, which stands for PHP Extension and Application Repository, may already be installed, as it is a common option when building PHP. Therefore, you should check to see if you have PEAR before running the script to install the manager.

In Linux, you can run this pithy command:

```
lynx -source http://go-pear.org/ | php
```

It basically executes the contents found on the go-pear.com web site.

In Windows, or if you do not have `lynx`, open `go-pear.org` in a web browser and save the contents as a file (for example, in a file named go-pear.php). Then execute the file from the PHP command line:

```
php go-pear.php
```

It will run through an installation process on the command line. The DB module should be installed.

At any time, you can use the manager to download or update PEAR packages using the `pear` script, as follows:

```
pear install <package_name>
```

Connecting to a Database

The PEAR::DB modules are accessed using object-oriented techniques. For example, once a query is issued, the result is an object. To retrieve data within the object, you call methods instead of passing a pointer to a function. It is also common to see a reference instead of an assignment operator for objects. This reference is an equal sign followed by an ampersand (=&).

Because PEAR::DB abstracts connections over a number of different database flavors, the connection string has been generalized. This string is referred to as the database source name (DSN). It follows a HTTP-looking format:

```
database_type://user:pass@host:port/database
```

For example, the DSN for the MySQL `duckwear` database would look like this:

```
mysql://root:pa55w0rd@localhost/duckwear
```

To connect, you issue the `connect()` function with your DSN as the parameter:

```
object = DB::connect(dsn, [options])
```

The *dsn* parameter can be either a well-formed DSN string or an array of connection settings. *options* are a named array of options: `'autofree'` Boolean for freeing the results after there are no more rows or `'persistent'` Boolean to use a persistent connection.

The result of the `connect()` function is a database object. Here is an example:

```php
<?php
require_once 'DB.php';
$dsn = 'mysql://root@localhost/duckwear';
$dbo =& DB::connect($dsn);
if (DB::isError($dbo))
    {
    die($dbo->getMessage());
    }
$dbo->disconnect();
?>
```

When you're using the DB library, the error handling is similar to when you're using the native PHP functions. First, check the result object or link to see if it is in an error state. If it is, process the error, and `die` or `exit`.

Executing Queries

In many languages, when communicating with a database, SQL statements are sometimes prepared and then executed. This concept exists in the PEAR::DB. The `prepare()` and `execute()` methods are usually called together. This offers the most flexibility, as a prepared statement can be executed any number of times and with different binding parameters.

The `prepare()` method has the following syntax:

resource = $result->prepare(*sql*)

sql is a string that contains the SQL statement to prepare. The following two common binding parameters are acceptable:

?	Values will be quoted before used.
!	Values will not be quoted and will be used as entered.

The `execute()` method has the following syntax:

object = $result->execute(*resource*, [*data*])

The *resource* parameter is an object that is a resource from a prepared statement. The *data* parameter is an array containing the bound data for substitution.

The following is an example of using the two methods to insert binding data. It leaves out the error checking in order to focus more clearly on the commands.

```php
<?php
    require_once 'DB.php';
    $dsn = 'mysql://root@localhost/duckwear';
    $dbo =& DB::connect($dsn);
    $sql = 'INSERT into duck_cust (cust_first, cust_last)
        VALUES (?, ?)';
    $sth =& $dbo->prepare($sql);
    $result = $dbo->execute($sth, array('Al', 'Lange'));
    $result = $dbo->execute($sth, array('Kyle', 'Sexton'));
    $result = $dbo->execute($sth, array('Terry', 'Crane'));
?>
```

This is a fast technique for inserting or updating multiple rows of information at once. However, if you do not need this flexibility, you can save some coding time and use the query() method. This basically combines the prepare() and execute() into one call. Issuing a simple query is similar to using the native PHP mysql_query() function. In this case, any binding parameter may be passed in as a second optional argument. In the background, it runs a prepare() and an execute() in one step.

The query() method has the following syntax:

object = $result->query(*sql*, [*mode*])

sql is a string that contains the SQL statement to issue. *mode* is one of the available fetching modes: DB_FETCHMODE_ORDERED, DB_FETCHMODE_ASSOC, or DB_FETCHMODE_OBJECT. If a mode is not supplied, query() will use the default mode: DB_FETCHMODE_ORDERED.

Here is an example of using the query() method:

```php
<?php
    require_once 'DB.php';
    $dsn = "mysql://root@localhost/duckwear";

    $dbo =& DB::connect($dsn);
    if (DB::isError($dbo))
        {
        die($dbo->getMessage());
        }
    $result =& $dbo->query("SELECT * FROM duck_cust");
    if (DB::isError($result))
        {
        die($result->getMessage());
        }
    $dbo->disconnect();
?>
```

Fetching Results

Two ways to deal with the results from a query (or prepare/execute) are the `fetchInto()` and `fetchRow()` methods. The `fetchRow()` method is similar to the `mysql_fetch_array()` function. It takes an optional parameter that sets the result mode, using the following syntax:

```
array = $result->fetchRow([mode])
```

The *mode* parameter is one of the available fetching modes: DB_FETCHMODE_ORDERED, DB_FETCHMODE_ASSOC, or DB_FETCHMODE_OBJECT. If a mode is not supplied, `fetchRow()` will use the default mode: DB_FETCHMODE_ORDERED, which is similar to the MYSQL_NUM mode you saw previously in the `mysql_fetch_array()` function.

The `fetchInto()` method allows you to fill a target variable with the row of data. It has the following syntax:

```
integer = $result->fetchInto(target, [mode], [row])
```

The *target* parameter is a reference to the target variable. The *mode* parameter is one of the available fetching modes, with the same options and default as `fetchRow()`. The *row* parameter is an integer data type that specifies to jump to a specific row.

The following is an example of using fetching results:

```php
<?php
   require_once 'DB.php';
   $dsn = 'mysql://root@localhost/duckwear';
   $dbo =& DB::connect($dsn);
   if (DB::isError($dbo))
      {
      die($dbo->getMessage());
      }
   $sql = 'SELECT cust_last, cust_first, cust_city,
      cust_state FROM duck_cust';
   echo "\n\nFetching all the rows using fetchRow():\n";
$result =& $dbo->query($sql);
   if (DB::isError($result))
      {
      die($result->getMessage());
      }
   while ($row = $result->fetchRow(DB_FETCHMODE_ORDERED))
      {
      echo "\t".$row[0];
      echo "\t".$row[1];
      echo "\t".$row[2];
```

```
        echo "\t".$row[3];
        echo "\n";
        }
// Free the result (the 'autofree' defaults to false)
    $result->free();
    echo "\n\nFetching all the rows using fetchInto():\n";
    $result =& $dbo->query($sql);
    if (DB::isError($result))
        {
        die($result->getMessage());
        }
    while ($result->fetchInto($row, DB_FETCHMODE_ASSOC))
        {
        echo "\t".$row['cust_last'];
        echo "\t".$row['cust_first'];
        echo "\t".$row['cust_city'];
        echo "\t".$row['cust_state'];
        echo "\n";
        }
    $dbo->disconnect();
?>
```

In this example, both methods display the entire database on the web page. However, fetchInto() allows you to specify a particular row to jump to, instead of taking the next row in line.

There are many shortcuts in the PEAR::DB library to make your life even easier. You should familiarize yourself with the library and consider using it in your applications.

This skill and the previous one only touched on some of the many methods you can use with PHP and MySQL. These examples gave you a taste of what MySQL and PHP can jointly accomplish and introduced some useful libraries. Now you have a basic foundation to further explore the possibilities of the PHP scripting language.

CRITICAL SKILL
7.3 Import MySQL Data into Access and Excel

Many new users have chosen to learn MySQL because they have outgrown their current manner of maintaining their data. Whether you've kept business records in a handwritten accounting ledger or stored your records in a spreadsheet or basic database, the moment often comes when that system becomes inadequate for a variety of reasons. Occasionally, however, you might want to manipulate data outside MySQL in an already familiar environment, frequently in Microsoft Excel or Access. This skill will cover how to get MySQL data into these programs.

NOTE

Excel is a widely available spreadsheet that is often a user's first attempt at storing data in a meaningful and manipulatable format; however a spreadsheet is not as functional as a database. If you want to get data from Excel into MySQL, you can write standard SELECT commands or save the data in Excel into a text file and use the LOAD DATA INFILE, as described in Module 2.

Importing MySQL Data into Excel

You can transfer MySQL data into Excel in two ways: by first exporting a file from MySQL and then opening that file in Excel, or by importing the data into Excel using ODBC.

Exporting from MySQL

MySQL allows you to export data, by using the SELECT INTO OUTFILE function, into a file that can be imported into Excel, with varying levels of difficulty. MySQL will export the contents of a table into a text file. You can use a variety of methods to divide the fields in the table when writing to the text file. The most basic syntax is as follows:

```
USE <database_name>;
SELECT *
INTO OUTFILE "<file_name.txt>"
FROM <table_name>;
```

This syntax results in a file where the fields are separated by tabs, which is the default when a delimiter is not specified.

Another common delimiter is a space, and in fixed-length fields, this results in a file that can be easily read. The following syntax shows how to specify a fixed-width delimiter by using single quotes with nothing, not even a space, between them to signify the field's contents should be padded with spaces to a fixed width. This makes all the fields appear in right-justified columns.

```
USE <database_name>;
SELECT *
INTO OUTFILE "<file_name.txt>"
FIELD TERMINATED BY ''
FROM <table_name>;
```

NOTE

If you receive an error using this syntax, try using the backtick (`) instead of the single quote (') on the FIELD TERMINATED BY line.

The most compatible way to format a file for Excel is to use comma delimiters. Excel even recognizes a special filename extension for a comma-delimited file, .csv. Naming a comma-delimited file in the *file_name*.csv format makes Excel think that the file is an actual Excel file and treat it accordingly. The syntax for creating such a file follows:

```
USE <database_name>;
SELECT *
INTO OUTFILE "<file_name.csv>"
FIELD TERMINATED BY ','
FROM <table_name>;
```

To import any file you exported from MySQL using the SELECT INTO OUTFILE function into Excel, simply choose to open a file in Excel (by using the File | Open option or clicking the Open File button on the toolbar). In the Open dialog box, browse for the file. MySQL saves the result of the OUTFILE command into the database folder in the Data folder in MySQL. For instance, the path for an OUTFILE result for the duck_cust table in the duckwear database would be C:\mysql\data\duckwear. Click the name of the exported file, and then click the Open button.

For any .txt file, a wizard will open to guide you through the rest of the process. Depending on the way the file was generated, you must select either Delimited, if characters were used to separate the fields, or Fixed Width, if spaces were used to pad the data into fixed width fields.

- If you choose Delimited, you must next indicate which character the file uses: Tab, Semicolon, Comma, Space, or Other. The Other choice allows you to input the specific character. You are also given options to treat consecutive delimiters as one and to indicate what, if any characters signify the status of what is held within them as text.

- If you choose Fixed Width, the second wizard window allows you to create new columns or move the position of the existing columns.

The third screen of the wizard allows you to select each column and specify whether the contents are General, Text, or Date in nature, or to skip importing that specific column. The Advanced button allows you to specify which characters you use for indicating decimal points and thousands. Once you've made all these decisions, click the Finish button, and your data will be imported into an Excel sheet.

If you use specified comma delimiters and named the file with a .csv filename extension when you exported from MySQL (as in the third OUTFILE example shown earlier in this section), Excel perceives the file as an Excel file type and opens it immediately.

Importing to Excel Using ODBC

Before you can use ODBC to import data from inside the Excel program, you need to create a Data Source Name (DSN), which is usually the same as the database name. Since you installed the ODBC drivers in Module 1, making the connection is simple. See Project 7-3 for step-by-step instructions for creating a DSN.

After you've set up the DSN, follow these steps to import the MySQL data into Excel:

1. Open Excel and select Data | Import External Data | Import Data | New Source.

2. Choose ODBC DSN and click the Next button.

3. Enter the DSN name and click the Next button.

4. Enter the database name and the table name that you want to import, and then click the Next button. The filename is *<database_name> <table_name>*.odc.

5. Click the Finish button.

6. Select the file you want to import (*<database_name> <table_name>*.odc) and click Open.

7. Select existing worksheet @ =a1, and then click OK.

Importing MySQL Data into Access

You can get data from MySQL into Access by importing the data directly into Access tables. You can also link to a MySQL table from Access. The question that might be occurring to you is, "Why would I want to do either of those things?" Importing data into Access or linking directly to a MySQL table from Access allows you to use Access to build queries, forms, and reports on the data. This lets users who are already familiar with Access continue to use its form-creation processes instead of writing HTML-based forms.

The DSN, discussed in the previous section in relation to importing into Excel, is also used to facilitate the connection between MySQL and Access. Access has a Get External Data link under the File drop-down menu that allows you to choose between importing and linking outside data.

Linking to the database from Access allows you to view the data in what is effectively real-time. Changes made to the data within Access will be reflected within the MySQL database; however, you cannot change the format of the table. Since Access has different data types than MySQL, it interprets the MySQL data types to the ones closest to its own data types. Access also uses a different icon from the normal Access table icon to represent the directly linked version.

Project 7-3 Import and Link MySQL Data in Access

This project will give you experience making a DSN connection using ODBC, and then using it to import and link MySQL data in Access.

Step by Step

1. In Windows, select Start | Settings | Control Panel. Double-click Administrative Tools, and then open Data Sources (ODBC) by double-clicking it.

(continued)

2. Click the System DSN tab, and then click the Add button.

3. Scroll down to the MySQL ODBC driver and select it. (If the MySQL ODBC is not listed, see the instructions for installing MyODBC drivers in Module 1.) Then click Finish.

4. For the Data Source Name, enter **duckwear** (so it will be easy to remember to which database the particular connection refers).

5. For the Host/Server Name (or IP Address), enter **localhost**, or enter the IP address of the MySQL Server if MySQL and Access are not on the same machine.

6. For the Database Name, enter **duckwear**.

7. Enter your user name and password for the MySQL database. Click the OK button.

8. Now that the DSN connection has been created, open Access to import the data. Select File | Get External Data | Import.

9. When the Open dialog box opens, change the File Type to ODBC Databases().

10. Click the Machine Data Sources tab, highlight the duckwear DSN, and then click the OK button.

11. Click the `duck_sales` table.

NOTE

The Select All button will allow you to select all the tables at once rather than selecting them individually.

12. Click the OK button. Now you have a separate copy of your data in your local Access database.

CAUTION

When you add records in the local copy in Access, the changes will not be reflected in your MySQL database.

13. To link to the MySQL data, from Access, select File | Get External Data | Link Tables.

14. In the dialog box, change the File Type to ODBC Databases().

15. Click the Machine Data Sources tab, highlight the duckwear DSN, and then click the OK button.

16. Click the `duck_sales` table, and then click the OK button. You now have a link to your MySQL table data from the Access program. Any changes you make to the data here will be reflected in your MySQL database.

Project Summary

This project showed you how to make a DSN connection using MyODBC and use it to import data directly from MySQL to Access and to link to the data in MySQL from inside Access. Importing the data allows you to manipulate and examine it outside your database environment. This can be useful for two reasons: By placing the data in a separate environment, you remove the risk of corrupting the original data. Linking to MySQL through Access also allows a person familiar with Access to examine and *change* the data in MySQL (but not the table format) without having to learn another GUI. While this is not a long term solution—a MySQL-specific GUI like MySQLCC will be an all-around better choice, practically speaking—it may be the quickest way for users to work with data that has been migrated from Access to MySQL. Data stored in Access can be migrated to MySQL by exporting it to a delimited file and then importing that file into MySQL using the file as input in the normal manner.

✓ *Module 7 Mastery Check*

1. What do the acronyms PHP and HTML stand for?

2. What does the following line of code do?

```
$link = mysql_connect('localhost', 'ron', 'sc0rpio');
```

3. What symbol do you add to the beginning of a function name to suppress the warning output?

4. What is the PHP equivalent of the MySQL command SHOW TABLES?

5. What do the PHP functions for forcing type casting do?

6. What security issue does the `mysql_escape_string()` function guard against?

7. What two methods in PEAR::DB are used to deal with the results from a query (or prepare/execute)?

8. What is database abstraction?

9. What are the two ways to export data from MySQL and import data into Microsoft Excel?

10. How can Microsoft Access be directly linked to MySQL in order to view its data?

Module 8

Basic Administration and Backups

From an administrator's perspective, securing a database means several things. You need to protect it by restricting access to the database server itself, and to the tables in its individual databases to only authorized users. You also need to be able to recover from a catastrophic database failure, no matter what the cause. This module will explain how to manage user accounts with regard to access and privileges, as well as how to back up your data using various processes and how to restore your database to health after a failure occurs.

Set Privileges

Privilege can be defined as a right granted for a specific reason. Setting privileges lets database administrators maintain the security of the data, while allowing users to access necessary information independently. If an administrator is the only person allowed to access a busy database, requests for information from it can become an overwhelming demand on that administrator's time. Setting privileges so that users are allowed to access only information applicable to their jobs, or to view but not alter the data, is a way for an administrator to delegate specific routine requests for information into an automatic process controlled by user names and passwords.

Understanding the Levels of Security

At its most basic level, setting privileges on a database is a matter of letting some users in and keeping some users out, but the more users you have and the more varied the data you store, the more levels of access you may find necessary. Security can be set at three levels: database, file, and client access.

Database Security

Database security revolves around setting user name/password combinations to allow access to approved users and deny access to all others. At the very least, a password should be set for the root user. If you followed the installation instructions in Module 1, you set the root user password as soon as you made your first connection to your database.

If, at some point, you forget the password for the root user, you can regain access to the database. In MySQL, user security information is stored in grant tables. You can start the server without accessing the grant tables, which means no password is required to log in. Once inside the server, the root user password can be reset, allowing secure access to the database server again. The precise process for resetting the root password depends on your OS. The following sections give specific steps to reset the root password on both Windows- and Linux-based MySQL Servers.

Resetting the Root Password on a Windows System   Before you can reset the root password, you must stop the MySQL Server. The following is the procedure for stopping the MySQL Server and resetting the password on a Windows computer.

1. Open the Control Panel in Windows, double-click the Administrative Tools icon, and then double-click the Services icon. In the Services window, locate the MySQL process, right-click it, and choose Stop from the menu to terminate the MySQL Server. Leave the Services window open; you will return here to restart the server.

2. Open a command-line window and enter the following command:

```
\mysql\bin\mysqld --skip-grant-tables
```

The cursor will move down a line but will not return a prompt.

3. Open another command-line window and enter the following commands:

```
\mysql\bin\mysqladmin -u root flush-privileges password "<new password>"
\mysql\bin\mysqladmin -u root
```

MySQL will prompt you for a password. Use the password you entered in place of *<new password>* in the preceding code.

4. Go back to the Services window, right-click the MySQL process, and choose Start from the menu. MySQL is now running in normal mode, and your root password has been reset.

You can also stop the MySQL Server by issuing the NET STOP MYSQL command in the command-line window, and restart it by issuing the NET START MYSQL command in the command-line window.

Resetting the Root Password on Linux   Before you can reset the root password, you must stop the MySQL Server. The following is the procedure for stopping the MySQL Server, and then resetting the password on a Linux computer.

1. If the MySQL server is not running, then skip to step 3. If the MySQL server is running it must be terminated by force. Make sure you are logged in to your computer as root and locate the file containing the process identification (PID) number. The .pid file is usually named in one of two formats: mysqld.pid or *<hostname>*.pid. For instance, if your Linux computer is named Doc, your .pid file may be named Doc.pid or mysqld.pid. The directory where the .pid file is located varies depending on the brand of Linux you are running; the following are common locations:

- /var/run/mysqld
- /var/lib/mysqld
- /var/lib/mysql
- /usr/local/mysql/data

2. Once you have located the correct directory and ascertained the .pid filename, execute the following command:

```
kill `cat /<path to correct directory>/<filename>.pid`
```

NOTE

Make sure you use backticks—the same key as the tilde (~)—in the preceding command. Single quotes may not work.

You should get a return line that indicates mysqld is ended, although you may need to press the ENTER key to return to the command-line prompt.

3. Enter the following commands to open MySQL without the grant tables:

```
mysql_safe --skip-grant-tables &
```

You should get a return indicating that the mysqld daemon is starting.

4. Enter the following command to reset the root password:

```
mysqladmin -u root flush-privileges password "<new password>"
```

5. You should be able to log in to MySQL now using the new password by entering the following command and then the new password when prompted.

```
/usr/bin/mysql -p
```

File-Level Security

Even if your users have access to your database, there are some areas of information to which you may not want to give them access. Obviously, the data files should be protected. If a user only needs to view data, give that user only viewing privileges. You may want to allow a user to insert data but not to delete data. A user may need access, at whatever level, to one table in a database and not to another. A good administrator examines a new user's role in interfacing with the database before setting up that user's access parameters.

Log files also need to have adequate security. These files can have sensitive information in them that should not be made available to all users. Many log file entries contain harmless information that may not be considered informative to anyone but an administrator; however, a log file that stores queries, for instance, can contain user name and password information and should be protected from general access.

In the Windows and Linux environments, file-sharing criteria can be set within the OS, and user privileges can be set within the MySQL Client.

Client-Access Security

Users can be given access to the MySQL Client in two different categories: server access and query access. Server access, as previously mentioned, involves a user name/password combination that allows access to the MySQL Client that interfaces with the MySQL Server. Query access functions inside the MySQL Client and involves varying levels of privilege regarding the user's use of queries and commands. A user may have all available privileges or a handpicked set of them designed specifically to balance that user's needs and the database's security.

Privileges are set by using the GRANT command, as described in the next section. The privilege settings, in combination with a user name and password, are stored in the grant tables, which MySQL consults whenever a user tries to execute a query. If a user has no privileges on a database, that database will not be listed when that user runs the SHOW DATABASES command. The same is true for tables within databases. If a database has 20 tables, but the user has privileges for only 5 of them, that user will see only those 5 tables listed when she or he runs the SHOW TABLES command.

Granting and Revoking User Privileges

MySQL allows you to grant certain privileges to a user. Creating a user account grants the new user the USAGE privilege as part of the account creation process. The USAGE privilege merely allows the user to log in to the MySQL server; it does not grant any other access. Even if all privileges are taken away from that user, the USAGE grant remains until the user is deleted from the system.

The GRANT function creates new users and grants privileges to existing users. The basic syntax is as follows:

```
GRANT <privilege_type> [<column_name or list of names>]
[, <privilege_type> [<column_name or list of names>]] ON
{ *| *.* | <database_name>.* | <database_name>.<table_name> }
TO <user_name> IDENTIFIED BY "<password>" [WITH GRANT OPTION};
```

NOTE

The text in the syntax surrounded by curly braces ({ }) is a list of possible choices, one of which must be selected for the command.

Privileges can be revoked for a variety of reasons. As part of the set up of a new user, you can grant all privileges, and then revoke the ones the user does not need. When a user's job description changes, you may need to revoke some privileges and grant others. In the case of database misuse or a user who is no longer with your company, revoking privileges is the first step to removing the user entirely.

The REVOKE function has a marginally simpler syntax than GRANT, and you can use the SHOW GRANTS FOR <user_name> command to verify the exact syntax needed to revoke a specific privilege.

```
REVOKE <privilege_type> [<column_name or list of names>]
[, <privilege_type> [<column_name or list of names>]] ON
{ *| *.* | <database_name>.* | <database_name>.<table_name> }
FROM <user_name>;
```

Privilege Levels

Privileges can take place on four levels: global, database, table, and column.

Global Privileges
Privileges granted on a global level apply to all of the databases in your MySQL Server. This includes the `mysql` database containing information used for MySQL's operation. Rarely do any users, other than those with administrative duties, require access to the `mysql` database. To grant or revoke all privileges on a global level, use the following partial syntax:

```
GRANT ALL ON *.*
REVOKE ALL ON *.*
```

Database-Level Privileges
Privileges granted on a database level apply to the specified databases in your MySQL Server. This includes access to all tables within the specified database and allows you to restrict a user's access to only that database. To grant or revoke all privileges on a database level, use the following partial syntax:

```
GRANT ALL ON <database_name>.*
REVOKE ALL ON <database_name>.*
```

Table-Level Privileges
Privileges granted on a table level apply to the specified table in your MySQL Server. This includes access to the specific table and all of its columns within the specified database, and allows you to restrict a user's access to only that table. To grant or revoke all privileges on a table level, use the following partial syntax:

```
GRANT ALL ON <database_name>.<table_name>
REVOKE ALL ON <database_name>.<table_name>
```

Column-Level Privileges
Privileges granted on a column level apply to the specified column within a specific database and table in your MySQL Server. This includes access to only the specific column and allows you to restrict a user's access to all other columns in that table. To grant or revoke all privileges on a column level, use the following partial syntax:

```
GRANT ALL (<column_name>) ON <database_name>.<table_name>
REVOKE ALL (<column_name>) ON <database_name>.<table_name>
```

Privilege Types
Table 8-1 lists the types of privileges you can grant. As you peruse the table, notice the commentary on which privileges it might be wise to grant on a restricted basis. Any privilege that has been granted can also be revoked. In many circumstances, it may be easier to grant a new user ALL PRIVILEGES, and then revoke the ones deemed unnecessary, depending on that user's required interaction with the database.

Privilege Type	Description	Comments
ALL	Grants all privileges, except WITH GRANT OPTION	Using the reserved word PRIVILEGES after ALL is optional.
ALTER	Grants use of ALTER TABLE	Renaming tables should be reserved for administrators only whenever possible.
CREATE	Grants use of CREATE TABLE	
CREATE TEMPORARY TABLES	Grants use of CREATE TEMPORARY TABLE	Users who access data in order to make reports may need this privilege.
DELETE	Grants use of DELETE	Only users involved in data maintenance should have this privilege.
DROP	Grants use of DROP TABLE	Dropping tables should be reserved for administrators only whenever possible.
EXECUTE	Grants use of stored procedures (new in MySQL version 4.0.2)	Depending on the stored procedures, this privilege may be better reserved for administrators only.
FILE	Grants use of SELECT INTO OUTFILE and LOAD DATA INFILE	Depending on the level of data security desired, this privilege may be better reserved for administrators only whenever possible.
GRANT OPTION	Used to revoke WITH GRANT OPTION	
INDEX	Grants use of CREATE INDEX and DROP INDEX	Only users involved in data maintenance should have this privilege.
INSERT	Grants use of INSERT	Only users involved in data maintenance should have this privilege.
LOCK TABLES	Grants use of LOCK TABLES on tables on which the user already has the SELECT privilege	Only users involved in data maintenance should have this privilege.
PROCESS	Grants use of SHOW FULL PROCESSLIST	Viewing the process list should be reserved for administrators only whenever possible.
RELOAD	Grants use of FLUSH	Only users involved in data maintenance should have this privilege.

Table 8-1 MySQL Privilege Types

Privilege Type	Description	Comments
REPLICATION CLIENT	Grants ability to ask where the slaves/masters are	Viewing replication servers locations should be reserved for administrators only whenever possible.
REPLICATION SLAVE	Grants ability of the replication slaves to read information from master	This privilege should be reserved for administrators only whenever possible.
SELECT	Grants use of SELECT	Any user who needs to view data will need this privilege.
SHOW DATABASES	Grants use of SHOW DATABASES	This privilege shows users only the databases to which they are granted access; most users can have this privilege.
SHUTDOWN	Grants use of MYSQLADMIN SHUTDOWN	This privilege should be reserved for administrators only whenever possible.
SUPER	Grants the user one connection, one time, even if the server is at maximum connections limit, and grants use of CHANGE MASTER, KILL THREAD, MYSQLADMIN DEBUG, PURGE MASTER LOGS, and SET GLOBAL	This privilege should be reserved for administrators only.
UPDATE	Grants use of UPDATE	Only users involved in data maintenance should have this privilege.
USAGE	Grants access to log in to the MySQL Server but bestows no privileges	All users, once defined, have this privilege.
WITH GRANT OPTION	Grants ability for users to grant any privilege they possess to another user	This privilege should be reserved for administrators only whenever possible.

Table 8-1 MySQL Privilege Types *(continued)*

More than one privilege type, with or without an accompanying column name or list of names, can be included in a single GRANT command, as shown by the syntax before the ON reserved word. The column name or list of names option is used only when setting privileges on the column level. The optional privilege type WITH GRANT OPTION is used only if the user is allowed to pass on the granting of privileges.

CAUTION

Giving a user the WITH GRANT OPTION in regards to a privilege also allows that user to grant others any other privilege the user might have at the same level as the one where WITH GRANT OPTION is bestowed.

User Names

It is also important to note that in MySQL, the host is part of the user name. If access to the database will always be made, or restricted to, the host that the database is running on, the host can be referred to as *localhost*, as in root@localhost or lorne@localhost. On the other hand, if a database will always be accessed, or restricted from access, from a network, the host can be specified as part of the local domain. For instance, if the local domain will always be *xxx.yyy.zzz*.[0-255], you can use a wildcard for the final set of numbers, so that the user name is in the format *name*@xxx.yyy.xxx.%, as in lorne@%.mydomain.com. You can also use the percent sign wildcard to allow a user to access the database from any host: lorne@%.

The wildcard symbols percent sign and underscore (% and _) are allowed in database names on the global and database levels. If a GRANT command has either of them in the database name, they must be offset by preceding them with a backslash (\) to indicate that MySQL should not interpret them as wildcards. For example, if your database login name is donut_boy, and you are granting privileges on the global or database level, the database name in the GRANT command should be `donut\_boy`.

If user names or host names contain special characters, they must be put between quotes in the GRANT command. For instance, queen_c@sun-e-dale.com has the special characters underscore and dash, so it would need to be typed in as `queen_c`@`sun-e-dale.com`. In other words, the parts of the user name that have special characters must be treated as a string and placed between quotes to indicate that no special meaning should be attached to the special characters, but the at symbol (@) must be outside the quotes so that it is still perceived as a special character connecting a user name and host name.

Grant Information Storage

The mysql database contains five tables that store grant information and are collectively referred to as the *grant tables:*

- The user table stores the users, including their hosts and passwords that allow them to connect to the MySQL Server.

- The db table stores the users and the database-specific privileges that exist, indicating whether each user has access to each privilege.

- The host table is used in combination with the db table to control access from specific hosts; however, it does not reflect the information generated by GRANT and REVOKE commands, so it usually remains empty and unused.

- The tables_priv table stores specific privileges in relation to a specific user and table, and the indicated privilege applies to the entire table.

- The columns_priv table stores the specific column and privilege in relation to the specific user, and the indicated privilege applies only to that specific column in that specific table.

CAUTION

It is possible to change the grant tables without using the GRANT command. That is one of the reasons why the mysql database should have extremely restricted access. The privilege tables should *never* be altered manually. For consistency and security, *always* use the GRANT command.

Removal of User Privileges and Users

The basic syntax for the REVOKE command is shown at the beginning of this section. Starting with MySQL version 4.1.2, you will be able to revoke all privileges on all levels, from a user or list of users, with one command, using the following syntax:

```
REVOKE ALL PRIVILEGES, GRANT OPTION FROM <user_name>[, <user_name>, ...];
```

There is a specific list of privileges that can be used in the privilege type field of the REVOKE function for a table: SELECT, INSERT, UPDATE, DELETE, CREATE, DROP, GRANT OPTION, INDEX, and ALTER. If the REVOKE function is for a column, the privileges specified in the privilege type field can be only SELECT, INSERT, and UPDATE.

Ask the Expert

Q: Why should I restrict my users' access to some of the MySQL commands?

A: The most common type of failure is user failure. This type of damage is seldom intentional, but unrestricted users may drop or corrupt data by mistake. You can reduce the possibility of user-corrupted data by limiting what users are allowed to do in the database. As of MySQL version 4, an administrator can limit privileges on a per-user basis. Limiting users in this way creates a better security policy and reduces the potential load on the machine. Another way to increase security for your database is to use SSL transport-layer encryption. This prevents your usernames and passwords from being passed in the open across the network.

Once all privileges have been revoked from a user, the user still has the USAGE privilege, which allows the user to log in to the database but not do anything once there. In order to remove the user from the database, you must execute the following commands:

```
DELETE FROM mysql.user
WHERE USER="<user_name>"
AND HOST="<host_name>";
FLUSH PRIVILEGES;
```

The FLUSH PRIVILEGES command causes MySQL to refresh the privileges in the cache where they are held in memory, thereby setting the latest version of privileges in place. Since the DELETE syntax for removing users is specific to the user name and host name, you must delete each instance of user permissions. For instance, if a particular user has access privileges from localhost and from the *.sun-e-dale.com host, you must execute a DELETE command for both instances in order to completely remove the user from the system.

Privilege Management

Here, we will look at some common considerations regarding privilege management that every administrator should consider.

Passwords   The most important factor in privilege management is that all users should have passwords in order to maintain the security of the database. When creating an administrator user, the GLOBAL privilege is granted by using the following syntax in the GRANT command:

```
ON *.*.
```

The WITH GRANT OPTION   If a specific user makes decisions about who has access to a particular database, giving that user the WITH GRANT OPTION privilege allows you to delegate the grant-access process to him or her, saving both of you time and effort. The syntax for doing so follows:

```
GRANT ALL ON <database_name>.* TO <user_name>
WITH GRANT OPTION;
```

Temporary Tables   If you have users who need to create temporary tables on a regular basis, the most secure way to allow this is to create a designated database to hold these tables and give those users, or all users, the necessary privileges to that database. Grouping all of the temporary tables within a database that holds no permanent tables removes the chance that a user might inadvertently or intentionally misuse privileges and corrupt the rest of the database.

Administrator-Only Privileges   Any users who have modifying privileges in the mysql database can give themselves GLOBAL privileges. As explained earlier, the grant tables where all access-related information is stored are in the mysql database, and these can be edited manually to modify privileges. Therefore, only administrators should be allowed access to the mysql database.

As noted in Table 8-1, several privilege types should be restricted to administrators whenever possible:

- Having the FILE privilege allows a user to write to or read a file nearly anywhere in the system. This includes all of the databases.

- The ALTER privilege, which allows a user to rename tables, can be used to gain access to a table the user does not have privileges on by changing its name to a table the user does have privileges on.

- The PROCESS privilege allows the use of the SHOW FULL PROCESSLIST command, which displays the list of currently running processes. On a busy system, it allows the user to see the text of any currently executing query, including plain text passwords in SET, CHANGE, or GRANT queries. It is not a guaranteed or efficient way to acquire other users' passwords, but it should still be guarded against.

- The SHUTDOWN privilege causes the entire database to stop running, which can be inconvenient or even catastrophic, depending on what is happening at that moment. Few, if any, users other than administrators should have this privilege.

- The DROP privilege allows the removal of an entire table and its data from the database. If the table does not exist on a backup, there is no way to recover it. This privilege is potentially so destructive that it should be reserved for administrator use only.

- The SUPER privilege allows the use of several privileges aimed at administrative tasks; it also allows access to the database even when the maximum number of connections is being used. No one other than an administrator needs this privilege.

Progress Check

1. What command do you use to create a new user?

2. What command do you use to give an existing user new privileges?

3. What command do you use to take away a user's privileges?

4. When you execute REVOKE ALL, does that remove all privileges?

5. What command removes the USAGE privilege?

---

1. The GRANT command creates new users.
2. The GRANT command gives existing users new privileges.
3. The REVOKE command takes away privileges.
4. No, the USAGE privilege still remains.
5. You must use the DELETE command to remove the user from the mysql.user table and then use the FLUSH PRIVILEGES command.

Project 8-1 Set Privileges

This project will allow you to gain experience granting user accounts and setting the privileges for them to access your database.

Step by Step

1. Open a command-line window and log in to the MySQL client as root.

2. Create a user named `second` with the password `pa552` and grant all privileges when logging in from any host.

```
GRANT ALL ON *.* TO second@'%' IDENTIFIED BY "pa552";
```

NOTE

Using a wildcard symbol (* or %) for the user or host requires that it be surrounded by single quotes.

3. Verify the grant.

```
SHOW GRANTS FOR second@'%';
```

```
Command Prompt - \mysql\bin\mysql -u root -p                          _□X
mysql> grant all on *.* to second@'%' identified by "pa552";
Query OK, 0 rows affected (0.00 sec)

mysql> show grants for second@'%';
+----------------------------------------------------------------+
| Grants for second@%                                            |
+----------------------------------------------------------------+
| GRANT ALL PRIVILEGES ON *.* TO 'second'@'%' IDENTIFIED BY PASSWORD '5dd0c2f709
aa6293' |
+----------------------------------------------------------------+
1 row in set (0.00 sec)
```

4. Create a user named `joss` with the password `f1refly`, logging in from the localhost only, with all privileges plus GRANT OPTION on the `duck_sales` table only.

```
GRANT ALL ON duckwear.duck_sales TO joss@localhost
IDENTIFIED BY "f1refly" WITH GRANT OPTION;
```

```
Command Prompt - \mysql\bin\mysql -u root -p                          _□X
mysql> grant all on duckwear.duck_sales to joss@localhost identified by "f1refly
" with grant option;
Query OK, 0 rows affected (0.02 sec)

mysql> show grants for joss@localhost;
+----------------------------------------------------------------+
| Grants for joss@localhost                                      |
+----------------------------------------------------------------+
| GRANT USAGE ON *.* TO 'joss'@'localhost' IDENTIFIED BY PASSWORD '3ea2aaa362ba4
5b1' |
| GRANT ALL PRIVILEGES ON `duckwear`.`duck_sales` TO 'joss'@'localhost' WITH GRA
NT OPTION |
+----------------------------------------------------------------+
2 rows in set (0.00 sec)

mysql>
```

(continued)

5. Open a new command-line window and log in as `joss`. Execute the following commands to demonstrate that the user `joss` has access to the `duck_sales` table only.

```
SELECT * FROM duck_cust LIMIT 3;
SELECT * FROM duck_sales LIMIT 3;
```

You will get an error when the user `joss` tries to access the `duck_cust` table. (The `LIMIT` option is used only to make the return a manageable size for the illustration.)

```
Command Prompt - mysql -u joss -p                                    _ □ X
C:\Documents and Settings\Michael Grey>cd \mysql\bin

C:\mysql\bin>mysql -u joss -p
Enter password: *******
Welcome to the MySQL monitor.  Commands end with ; or \g.
Your MySQL connection id is 51 to server version: 4.0.18-nt-log

Type 'help;' or '\h' for help. Type '\c' to clear the buffer.

mysql> use duckwear;
Database changed
mysql> select * from duck_cust limit 3;
ERROR 1142: select command denied to user: 'joss@localhost' for table 'duck_cust
'
mysql> select * from duck_sales limit 3;
+-----------+-------------+--------------+-------------+-------------+--------
-----+-----------------+
| design_num | design_name | winter_sales | spring_sales | summer_sales | fall_s
ales | design_category |
+-----------+-------------+--------------+-------------+-------------+--------
-----+-----------------+
|         1 | Santa_Duck  |         1067 |          200 |          150 |
 267 | Holiday         |
|         2 | Dr_Duck     |          970 |          770 |          561 |
 486 | Profession      |
|         3 | Duckula     |           53 |           13 |           21 |
 856 | Literary        |
+-----------+-------------+--------------+-------------+-------------+--------
-----+-----------------+
3 rows in set (0.01 sec)

mysql>
```

6. Create a user named `marti` on localhost with a password of `tick3t`, who has `ALL` privileges on the `duck_sales` table, and then revoke the `DELETE`, `DROP`, and `ALTER` privileges.

```
GRANT ALL ON duckwear.duck_sales TO marti@localhost IDENTIFIED BY "tick3t";
REVOKE DELETE, DROP, ALTER ON duckwear.duck_sales FROM marti@localhost;
SHOW GRANTS FOR marti@localhost;
```

```
Command Prompt - \mysql\bin\mysql -u root -p                          _ □ X
mysql> grant all on duckwear.duck_sales to marti@localhost identified by "tick3t
";
Query OK, 0 rows affected (0.00 sec)

mysql> show grants for marti@localhost;
+----------------------------------------------------------------------------+
| Grants for marti@localhost                                                 |
+----------------------------------------------------------------------------+
| GRANT USAGE ON *.* TO 'marti'@'localhost' IDENTIFIED BY PASSWORD '6aba326c7cac
8ab6' |
| GRANT ALL PRIVILEGES ON `duckwear`.`duck_sales` TO 'marti'@'localhost'      |
+----------------------------------------------------------------------------+
2 rows in set (0.00 sec)

mysql> revoke delete, drop, alter on duckwear.duck_sales from marti@localhost;
Query OK, 0 rows affected (0.00 sec)

mysql> show grants for marti@localhost;
+----------------------------------------------------------------------------+
| Grants for marti@localhost                                                 |
+----------------------------------------------------------------------------+
| GRANT USAGE ON *.* TO 'marti'@'localhost' IDENTIFIED BY PASSWORD '6aba326c7cac
8ab6' |
| GRANT SELECT, INSERT, UPDATE, CREATE, REFERENCES, INDEX ON `duckwear`.`duck_sa
les` TO 'marti'@'localhost' |
+----------------------------------------------------------------------------+
2 rows in set (0.00 sec)

mysql>
```

7. Have the user `joss` grant the `DELETE` privilege to `marti@localhost`.

```
GRANT DELETE ON duckwear.duck_sales TO marti@localhost;
SHOW GRANTS FOR marti@localhost;
```

8. Have the root user show the change.

```
SHOW GRANTS FOR marti@localhost;
```

Compare the results with those received in step 6.

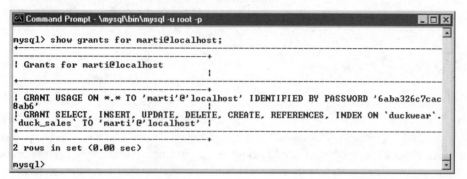

9. Revoke `ALL` privileges from the user `second`, delete the user, and then verify the removal.

```
REVOKE ALL ON *.* FROM second@`%`;

DELETE FROM mysql.user
WHERE USER="second"
AND HOST= "%";

FLUSH PRIVILEGES;

SHOW GRANTS FOR second@'%';
```

(continued)

Project Summary

This project gave you hands-on experience with creating new users and setting and revoking their privileges. You created a user using `WITH GRANT OPTION`, and then had that user grant another user a specified privilege. You created users that had only table-specific access to a database, as well as a user with all privileges to all databases. You also revoked that user's privileges, which left the user with only the `USAGE` privilege, and then took that away by deleting the user from the `mysql.user` table and flushing the privileges tables to remove the previous reference to the now deleted user.

CRITICAL SKILL
8.2 # Make Backups

Backups are an important part of database administration, because no matter how careful you might be, accidents happen. A regularly scheduled backup procedure will go a long way toward making recovery from a database failure quick and easy. This section will cover how to go about making a backup, how to use a backup to recover from a failure, how to monitor the health of your tables, and how to repair tables in the event that they become corrupted.

Reviewing the Causes of System Failure

A failure of a database may be caused by a user's mistake like issuing a command accidentally or inadvertently clicking the wrong button, or it may be the result of forces you cannot control like the weather or the power company. No matter what the root cause of the failure, it always fits into one of two categories: hardware failure or user failure.

Hardware Failures

Hardware failures can be caused by mechanical or electrical means. When a component of the computer your database is running on dies, it can often result in data being lost. Loss of power, for whatever reason, can also lead to a system crash. Having an Uninterruptible Power Supply (UPS) for your computers is the best way you can back up the power requirements for your database's operation; however, a UPS is simply a large battery with a finite life span, so its protection lasts for only a certain number of hours.

When a hardware failure causes data loss or corruption, a backup of data taken at regular intervals will allow you to restore the database as quickly as possible with the least amount of effort.

User Failures

User failures come in varying guises. Using a `DROP TABLE` or `DELETE FROM` command may result in the unintentional loss of data. Editing tables can result in data loss, especially if the user leaves off a qualifying `WHEN` clause or uses a wildcard symbol in an inappropriate place, thereby changing or deleting all the data in a column or table, instead of affecting only the intended data. Users can also make mistakes when removing cables or turning off power, resulting in data loss due to interruption of processes. Even if you are the only person to use your database, statistically speaking, you will eventually make a critical mistake that leads to data loss or corruption, making backups a necessity and your salvation.

Planning and Preparing for Backup

There are a variety of ways to make a backup in MySQL, but before you decide which one is right for your situation, there are some basic backup fundamentals to consider. A good backup relies on forethought and planning to provide you with the information needed to restore your system, no matter what the cause of your database failure.

Deciding How Often to Perform Backups

Backups need to be performed on a regular basis. If your database is extremely busy and changes are being made constantly, you might want to back up your database once a day, although that is probably excessive in most cases. Certainly, backing up once a week is not unreasonable. If you database is merely an information repository, and updates and additions rarely happen, backing up once a month or even less may be acceptable. Consider that you will need to re-create all the transactions that occurred after the backup was taken in order to return your system to its current status, so the number of transactions that have occurred since backup can affect how long the restoration will take to complete.

Turning On the Binary Update Log

The binary update log needs to be turned on in order to restore the database without losing any of its data. This log stores only queries that actually change the data in the database. A restore operation will consult this log to re-create the changes in the database that occurred after the last backup. If you have a backup but do not turn on the binary update log, all of the post-backup changes will need to be re-created by hand—if you can be sure of what those changes were. You should also synchronize your update log file with your backup files, by using the FLUSH LOGS command, so that the only listings in the update logs have occurred after the last backup was made.

Naming Backup Files Consistently

You should name your backup files consistently and always include the date on which they were made. For instance, a backup of the database for the DuckWear Company might be named duckwear.*YYYYMMDD*.bkp, where the *Y*, *M*, and *D* characters stand for the year, month, and day the backup occurred. Listing the year first makes sure that all of the backup files for that year will be together in an alphanumeric directory listing, which makes scanning for a specific date's backup easier.

Storing Your Backups

Since sometimes you need a backup because of a hardware failure, you should always store your backup files on a different file system than your database. You should also make copies of the backup files and store them on another computer entirely or on a removable data storage device like a tape drive, floppy disk, or a CD-R, or DVD-R.

CAUTION

For long-term data integrity, recent studies have proven that low-quality CD-Rs are not extremely reliable and are susceptible to degradation over time.

Understanding the Backup Methods

The backup methods fall into two broad categories:

- File and data copies

- Table copies

Making File and Data Copies

The file and data copy methods work by making copies of the files specified for backup. Three methods that fit into this category are the BACKUP TABLE command, the mysqlhotcopy script, and the direct-data copy.

The BACKUP TABLE Command   The BACKUP TABLE command works only for MyISAM tables. It copies the .MYD and .frm files to the specified location. The .MYD files hold the actual data from the MyISAM tables, and the .frm file contains the format description of the table. The BACKUP TABLE command causes a lock to be placed on all reads for the duration of the function's execution. This means that while BACKUP TABLE is executing, nothing else can access the table in question.

The syntax for a BACKUP TABLE command is as follows:

```
BACKUP TABLE <table_name>[, <table_name>, . . .]
TO `<path to save directory>`;
```

Figure 8-1 shows an example of using the BACKUP TABLE command to back up the duck_sales table.

CAUTION

The slash marks delineating the path for the BACKUP TABLE command must be forward slashes (/), even on the Windows operating system where back slashes are the norm.

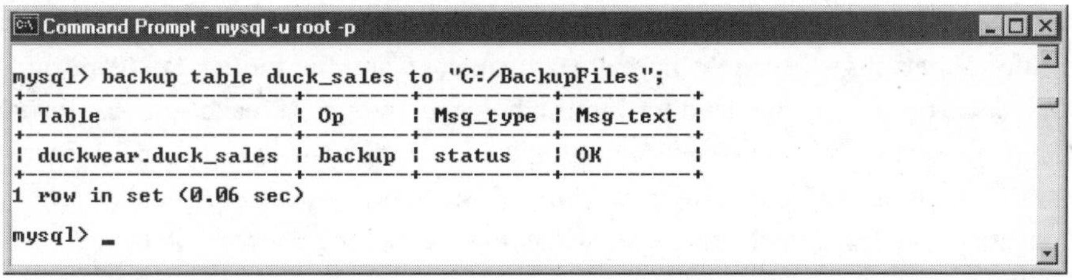

Figure 8-1 Using BACKUP TABLE

The BACKUP TABLE command will not overwrite already existing files. If files already exist in the desired directory, delete, move, or rename them (preferably reflecting their backup date) before attempting to make a current backup of the .MYD and .frm files, as shown in Figure 8-2.

The mysqlhotcopy Script   The mysqlhotcopy script is written in Perl and allows you to easily backup databases. It can, however, be run only on databases that are located on the same computer on which the script is running. It performs the following steps:

● Executes a LOCK TABLES command.

● Executes a FLUSH TABLES command.

● Copies the specified table files to the specified location, using either cp or scp.

● Executes the UNLOCK TABLES command.

The syntax for executing the mysqlhotcopy script is as follows:

```
MYSQLHOTCOPY <database_name> TO <path to save directory>;
```

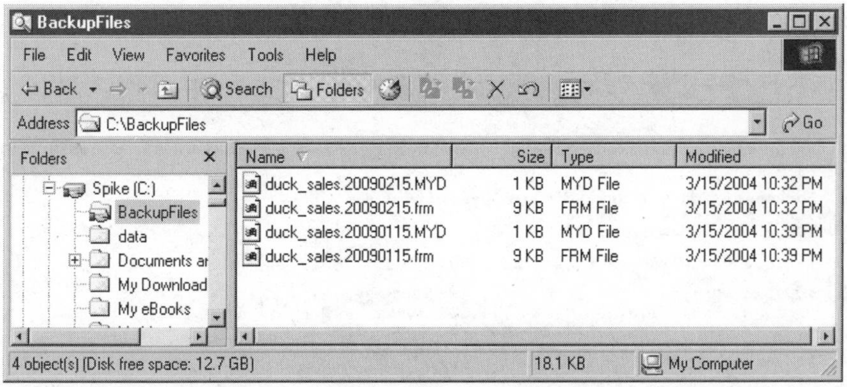

Figure 8-2 Renamed backup files reflecting their backup date

Direct-Data Copy   The direct-data copy method is simply to make a copy of the data files in the mysql/data directory in the normal way you copy any file for that OS (copy and paste for Windows or the `cp` command for Linux); however, you must make sure that the tables are *not being used* when you make the copy. If you are the only one to use your database, that is probably not all that difficult. However, if other users may be accessing the database, you can ensure the tables are not being used while you are making the copy by using one of the following methods:

- Stop the database, copy the files, and start the database again after you are finished copying. If your database cannot be stopped due to usage constraints, use the following method.

- Execute a `LOCK TABLES` command, copy the files, and then execute an `UNLOCK TABLES` command. This is essentially what the `mysqlhotcopy` script does, but you do it by hand.

Making Table Copies

The table copy methods work by making copies of the tables specified for backup. Two techniques for making table copies are using the `mysqldump` script and using the `SELECT INTO OUTFILE` command.

The mysqldump Script   The `mysqldump` script makes a file containing the SQL commands necessary to re-create the database. Its commands will make and fill the tables in the database. It is most often used when you are trying to re-create the database on another MySQL Server. For instance, you can use it to load a copy of a database onto a laptop, so that you can access the database while you're away from the main database's location and don't have the facilities to log in. Any changes you make and want to save can be dumped and transferred back to the original database when you return.

You run the `mysqldump` script from the OS command line, not inside the MySQL Client, as shown in Figure 8-3.

The syntax for the `mysqldump` script allows you to back up the entire database:

```
mysqldump <database_name> > <backup_name_with_date>.sql;
```

Figure 8-3 Running the mysqldump script from the OS command line

Alternatively, you can specify tables, instead of dumping the entire database:

```
mysqldump <database_name> [table or list of tables] >
<backup_name_with_date>.sql;
```

Figure 8-4 shows the file resulting from using the `mysqldump` script to back up the `duck_cust` table.

Adding the `--opt` option will allow you to get a quick dump that can be loaded into a MySQL Server rapidly. It is an abbreviation for all of the following options: `--quick`, `--add-drop-table`, `--add-locks`, `--extended-inserts`, and `--lock-tables`. Speed and increased compatibility with MySQL is the upside to using the `--opt` option; however, it results in a file that works with only MySQL. Without the `--opt` option, the resulting file will work with any DBMS system. The syntax for using options with `mysqldump` is as follows:

```
mysqldump [--option] <database_name> > <backup_name_with_date>.sql;
```

Figure 8-5 shows an example of the file resulting from using the `--opt` option when backing up the `duck_cust` table.

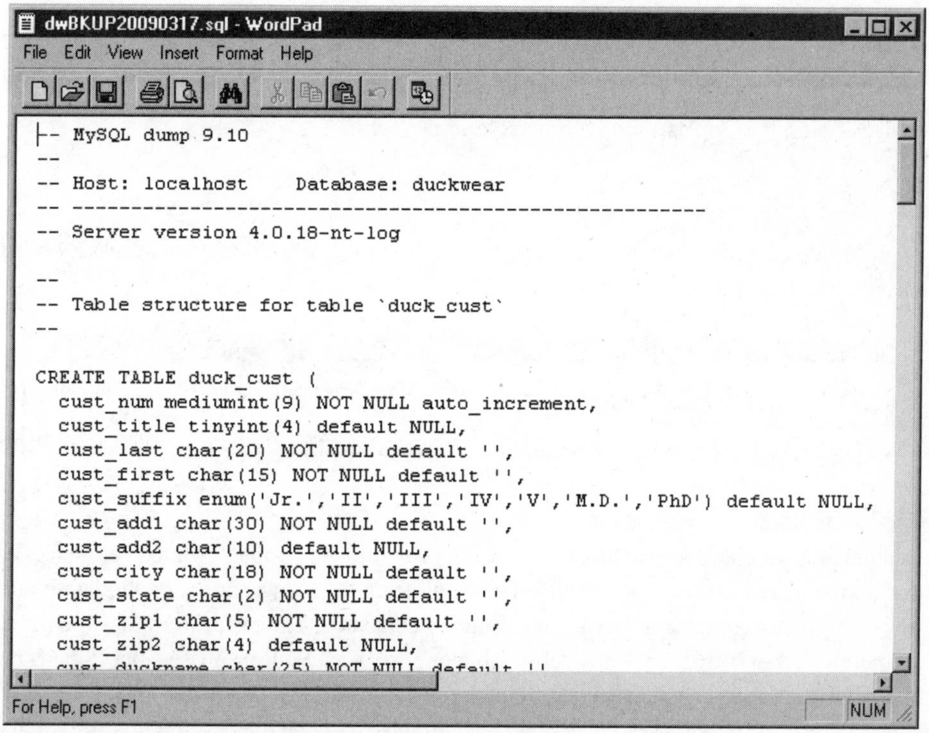


```
-- MySQL dump 9.10
--
-- Host: localhost    Database: duckwear
-- ------------------------------------------------------
-- Server version 4.0.18-nt-log

--
-- Table structure for table `duck_cust`
--

CREATE TABLE duck_cust (
  cust_num mediumint(9) NOT NULL auto_increment,
  cust_title tinyint(4) default NULL,
  cust_last char(20) NOT NULL default '',
  cust_first char(15) NOT NULL default '',
  cust_suffix enum('Jr.','II','III','IV','V','M.D.','PhD') default NULL,
  cust_add1 char(30) NOT NULL default '',
  cust_add2 char(10) default NULL,
  cust_city char(18) NOT NULL default '',
  cust_state char(2) NOT NULL default '',
  cust_zip1 char(5) NOT NULL default '',
  cust_zip2 char(4) default NULL,
```

Figure 8-4 Results of using mysqldump to back up the duck_cust table

```
📄 dwoptBKUP20090317.sql - WordPad                          _ □ ✕
File  Edit  View  Insert  Format  Help

 🗋 🖆 🖫  🖨 🔍  🗛   ✂ 🖹 📋 ↺  🔃

/*!40000 ALTER TABLE duck_cust DISABLE KEYS */;
LOCK TABLES duck_cust WRITE;
INSERT INTO duck_cust VALUES (1,8,'Salisbury','Jenny','','9 Wishing Well
UNLOCK TABLES;
/*!40000 ALTER TABLE duck_cust ENABLE KEYS */;

--
-- Table structure for table `duck_sales`
--

DROP TABLE IF EXISTS duck_sales;
CREATE TABLE duck_sales (
  design_num mediumint(9) NOT NULL auto_increment,
  design_name char(20) NOT NULL default '',
  winter_sales int(11) NOT NULL default '0',
  spring_sales int(11) NOT NULL default '0',
  summer_sales int(11) NOT NULL default '0',
  fall_sales int(11) NOT NULL default '0',
  design_category char(13) NOT NULL default '',
  PRIMARY KEY  (design_num)
) TYPE=MyISAM;

For Help, press F1                                           NUM
```

Figure 8-5 Using the --opt option with mysqldump

If MySQL refuses to allow the mysqldump --opt access, it may be necessary to supply a user name and password.

```
Command Prompt                                              _ □ ✕
C:\Documents and Settings\Michael Grey>\mysql\bin\mysqldump -u root -p --opt duc
kwear > dwoptBKUP20090317.sql
Enter password: ********
```

Evaluating Backup Methods

Deciding on which backup method is right for you ultimately boils down to preference, but the main criteria are speed and portability. The result from the mysqldump method without the --opt option is portable across a wide range of databases. The result from the mysqldump method with the --opt option is compatible only with MySQL databases, but it loads much faster. On the other hand, any of the file copying methods are much faster to execute than mysqldump, so if time is of the essence, one of those may be the best method for you to choose.

Progress Check

1. What are three methods of making file and data backup copies?

2. What are two methods of making table backup copies?

3. What is the basic syntax for the BACKUP TABLE command when only one table is backed up?

4. What is the basic syntax for the mysqldump script when one database is backed up and no options are specified?

Project 8-2 Back Up a Database

This project gives you experience backing up both an entire database and specified tables within a database, by using the BACKUP TABLE command and the mysqldump script.

Step by Step

1. Open a command-line window and log in to the MySQL Client as root.

2. Change to the duckwear database. Back up the duck_cust and duck_title tables using the BACKUP TABLE command, saving the results to a directory called BackDuck. The following commands show the BackDuck directory located on a different hard drive (D:\) than the database hard drive (C:\) for increased data security. Your command may need to indicate the path to another location.

```
USE duckwear;
BACKUP TABLE duck_cust, duck_title TO "D:/BackDuck/";
```

Project
8-2

Back Up a Database

```
Command Prompt - mysql -u root -p
mysql> use duckwear;
Database changed
mysql> backup table duck_cust, duck_title to "D:/BackDuck";
+--------------------+--------+----------+----------+
| Table              | Op     | Msg_type | Msg_text |
+--------------------+--------+----------+----------+
| duckwear.duck_cust | backup | status   | OK       |
| duckwear.duck_title| backup | status   | OK       |
+--------------------+--------+----------+----------+
2 rows in set (0.13 sec)
```

(continued)

---

1. The three methods of making file and data backup copies are the BACKUP TABLE command, the mysqlhotcopy script, and direct file copying.

2. The two methods of making table backup copies are the mysqldump script and the SELECT INTO OUTFILE function.

3. The basic syntax for the BACKUP TABLE command is as follows:

```
BACKUP TABLE <table_name> TO `<path to save directory>`;
```

4. The basic syntax for the mysqldump script is as follows:

```
mysqldump <database_name> > <backup_name_with_date>.sql;
```

CAUTION

The directory that you indicate as the location to place the files resulting from a BACKUP TABLE command must exist *before* you run the command. It will *not* create it for you.

3. Open your system's file navigation tool, such as Windows Explorer, and examine the contents of the directory you indicated in the command in step 2.

```
BackDuck                                                            _ □ ×
 File   Edit   View   Favorites   Tools   Help                           

 ← Back  ▾  ⇒  ▾  ⬚  │ ❑Search  🗁Folders  ❸  │ ❖ ❖ ✕ ↻  │ ▦▾
 Address │ 🗀 D:\BackDuck                                          ▾  ⬚ Go

 Folders               ✕    Name  △              Size  Type        Modified
 ⊟ 💾 Spike (D:)          ▲   📄 duck_cust.frm       9 KB  FRM File    3/17/2004 11:18 PI
    🗀 ADJECT               📄 duck_cust.MYD       2 KB  MYD File    3/17/2004 11:18 PI
    🗀 apics                📄 duck_title.frm      9 KB  FRM File    3/17/2004 11:18 PI
    ⊞ 🗀 AtomTime           📄 duck_title.MYD      1 KB  MYD File    3/17/2004 11:18 PI
    🗀 BackDuck
    ⊞ 🗀 C on Spike     ▼
 ◀                    ▶    ◀                                              ▶

 4 object(s) (Disk free space: 53.7 GB)          │19.1 KB  │ 💻 My Computer
```

4. Exit from the MySQL Client to the command-line prompt. If you are not already in the /mysql/bin/ directory, go there.

5. Make a backup of the duckwear database using the following mysqldump command:

```
MYSQLDUMP duckwear > dw20090317.sql
```

The resulting file will be saved in the /mysql/bin/ directory.

```
Command Prompt                                                     _ □ ×
mysql> exit
Bye

C:\mysql\bin>mysqldump duckwear > dw20090317.sql

C:\mysql\bin>dir dw2*
 Volume in drive C is Spike
 Volume Serial Number is 4019-A80E

 Directory of C:\mysql\bin

03/18/2004  12:19a              6,504 dw20090317.sql
               1 File(s)         6,504 bytes
               0 Dir(s)  13,735,075,840 bytes free

C:\mysql\bin>_
```

Project Summary

This project produced backup files for the duck_cust and duck_title tables and for the entire duckwear database. You will use these files in Project 8-3 to restore tables, after you simulate damage to the database.

CRITICAL SKILL
8.3 Recover from a Disaster

No one likes the sound of the phrase "disaster recovery," but the best thing to do is focus on the "recovery" part. If you have been faithfully making backups and synchronizing your binary update log each time, MySQL makes it fairly easy to quickly and cleanly get your database back to where it was before your particular disaster struck.

Once you have ascertained the cause of your disaster, you can take steps to recover from it. Obviously, if it is a hardware failure, you will need to replace the hardware and reload the appropriate programs onto your machine. If it was human error in the form of unfortunate queries that resulted in table damage, you need to locate those queries in your binary update log so that you do not execute them again during the recovery process and duplicate the error. If it was something uncontrollable, like a power outage, then weigh what your downtime is costing you compared to the price of a suitable UPS, and if the downtime is more costly, put one in the loop before recovering your database.

Knowing the Restore Procedure

The following is the basic procedure for recovering from a database failure:

1. Make a copy of the damaged database.

2. Put your most current backup in the data directory.

3. Use the binary update log to execute the queries that had been run since the backup was taken.

The following sections describe how to accomplish each of these steps.

Copying the Damaged Database

If you still have a current but damaged copy of your database, make a copy of it that is clearly marked as damaged. It is possible that you may want to examine the damage during the restoration process. It may be that the causes of the disaster were more complex than you first realized, so in the unlikely event that the recovery fails, you will still need the damaged database to examine.

Putting Your Backup in the Data Directory

Next, you need to put your most current backup in the data directory. How you do this depends on how the data was backed up.

If you used the direct-copy data file method, copy the backup files into the data directory using the same OS-specific file-copy techniques.

If you used the BACKUP TABLE command, use the reciprocal RESTORE TABLE command. Like BACKUP TABLE, RESTORE TABLE can be used only on MyISAM tables. When you use the RESTORE TABLE command, it copies the .MYD and .frm files into the data directory and re-creates the index (.MYI), if there was one in the original table. The syntax for the RESTORE TABLE command is as follows:

```
RESTORE TABLE <table_name or list of names> FROM <path to backup files>
```

NOTE

The RESTORE TABLE command will not allow you to write over any already existing files. The old files must be removed from the data directory, or the command will return an error.

If you used either of the methods that result in a file of SQL commands, run those commands, preferably using a GUI to import the file or to paste the file information into an SQL editor window to run.

Executing Queries with the Binary Update Log

Once the backup is installed into MySQL, use the binary update log to execute the queries that had been run after the backup was taken. mysqlbinlog is another script that must be run from the command line, and its syntax is as follows:

```
MYSQLBINLOG <update_log_name> | MYSQL --ONE-DATABASE <database_name>
```

The --ONE_DATABASE option allows MySQL to ignore any SQL statements in the update files for any but the specified database.

Dealing with Damaged Tables

If you have a damaged table, the logical reaction would seem to be restoring just that table; however, restoring a table can be much more complicated than restoring an entire database. When you restore a database, MySQL searches through the binary update file for all queries pertaining to that database. If you have multiple databases, that can be a complicated search. If you are restoring one table within a specific database, the binary update file must be searched one level deeper, looking for only the queries pertaining to that specified table.

It is often easier to restore the entire database than take the time to restore just one table within it. Remember that the mysql and test databases are installed with MySQL, so even if you store all your data within one other database, there are still queries to more than one database happening within the binary update log. The more databases you have, the more complex a mixture of queries will reside in your binary update file. That being said, you may still decide to deal with database damage on a table level.

There are several ways a table can become damaged. During the operation of a `mysqld` process, the interruption of a write will result in a damaged table. Such an interruption can be caused by a power failure, a crash of the OS, a hardware error, or a `kill` command issued on the process. Using a script to interface with MySQL without locking the tables first can also result in table damage.

The classic signs of table damage are if MySQL suddenly stops working for no apparent reason or if one process thread begins to use up all of your CPU activity. When either of those events occurs, it may be advisable to use the CHECK TABLE command.

Using the CHECK TABLE Command

The CHECK TABLE command works on MyISAM and InnoDB tables. It operates by first locking tables, and then checking for errors in the data or table structure before unlocking the tables again. On MyISAM tables, it corresponds with the `myisamchk` script when using the -m option, as discussed in the next section.

The syntax for the CHECK TABLE command is as follows:

```
CHECK TABLE <table_name or list of names> [option]
```

You can run CHECK TABLE with any of the five options shown in Table 8-2.

Specifying no options in the CHECK TABLE command causes the command to use the default value, MEDIUM. You may also specify multiple options, if desired.

If the command line returns anything other than OK or Table is already up to date, you need to repair the table.

Diagnosing and Repairing with the myisamchk Script

The `myisamchk` script works only with MyISAM tables. It can check a table for errors, and it can also repair, optimize, and gather information about a table. Including options in the command syntax controls the various levels of operation.

Option	Description
QUICK	Does not scan rows for broken links
FAST	Does not scan tables that have closed properly
CHANGED	Does not scan unaltered or properly closed tables
MEDIUM	Scans rows to verify deleted links are correct and runs a checksum verification on rows (default value)
EXTENDED	Does a full key lookup for all keys on all rows (time-consuming)

Table 8-2 Options for the CHECK TABLES Command

The `myisamchk` script does not communicate with the MySQL Client, however; so running it without locking the database tables is dangerous and can lead to damage. Therefore, you must take the following steps when using `myisamchk`:

1. Open two command-line windows and log in to the MySQL Client in one of them.

2. Perform the following commands in the MySQL Client window:

```
LOCK TABLE <table_name> READ;
FLUSH TABLES;
```

3. In the other command-line window, change to the data directory of the database holding the table you wish to check and execute the `myisamchk` command, using the following syntax:

```
MYISAMCHK [option] <table_name>
```

4. When you have completed using `myisamchk`, return to the window where you are still logged in to the MySQL Client and execute the following command:

```
UNLOCK TABLES;
```

You can perform this task from one command-line window by logging in and out of the MySQL Client when necessary, but the dual-window method makes it less likely that you will forget to unlock the tables after you are finished checking them.

There are many options for the `myisamchk` script, which can be listed by running `myisamchk --help` from the command line. The most commonly used options for checking tables are shown in Table 8-3.

The `myisamchk` script will also repair tables using the `-r` and the `-o` options. The `-r` option is the basic way to repair a table and fixes most errors; the `-o` option does a more thorough check and can sometimes repair errors that the `-r` option does not. The `-q` option can be used to speed the repair by not modifying the data.

Option	Description	Level/Use
No option	Default table check	Finds most errors
`-m` or `--medium-check`	Corresponds to CHECK TABLE MEDIUM	More thorough check
`-e` or `--extend-check`	Corresponds to CHECK TABLE EXTENDED	Most thorough check
`-s` or `--silent`	Returns only error messages	Handy for use in scripts
`-r` or `--recover`	Default table repair	Fixes most errors
`-o` or `--safe-recover`	Slower but more thorough table repair	Fixes errors that `-r` does not fix.
`-q` or `--quick`	Faster but limited table repair	Fixes a table but not a table's data

Table 8-3 Commonly Used Checking and Repairing Options for myisamchk

As when you use the `myisamchk` script to check tables, you must remember to lock, flush, and unlock the tables, or the process may result in a false result or even damage the tables.

NOTE

The easiest way to avoid difficulties with unlocked tables when performing checks or repairs is to use the CHECK TABLE or REPAIR TABLE command instead of the `myisamchk` script, because it handles the locking and unlocking steps for you.

Repairing on the Table Level

If your database has multiple, large tables, it may be more efficient to repair damage on the table level. The REPAIR TABLE command, like the BACKUP TABLE and CHECK TABLE commands, works only on MyISAM tables. It also handles the locking and unlocking steps automatically. The command corresponds to the `myisamchk -r` script option.

The basic syntax for the REPAIR TABLE command is as follows:

```
REPAIR TABLE <table_name> [option];
```

REPAIR TABLE has two options: QUICK and EXTENDED. The QUICK option attempts to repair the table by examining and repairing its index only. The EXTENDED option repairs the index by examining the table a row at a time.

On an extremely large table, the REPAIR TABLE command with the EXTENDED option may never complete. If it continues interminably, you should abort the attempt and use the backup to recover the table.

The recommended procedure for repairing tables is to start with the fastest method and then proceed to the slower methods if the original attempt does not work. In most cases, the basic, fast method will result in the table being fixed.

Occasionally, the normal repair methods do not work. In that case, it may be because the index file (.MYI) is damaged beyond repair or missing entirely, or your table description file (.frm) could be damaged or missing. If it is the index file that is damaged or missing, and you are running MySQL version 4.0 or newer, you can create a new index file by using the following command syntax:

```
REPAIR TABLE <table_name> USE_FRM;
```

If you are running a MySQL version prior to 4.0, you can make a safety copy of the data file in another directory, use the TRUNCATE <table_name> command to empty the data and index from the table, and then copy the safety copy of the data back into the original directory. Once that has been accomplished, run a REPAIR TABLE command to verify the table's condition.

If your description file is damaged or missing, you can either restore the table from the latest backup or create a new description file by making a safety copy of the data and index files in another directory, executing a CREATE TABLE command, and then copying the index and data file back into the original directory.

Ask the Expert

Q: How can I recover from a failure as quickly as possible?

A: Often, it is faster and easier to rebuild from a backup than to fix a corrupt database. When performing backups always remember to run the flush logs command. Flushing the logs makes the MySQL server start a new binary log file. That means the most current log file contains only the transactions performed since the last backup, which allows you to apply it to the most current backup and re-create your database. Even though the default MySQL table type (MyISAM) does not have transactional capability, you should be able to bring the database back to its prefailure state in a matter of minutes if you have backed up the database and flushed the logs at regular intervals. If you write a script or create a batch file to perform this recovery process, the restoration may take only seconds. Once the process is semiautomated using a script or batch file, the key factors affecting restoration speed are file size and the number of statements that need to be rerun to bring the system up to date.

If both the index and description files are damaged or missing, you should first re-create the description file, and then re-create the index file.

Performing Preventative Maintenance: A Stitch in Time

As the preceding sections make clear, recovering your database from a disastrous failure is almost always possible, and MySQL gives you many tools to achieve those ends. However, prevention is always preferable to repair or recovery.

Corrupted tables can cause system failure. MySQL provides you with maintenance tools, whose regular use can help avoid that undesirable end. Checking your tables once a week is considered a reasonable interval. Linux users can set up a `cron` job to do it automatically, and Windows users can set up a process in the Windows Scheduler.

CAUTION

If the MySQL Server is running as usual (without locking the tables), it is possible to get an error result from checking a table, even when the table in question is actually okay.

Using Startup Table Check

If your MySQL Server is stopped and started regularly, you can place a `myisam-recover` option under the `[mysqld]` section in your `.cnf` or `.ini` configuration file, which will cause MySQL to check the tables automatically each time it starts up. When a table is opened, it will be checked and repaired if necessary. You can go one step further and change the syntax in the configuration file to read `myisam-recover=BACKUP`, which will cause backups of any changed data files to be saved under the default filename `<table_name>_<datetime function>.BAK`.

Using the OPTIMIZE TABLE Command

The `OPTIMIZE TABLE` command allows you to clean up after the changes made in a table during routine operation. It accomplishes four basic tasks:

- Unused space is made usable.
- Data files are defragmented.
- Index pages are sorted.
- Statistics are updated.

Any time you delete large parts of any table, or you have many changes to a variable-length table, you should run `OPTIMIZE TABLE` to do the basic housekeeping that keeps your tables less vulnerable to damage.

The `OPTIMIZE TABLE` command works with MyISAM and BDB tables. Its syntax is as follows:

```
OPTIMIZE TABLE <table_name or list of names>;
```

The `OPTIMIZE TABLE` command corresponds to running the `myisamchk` script with these options: `--QUICK`, `--CHECK-CHANGE-TABLES`, `--SORT-INDEX`, and `--ANALYSE`.

Project 8-3 Simulate Damage and Restore a Table

In this project, you are going to simulate damage to your database and use a variety of methods to verify that damage and repair it. You will use the `CHECK TABLE`, `REPAIR TABLE`, `OPTIMIZE TABLE`, and `RESTORE TABLE` commands, as well as use the MySQLCC GUI to restore a database.

Step by Step

1. Either from the command line or from the MySQL Administrator, stop your MySQL Server. Open a window to view the /mysql/data directory. Make a copy of the entire duckwear directory, saving it outside the /mysql path.

2. Open the duck_cust.myi file in a word processor. It should look like gibberish. Delete four or five characters from the middle of the file, save the changes, and then close the file. If the word processor asks if it is all right to save the file as .txt and lose all formatting, agree. Using whatever method you choose, restart your MySQL Server.

(continued)

3. Open a command-line window and log in to the MySQL Client as root. Run the following commands:

```
USE duckwear;
CHECK TABLE duck_cust, duck_title, duck_sales QUICK;
```

You will see that `duck_title` and `duck_sales` check out okay, but `duck_cust` returns errors and is identified as corrupt.

```
Command Prompt - mysql -u root -p                                         _ □ ×

mysql> check table duck_cust, duck_title, duck_sales quick;
+------------------------+-------+----------+-----------------------------
| Table                  | Op    | Msg_type | Msg_text
+------------------------+-------+----------+-----------------------------
| duckwear.duck_cust     | check | warning  | Size of indexfile is: 2050      Shoul
d be: 2048              |
| duckwear.duck_cust     | check | error    | Found key at page 1024 that points to
 record outside datafile |
| duckwear.duck_cust     | check | error    | Corrupt
| duckwear.duck_title    | check | status   | OK
| duckwear.duck_sales    | check | status   | OK
+------------------------+-------+----------+-----------------------------
5 rows in set (0.02 sec)

mysql>
```

4. Execute the following `REPAIR TABLE` command to attempt to repair `duck_cust`, and then check the tables again to verify the repair.

```
REPAIR TABLE duck_cust USE_FRM;
CHECK TABLE duck_cust, duck_title, duck_sales QUICK;
```

The `REPAIR TABLE` command should return that the repair status is `OK`, and then all three tables should show that check status is `OK`.

```
Command Prompt - mysql -u root -p                                         _ □ ×

mysql> repair table duck_cust use_frm;
+------------------------+--------+----------+-----------------------------------+
| Table                  | Op     | Msg_type | Msg_text                          |
+------------------------+--------+----------+-----------------------------------+
| duckwear.duck_cust     | repair | warning  | Number of rows changed from 0 to 14 |
| duckwear.duck_cust     | repair | status   | OK                                |
+------------------------+--------+----------+-----------------------------------+
2 rows in set (0.03 sec)
mysql> check table duck_cust, duck_title, duck_sales quick;
+------------------------+-------+----------+----------+
| Table                  | Op    | Msg_type | Msg_text |
+------------------------+-------+----------+----------+
| duckwear.duck_cust     | check | status   | OK       |
| duckwear.duck_title    | check | status   | OK       |
| duckwear.duck_sales    | check | status   | OK       |
+------------------------+-------+----------+----------+
3 rows in set (0.00 sec)
mysql> _
```

5. Use the OPTIMIZE command on the duck_cust table.

```
OPTIMIZE TABLE duck_cust;
```

None of the tables you have made so far have had enough transactions to require optimization, so the result should show that the optimize status is OK.

```
Command Prompt - mysql -u root -p                              _ □ ×
mysql> optimize table duck_cust;
+-------------------------+----------+----------+----------+
| Table                   | Op       | Msg_type | Msg_text |
+-------------------------+----------+----------+----------+
| duckwear.duck_cust      | optimize | status   | OK       |
+-------------------------+----------+----------+----------+
1 row in set (0.02 sec)

mysql> _
```

6. Once again, shut down the MySQL Server so you can simulate damage. When it is stopped, go to the /mysql/data.duckwear directory and delete the duck_title.MYD, duck_title.frm, and duck_title.MYI files. Restart the server.

7. In the MySQL Client, execute a SHOW TABLES command. The return will indicate the server has been disconnected—a result of stopping the server—but sending the same command again will usually result in a new connection. The duck_title table will no longer be listed in the SHOW TABLES report.

8. Begin repairing the duckwear database by using the RESTORE TABLE command in conjunction with the backup files that resulted from the BACKUP TABLE command you used in Project 8-2. The following code uses the path in the example in Project 8-2. Your path to the backup files may be different.

```
RESTORE TABLE duck_title FROM "D:/BackDuck";
SHOW TABLES;
```

The return of the RESTORE TABLE command should indicate that the restore status is OK, and the return of the SHOW TABLES command should list the duck_title table once more.

```
Command Prompt - mysql -u root -p                              _ □ ×
mysql> restore table duck_title from "D:/BackDuck";
+-------------------------+----------+----------+----------+
| Table                   | Op       | Msg_type | Msg_text |
+-------------------------+----------+----------+----------+
| duckwear.duck_title     | restore  | status   | OK       |
+-------------------------+----------+----------+----------+
1 row in set (0.03 sec)

mysql> show tables;
+-------------------+
| Tables_in_duckwear |
+-------------------+
| duck_cust         |
| duck_sales        |
| duck_title        |
| empty             |
| here              |
| lazertag          |
| there             |
+-------------------+
7 rows in set (0.00 sec)

mysql> _
```

(continued)

9. Stop the MySQL Server and go to the /mysql/data/duckwear directory. Delete the duck_sales.MYD, duck_sales.frm, and duck_sales.MYI files. Restart the MySQL Server.

10. Open the MySQLCC GUI and connect to your MySQL Server. Click the SQL icon button, which is the third button from the left side of the toolbar. The Query window should open.

11. Select File | Open or click the Open folder icon button. Browse to /mysql/bin and select the dw20090317.sql file, from the `mysqldump` script you used in Project 8-2. Click the Open button, and the file will open in the main viewing area of the Query window.

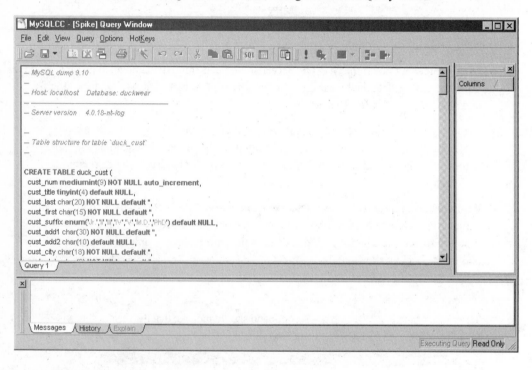

NOTE

The file will be clearly color-coordinated in the Query window to make the SQL command it contains easy to read.

12. Click the button with the exclamation mark icon (the fifth button from the right side of the toolbar) to execute the SQL commands in the .sql file. In the Messages area of the Query window, you will see a variety of error messages regarding the tables that are still there and do not need to be restored, and you may hear an error sound.

13. Send the SHOW TABLES command to the MySQL Client. You will get a disconnected message. Send the command again, and it will connect and return the list of tables. The duck_sales table is present once again.

```
Command Prompt - mysql -u root -p                          _ □ ×
mysql> show tables;
+-------------------+
| Tables_in_duckwear |
+-------------------+
| duck_cust         |
| duck_sales        |
| duck_title        |
+-------------------+
3 rows in set (0.00 sec)

mysql>
```

Project Summary

This project gave you hands-on experience with CHECK TABLE, REPAIR TABLE, RESTORE TABLE, and OPTIMIZE TABLE. You also used the file from the mysqldump script in conjunction with the MySQLCC GUI to restore a missing table. These examples are simple because of the relatively small size of the database you are working with, but the ease of recovery is similar on larger databases.

✓ *Module 8 Mastery Check*

1. What does the following command accomplish?

   GRANT ALL ON monsters.* TO vanhelsing@'%' IDENTIFIED BY "4ber4h4m";

2. What command allows the new user giles to log in only from the local host using the password fyar168 and to look up or look at all databases and tables but nothing else?

3. What command allows you to remove the ALTER, INDEX, DELETE, and DROP privileges from the user morgan@kelson.org on the swords table of the arsenal database?

4. What series of commands removes all of the user privileges of woodchuck@dandd.com and then deletes the user account and wipes it from the system?

5. What are the possible privileges that can be removed from a user with the REVOKE command?

6. What must you always do before and after using the myisamchk script to avoid further damage to the database?

7. What types of backup files are used with the RESTORE command?

8. What type of backup file does the mysqldump script produce?

9. What command should you use to initially check the tables sandstorms, sandworms, and watercustoms?

10. What command should you use any time your database has had a great deal of changes made or a large amount of data deleted?

Appendix  A

Answers to
Mastery Checks

Module 1: Installing MySQL

1. **Which pairs of the following words mean the same thing:** *row, field, key, record, index, column*?

   Row and *record* both refer to the sets of connected data in a table. *Field* and *column* refer to the individual pieces of data that form those sets. *Key* and *index* both refer to a field set as the specific piece of a record used for indexing the data for quicker retrieval.

2. **What is the distinguishing feature of a relational database?**

   Row and *record* both refer to the sets of connected data in a table. *Field* and *column* refer to the individual pieces of data that form those sets. *Key* and *index* both refer to a field set as the specific piece of a record used for indexing the data for quicker retrieval.

3. **Is open source software always free of cost?**

   The key, which allows for indexing, is the distinguishing feature of a relational database.

4. **What are the seven criteria you should use to evaluate operating systems?**

   The seven criteria for evaluating an OS are ease of use, reliability, speed, functionality, price, integration with Microsoft technologies, and availability of free/open source software.

5. **Of the seven criteria used to evaluate operating systems, which show the most difference?**

   The price criterion displays the widest range of differences, often making it the deciding factor.

6. **In Windows, if you require tables larger than 4GB, on what type of file system will you need to install MySQL and what commands must be used when creating the tables?**

   The file system must be NTFS or newer, and the tables must be made using the `max_rows` and `avg_row_length` commands.

7. **In Linux, what is the command syntax for installing an .rpm file?**

   The proper syntax is either rpm -i *<server filename>* <client filename> or:

   ```
   rpm -Uvh < server filename >
   rpm -Uvh < client filename >
   ```

8. **In Linux, what is the syntax on the two commands to set a password?**

   The proper syntax for setting the MySQL password consists of these two lines:

   ```
   usr/bin/mysqladmin -u root password <your password>
   /usr/bin/mysqladmin -u root -h `hostname` password <your password>
   ```

9. **What does ODBC stand for and which OS is most likely to require it?**

   ODBC stands for Open Database Connectivity, a database abstraction layer that allows (mostly Windows) applications to access the database.

10. **Why does this guide initially choose to use the command line to interface with MySQL instead of a GUI?**

For the beginning learning process, typing the syntax on the command line has proved more conducive to long-term learning than the point-and-click environment of a GUI.

Module 2: Defining a Database

1. **Which TABLE type is the MySQL DEFAULT?**

The MySQL DEFAULT TABLE type is MyISAM.

2. **Which data types would you use to display the Date in one column and the Time in a separate column?**

The one column would be defined as the DATE type and the other column would be defined as the TIME type.

3. **How does the VARCHAR data type differ from the CHAR data type?**

Both CHAR and VARCHAR have an defined limit to the length of string value they may hold, but the VARCHAR data type varies in length if the string value placed in it is shorter than the defined limit. The CHAR data type is always the length of its defined limit.

4. **What are the two main rules for naming a TABLE?**

The two main rules for naming a table are:

A. A Table name may only have up to 64 characters

B. A Table name may not include characters backslash (\), forward slash (/) or period (.).

5. **What is the syntax to create a database called `Angel` and a table in it called `Wesley` with a `TINYINT` column called `Fred`?**

The following is the syntax to create a database called `Angel` and a table in it called `Wesley` with a `TINYINT` column called `Fred`:

```
CREATE DATABASE Angel;
USE Angel;
CREATE TABLE Wesley(
Fred TINYINT)
TYPE=MyISAM;
```

6. **How do you display the databases in your MySQL Server?**

To display the databases in your MySQL Server, use the command SHOW DATABASES;.

7. How do you display the tables in a database called Jet?

To display the tables in a database called Jet, use the following syntax:

```
USE Jet;
SHOW TABLES;
```

or

```
SHOW TABLES FROM Jet;
```

8. How do you display the layout or specifications of a table called Wraith if you are already using the database in which it is housed?

To display the layout or specifications of a table called Wraith if you are already using the database in which it is housed, use the command DESC Wraith;.

9. How do you display the contents of a table called horse if you are already using the database in which it is housed?

To display the contents of a table called horse if you are already using the database in which it is housed, use the command SELECT * FROM horse;

10. If the horse table has the columns bridle, saddle, and blanket, how do you display the contents of saddle only?

To display only the saddle column in the horse table, use the command SELECT saddle FROM horse;

Module 3: Manipulating a Database

1. How do you make a copy of the table wolfhounds, including its data?

Use the following to make a copy of the wolfhounds table and its data:

```
CREATE TABLE copy_wolfhounds
SELECT * FROM wolfhounds;
```

2. If you have a table called sport and it has the fields football, basketball, soccer, and hockey, how do you make a table called ballgames without the hockey field?

To make a ballgames table without the hockey field, use the following:

```
CREATE TABLE ballgames
SELECT football, basketball, soccer FROM sports;
```

3. What kind of table resides in memory and lasts only as long as the MySQL Client's current connection?

A TEMPORARY table resides in memory and lasts as long as the MySQL Client's current connection.

4. **What does the following command accomplish?**

```
LOAD DATA INFILE '\documents\games_stats.txt'
INTO TABLE stat_sheet
FIELDS TERMINATED BY ':'
LINES TERMINATED BY '\r\n';
```

It places data separated by colons from a file called game_stats.txt into an already existing table called `stat_sheet`.

5. **What are the four options for the `ALTER TABLE` command and what to they do?**

The four options that can be used with `ALTER TABLE` are ADD, MODIFY, CHANGE, and DROP. ADD inserts a new field definition into a table. MODIFY changes the format of an existing field. CHANGE renames an existing field. DROP deletes an existing field or index from a table.

6. **What command inserts only entire records into a table?**

The `REPLACE INTO` command inserts, or deletes and inserts, entire rows (or records).

7. **What does a table need to have in order to use the `REPLACE INTO` command and avoid inserting duplicate records?**

If a table has a `UNIQUE` index or `PRIMARY` key, then `REPLACE INTO` will delete an existing record with a duplicate key or index field, and then insert the new record.

8. **What do you type on the command line to temporarily turn off the `safe-updates` option?**

To temporarily turn off the `safe-updates` option, type the following at the command line:

```
--safe-updates=0
```

9. **Which command allows you to insert data into specific fields within records?**

The UPDATE command allows you to insert data into a single or multiple specific fields in one or more records.

10. **What does the following command do?**

```
UPDATE wine_list
SET color="red"
WHERE variety="Merlot";
```

It searches the `wine_list` table, and in every record where it finds the string `"Merlot"` in the `variety` field, it places the string `"red"` in the `color` field.

11. **Which command(s) removes a table and which command(s) removes only the data in the table?**

The DROP command removes the entire table. The DELETE and TRUNCATE commands get rid of the data while leaving the table structure.

12. How is TRUNCATE different from DELETE?

The DELETE command removes the data one record at a time, leaving the table intact. The TRUNCATE command drops the entire table all at once, and then re-creates the table structure from the file where its definitions are saved.

13. What does the following command do?

```
ALTER TABLE horse_gear
MODIFY num_code MEDIUMINT(9) PRIMARY KEY NOT NULL AUTO_INCREMENT,
MODIFY feed CHAR(15) NOT NULL,
CHANGE saddles_bridles tack CHAR(20) NOT NULL,
ADD blanket ENUM('Yes', 'No')
DROP color;
```

This ALTER TABLE command changes the horse_gear table in the following manner:

- It makes the existing field num_code a MEDIUMINT type that is nine characters long and defines it as an auto-incrementing primary key with a NOT NULL default.

- It changes the field feed from whatever it used to be into a CHAR type that is 15 characters long and has a NOT NULL default.

- It changes the name of the field saddles_bridles to tack.

- It adds an enumerated list field called blanket, which can hold only the values Yes or No.

- It removes a field called color.

Module 4: Basic Reporting

1. What is the command to list all the data in the monsters table?

The correct code is:

```
SELECT * FROM monsters;
```

2. What is the command to list only the records with the values "vampire" and "werewolf" in the m_types field of the monsters table?

The correct code is:

```
SELECT * FROM monsters
WHERE m_types="vampire" AND m_types="werewolf";
```

3. What does the following command do?

```
SELECT m_types FROM monsters LIMIT 13;
```

It lists the contents of the m_types column for the first 13 records in the monster table.

4. How do you view the records for the m_active field in the monsters table, starting with record 9 and listing the next 13 records?

The simplest correct code is:

```
SELECT m_active FROM monsters
LIMIT 8,13;
```

5. How do you list each unique entry in the m_types field of the monsters table?

The simplest correct code is:

```
SELECT DISTINCT m_types FROM monsters;
```

6. What is the code for listing the m_names, m_types, and m_active fields in the monsters table, using the headers Monster Names, Kind of Monster, and Day/Night/Both, respectively.

The code for such a list is:

```
SELECT m_names AS "Monster Names", m_types AS "Kind of Monster",
 m_active as "Day/Night/Both" FROM monsters;
```

7. What are the two types of operators used for comparisons in the WHERE clause?

The two types of operators used for comparison in WHERE clauses are arithmetic and logical.

8. What are the four basic commands for viewing databases and tables?

9. The four most basic commands to view databases and tables are:

```
SHOW DATABASES;
USE <database_name>;
SHOW TABLES;
DESC <table_name>;
```

10. What are two different ways that a WHERE clause could specify a numeric range of data between 42 and 113 in the field some_number?

The range can be specified in a WHERE clause any of the following ways:

```
WHERE some_number>=42 AND some_number<=113;
WHERE some_number BETWEEN 42 AND 113;
WHERE some_number >41 and <114;
```

11. How can you display entire records from the monsters table that contain "vampire" in the m_types field and a name beginning with the letter _D_ in the m_names field?

Use the following code:

```
SELECT * FROM monsters
WHERE m_types="vampire" AND m_names LIKE "D%";
```

12. How do you list m_numbers and m_names fields of every instance in the monsters table where you know the m_creators field should read "Joss" but due to a typo, the m_creators entry is not capitalized?

Use the following code:

```
SELECT m_numbers, m_names FROM monsters
WHERE BINARY m_creators="joss";
```

Module 5: Advanced Reporting

1. What does the following command return?

```
SELECT ep_title AS Album, Band,
IF(Release>1964 and Release<=1969, "60's"," ") AS Beatles Era,
IF(Release>1979 and Release<1990, "New Wave"," ") AS "Hair Band Era",
FROM RecordCollection
ORDER BY Band;
```

It returns a report with the headers Album, Band, Beatles Era, and Hair Band Era, arranged by sorting the Band column and putting either 60's or a space in the Beatles Era column and New Wave or a space in the Hair Band Era.

2. What is the purpose of the CASE...WHEN function?

It controls the flow of data to the resulting output report.

3. What are the four ways to control how a column of fields rounds off numeric content?

ROUND, CEILING, FLOOR, and TRUNCATE all allow you to control the way a numeric field is rounded.

4. What does the code LPAD sale_price, 5, "$" return, when sale_price contains a string value of 9.95?

It returns the string $$$$$9.95.

5. From a table called cust_orders that has the columns cust_num, design_num, design_name, quantity, and price, make a report that shows the total quantity of outfits bought by cust_num 13.

The code would look like this:

```
select sum(quantity)
from cust_orders
where cust_num=13;
```

6. What would the following code return?

```
concat_ws(" ... ", "There can be", "Only ONE")
```

It would return the string There can be ... Only ONE.

7. **When is it required that you use the `table_name.field_name` syntax in your JOIN clause?**

   You must use the `table_name.field_name` syntax when you are selecting a field that has exactly the same field name from each table.

8. **Can you use only the ORDER BY clause in the SELECT syntax?**

   No, the GROUP BY clause must always come before ORDER BY clause in the SELECT syntax.

9. **Which function returns the current date and time on the computer on which you are working?**

   The NOW function returns the current date and time.

10. **What does the following command do?**

    ```
    SELECT Range, AVG(height) FROM Mountains GROUP BY Range
    HAVING Range="Rockies";
    ```

    It returns an average of the height of the peaks listed in the Rockies table.

Module 6: GUI Interfaces for Data Handling and Administration

1. **What is an Alpha version release?**

   An Alpha version means that the program is still in the development stage and that bugs can be expected. Sections of the code may not be written or entirely completed.

2. **How do MySQLCC and MySQL Administrator differ?**

   MySQL Administrator is aimed at administering database functions and design. MySQLCC does some administration, but it also allows you to edit, delete, and add to the contents of a database, as well as adjust its format.

3. **How can you change or set Hot Keys with MySQLCC?**

   The Hot Key link in the Control Center dropdown menu or Toolbar button gives access to the Hot Key Editor where existing Hot Keys can be altered or new Hot Keys defined.

4. **What happens when you select different levels on the tree pane of MySQLCC?**

   The toolbar buttons change to reflect functions that relate to that particular selection.

5. **What is the MySQL recommendation for buffer size?**

   The recommended buffer size is 25 percent of your system's available RAM.

6. **Which of these two GUIs allows you to start and stop the MySQL server by pressing a button?**

   MySQL Administrator allows you to start and stop the server by pressing a button.

7. **What four areas of system health can you monitor with MySQL Administrator?**

The four areas you can monitor in the Health section of MySQL Administrator are Connection Health, Memory Health, Status Variables, and System Variables.

8. **Where do you go in MySQL Administrator to set up a variety of system logs?**

The Log Files tab of the Startup Variables section in MySQL Administrator allows you to set up Binary, Query, Error, Slow Queries, Update, and ISAM log files.

9. **How do you change the main display window in MySQLCC?**

Selecting a database or table from the Console Manager listing changes the main console window to reflect data pertaining to your selection?

10. **What causes buttons to appear and disappear from the toolbar in MySQLCC?**

Choosing a server, database, or table in the Console Manager listing can cause buttons to appear or disappear from the toolbar, depending on whether or not they pertain to the selected item.

Module 7: Interfacing with Programs

1. **What do the acronyms PHP and HTML stand for?**

PHP stands for Pre-Hypertext Processor, and HTML stands for Hypertext Markup Language.

2. **What does the following line of code do?**

```
$link = mysql_connect('localhost', 'ron', 'sc0rp1o');
```

It creates a link to a MySQL database housed on the localhost server for a user called ron with a password of sc0rp1o.

3. **What symbol do you add to the beginning of a function name to suppress the warning output?**

You add an at symbol (@) to the beginning of a function if you want to suppress the warning output.

4. **What is the PHP equivalent of the MySQL command SHOW TABLES?**

The PHP equivalent of SHOW TABLES is mysql_list_tables().

5. **What do the PHP functions for forcing type casting do?**

The PHP functions to force type casting set a variable to a specific type, such as Boolean, integer, float, string, array, object, or null.

6. **What security issue does the mysql_escape_string() function guard against?**

The mysql_escape_string() function guards against SQL injections.

7. **What two methods in PEAR::DB are used to deal with the results from a query (or prepare/execute)?**

The `fetchInto()` and `fetchRow()` methods in PEAR::DB deal with the results from a query (or prepare/execute).

8. **What is database abstraction?**

Database abstraction is the separation between application code and database-specific functions in a mixed environment, which makes these issues more manageable.

9. **What are the two ways to export data from MySQL and import data into Microsoft Excel?**

The two ways in which you can export data from MySQL and import data to Excel are by file and by ODBC connection.

10. **How can Microsoft Access be directly linked to MySQL in order to view its data?**

Microsoft Access can be directly linked to a MySQL database using ODBC, allowing you to view its data and manipulate it in the database, but not change the table's format.

Module 8: Basic Administration and Backups

1. **What does the following command accomplish?**

```
GRANT ALL ON monsters.* TO vanhelsing@'%' IDENTIFIED BY "4ber4h4m";
```

It creates a user named `vanhelsing` who can connect from any host to any table in the `monsters` database and whose password is `4ber4h4m`.

2. **What command allows the new user `giles` to log in only from the local host using the password `fyar168` and to look up or look at all databases and tables but nothing else?**

The command is as follows:

```
GRANT SELECT, SHOW ON *.* TO giles@localhost INDENTIFIED BY "fyar168";
```

3. **What command allows you to remove the `ALTER`, `INDEX`, `DELETE`, and `DROP` privileges from the user `morgan@kelson.org` on the `swords` table of the `arsenal` database?**

The command is as follows:

```
REVOKE ALTER, INDEX, DELETE, DROP, ON arsenal.swords FROM morgan@kelson.org;
```

4. **What series of commands removes all of the user privileges of `woodchuck@dandd.com` and then deletes the user account and wipes it from the system?**

The commands are as follows:

```
REVOKE ALL ON *.* FROM woodchuck@dandd.com;
DELETE FROM mysql.user
WHERE USER="woodchuck"
AND HOST= "dandd.com";
FLUSH PRIVILEGES;
```

5. **What are the possible privileges that can be removed from a user with the REVOKE command?**

The privileges that can be removed using the REVOKE command are SELECT, INSERT, UPDATE, DELETE, CREATE, DROP, GRANT OPTION, INDEX, and ALTER.

6. **What must you always do before and after using the myisamchk script to avoid further damage to the database?**

You should always issue the LOCK TABLE command before using the myisamchk script and the UNLOCK TABLE command after using it.

7. **What types of backup files are used with the RESTORE command?**

The RESTORE command uses .frm and .MYD files.

8. **What type of backup file does the mysqldump script produce?**

The mysqldump script results in a .sql file.

9. **What command should you use to initially check the tables sandstorms, sandworms, and watercustoms?**

The following CHECK TABLE command, with the QUICK option, should be tried first:

```
CHECK TABLE sandstorms, sandworms, watercustoms QUICK;
```

10. **What command should you use any time your database has had a great deal of changes made or a large amount of data deleted?**

You should run the OPTIMIZE TABLE command when a lot of transactions have taken place or when sections of data have been deleted from a table.

Appendix B

Reserved Words

MySQL has a list of reserved words that are used as commands or options and clauses in commands. These words should be avoided when naming columns, tables, or databases within your MySQL server. Table B-1 has been provided as a reference to help avoid such unrecommended usage, as well as provide easy access to these words for syntax verification.

ADD	COLUMNS	DISTINCTROW	HOUR_MINUTE
ALL	CONDITION	DIV	HOUR_SECOND
ALTER	CONNECTION	DOUBLE	IF
AND	CONSTRAINT	DROP	IGNORE
AS	CONTINUE	ELSE	IN
ANALYZE	CREATE	ELSEIF	INDEX
ASC	CROSS	ENCLOSED	INFILE
ASENSITIVE	CURRENT_DATE	ESCAPED	INNER
AUTO_INCREMENT	CURRENT_TIME	EXISTS	INNODB
BDB	CURRENT_TIMESTAMP	EXIT	INOUT
BEFORE	CURSOR	EXPLAIN	INSENSITIVE
BERKELEYDB	DATABASE	FALSE	INSERT
BETWEEN	DATABASES	FETCH	INT
BIGINT	DAY_HOUR	FIELDS	INTEGER
BINARY	DAY_MICROSECOND	FLOAT	INTERVAL
BLOB	DAY_MINUTE	FOR	INTO
BOTH	DAY_SECOND	FORCE	IO_THREAD
BY	DEC	FOREIGN	IS
CALL	DECIMAL	FOUND	ITERATE
CASCADE	DECLARE	FRAC_SECOND	JOIN
CASE	DEFAULT	FROM	KEY
CHANGE	DELAYED	FULLTEXT	KEYS
CHAR	DELETE	GRANT	KILL
CHARACTER	DESC	GROUP	LEADING
CHECK	DESCRIBE	HAVING	LEAVE
COLLATE	DETERMINISTIC	HIGH_PRIORITY	LEFT
COLUMN	DISTINCT	HOUR_MICROSECOND	LIKE

Table B-1 Reserved Words

LIMIT	OUT	SPECIFIC	TRAILING
LINES	OUTER	SQL	TRUE
LOAD	OUTFILE	SQLEXCEPTION	UNDO
LOCALTIME	PRECISION	SQLSTATE	UNION
LOCALTIMESTAMP	PRIMARY	SQLWARNING	UNIQUE
LOCK	PRIVILEGES	SQL_BIG_RESULT	UNLOCK
LONG	PROCEDURE	SQL_CALC_FOUND_ROWS	UNSIGNED
LONGBLOB	PURGE	SQL_SMALL_RESULT	UPDATE
LONGTEXT	READ	SQL_TSI_DAY	USAGE
LOOP	REAL	SQL_TSI_FRAC_SECOND	USE
LOW_PRIORITY	REFERENCES	SQL_TSI_HOUR	USER_RESOURCES
MASTER_SERVER_ID	REGEXP	SQL_TSI_MINUTE	USING
MATCH	RENAME	SQL_TSI_MONTH	UTC_DATE
MEDIUMBLOB	REPEAT	SQL_TSI_QUARTER	UTC_TIME
MEDIUMINT	REPLACE	SQL_TSI_SECOND	UTC_TIMESTAMP
MEDIUMTEXT	REQUIRE	SQL_TSI_WEEK	VALUES
MIDDLEINT	RESTRICT	SQL_TSI_YEAR	VARBINARY
MINUTE_MICROSECOND	RETURN	SSL	VARCHAR
MINUTE_SECOND	REVOKE	STARTING	VARCHARACTER
MOD	RIGHT	STRAIGHT_JOIN	VARYING
NATURAL	RLIKE	STRIPED	WHEN
NOT	SECOND_MICROSECOND	TABLE	WHERE
NO_WRITE_TO_BINLOG	SELECT	TABLES	WHILE
NULL	SENSITIVE	TERMINATED	WITH
NUMERIC	SEPARATOR	THEN	WRITE
ON	SET	TIMESTAMPADD	XOR
OPTIMIZE	SHOW	TIMESTAMPDIFF	YEAR_MONTH
OPTION	SMALLINT	TINYBLOB	ZEROFILL
OPTIONALLY	SOME	TINYINT	
OR	SONAME	TINYTEXT	
ORDER	SPATIAL	TO	

Table B-1 Reserved Words *(continued)*

Appendix C

PHP Installation and Basic Syntax

PHP began when Rasmus Lerdorf, in 1995, wrote a set of Perl scripts to track his online resume. The acronym PHP referred to using the scripts as his "Personal Home Page" tools. Subsequently, PHP/FI (Personal Home Page/Forms Interpreter) was released to the public. It has evolved into a popular and efficient language for web applications.

One of the reasons for PHP's popularity is that it can be easily integrated into web page HTML code. HTML tags directly identify the PHP code to be interpreted when viewed with a web server supporting PHP. Two of the most popular web servers that support PHP are Apache and Internet Information Services (IIS). The HTML tags that identify PHP code are standard, allowing the interface between the HTML web page source and the PHP application to be very efficient and convenient to maintain across various server platforms.

PHP is described as a *web-embedded language*, which means that the PHP code is embedded in, or inserted as a part of, the HTML source code. In addition to tying in closely with HTML, the PHP code is executed on a web server in the client/server architecture. The combination of HTML and PHP code in a web page is interpreted and executed when a page is requested by a browser viewing the page. In that way, it supports dynamic web page responses, which means that web pages can change depending on user input or other variable information. Any time you have looked at a web page with the current date and time, for instance, you have viewed a dynamic web page.

PHP and MySQL

PHP, like MySQL, is an open-source product with all the reliability and affordability that usually implies. PHP and MySQL also combine in a way that makes them ideal for a data-driven web site.

NOTE

The PHP open source, as well as a great deal of useful information, is available from the PHP web site at http://www.php.net.

MySQL does not take up storage space or use large amounts of your CPU's resources; therefore, while it is ideal for small and medium database applications, it is also scalable for larger applications with little impact on its performance. In addition, MySQL's performance is outstanding, which makes it ideal for dynamic web applications.

The PHP server-side scripting language is easy to code, and all of its output goes directly to the browser, including errors. This makes it a great fit for dynamic web applications also.

The MySQL/PHP combination is collaborative. You'll find a wealth of documentation and support. Bugs are rapidly fixed. New features are openly considered.

PHP Setup

PHP resides on the web server. For most web servers, PHP support is active; however, for some stand-alone systems, especially Windows, you might need to activate or install the PHP support. Activation of PHP on Linux systems is usually taken care of during installation. Refer to the documentation for your specific version of Linux for details regarding PHP installation.

Checking for PHP Activation

On Windows systems, you can check to see if PHP is activated as follows:

1. Select the Add/Remove Programs icon in the Control Panel.

2. Select Add/Remove Windows Components.

3. PHP is included in the list of Windows components that appears. If its check box is checked, the PHP component is already installed. If IIS is checked, IIS is already active.

4. If the IIS check box isn't selected, choose it and continue with its installation, inserting the Windows operating system CD if requested.

In addition to many other functions, IIS will recognize files with the .php extension as being files that contain PHP code.

Verifying PHP Installation

If you want to verify whether a specific server has PHP installed in its configuration, you can run a simple PHP command, embedded in an HTML page, and the resulting web page will print information if PHP is installed. This simple verification works with any operating system.

Open a word processing program and type in the following code:

```
<?php
    phpinfo();
?>
```

Save the text as a **.php** file into your Internet directory. The Internet directory on Linux is public_html. On Windows, if you are using Apache for a web server, the Internet directory is C:\Program Files\Apache Group\Apache2\htdocs. If you are using IIS as the web server, the directory is C:\Inetpub\wwwroot, which you can access by entering **localhost** into the browser.

Now, look at your .php file in a web browser. If PHP is installed on your operating system and your web server is activated, you will see a list of information about PHP on your machine, as shown in the example in Figure C-1. If PHP is not installed, you will see the code from the .php file displayed in the browser window.

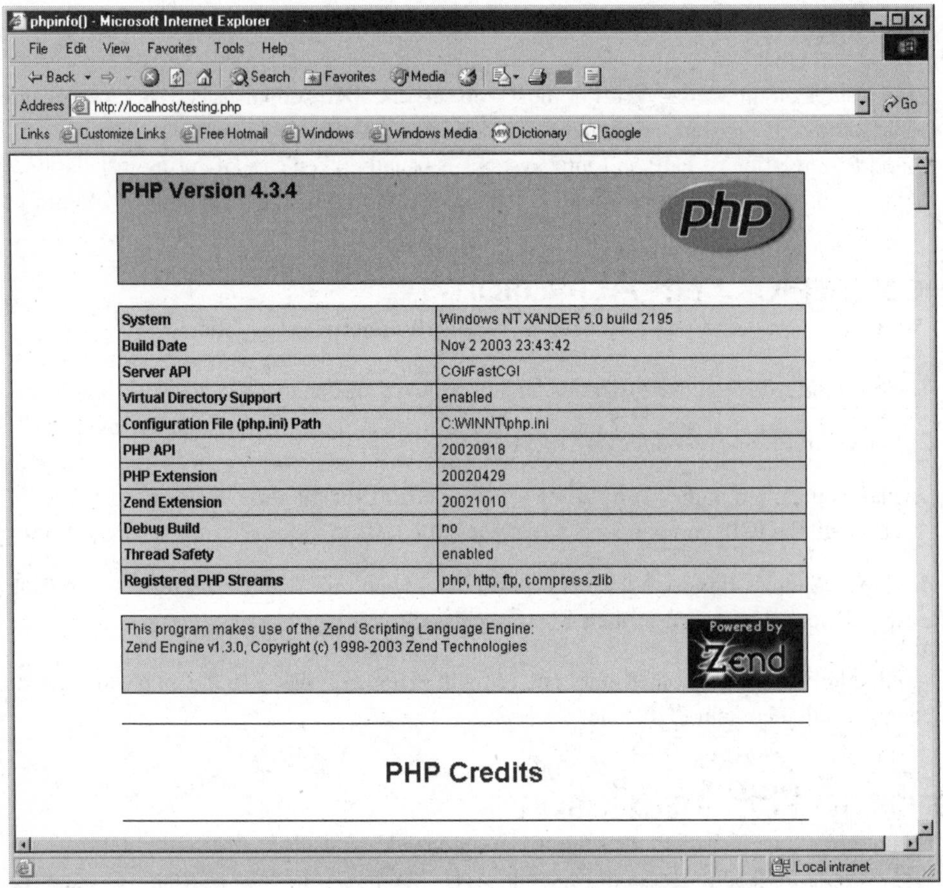

Figure C-1 If PHP is installed, you'll see a page of information similar to this.

PHP in HTML

Within HTML source code, start and end tags identify the PHP code. The standard PHP tag is recommended, but any one of the following tags can designate PHP:

Standard PHP tag	`<?php <PHP_code> ?>`
Shortcut PHP tag	`<? <PHP_code> ?>`
ASP-style PHP tag	`<% <PHP_code> %>`
Script PHP tag	`<script language="PHP"> <PHP-code> </script>`

Since these tags are HTML constructs, they are not case-sensitive; however, it is most common and recommended that you use the standard tags with lowercase `<?php ?>`. Most web servers are configured to use the filename extension .php, rather than .html, for a file containing PHP. This tells the web server to use the PHP interpreter on the file before displaying it.

CAUTION

While the PHP tags themselves are not case-sensitive, the code that is enclosed within them *is* case-sensitive.

You can use the HTML `<FORM>` tag to define boxes for user input. A global array variable called _POST gets an entry for each input name in the form. This _POST array is a data link between the HTML forms and PHP, and it can be used in the PHP code in the same way as any other variable defined in the PHP block. The following is an example of an HTML `<FORM>` that creates a text _POST array entry called `userinput`.

```
<FORM METHOD="post">
Enter Data:
<INPUT TYPE="text" NAME="userinput">
</FORM>
```

If the `<FORM>` has only one text-entry field, pressing the ENTER key will submit the form. However, when there are multiple text-entry fields, a submit button is needed. You can create a submit button within a `<FORM>` input block with the code `TYPE=SUBMIT`.

PHP Syntax

For general PHP syntax, all statements are terminated with a semicolon (`;`). In the PHP source code, any line starting with a double forward slash (`//`) signifies a comment, causing everything to the end of that line to be ignored by the PHP interpreter and by the HTML browser. For multiple-line comments, the comment line begins with a forward slash asterisk (`/*`) and ends, on another line, with an asterisk forward slash (`*/`). Everything in between that pair of tags will be considered a comment.

NOTE

Comments are intended for documentation purposes and enable the programmer to insert reminders of the code's purpose.

Variables

PHP variables start with a dollar sign ($), followed by either an underscore (_) or a letter. After that, the variable can have any amount or combination of letters, numbers, or underscores. As in MySQL, a letter is defined as any lowercase or uppercase character *a* through *z*, as well as any character with an ASCII value of 127 to 255. Variables *are* case-sensitive; thus $ABC and $abc are different variables.

PHP variables are *pseudo-typeless*, which means that their types are determined by context. So, if a variable is assigned a string, it becomes a string type. However, variables may be *cast*—forced to a certain type—using this syntax:

```
$s_string = set_type('string', $s_string);
```

Or variables can be cast using the C-style syntax:

```
$s_string = (string);
```

Empty variables can be defined by the VAR statement when they are within a class construct for an object, but not when they are in free-standing procedural code:

```
VAR $PHPvariable1;
```

Variables can also be defined when they are used:

```
$PHPvariable2="value2";
```

The data types of a PHP variable include INTEGER, FLOATING POINT, STRING, OBJECT, and ARRAY. If the type is not specifically defined, the variable is typed by the context in which it is used.

INTEGER Variables

The INTEGER is any whole number between –2 billion and +2 billion, using decimal, octal, or hexadecimal notation. For instance, all of the following variable definitions equal 100 in decimal, octal, and hexadecimal, respectively.

```
$vdec=100;
$voct=0144;
$vhex=0x64;
```

FLOATING POINT Variables

The FLOATING POINT is a number with a decimal portion, in either decimal or scientific notation. FLOATING POINT variables are sometimes misleading, because values may not always be stored literally in a binary architecture; for instance, the fraction one-third cannot be precisely represented in binary. The following FLOATING POINT notations are for the same number in both decimal and scientific notations.

```
$vfdec=1.23;
$vfsci=123e1;
```

STRING Variables

The STRING is any combination of letters, numbers, and/or special characters. When the STRING value is assigned to a STRING variable, the STRING value is surrounded by quotation marks (quotes). You can use either single quotes or double quotes, but you must be consistent, and there is a subtle difference. If single quotes surround the STRING, the assigned STRING value is exactly as it appears between the single quotes. If double quotes surround the STRING, the STRING is checked for any embedded PHP variables, and then those variables' values are put into the code in place of the embedded variable name. The following variable examples show this difference:

```
$vstring0 = "4";
$vstring1 = 'The value assigned is $vstring0'
$vstring2 = "The value assigned is $vstring0"
```

The value assigned to $vstring1 is The value assigned is $vstring0; the value assigned to $vstring2 is The value assigned is 4, because the double quotes in the $vstring2 definition cause it to insert the assigned value of the variable $vstring0.

You may need to include special characters in a quoted STRING. To achieve this, you use the backslash (\), which is the *escape* character, to indicate that the following special character is to be interpreted literally, without any substitution that it might normally indicate:

```
$vstring3 = 'The value assigned is \"ESCAPE\"'
```

The value assigned to the PHP variable $vstring3 is The value assigned is "ESCAPE". The backslashes allow the double quotes to be shown, instead of interpreted as STRING indicators. Common escape sequences for special characters are listed in Table C-1.

NOTE

Escape characters work when printing to the display or to a file, but they do not work correctly when printing to HTML for viewing through a browser. In this case, you must use HTML format tags, such as the <BR> tag for a new line.

Escape Sequence	Meaning
\n	Start a new line
\r	Insert a carriage return
\t	Insert a tab character
\\	Print a backslash character
\"	Print a double quote within a string
\$	Print a dollar sign
\0 (zero)	Print an octal value
\x	Print a hexadecimal value

Table C-1 Escape Sequence Meanings

ARRAY Variables

An ARRAY variable is a single name that can reference a set of values by using the array name and an index. PHP has two types of arrays: anonymous (an integer index) and hash key (some string that can be used as an index). A simple example of an anonymous array that initializes an ARRAY variable named $varray with four values follows:

```
$varray = array("value1", "value2", "value3","value4");
```

Indexes start at zero, so $varray[0] has the value value1 and $varray[3] has the value value4. In addition, the ARRAY can be expanded by assigning new values. The value is added after the last array entry.

```
$varray[ ] = "value5";
```

Here is an example of a hash key array:

```
$vhash = array ('size' => 'medium', 'color' => 'blue', 'temp' =>
'warm');
```

OBJECT Variables

An OBJECT is an instance of a class. To create an OBJECT, a class must first exist. The following is a trivial example using PHP to define the class with a member variable and two class functions: one to set the value and one to retrieve the value. Member values are typically not accessed directly. PHP creates the variable $this, which is available anywhere within the class to reference a created object itself.

NOTE

This example uses a special form of comments called *PHPDoc*, which is used in many PHP object-oriented code projects. It is very similar in syntax to JDoc and is highly recommended when writing code for large projects.

```php
<?php
   class php_object
      {
      var $php_var;
//This is called a constructor
// Constructors have the same name as the class
// in PHP4.  This constructor initialized our
// variable to null.
      function php_object()
         {
         $this->php_var = null;
         }

// getvar() returns our variable
function getvar()
         {
         return $this->php_var;
         }
// setvar() sets our variable
function setvar($setvalue)
         {
         $this->php_var = $setvalue;
         }
      }
?>
```

You can create a new OBJECT or instance of the php_object class with the following PHP code. The $a_php_object variable keeps the reference to the new OBJECT.

```php
<?php
   $a_phpobject =& new php_object();
?>
```

Any variable or function in the OBJECT can now be accessed, as the following example shows:

```php
<?php
   $a_phpobject->setvar(4);
   echo $a_phpobject->getvar();
?>
```

OBJECT member variables are typically not accessed directly. The setvar class function call with the new object will assign the $a_phpobject object's php_var variable to the value 4. The getvar class function will fetch the value of the $a_phpobject object's php_var variable for the PHP ECHO command to display.

The PHP PRINT and ECHO commands achieve the same basic result: they produce output on the screen. There is, however, one slight difference: The PRINT command can return a TRUE/FALSE result, whereas the ECHO command cannot. Because of this minor difference, the ECHO command is sometimes said to be slightly faster.

PHP variable data types can change from one assignment operation to the next, a characteristic referred to as *loosely typed*. To control the data type of an assignment, PHP supports the concept of typecasting. When a variable is assigned a value, a data type can also be specified. This data type can be different from that of the source data type. The target type appears within parentheses after the equal sign with one of the following values: (INT), (ARRAY), (OBJECT), (STRING), (REAL), (DOUBLE), or (FLOAT). The following example resets the data type of the already assigned variable $vinteger to an INTEGER rather than the REAL value of its source.

```
$vinteger = (int) $vreal ;
```

This can also be accomplished using the settype function:

```
$vinteger = $vreal;
settype($vinteger, 'integer');
```

Operators

PHP supports familiar operators, including arithmetic, logical, concatenation, and comparison operators.

Arithmetic Operators

The following are some of the common arithmetic operators.

Arithmetic Operator Example	Explanation
$a + $b	Adds variables $a and $b
$a - $b	Subtracts variable $b from $a
$a * $b	Multiplies $a and $b
$a / $b	Divides $a by $b
$a % $b	Returns modulus (remainder) of $a divided by $b

Logical Operators

Logical operators evaluate values and determine whether they are true or false according to the specified criteria. The following are some examples.

Logical Operator Example	Explanation
`$a and $b` `$a && $b`	AND operation means both values must be true.
`$a or $b` `$a || $b`	OR operation means one or the other value must be true.
`Not $a` `! $a`	NOT operation means the value cannot be true.

Concatenation Operator

The concatenation operator takes two string values and combines them, in the specified order, into one string value. For example, `$a . $b` concatenate the text values of variable `$a` with that of `$b`.

Comparison Operators

Comparison operators determine the relationship between two variables or expressions and return TRUE or FALSE. The following are some examples.

Comparison Operator Example	Explanation
`$a < $b`	Less than: if `$a < $b`, then the result is TRUE; otherwise it's FALSE
`$a > $b`	Greater than: if `$a > $b`, then the result is TRUE; otherwise it's FALSE
`$a <= $b`	Less or equal: if `$a <= $b`, then the result is TRUE; otherwise it's FALSE
`$a >= $b`	Greater or equal: if `$a >= $b`, then the result is TRUE; otherwise it's FALSE
`!$a`	NOT: negate the logical TRUE/FALSE value of `$a`
`$a == $b`	Equality: if `$a` and `$b` are equal, then TRUE; otherwise FALSE

Operator Precedence

Operators have *precedence* levels. That means that there is an order in which PHP deals with them, some getting preferential consideration over others.

All operations at the same precedence level can be completed in any sequence without changing the result. Addition and subtraction, for instance, are at the same precedence level.

When both addition and subtraction occur, the operations are performed in order of their appearance in an expression. Similarly, multiplication and division are at the same level.

When operations of different precedence are in the same expression, all operations of a higher precedence are done before those of a lower precedence, regardless of their order of appearance. Multiplication and division are done before any addition or subtraction.

You can use parentheses to override or impose a desired sequence of operator processing. Parentheses are also useful to document and clarify the sequence of calculation in an expression. Table C-2 gives more detail about operators and the operator precedence in PHP.

Precedence Level	Operator	Description	Evaluation Sequence (R=Right; L=Left)
1	`new`	Create new object	R to L
2	`.`	Property access (dot notation)	L to R
2	`[ ]`	Array index	L to R
2	`( )`	Function call	L to R
3	`!`	Logical NOT	R to L
3	`~`	Bitwise NOT	R to L
3	`++, --`	Increment and decrement operators	R to L
3	`+, -`	Unary plus and negation	R to L
3	`(int), (double), (string), (array), (object)`	Cast operators	R to L
3	`@`	Inhibit errors	R to L
4	`*, /, %`	Multiplication, division, modulo (remainder)	L to R
5	`+, -`	Addition, subtraction	L to R
5	`.`	Concatenation	L to R
6	`<<, >>`	Bitwise-shift left, bitwise-shift right	L to R
7	`<, <=, >, >=`	Comparison operators: less than, less than or equal to, greater than, greater than or equal to	L to R
8	`==, !=`	Equality, inequality	L to R
8	`===, !==`	Identity, nonidentity	L to R

Table C-2 Operators, with Their Precedence and Description

Precedence Level	Operator	Description	Evaluation Sequence (R=Right; L=Left)
9	&	Bitwise AND	L to R
10	^	Bitwise XOR	L to R
11	|	Bitwise OR	L to R
12	&&	Logical AND	L to R
13	||	Logical OR	L to R
14	? :	Conditional (ternary)	R to L
15	=	Assignment	R to L
15	*=, /=, %=, +=, -=	Assignment with operation	R to L
16	and	Logical AND	L to R
17	xor	Logical XOR	L to R
18	or	Logical OR	L to R
19	,	List separator	L to R

Table C-2 Operators, with Their Precedence and Description *(continued)*

Functions

Functions are traditional language constructs that allow repeated tasks to be defined with customized parameters and to return the results to the point of the function call in the program's logic. PHP supports user-defined functions, as well as many standard-language functions.

User-Defined Functions

When you have a series of commands that you are going to perform repeatedly, you can choose to turn those commands into a function. This means that instead of typing in multiple lines of code whenever you need to achieve that result, you need to type those lines only once (in the function definition), and then you put the much shorter function call into your code wherever you need it. PHP allows users to create customized functions using the following syntax:

```
function <function_name>(<function_parameters>) {
   (<PHP_function_code>)
}
```

Built-in Functions

Built-in functions are repeatedly used pieces of code that have already been written and tested. Instead of typing multiple lines of code to accomplish a commonly executed task, you call the function by using its name and parameters. For a list of the built-in PHP functions and examples of their use, refer to http://www.php.net/manual/en/funcref.php.

Some built-in functions are so common that they are often thought to be part of the command syntax. ECHO, for instance, is actually a built-in function that takes its input text and places it in the HTML at the current location, but it is so commonly used that most users assume it is part of the command syntax.

Control Structures

Most languages assume the sequential flow from one statement to the next unless some language-dependent control structure imposes a change. PHP supports a number of common control structures, such as IF, WHILE, FOR, SELECT, and some variations.

IF/IFELSE Control Structures

One variation of the IF conditional control structure is the IFELSE extension, which allows several return conditions to result in actions that are specified for each unique return, one of which is executed at the same point of the program logic flow.

The following is the basic syntax for an IFELSE control structure:

```
<?php
    if (<expression1)
        {
        <statement1>;
        }
    elseif (<expression2>)
        {
        <statement2>;

        }
    else
        {
        <statement_default>;
        }
?>
```

You use an IFELSE keyword to define blocks of statements, as well as the precedence order of the condition expression associated with the block of code. A single statement or block of statements is executed if its specified condition is true and all previous condition expressions were false. If all condition expressions are false, the default statement after the

ELSE keyword is executed. In other words, the series of IF conditions is evaluated one after another, and the first one of them that evaluates as true sends the program's path to its block of statements. If none of the IF conditions evaluate to true, the logic path falls all the way through, and the ELSE statements are executed.

WHILE Control Structures

The WHILE construct is a loop that allows a block of code to be repeated until some condition is satisfied. The syntax for the basic WHILE control structure is as follows:

```php
<?php
   while (<condition>):
      (<PHP_statements>)
   endwhile;
?>
```

The condition is tested at the beginning of the WHILE block, and if it evaluates to true, the block of code it contains is executed. Otherwise, it proceeds through the WHILE loop until it reaches the end. At the end of each loop through the block of code, the condition is tested again to see if it is still true and if it should continue with another iteration, or if it is now false and should exit to the statement that follows the WHILE loop. The condition expression might evaluate to false in the middle of the code block, but even if it does, the execution will continue until the test at the end of the code block.

FOR and FOREACH Control Structures

The FOR control structure loops through a block of code for some specified number of iterations. An index variable is frequently used so that it can get its initial value, and then increment with each iteration, which is compared with an exit value. The basic syntax appears simple, but the logic expressed within this control structure can be very complex:

```php
<?php
   for (expression1; expression2; expression3)
      {
      (<PHP_statements>)
      }
?>
```

In a FOR control structure, the three expressions are as follows:

● The first expression is the starting value for the loop counter.

● The second expression is the evaluation criteria that the loop counter is compared against.

● The third expression is the incremental increase for the loop counter.

So, the block of code within the loop, in this case one or more PHP commands, is executed until *expression1* has been incremented by the definition in *expression3* and meets the evaluation criteria used for comparison in *expression2*. In other words, it allows you to specify exactly how many times a particular block of code is executed.

The FOREACH control structure is a common variation of the FOR loop and is especially useful for iterating through arrays. It can be run for anonymous arrays or array hashes. Here is an example for an anonymous array:

```php
<?php
    foreach ($array as $value)
        {
        (<PHP code>)
        }
?>
```

And here is an example of the FOREACH structure to iterate through a hash array:

```php
<?php
    foreach ($hash as $key => $value)
        {
        (<PHP code>)
        }
?>
```

SWITCH Control Structures

The SWITCH control structure allows you to map out several paths that branch from a single place in your code, allowing you to choose one path depending on the circumstances. The SWITCH control structure has the following syntax:

```php
<?php
switch (<expression>)
    {
    case <value1>:
        <block_of_code_1>;
        break;
    case <value2>:
        <block_of_code_2>;
        break;
    <as_many_CASE_values_as_needed>
    default:
    <statement_default>;
    }
?>
```

A specific expression is hard-coded into the program, and the value of that expression is compared to any number of other values defined as CASE statements. Each CASE statement has its own corresponding block of code, which may be one or more lines of code. If the expression matches a particular CASE value, that CASE value's code is executed. Once the BREAK at the end of that block of code is reached, the SWITCH control structure is finished, and the program continues. If the expression does not equal any of the CASE values, it falls through the code and either proceeds without executing any code or executes the default block of code if one is defined.

Using a BREAK at the end of each CASE will terminate the SWITCH after a successful match of the CASE value with the expression. If a BREAK is not included, the SWITCH will continue executing all statements until the end of the SWITCH. This means that the default, if one were defined, would always be executed; so unless that is your intention, remember to insert a BREAK at the end of each CASE block of code.

Project C-1 Displaying and Inserting Data in MySQL

You can observe many of the basic PHP syntax features by coding the "Hello World" test. You can study the client/server environment in which it runs. Most important, however, is that you will be able to see the integration of PHP with HTML. You will then proceed to use PHP to read and display the contents of a MySQL table in a web page, and then use a web page interface to insert data into a MySQL table.

NOTE

To do this project, you will need the database you created in the projects in Modules 1 through 5.

Step by Step

1. Open a word processor that allows you to save a file in plain text. Enter the following PHP code, which is embedded in an HTML page.

```
<HTML>
    <BODY>
        <?php
            $howdy = "Hello World:    " . date("m/d/y    -    H:m:s");
            echo $howdy;
        ?>
    </BODY>
</HTML>
```

(continued)

2. Save the page in your Internet directory (/Inetpub/wwwroot/ for Windows and /public_html/ for Linux) as **HW1.php**.

CAUTION

Some word processors will automatically put a file type extension on your filename, such as .txt or .doc. If this happens, you must manually remove it, because the filename extension must be .php in order for the web server and browser to interpret it correctly. Doing this may cause a warning to pop up, cautioning against changing file type extensions. Indicate that you do want to change the file type.

3. Open your web browser to the localhost or public_html directory and view the web page, which should return the traditional message, "Hello World," followed by the current date and time.

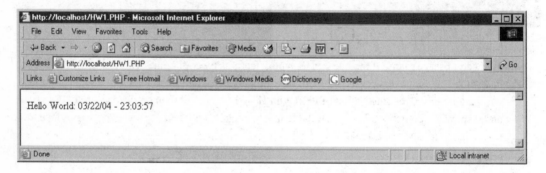

4. The following code adds an HTML form with a submit button to create a variable for user input of a temperature in centigrade, convert if to Fahrenheit, and display it. Alter the HW1.php file in a word processor and save it as **HW2.php**.

```
<HTML>
   <BODY>
   <FORM METHOD="POST">
      Enter Centigrade:
      <INPUT TYPE="TEXT" NAME="centigrade">
      <INPUT TYPE="SUBMIT">
   </FORM>
<BR>
<?php
   $howdy="Hello World: ". date("m/d/y   -   H:m:s");
```

```
      echo $howdy."<br>";
      if(isset($_POST["centigrade"]))
          {
          $ctemp=$_POST["centigrade"];
          $ftemp=32+$ctemp*9/5;
          echo $ctemp." Centigrade = ".$ftemp." Fahrenheit";
          }
  ?>
      </BODY>
  </HTML>
```

5. View the web page, enter the value **45** into the form box, and click the submit button. You'll see the web page change. You can also try entering 0 centigrade, which equals 32 Fahrenheit, for verification.

6. Enter the following code in your word processor and save it as **dbconnect.php** in the Internet directory.

```
<?php
  unset($dbfailed);

  if(mysql_connect("localhost","root"))
      {
      mysql_select_db("duckwear")or $dbfailed=mysql_error();
      }
  else
      {
      $dbfailed="Could not connect to database";
      }
```

(continued)

```
    if(isset($dbfailed))
        {
        echo $dbfailed;
        }
?>
```

This text creates a routine for connecting to your MySQL database and indicates what the program should do if it cannot connect. It is included in the file you will create in the next step.

7. Type the following code into a file and save the file as **usedata.php** in your Internet directory.

```
<?php
    include 'dbconnect.php';
?>
<HTML>
    <BODY>
<?php
    $rs=mysql_query("select * from duck_sales")
    or die(mysql_error());
    $num=mysql_num_rows($rs);
    echo "There are $num rows<BR>";
?>
    <h1>Sales Report</H1>
<TABLE cellpaddig=2 border=1>
<TR><TH>Design</TH><TH>Winter</TH><TH>Spring</TH>
    <TH>Summer</TH><TH>Fall</TH></tr>
<?php
    while($row=mysql_fetch_array($rs))
        {
        echo
"<TR><TD>$row[design_name]</TD><TD>$row[winter_sales]</TD>
        <TD>$row[spring_sales]</TD><TD>$row[summer_sales]</TD>
         <TD>$row[fall_sales]</TD></TR>";
        }
?>
</TABLE>
    </BODY>
</HTML>
```

8. View the page in your web browser. It should display the contents of your `duck_sales` table in your `duckwear` database.

```
http://localhost/USEDATA.php - Microsoft Internet Explorer
File   Edit   View   Favorites   Tools   Help
Back  ▼  →  ▼  🗙  🗋  🏠   🔍 Search   📑 Favorites   📷 Media   🔊
Address 🗋 http://localhost/USEDATA.php
Links  🔗 Customize Links   🔗 Free Hotmail   🔗 Windows   🔗 Windows Media
```

There are 9 rows

Sales Report

Design	Winter	Spring	Summer	Fall
Santa_Duck	1067	200	150	267
Dr_Duck	970	770	561	486
Duckula	53	13	21	856
Fire_Duck	782	357	168	250
Bunny_Duck	589	795	367	284
Duckspeare	953	582	336	489
Sherlock_Duck	752	657	259	478
Duck_O_Lantern	67	23	83	543
Rodeo_Duck	673	48	625	52

```
Done
```

9. Enter the following code into a file and save it as **enterdata.php**.

```php
<?php
   include 'dbconnect.php';
   ?>
<html>
   <body>
      <h1>Enter Design</h1>
   <form method="post">
   Design:<input type="text" name="design"><br>
   Category:<input type="text" name="cat"><br>
   Winter:<input type="text" name="winter"><br>
   Spring:<input type="text" name="spring"><br>
   Summer:<input type="text" name="summer"><br>
   Fall:<input type="text" name="fall"><br>
   <input type="submit">
   </form>
```

(continued)

```php
<?php
if(isset($_POST["design"])){
    $sql = "insert into duck_sales
        values(0,'".$_POST["design"]."'",".$_POST["winter"].",
        ".$_POST["spring"].",".$_POST["summer"].",".$_POST["fall"].",
        '".$_POST["cat"]."')";
if(mysql_query($sql)){
    echo "record inserted";
    }else{
    echo mysql_error();
    }
    }
?>
</body>
</html>
```

10. View the page in your web browser. As you can see, it will allow you to insert records into the duck_sales table in the duckwear database.

CAUTION

To express these concepts simply, this script allows user-provided input to be placed directly into a SQL query. Under *no* circumstances should this be done in a real-world script. It produces a condition called *SQL injection* and can be a serious security problem. Once you understand the PHP basics in this appendix, return to the advanced topics in Module 7, which will cover how to avoid SQL injection.

11. Insert a new record using the following information: **Rock_Duck**, **Profession**, **98**, **87**, **76**, **65**. Then press the ENTER key. A "Record Inserted" statement will appear.

12. In your browser, return to the usedata.php page. If necessary, click the Refresh button. The page should show the Rock_Duck addition to the `duck_sales` table.

Project
C-1

http://localhost/USEDATA.php - Microsoft Internet Explorer

File   Edit   View   Favorites   Tools   Help

Back • → • ⊗ ⊗ ⌂ ⊗Search ⊗Favorites ⊗Media ⊗

Address ⊗ http://localhost/USEDATA.php

Links ⊗Customize Links ⊗Free Hotmail ⊗Windows ⊗Windows Media ⊗

There are 10 rows

Sales Report

Design	Winter	Spring	Summer	Fall
Santa_Duck	1067	200	150	267
Dr_Duck	970	770	561	486
Duckula	53	13	21	856
Fire_Duck	782	357	168	250
Bunny_Duck	589	795	367	284
Duckspeare	953	582	336	489
Sherlock_Duck	752	657	259	478
Duck_O_Lantern	67	23	83	543
Rodeo_Duck	673	48	625	52
Rock_Duck	98	87	76	65

Done

Project Summary

This project gave you experience with creating PHP code to put text on a web page. You also saw how to post data to and from a web page, use a web page interface to view data in a MySQL database, and insert data into a MySQL database.

Index

S

INTERNATIONAL CONTACT INFORMATION

AUSTRALIA
McGraw-Hill Book Company
Australia Pty. Ltd.
TEL +61-2-9900-1800
FAX +61-2-9878-8881
http://www.mcgraw-hill.com.au
books-it_sydney@mcgraw-hill.com

CANADA
McGraw-Hill Ryerson Ltd.
TEL +905-430-5000
FAX +905-430-5020
http://www.mcgraw-hill.ca

**GREECE, MIDDLE EAST, & AFRICA
(Excluding South Africa)**
McGraw-Hill Hellas
TEL +30-210-6560-990
TEL +30-210-6560-993
TEL +30-210-6560-994
FAX +30-210-6545-525

MEXICO (Also serving Latin America)
McGraw-Hill Interamericana Editores
S.A. de C.V.
TEL +525-1500-5108
FAX +525-117-1589
http://www.mcgraw-hill.com.mx
carlos_ruiz@mcgraw-hill.com

SINGAPORE (Serving Asia)
McGraw-Hill Book Company
TEL +65-6863-1580
FAX +65-6862-3354
http://www.mcgraw-hill.com.sg
mghasia@mcgraw-hill.com

SOUTH AFRICA
McGraw-Hill South Africa
TEL +27-11-622-7512
FAX +27-11-622-9045
robyn_swanepoel@mcgraw-hill.com

SPAIN
McGraw-Hill/
Interamericana de España, S.A.U.
TEL +34-91-180-3000
FAX +34-91-372-8513
http://www.mcgraw-hill.es
professional@mcgraw-hill.es

**UNITED KINGDOM, NORTHERN,
EASTERN, & CENTRAL EUROPE**
McGraw-Hill Education Europe
TEL +44-1-628-502500
FAX +44-1-628-770224
http://www.mcgraw-hill.co.uk
emea_queries@mcgraw-hill.com

ALL OTHER INQUIRIES Contact:
McGraw-Hill/Osborne
TEL +1-510-420-7700
FAX +1-510-420-7703
http://www.osborne.com
omg_international@mcgraw-hill.com

Sound Off!

Visit us at **www.osborne.com/bookregistration** and let us know what you thought of this book. While you're online you'll have the opportunity to register for newsletters and special offers from McGraw-Hill/Osborne.

We want to hear from you!

Sneak Peek

Visit us today at **www.betabooks.com** and see what's coming from McGraw-Hill/Osborne tomorrow!

Based on the successful software paradigm, Bet@Books™ allows computing professionals to view partial and sometimes complete text versions of selected titles online. Bet@Books™ viewing is free, invites comments and feedback, and allows you to "test drive" books in progress on the subjects that interest you the most.